Being Modern in the Middle East

Being Modern in the Middle East

REVOLUTION, NATIONALISM, COLONIALISM, AND THE ARAB MIDDLE CLASS

Keith David Watenpaugh

PRINCETON UNIVERSITY PRESS

PRINCETON AND OXFORD

Copyright © 2006 by Princeton University Press
Published by Princeton University Press, 41 William Street,
Princeton, New Jersey 08540
In the United Kingdom: Princeton University Press,
3 Market Place, Woodstock, Oxfordshire OX20 1SY

Library of Congress Cataloging-in-Publication Data

Watenpaugh, Keith David, 1966–
Being modern in the Middle East : revolution, nationalism, colonialism,
and the Arab middle class / Keith David Watenpaugh.—1st ed.

p.   cm.
Includes bibliographical references and index.
ISBN-13: 978-0-691-12169-7 (alk. paper)
ISBN-10: 0-691-12169-9 (alk. paper)
1. Arab nationalism. 2. Middle class—Arab countries. 3. Revolutions.
4. Social conflict—Arab countries. 5. Civil society—Arab countries. I. Title.
DS63.6.W38 2006
956′.03′08622—dc22   2005021431

British Library Cataloging-in-Publication Data is available

This book has been composed in Sabon

Printed on acid-free paper. ∞

pup.princeton.edu

Printed in the United States of America

10 9 8 7 6 5 4 3 2 1

For Heghnar

Contents

Preface and Acknowledgments

The prevailing image of the Middle East includes neither the middle class nor modernity.

Not only popular media, but even a great deal of serious academic writing, portray the region as the definitive realm of irrationality, extremism, and senseless violence, where vast, undifferentiated, and inherently backward societies are ruled by kleptocratic dictators, nationalist demagogues, turbaned fundamentalist clerics, or oil-rich petty monarchs. As a consequence, contemporary Middle Eastern social, intellectual, and cultural history has been excluded, from the global study of class, liberalism, and historical thought. The reasons for this exclusion are manifold and have as much to do with the corrosive political situation in the region as they do with the culture of Middle East studies in the American academy.

This book challenges that exclusion not just by writing a history of the middle class of Aleppo in the period 1908–1946, but also by situating that history against the question of modernity in a way that secures a place for contemporary Middle Eastern history in the study of urban society, class conflict, colonialism, and ideas.

Part of that challenge is creating new descriptive vocabularies of geography: hence my adoption of the term Eastern Mediterranean, which in this work means the cities and countryside facing the sea and bounded at the north by the mountains of Anatolia, the west by Mesopotamia, and the south by the deserts of the Arabian Peninsula. This was a part of the world connected by history, culture, and networks of trade and education that also possessed tremendous linguistic, ethnic, and religious heterogeneity. About the size of Iberia, it makes more sense as a geographical construct than the Middle East—a term that can describe a much larger and even more diverse area and carries with it residues of colonialism and an obvious Eurocentrism. That said, the issues raised in this book have a larger resonance for that part of the world labeled by Western historical and political thought the "Middle East" and hence its place in the title and other moments in the work.

I have also chosen to write about the middle class because it has been largely invisible to history. Putting a human face on it—the way its members thought, remembered, organized themselves, related to power, experienced anxiety and joy—is my modest contribution to the creation of a Middle East in which the middle class does more than just survive or emigrate, but rather is empowered to construct a peaceful and better world for itself and its children.

Moreover, I write about the middle class because I had the opportunity to live in a middle-class community in Aleppo. I watched middle-class families live unremarkable lives of great beauty, community, heartbreak, ambition, and sorrow, and I never could have written this book without their help. In particular I thank the extended Baronian-Homsy-Zobian family, especially Koko Zobian. I am thankful that I met and was able to spend time with Dr. Robert Jebejian before he died in 2001 nearing his ninety-third birthday. Dr. Jebejian was the careful guardian of the history of Aleppo's vast Armenian community, and he allowed me to wander the collection of the Violette Jebejian Library and Archive at will. I am indebted as well to those Aleppines who granted me oral history interviews and shared with me their private collections of books, photographs, and papers.

As this book evolved from a UCLA doctoral dissertation in history, senior colleagues helped me to sharpen ideas and ask the right questions, in particular, Afaf Marsot, Hasan Kayalı, Philip Khoury, Elizabeth Thompson, Geoff Eley, Palmira Brummett, Virgina Aksan, Leila Fawaz, Juan Cole, Kenneth Cuno, Elizabeth Picard, James Gelvin, Nadine Méouchy, Michael Morony, Carole Pateman, and especially, Peter Sluglett. Roger Owen and Cemal Kafadar secured time for me to complete the final revisions of this book as a visiting scholar at Harvard University's Center for Middle East Studies (2004–2005), and Brigitta van Rheinberg of Princeton University Press made this book a reality.

My family played a tremendous role in this work, especially my father, who in addition to reading an earlier draft of this book sparked my original interest in the Middle East. He had lived in Iraq and Lebanon for much of the 1950s and remembers these places in a way I imagine any bright American teenager would have in the middle of the last century: confidently optimistic and with real affection for the people who always treated his family with courtesy and kindness. His memories are colored by the exotic and the biblical and reinforced by beautiful trinkets, carpets, antiquities, and most of all by slide transparencies. My father's slide collection is immense. And these images became part of my own memories of childhood.

Thus unlike most Americans of my generation, whose earliest childhood encounters with the Middle East were images of the Iranian hostage crisis, the Israeli invasion of Lebanon, or Hizbullah's bombing of the marine corps barracks in Beirut, the Middle East I grew up with was a more humane and knowable place, home of real people with hopes and dreams. I have tried to capture in the following pages something of their lives.

My deepest gratitude goes to my wife Heghnar Zeitlian Watenpaugh, a brilliant scholar and beloved companion; this work and my life are the richer because of her. I dedicate this book to her.

Some of the material in this work is drawn from articles and book chapters I have published elsewhere and is used here by permission.

"Steel Shirts, White Badges and the last *Qabaday*: Fascist Forms and the Transformation of Urban Violence in French Mandate Syria" in *France, Syrie et Liban, 1918–1846—les dynamiques et les ambiguïtés de la relation mandataire*, Nadine Méouchy, ed. (Damascus: Institut Français d'Études Arabes de Damas Press, 2002), 325–347.

"Middle-class Modernity and the Persistence of the Politics of Notables in Interwar Syria," *The International Journal of Middle East Studies* 35:2 (2003): 257–286.

"Colonial Cooperation and the *Survivors' Bargain*—The Post-Genocide Armenian Community of Syria under French Mandate," in *The British and French Mandates in Comparative Perspective*, Nadine Méouchy and Peter Sluglett, eds. (Leiden: Brill, 2004), 597–622.

"Cleansing the Cosmopolitan City: Historicism, Journalism and the Arab Nation in the Post-Ottoman Eastern Mediterranean," *Social History* 30 (2005): 1–24.

The text is followed by a selected bibliography that lists archives consulted, several of the more important works on the history of Aleppo, and sources used to guide my theoretical discussions of class and modernity. Whenever a source is used for the first time in the text, I have given it a complete footnote.

Note on Translation and Transliteration

While appearing neutral, any transliteration of Arabic written symbols and speech sounds into a Latin alphabet carries with it the potential for anachronism and political manipulation.

This book employs documents and literary works from two different languages—modern Arabic and Ottoman Turkish—that used the same alphabet, and it discusses people who would have known several languages and employed them according to the situation. I have chosen, for the most part, to transliterate according to the language of the original text or historical context. For this process, I have used the modified transliteration scheme of the *International Journal of Middle East Studies*; words of Ottoman Turkish origin are translated into a modified modern Turkish spelling. For example, when a name appears in a telegram written in Ottoman Turkish and sent to the Sublime Porte, the name is rendered in modern Turkish; if the telegram is in Arabic, its text and signatories are transliterated according to the Arabic scheme. Ranks, bureaucratic postings, and religious positions in the period before 1918 are in their Ottoman form, hence *kadı* rather than *qadi*. After 1918, unless indicated otherwise by the context, transliteration is made from modern Arabic. When individuals have expressed a preference as to the way their names should be spelled in a European language, I have respected that decision: hence the Gallicized Edmond Rabbath, rather than Idmun al-Rabbat. Generally well-known Anglicized spellings of places, concepts, and texts are rendered according to convention.

All translations from Arabic, Ottoman Turkish, Turkish, French, or Armenian are my own unless noted otherwise.

Abbreviations and Acronyms

AHR	*The American Historical Review*
BBA DH-MTV	Başbakanlık Arşivi (Prime Ministry Archives), Dahilye Nezareti (Interior Ministry) Mütenevvî (Various), Istanbul, Turkey
BBA DH-MUI	Başbakanlık Arşivi (Prime Ministry Archives), Dahilye Nezareti (Interior Ministry) Muhâberât-i Umûmiye Idaresi (General Intelligence Bureau), Istanbul, Turkey
BEO	*Bulletin d'Études Orientales*
CADN-MAE	Centre des archives diplomatiques Nantes, Ministère, des affairs etrangères
CHEAM	Centre de Hautes Études Administratives sur l'Afrique et l'Asie Modernes, Paris, France
CSSH	*Comparative Studies in Society and History*
EI²	*The Encyclopedia of Islam*, 2nd ed., Leiden: E. J. Brill, 1956–present
IJMES	*International Journal of Middle East Studies*
MD-SHAT	Ministère de la Défense: Service historique de l'armée de terre, Vincennes, France
MWT-QKh	Markaz al-watha'iq al-tarikhiyya (Center for Historical Documents), Al-Qism al-khass (Special Section), Damascus, Syria
Notables	Raghib al-Tabbakh, *I'lam al-nubala' bi-tarikh Halab al-shahba'*, 2nd ed., 7 vols. and index volume, edited by Muhammad Kamal (Aleppo: Arab Pen Press, 1988–1992) [orig. ed. Aleppo: Maronite Press, 1923–1926].
PRO FO	Public Record Office, Foreign Office, Kew, United Kingdom
REMMM	*Revue du Monde Musulman et de la Méditerranée*
River	Kamil al-Ghazzi, *Kitab Nahr al-Dhahab fi Tarikh Halab*, 2nd ed., 3 vols., edited and introduced by Shawqi Sha'th and Mahmud Fakhuri (Aleppo: Arab Pen Press, 1991–1993) [orig. ed. Aleppo: Maronite Press, 1923–1926].
USNA II	United States National Archives, Department of State, College Park, Maryland

Being Modern in the Middle East

ONE

Introduction: Modernity, Class, and the Architectures of Community

> They hold a refracted mirror in front of that which is civilized out of which a caricature of its obverse essence stares back.
> —Siegfried Kracauer, 1925

On the evening of 2 January 1910, Fathallah Qastun, a newspaper editor in Aleppo, one of the most important cities of the Ottoman Empire, addressed the inaugural meeting of the Mutual Aid Society. Simply titled "Becoming Civilized," the text of the speech, complete with parenthetical notations of spontaneous applause, was published in Qastun's own Arabic-language newspaper, *al-Sha'b* [The People]. Qastun began his speech by asking: "Why have we not yet become fully civilized and in particular, why have we not borrowed more from Europe?" He answered his own question by arguing:

> I say we have not become fully part of Western Civilization because we have only taken from it what is in conformity with the traditions and customs of the various races which make up our state. This has caused both material and cultural harm. . . . For if we just copy Europeans, we will disavow our origins and acquire an antipathy toward our [past]. Instead, we should follow them as closely as possible in the way in which they protect their own race and homeland. We should strive to protect our noble language and ways just as they protect their languages and ways.[1]

Beyond distinguishing between the mere reproduction of the superficial trappings of European manners and fashions and the complete adoption of the bases of what the editor would later call "true civilization" (*al-madaniyya al-haqqa*), the most striking feature of this lecture is Qastun's conclusion that incorporation of the "essence" of the West and not just its material culture was vital to the survival of his society. Moreover, the preeminent threat was not only that West (although it clearly remained a pressing concern), but rather, in his estimation, an *irrational* attachment

[1] *al-Sha'b* (Aleppo), 3 January 1910.

to tradition and custom by his fellow citizens prevented them from joining the ranks of the "fully civilized."

The content of Qastun's speech was not especially unique in 1910: questions about civilization, political legitimacy, social reform, the place of the peoples of the Ottoman Empire in the passage of history, and, ultimately, what it meant to be modern had become commonplace in the few short months since the Revolution of 1908 and were being asked in the several languages of the Eastern Mediterranean—Ottoman Turkish, Arabic, Armenian, Greek, and Ladino—on the pages of newspapers and from podiums throughout the region. The Revolution of 1908, also known as the Young Turk Revolution, ended the autocratic and paranoid rule of Sultan Abdülhamid II and led to the reinstatement of the quasi-liberal Ottoman Constitution of 1876. Unlike the prerevolutionary government, which had generally proscribed such forms of association and made the publishing of private newspapers difficult, if not impossible, the new régime, dominated by the reform-minded officers and bureaucrats of the Ottoman Committee for Union and Progress (CUP), the so-called Young Turks, had created an atmosphere in which civil society flourished, and voluntary associations and newspapers had become the most visible manifestations of the full measure of change.

As important as the content of the speech was its audience. The lawyers, bureaucrats, bankers, petty capitalists, high school teachers, doctors, agents of European and American companies, fellow journalists, and others who sat in rows of straight-backed chairs while they listened to Qastun employ a novel political and historical vocabulary to conjure a vision of the beguiling and dangerous aspects of the West were members of a distinct new urban middle class that owed its existence to the material, economic, and political transformations of the late nineteenth and early twentieth centuries. The men, dressed in coats and trousers of British wool, French cravats, and starched white collars, and the few women, faces uncovered, wearing linen blouses over corsets, tailored skirts, and Italian felt hats, had gathered, in part, to make sense of the rapid and accelerating change of those last few decades. But they had also come, in what was their leisure time, to see and be seen, enjoy an evening's entertainment masquerading as education, revel in one another's company, socialize, gossip, make business deals, scout out potential mates for their children, and, moreover, reinforce those particular cultural and social bonds that distinguished them from the city's poor and its "old social class" of Sunni Muslim aʿyan, a politically and culturally tenacious semifeudal landed elite.

Some had traveled by automobile to the society's hall, located on a wide, straight thoroughfare in a recently built district far beyond the narrow streets and blind alleys of Aleppo's walled old city; most had walked or taken a streetcar from their single-family homes and flats in a suburb nearby, their way having been lit by gas streetlamps. The warm glow of electric light bulbs illuminated the proceedings and allowed the discussion that followed the talk to pass well into the evening. Many of those in the hall—filled with the smoke of machine-rolled cigarettes of American and Turkish tobaccos—were graduates of local Christian missionary or Western-style state schools, and a few had attended university in Istanbul, Beirut, or even Europe and the United States. They knew foreign languages, usually French, learned in the course of their education, but also as a necessity of doing business in a marketplace increasingly dominated by commerce with cities like Marseilles and Manchester. Those in government employ had mastered bureaucratic Ottoman Turkish in addition to Arabic.

In the months since the Revolution of 1908, the partial lifting of censorship meant that they could glean from their afternoon papers a less filtered view of their society and the wider world than had previously been the case; they could also follow spirited debates between editors of different papers, sometimes vicious arguments, and personal attacks by journalists on one another or those in positions of authority. The telegraph, which had already been in use for several decades, brought much of that news, but the introduction of a modest telephone network added even more. Bookshops carried domestic journals in the several languages of the empire, and magazines, full of advertisements and imported directly from Paris, London, Rome, or Vienna, made them aware—at about the same time as their Western counterparts—of the availability of consumer goods, musical instruments, and labor-saving devices, as well as *au courante* European fashion and cuisine. Equally consumed were serialized novels and poetry—in their original and translated versions—and cutting-edge scientific, medical, and literary journals. Local boutiques and department stores, some owned or managed by members of Qastun's audience, made certain that these items were readily available. Most recently, images of the world beyond the city had come in the form of an outdoor cinema set up by a local representative of the Pathé Frères, weather permitting, in a gated public park.

While Qastun's *al-Sha'b* may have been just one of the dozens of new newspapers of Aleppo, and the Mutual Aid Society indistinct from the hundreds of other European-style benevolent and cultural organizations taking shape in the cities of the region, collectively, the organizations, newspapers, seemingly familiar patterns of consumption, forms of sociability, and ways of thinking of the people who inhabited those new spaces or inscribed their thoughts on newsprint bespoke a fundamental cultural and political turn in the contemporary history of the Middle East. For the first time in the lives of anyone in that room, they could *imagine* connecting the ideas being expressed, discussed, and debated to what they would have considered the actual material and moral progress of their community. This optimistic connection was not only a function of the restoration of liberal constitutionalism and the reintroduction of electoral politics by the revolutionary régime; rather the adoption of new technologies that increasingly collapsed space and time, the seeming embrace of secular citizenship by the Young Turks, the knowledge of organizational and intellectual tools like public opinion and nationalism, and the growing cultural and economic penetration by the West in various forms meant, for members of the emerging middle class, the possibility of changing their society and their role in it to such a degree and in such a fashion as to make it, in the way they understood the concept, *modern.*

However, progress had come at the price of short-term political instability and a breakdown of customary social and religious hierarchies. Not only did war continue the territorial erosion of the Ottoman Empire, but Qastun, his listeners, and his readers were keenly aware of the horrific pogrom of the prosperous Armenian community of the nearby city of Adana in April 1909 during a short-lived period of counterrevolution. Eventually engulfing rural communities in the northern tier of the province of Aleppo, the violence, in which Ottoman officials, soldiers, and religious students played a part, underscored how fragile and unstable the new order truly was; that the perpetrators of the violence had as yet escaped punishment by the Young Turks added to the anxiety of those in the room. Tensions between liberal reform and brutal reaction would continue to beset the empire as it stumbled into World War I (1914–1918) and was then broken apart altogether at the behest of European states in the postwar period.

In posing reflective questions about civilization and the West, adjusting to rapid technological change, responding to the draw of European aesthetics and fashions, and balancing the revolution and liberalism with the possibility of mass atrocities and ferocious communal violence, the emerging middle class had come face to face with the reality of being and becoming, to borrow a phrase from Harry Harootunian's study of interwar Japan, "overcome by modernity."[2] For critics like Qastun there was no doubt that "we," primarily but not exclusively his middle-class listeners, had already embraced modernity and were in the process of becoming *just as modern* as Europeans while at the same time retaining their own unique identity and way of life. Consider his enumeration of successful moments of claiming modernity, from the second night's continuation of the speech:

> The most beautiful thing to take from the Westerners is the science of industry as it is the basis of all advancement and the foundation of civilization. . . . the

[2] Harry Harootunian, *Overcome by Modernity: History, Culture, and Community in Interwar Japan* (Princeton: Princeton University Press, 2000).

cultivation of the mind with science and law [also puts us] on the path of true civilization. Indeed we have established schools in all the corners of the kingdom, even villages have places of learning to instruct children in the basics of reading, writing, and arithmetic, moreover we have taken from the Europeans the cultivation of women. . . . We are nearing the summit of modern civilization, Europeans are amazed by our enterprise and our vigor . . . so much so that some have bowed their heads as if to say: he who wishes to attain real civilization let him follow the example of the Ottomans.[3]

By liberating Western civilization from Westerners, Qastun asserted that actual and understandable material and historical circumstance—primarily industrialization in the West and the reactionary autocracy and cultural backwardness of the Ottoman *ancien régime*—had created a temporary disparity. Casting blame in such a way, and centering reform on concrete issues of commerce, education, and industry, he also betrayed the overarching interests of his audience. These were not starry-eyed idealists conducting discussions of liberalism and political economy in the abstract, but instead many were businessmen and white-collar professionals, including members of his extended family, for whom interest rates, tariffs, monetary policy, official corruption, and nascent industrialization were the pressing realities of daily life.

More to the point, Qastun's acceptance of the underlying logos of Western civilization while asserting the ability of non-Westerners to resist the political and cultural hegemony of the West is the quintessential ambivalence at the center of the historical experience of modernity in the colonial and postcolonial non-West. Thus, in a telling paradox consonant with that ambivalence, the ultimate judges of whether Qastun and his audience had attained modernity were still external: the Europeans who "bowed their heads" and the "We" who were "nearing the summit of modern civilization" were doing so only after having crossed an axial barrier defined by the West, thereby folding themselves into a teleological narrative that had as its terminus the accomplishments of Western civilization.

The crossing of that boundary in the Middle East has often served as the organizing theme for historians of the Ottoman Empire's collision with modernity. Albert Hourani and Bernard Lewis, especially, assert the existence of a dialectical relationship between the commitment to modernization, which in this case means reaching a level of material and institutional equivalence with Europe, and a conservative reaction against modernity, in this context the ideation of the post-Enlightenment social and intellectual processes that led to the "rise of the West." This appears most clearly in Lewis's discussion of the *Tanzimat* period (1826–1878), during which the Ottoman Empire, when faced with overwhelming military

[3] *al-Shaʿb* (Aleppo), 5 January 1910.

threats from Europe, accelerated the process of defensive modernization, thereby opening the door ever more slightly to modernity. Reform was imposed from above, often on groups ill prepared for and suspicious of the new way. While the reforms produced cadres of *moderns*, the Ottoman Empire could never achieve modernity until it became a "real" European nation-state in the form of the Republic of Turkey, as reflected in the title of Lewis's most noteworthy book on the subject, *The Emergence of Modern Turkey*. The key moment in this process was not the reform movement of Kemal Atatürk's post-Ottoman régime as much as it was the sloughing off of the forms of an "Oriental" Islamic past. Far from challenging the linear master narrative of Progress and the unfolding of human freedom underpinning the historical consciousness associated with Western civilization, Lewis merely wrote a portion of the Ottoman Empire's population into it, and in so doing he excluded the rest of the population, primarily Arabs, from it.[4]

What remains cogent in his analysis is the possibility that modernization can occur without a simultaneous commitment to modernity. In other words, the grand nineteenth-century projects of modernization in Egypt and the Ottoman Empire—often involving the incorporation of recent technological and bureaucratic innovations—did not necessarily flow from an ideological engagement with modernity on the part of the reformers themselves. Furthermore, in drawing a distinction between the phenomenon of modernization and the idea of modernity, Lewis creates a way to account for the obvious attraction technology exerts on Islamists, the customary elite, even the poor, without a concomitant belief in emancipation, secularism, or rational epistemology.

For Hourani, writing from the perspective of Arabic-language authors in his seminal *Arabic Thought in the Liberal Age*, modernity followed from elite local-European interaction in the salons of Arabophile British and French expatriates and on the campuses of American missionary colleges. It was a consequence, as well, of journeys to the West by generations of Arab students and Muslim scholars.[5] The series of exchanges between the French intellectual Ernest Renan and Jamal al-Din "the Afghan" best exemplify Hourani's understanding of the dialectic. Jamal al-Din, an intellectual of extraordinary abilities, engaged Renan in a debate about the compatibility of Islam and rationality in which he argued that philosophy (West) and prophecy (Islam) arrive through different means at the same

---

[4] Bernard Lewis, *The Emergence of Modern Turkey* (Oxford: Oxford University Press, 1968), and *The Muslim Discovery of Europe* (New York: W. W. Norton, 1982).

[5] Albert H. Hourani, *Arabic Thought in the Liberal Age, 1798–1939* (Cambridge: Cambridge University Press, 1983), originally published by Oxford University Press in 1962. Also Donald M. Reid, "Arabic Thought in the Liberal Age Twenty Years After," *IJMES* 14:4 (1982): 541–557.

truth. As Hourani shows, there is little evidence that Jamal al-Din would have expounded these ideas outside of the relatively free discursive environment of 1880s' Paris. When he did so in a more limited way in Cairo and Istanbul, the Muslim religious establishment labeled his ideas tantamount to heresy and ostracized him.[6] Hourani, like Lewis, conceived the entry of modernity into the region from multiple points, culminating primarily in the broader adoption of a secular nationalism or nationalisms built within the confines of nation-states like Egypt. In emphasizing Arabism as the logical consequence of modernization, Hourani placed that ideology at the center of intellectual, social, and cultural change, thereby obscuring any discussions and movements otherwise unintelligible in the language of nationalism.

Residues of this dialectic, under the influence of 1960s' modernization theory,[7] continue to control discussions of modernity in the region. Moreover, as Deniz Kandiyoti observes about the prevailing trends in Turkish and Ottoman historiography on modernity, "The relative impoverishment of this field has not been altogether accidental. The polemical perspectives adopted both by apologists of Turkish modernization—Kemalists in particular—and by its critics have inadvertently limited our conceptual horizons by falling short of interrogating the notion of the 'modern' itself and charting its local specificities."[8] With a few notable exceptions, primarily scholarship on middle-class and elite feminism, her comments could equally apply to the historiography of the Arab Levant.[9]

Any account, however, that privileges a linear narrative of modernization or "Westernization"—and resistance thereto—can shed light on only larger institutional and political modifications; at the same time such accounts tend to reinforce Eurocentric prejudices about Arab and Muslim societies by putting the onus for change solely on the shoulders of Westerners and characterizing reform as a mimetic reaction to the West. To

[6] Nikki R. Keddie, *An Islamic Response to Imperialism: Political and Religious Writings of Sayyid Jamal ad-Din "al-Afghani,"* including a translation of the *Refutation of the Materialists* from the Persian by Nikki R. Keddie and Hamid Algar (Berkeley: University of California, 1968); Rudi Matthee, "Jamal al-Din al-Afghani and the Egyptian National Debate," *IJMES* 21:2 (1989): 151–169.

[7] Manfred Halpern, *The Politics of Social Change in the Middle East and North Africa* (Princeton: Princeton University Press, 1963). At the time, the inevitability of the rise of the "New Middle Class"—though not modernization theory per se—particularly in Egypt, was dismissed by, among others, Amos Perlmutter, "Egypt and the Myth of the New Middle Class: A Comparative Analysis," *CSSH* 10:1 (1967): 46–65.

[8] Deniz Kandiyoti, "Gendering the Modern: On Missing Dimensions in the Study of Turkish Modernity," in Sibel Bozdogan and Resat Kasaba, eds., *Rethinking Modernity and National Identity in Turkey* (Seattle: University of Washington Press, 1997), 129.

[9] Lila Abu-Lughod, "Introduction," in Lila Abu-Lughod, ed., *Remaking Women: Feminism and Modernity in the Middle East* (Princeton: Princeton University Press, 1998).

move beyond that narrative (but not reject elements of it altogether), I seek instead in this work to capture modernity as a lived historical experience and explore how it has colonized local politics, cultural practices, and everyday life by bringing into the discussion a consequence of modernity: modernity draws and redraws boundaries of class, and, critically, the ideas, institutions, and politics associated with modernity have given rise to a uniquely modern middle class.[10]

Based on archival, literary, visual, and oral historical evidence in several languages, including, Arabic, Ottoman and Modern Turkish, Armenian, and French—and an eclectic body of theoretical literature—I argue in this book that in the crucible of the Young Turk Revolution of 1908, World War I, and the imposition of colonial rule, a discrete middle class emerged in the cities of the Eastern Mediterranean that was defined not just by the wealth, professions, possessions, or levels of education of its members, but also by the way they asserted their modernity. To claim modernity, they incorporated into their daily lives and politics a collection of manners, mores, and tastes, and a corpus of ideas about the individual, gender, rationality, and authority actively derived from what they believed to be the cultural, social, and ideological praxis of the contemporary metropolitan Western middle classes. By *being modern*, members of this class distinguished themselves from the region's ruling Sunni Muslim oligarchy and subaltern class of urban and rural poor and evidenced how they conceived of themselves as a separate element of their society. Moreover, excluded by customary practices and political theory from structures of power, this class contested its exclusion and asserted its right to equality, citizenship, and political participation in the idiom of modernity. By being modern, its members declared their intention to take a preeminent role in the production of knowledge and culture, not just for themselves, but for society at large. The dedication to these ideas, praxis, and politics marks that middle class as both a distinct component and an unprecedented innovation in the social and cultural history of the Middle East, as well as a vital subject in the question of modernity in the non-West.

I trace not just what it meant to be modern for this class, but how the class's commitment to being modern shaped its attempts to create civil society and mold urban politics, the multiple ways it employed nationalism, history writing, and violence to make sense of the post–World War I

[10] A relevant example of this link, especially as it bears on questions of white-collar professionals, middle-class city people, and culture, is seen in Siegfried Kracauer's *The Salaried Masses*, trans. Quintin Hoare (London: Verso, 1998). Important to take from Kracauer is the idea that modernity constitutes a reproducible experience connected to worldview, consumption, technology, and taste as well as wealth, and in "the real world" it often has as much to do with ideas and attitudes as it does with material things and observable simulation.

world, and its engagement with—or resistance to—European imperialism. Likewise, I explain how the emergence of this middle class began to alter the ideological, social, and cultural topography of the contemporary Middle East, especially as it bears on questions of secularism, citizenship, and liberalism. And as this new class, like its cognates in South Asia, Latin America, and East Asia, was, and continues to be, a salient feature of so-called globalization, or what should correctly be termed neomoderniza-tion, understanding its origins and its historical background is a crucial—and until now missing—dimension of postcolonial studies.

These issues are examined primarily through the history of the modern-izing middle class in the city of Aleppo during the tumultuous period 1908–1946. Aleppo, a once cosmopolitan city at the southern edge of the Anatolian plateau, was one of the major provincial capitals of the Otto-man Empire and remains one the most populous urban centers in the Levant. In addition to its Sunni Muslim plurality, it possessed a substan-tial Arabic-speaking Christian population. Before 1948 a large and vi-brant Jewish community also resided in Aleppo, and the city became the main center of resettlement for vast numbers of Armenian Genocide survi-vors in the interwar period. It was home to a complex, emergent middle class, of which these non-Muslim groups represented significant portions. Like Aleppo's counterparts throughout the Ottoman Empire, members of its middle class were generally multilingual, literate, and European-centered in much of their cultural activity. More important, to paraphrase Marshal Berman, they sought to inscribe themselves into what they saw as the modern world as modern people, making themselves both objects and subjects of modernity.[11] And while members of this middle class never acquired the kind of political preeminence their opposite numbers gained in the West, they indelibly altered the society in which they were enve-loped. However, when their political or economic situation deteriorated, they often resorted to political quietism or chose emigration to Western Europe or the Americas.

Taking consummate modern moments from the lives of the members of the middle class like Qastun's speech—not just what was said, but also who was speaking and listening, who produced culture, knowledge, and history, and who claimed the right to be violent—this book brings into relief the way the inhabitants of places like Aleppo negotiated *for them-selves* the distillates of urban life, capitalism, liberalism, nationalism, the material needs of bourgeois aesthetics and fashion, and the increasing technologically driven aspects of a mass-participant society—all of which, like class formation, colonialism, and later fascism, collectively represent

[11] Marshall Berman, *All That Is Solid Melts into Air: The Experience of Modernity* (New York: Penguin, 1988), 5.

corollaries of modernity. In this way, being modern in the Middle East becomes an intelligible and understandable, albeit complex, historical process rather than just an inevitable consequence of imperialism or the region's integration into the global and hegemonic logic of high capitalism.

Still, it would be unwise to consider the region's modern middle class a purely localized occurrence, ignoring that logic altogether. Thus, as I explore the local transformations of modernity, I place the history of this new class firmly within the early moments of the formation of "middle-class modernity," a transnational phenomenon whereby being modern and being middle class became intertwined, if not one and the same thing, in the consciousness and praxis of members of emergent middle classes.

While this work is the first monograph to link the emergence of an urban middle class and the historical experience of modernity in the Eastern Mediterranean, by no means is it, nor indeed could it be, a comprehensive account of that process. Neither is it a narrative of Aleppo's political or economic history, especially as it devotes little attention to the calamitous financial impact of the division of the city from its hinterland in southern Anatolia and integration into an unprecedented French colonial construct, the Republic of Syria, in the interwar period. Likewise, this study does not divide the late-Ottoman (1908–1918), brief interwar Arab Kingdom (1918–1920), and French Mandate (1920–1946) periods into discrete units of investigation.[12] Writing the history of Aleppo and its inhabitants along those lines would represent a concession to nationalist and imperialist narratives. In those narratives, Aleppo is adjoined to the European imperialist construct of Syria as an Arab city and conversely, as it lay a few too many kilometers on the southern side of a boundary determined by the path of the Berlin-Baghdad railway, it is not depicted as a Turkish city. Often the current national designation of the subject acts to control the types of sources deemed legitimate for use.

To assert, likewise, the existence of a Syria or a Turkey in the prewar period is quite simply anachronistic, and to use the nation-state as a basis

---

[12] For contrasting periodization in English, see James Gelvin, *Divided Loyalties: Nationalism and Mass Politics in Syria at the Close of Empire* (Berkeley: University of California Press, 1998); also Stephen Hemsley Longrigg, *Syria and Lebanon under French Mandate* (London: Oxford University Press, 1958), and Elizabeth Thompson, *Colonial Citizens: Republican Rights and Paternal Privilege in French Syria and Lebanon* (New York: Columbia University Press, 2001). Philip Khoury argues for a high degree of elite political continuity in Damascus and Aleppo over the three periods in *Syria and the French Mandate: The Politics of Arab Nationalism 1920–1945* (Princeton: Princeton University Press, 1987) and "Continuity and Change in Syrian Political Life: The Nineteenth and Twentieth Centuries," *AHR*, 96:5 (December 1991): 1374–1395. See also Peter Sluglett, "Urban Dissidence in Mandatory Syria: Aleppo 1918–1936," in Kenneth Brown et al., eds., *Etat, ville et mouvements sociaux au Maghreb et au Moyen Orient/Urban Crises and Social Movements in the Middle East* (Paris: L'Harmattan, 1986), 301–316.

for this kind of study in the interwar period is also problematic. By rejecting the nationalist and imperialist definitions of the historical and political bounds of Aleppo, I can bring together evidence from Arab studies and Turkish studies, both of which have grown exclusionary in recent times. Gathering evidence from the diverse communities and various languages that contributed to the cosmopolitan nature of Aleppo produces a vivid and complex portrait of this remarkable city and its inhabitants at a moment of tremendous change.

Being Modern as a Historical Problem

Clearly, *being modern* was not a condition exclusive to the middle class of Aleppo in the period 1908–1946. Yet understanding the unique and the shared in their historical experience is a step toward claiming a position for the non-West (defined in modernist terms by what it is not) in the broader critique of the question of modernity. By doing so, it is possible to begin to understand the experience of modernity for those outside of the West as something more complex than mere colonial and postcolonial acts of imitation or mimicry. In this sense, my work rises to the task posed by Timothy Mitchell, to "find a way to theorize the question of modernity that relocates it within a global context, and at the same time, enables that context to complicate, rather than simply reverse, the narrative logic of modernization."[13] Crucial to that task is first unraveling how and why groups and individuals systematically adhered to a category of phenomena "Western," "modern," and "civilized," and then exploring the questions that arose in that particular social and cultural milieu because of that adherence.[14] Exemplary is the question occasioned by the internalization of "Weberian occidental reason" by putative "Orientals"—a question central not just to Qastun's speech, but also to Stefan Tanaka's *Japan's Orient: Rendering Pasts into History*—namely, "how to become modern while simultaneously shedding the objectivistic category of Oriental and not lose an identity?"[15]

[13] Timothy Mitchell, "The Stage of Modernity," in Timothy Mitchell, ed., *Questions of Modernity* (Minneapolis: University of Minnesota Press, 2000), 7.

[14] "What is important . . . is to explore how the notions of modernity have been produced and reproduced through being opposed to the nonmodern in dichotomies ranging from the modern/primitive of philosophy and anthropology to the modern/traditional of Western social theory and modernization theory, not to mention the West/non-West that is implied in most of these dichotomies." Abu-Lughod, *Remaking*, 7.

[15] Stefan Tanaka, *Japan's Orient: Rendering Pasts into History* (Berkeley: University of California Press, 1993), 3.

At stake in this critique, beyond affirming Arif Dirlik's conclusion that "modernity is incomprehensible without reference to Eurocentrism,"[16] is revising the prevailing Eurocentrism of the question of modernity. It challenges, as well, the continuing dominance of Europe, as currently constructed, in the articulation of social theory and contemporary class, intellectual, and cultural history writing. Writing a post-Eurocentric history that can still make sense of Europe in that history is among the most important dividends of this critique, as is understanding not just why the Ottoman Empire was created as modern Europe's definitive "other," but also how it has been excluded from the genealogy of modernity despite the "almost universal perception of [it] as a European state" in the early modern period.[17] The relatively recent "Europeaness" of the Ottoman Empire and its uninterrupted connection with those city-states, kingdoms, and merchant republics of far northwestern Eurasia that became Europe in the late eighteenth and nineteenth centuries, though now largely ignored by modern historians, crystallize the unique nature of Ottoman history into the question of modernity itself and, moreover, have considerable implications for any attempts to impose colonial theory derived from South Asia on the Eastern Mediterranean.

Three definitive aspects of modernity underlie the way it is employed in this work. First, what is "crucially distinctive about Modernity," observed Marshall G. S. Hodgson is that "Modernity has been not simply rational emancipation from custom, nor has it been simply the further unfolding of a bent for progress peculiar to the Western tradition; it has been a cultural transformation *sui generis*."[18] Hodgson's claim is particularly relevant as he was examining the transformative nature of modernity in parts of the world tangential to its place of origin. Consequently, conceptualizing modernity as a distinct cultural transformation is fundamentally important to both understanding world history from the last two centuries and decentering—or perhaps rationalizing—the presence of the West in that history.

Second, as a distinct cultural transformation, modernity possesses dimensionality. When historicized, it is buffeted by the conditional, the regional, and the subjective. However, in an often misunderstood paradox,

---

[16] Arif Dirlik, "Is There History after Eurocentrism? Globalism, Postcolonialism, and the Disavowal of History," in Arif Dirlik, Vinay Bahl, and Peter Gran, eds., *History after the Three Worlds: Post Eurocentric Historiographies* (Oxford: Rowman and Littlefield, 2000), 25.

[17] Daniel Goffman, *The Ottoman Empire and Early Modern Europe* (Cambridge: Cambridge University Press, 2002), 18.

[18] Marshall G. S. Hodgson, *The Venture of Islam: Conscience and History in a World Civilization* vol. 2, *The Expansion of Islam in the Middle Period* (Chicago: University of Chicago Press, 1974), 375.

its acolytes believe it embraces everything and everyone in simultaneous and absolute terms unrestrained by place and time.[19] Thus conceived, modernity presupposes an absolute subject position, one that does not—and cannot—acknowledge its own contingency. When modernity is dislocated from its self-defined universality and made contingent on time and place, its intrinsic limit and fragmentary nature comes into view.[20] The last assertion does not constitute an endorsement of the problematic suggestion that non-Western societies can exist out of historical time as a consequence of some kind of regionally conditioned immaturity, and that their modernity merely lies inchoate, waiting to be awakened. While observers and critics like Qastun may have regarded their societies as "behind" the West or "backward," they could not have imagined that they were in a historical moment outside of a global modern age, nor would they have conceded the existence of a unique "Ottoman" modernity—a modernity modified by an ethnic or national adjective would have made little sense to them nor have any utility; in fact, quite the opposite, as it would imply that Qastun and his counterparts, as non-Europeans, could never attain "true" modernity but rather were relegated to an inherently inferior local version thereof.

As Harootunian observes of a similar moment in Japan's encounter with modernity, "It is precisely this [concept] of time lag that produces the scandal of imagining modernities that are not quite modern—usually a euphemism for being 'not quite white'—and new . . . classifications like 'alternative modernities' . . . differentiated from the temporality of the modern West which, then, allow us to safely situate societies like Japan," and by extension the Ottoman Eastern Mediterranean, "in a historical trajectory derived from another's development."[21] Such formulations inadvertently play into modernity's ongoing process of universal-

---

[19] "This subject-centered reason claims for itself a singular universality by asserting its epistemic privilege over all other local, plural, and often incommensurable knowledges; it proclaims its own unity and homogeneity by declaring all other subjectivities as inadequate, fragmentary, and subordinate." Partha Chatterjee, *The Nation and Its Fragments: Colonial and Postcolonial Histories* (Princeton: Princeton University Press, 1993), xi. On this composite definition and the problem of defining "modernity," see Richard Rorty, "Habermas and Lyotard on Postmodernity," in Richard J. Bernstein, ed., *Habermas and Modernity* (Cambridge: MIT Press, 1985), 161–175; and Jean-François Lyotard, *The Postmodern Condition: A Report on Knowledge*, trans. Geoff Bennington and Brian Massumi (Minneapolis: University of Minnesota Press, 1984).

[20] "Modernity must be staged as that which is singular, original, present and authoritative. This staging does not occur only in the West . . . to be later imitated in the non-West. Its authority and presence can be produced only across the space of geographical and historical difference. . . . Modernity, like capitalism, is defined by its claim to universality. . . . Yet this always remains an impossible unity, an incomplete universal." Mitchell, *Questions*, 24.

[21] Harootunian, *Overcome*, xvi.

izing, and its constant search for places unmodern against which to define itself. Harootunian suggests as an alternative to "alternative modernities" the term "coeval." The use of this word emphasizes the real-time nature of the non-West's encounter with modernity. More to the point, the recognition of modernity's fragmentation that figures prominently in poststructuralism's critique of it is, on the one hand, relevant only in retrospect and from an exteriorized (often Eurocentric) view, and on the other, of limited value in the study of the historical experience of modernity. Important in understanding how people encountered and internalized modernity is probing the very lack of fragmentation in their perception; it is precisely the unity and coherence of modernity in the imagination and consciousness of those seeking to be modern that marks its overarching historical significance.

Clearly there is a measure of local adaptation—variations on the theme of modernity. However, anything claimed to be modern must maintain (or attempt to maintain) a transnational intelligibility to have any authority or power. To extend the linguistic metaphor further, modernity is a language that can acquire local dialects. However, were those dialects to lose coherence or a degree of lexical uniformity, they would no longer constitute modernity. I suspect what is often labeled "alternative modernity" is in fact these local idioms that at the most radical level are still comprised of the definitive components of modernity. An anxiety about the brutal homogenizing and flattening effect of neomodernization is the motive for identifying "alternative modernity," as though a not quite modern modernity could insulate indigenous societies and local knowledges from the hegemonic forces of high capitalism and neocolonialism. "Alternative modernity" is seductive, but it has the possible effect of rendering modernity itself an ahistorical essence rather than affirming its status as a historically contingent ideological construction with geographical origins in northwestern Eurasia.[22]

Third, the unreliability and instability of forms—the central cause of the "crisis of modernity"—was the shared cost of modernity's cultural transformations in the West and the non-West. As Georg Simmel noted in his uncharacteristically pessimistic 1918 essay "Der Konflikt der modernen Kultur," "What is happening [now] is not only a passive dying out of traditional forms, but simultaneously a fully positive drive towards life which is actively repressing these forms. Since this struggle, in extent and intensity, does not permit concentration on the creation of new forms, it makes a virtue of necessity and insists on fighting against forms simply

---

[22] I explore these issues further in my "Die Grenzen der 'Alternativen Moderne' in der Geschichte des spätosmanischen östlichen Mittelmeers," in "Westasien und die Moderne," special issue, *Periplus* 13 (2003): 138–149.

because they are forms."[23] Simmel's writings on this crisis, complicated by his contention that "The nineteenth century, with its motley variety of intellectual currents, did not produce any . . . all embracing guiding concept," seem to anticipate the sense of cultural emptiness and ennui that the fascism of the interwar period capitalized upon and what today neomodernization seeks to anesthetize.[24] In the decade after Simmel's essay appeared, Sami al-Kayyali, the editor of the Aleppine journal *al-Hadith* [The Modern], voiced a similar conclusion. "The appeal of the 'new' is that its meaning effaces and annihilates the 'old.' The proponents of the 'new' always fail to see the usefulness of the 'old' and reject it out of hand."[25] As a remedy to the summary rejection of the old, Kayyali suggested novelizing the biographies of important figures from the Islamic past for didactic purposes. The irony of such a proposal is that it clearly reflected the adoption of the aesthetics of fin-de-siècle bourgeois historicism and not the resurrection of old forms associated with Islamic learning. This slippage of the stable cultural and aesthetic forms of the past into the instability of modernity's present echoes Walter Benjamin's observation that it is "precisely the modern which always conjures up prehistory."[26] Moreover, it hints at how moderns often found temporary refuge from the moral and intellectual uncertainties occasioned by the rapidity of change in nostalgia. Nevertheless, finding a "traditional" justification for doing the modern thing is a trope suffusing modernization programs; far from saving tradition from the modern and/or authenticating the modern with reference to tradition, it merely simulates tradition within a purely modern space. The most relevant and obvious example of this phenomenon is nationalism's body of invented traditions.[27]

Left unanswered in Simmel's conclusion—especially when seen through the lens of Kayyali's anxiety about the effacement of the "old"— are the possible consequences of the destruction or destabilizing of forms in the context of the colonial encounters of the last two centuries. Clearly, the historical experience of modernity in the Eastern Mediterranean was shaded by the increasing influence of Western Europeans and their governments in the Ottoman Empire, and likewise by the growing impact of the centralizing Ottoman Empire on the lives of its subjects; however, to

---

[23] Georg Simmel, *The Conflict in Modern Culture, and Other Essays,* trans. with an introduction by K. Peter Etzkorn (New York: Teachers' College Press, 1968), 377.

[24] Ibid., 79.

[25] Sami al-Kayyali, "Introduction," *al-Hadith* 2:10 (December/January1927/1928): 2.

[26] Walter Benjamin, *Charles Baudelaire: A Lyric Poet in the Era of High Capitalism,* trans. H. Zohn (London: New Left Books, 1973), 171.

[27] See Partha Chatterjee, *Nationalist Thought and the Colonial World: A Derivative Discourse* (London: Zed Books, 1986); also, Deniz Kandiyoti, "Afterword: Some Awkward Questions on Women and Modernity in Turkey," in Abu-Lughod, ed., *Remaking,* 271.

ascribe an exclusive role to imperialism—Ottoman, French, British, or otherwise—in this experience denies the agency of inhabitants of the Eastern Mediterranean in playing an active role in confronting the crisis of modernity. Conversely, characterizing how the observable modernity of the colonized transforms the colonizer, regardless of the reciprocal recognition of that modernity, remains, if not the unacknowledged, at least the unanalyzed dimension of the colonial encounter.

Reduced to its fundamentals, being modern required either a passive or an active assent to the universal nature of modernity, a commitment to an assault on the forms of the past, and the incorporation of a specific, though in the end mutable and contingent, corpus of ideas and practices. Moreover, being modern had to be observable and reproducible, something that bisected the public and the private, often requiring the use of venues such as clubs, newspapers, Western consumer goods, and schools in which or with which to perform one's modernity. Interventions like Qastun's confirm the adoption of that corpus of ideas and practices, but more important, provide a basis for reconstructing what it meant to be modern *at that moment*. In a larger sense, being modern forced individuals into a series of new and complex dialogues and exchanges with elements of their society. Adopting the position of the modern, they embraced ideas, forms of knowledge, and practices and rejected others that would have engendered responses varying from outright acceptance to suspicion or even fear and animus from their neighbors, the elite of the old social classes, and even members of their own families. Unlike relatively stable early modern Ottoman-Islamic forms, the legitimacy of the new ideas and practices would be based on their modernity or their more mercurial status as European, and fundamentally domesticating that praxis brought the moderns into alignment with an alien, non-Muslim, and acquisitive West. While their acceptance of the promise of modernity often at its most unironic face value, their unabashed faith in what they saw as self-evident rationality and science, and their firm belief in the inevitability of emancipation and progress may have solidified for some their links with a centralizing and modernizing Ottoman Empire, as well as securing their position with the colonizing West, it also put them in conflict with other components of the larger Eastern Mediterranean milieu. Where Qastun could formulate the benefits and necessity of being modern, less apparent from his talk, but certainly in his mind and in the minds of his audience, were the inherent risks of doing so.

It would be a mistake to conceive of this historical moment as one in which modernity appears from over the horizon to seduce delusional and passive natives who, lacking the will to resist it, naively and without guile gave in to its Panglossian promise to deliver the best of all possible worlds. This is the flaw inherent in Lewis's conclusion that the moderns of late-

Ottoman society were motivated by a desire to "win the respect of Europe by conforming to European patterns of culture and organization."[28] Such a conceptualization precludes the possibility that reformers and members of insurgent classes could and would employ modernity for their own ends and do so in a way that went far beyond resistance to or collaboration with the West. Observations like Lewis's disallow the possibility that those being modern could be makers of their own history.[29]

MIDDLE-CLASS MODERNITY

This book approaches the Eastern Mediterranean's encounter with modernity through the historical lens of the emergence of an urban middle class. However, it takes shape in the context of very little scholarship on the middle class in the Eastern Mediterranean or elsewhere in the colonial non-West. When the middle class has appeared in the historiography of the region, it has only been in fleeting glimpses or footnotes and rarely in any systematic fashion: the way the literature has addressed the organizational and ideological role of the *effendiyya*—Western-style educated young men—in nationalist struggles, or the place of middle-class subordinates in elite-dominated feminist movements, are chief examples of this phenomenon.[30]

---

[28] Lewis, *Emergence*, 234.

[29] As Talal Asad suggests, crucial to understanding the colonial encounter, modernity, and historical change in the Middle East at the onset of the twentieth century "is the determination of [the] new landscape, and the degree to which the languages, behaviors, and institutions [that modernity] makes possible come to resemble those that obtain in the West European nation-states. This approach requires some reference to the necessities and potentialities of modernity as these were presented by Europeans and interpreted" by people in the region. Talal Asad, *Formations of the Secular: Christianity, Islam, Modernity* (Stanford: Stanford University Press, 2003), 217.

[30] "Out of the 'traditional' urban and rural middle classes there emerged by the beginning of the twentieth century a new social group, the *effendiyya*. These men were the product of modern education, wore western-style clothing, emulated European lifestyles, and worked in the new occupations to which capitalist development had given rise. This category included secondary and university students, teachers, lawyers, journalists and other professionals, white-collar employees, and lower and middle-level government functionaries. These effendis would, despite their relatively small numbers, play a central role in Egypt's political life before 1952." Joel Benin and Zachary Lockman, *Workers on the Nile: Nationalism, Communism, Islamism and the Egyptian Working Class, 1882–1954* (Princeton: Princeton University Press, 1987), 10. See also, Gelvin, *Divided*, in particular his discussion of the *mutanawirrun* (the enlightened), 16–17. Hanna Batatu's monumental study of Iraq, *The Old Social Classes and the Revolutionary Movements of Iraq: A Study of Iraq's Old Landed and Commercial Classes and of Its Communists, Ba'thists, and Free Officers* (Princeton: Princeton University Press, 1978), employs the term "middle class" in very much the same way I do in this work: "The term 'middle class,' as used in these pages, refers to that compos-

Perhaps neglected because of the visceral reaction that this "inauthentic," often comprador middle class evinces from those who claim solidarity with a more "authentically national" past, the centrality of the middle class to the shape of the contemporary world is by no means commensurate with the paltry amount of attention paid to it.[31] Or, as Arno Mayer argues in "The Lower Middle Class as Historical Problem,"

> social scientist[s] may question the authenticity of this . . . middle-class universe. They may also deprecate it for being an uninspiring mélange, not to say syncretism of the higher bourgeois and the lower working—class cultures. But even syncretisms have been known to develop striking and unmistakable structures as well as dynamic qualities; and they have also been known to leave indelible marks on the course of human history.[32]

From the perspective of the late-Ottoman and interwar Eastern Mediterranean, the most intriguing element of this seminal essay occurs again in a footnote: "The essay does not pretend to speak of the petit bourgeois phenomenon . . . in the developing nations of the non-Western world. At best it provides a starting point for the study of the character and

---

ite part of society which is plural in its functions but has in common a middling income or a middling status, and which includes merchants, tradesmen, landowners, army officers, students, members of professions, civil servants, and employees of private companies. It would be a mistake to make too sharp a distinction of this class and another, say, between army officers and tradesmen or landowners, for it must not be forgotten that the real unit of class is not the individual but the family, and that members of one middle-class family pursue different professions" (28 n.55 and 5–12 passim). Akram Khater links modernity to a middle class in the historically unique moment of Maronite peasants emigrating and returning to the mountains of Lebanon where they attempted to reconfigure their lives in accordance with new tastes and, more important, gender roles. In so doing he emphasizes the role of transnational mobility in the emergence of the middle class, but less the ideation of modernity. Akram Fouad Khater, *Inventing Home: Emigration, Gender, and the Middle Class in Lebanon, 1870–1920* (Berkeley: University of California Press, 2001).

[31] The exclusive link between the Eastern Mediterranean middle class and the impression that it slavishly modeled itself on its European cognate has proved a gnawing source of embarrassment for many in the field and has contributed to the paucity of work on this group; in standard narratives, the middle class—often dominated by non-Muslims—somehow falls short of a nationalist ideal of authenticity (arguably a middle-class value as well). Writers have held up this supposed act of unself-conscious reproduction as an unintended communal character flaw. Leila Fawaz concludes a section on the *embourgeoisement* of a Beiruti entrepreneurial middle class with the conclusion, "The new clothes and houses were accompanied by a new European cultural orientation, and a passion for all things European developed among the city's Christians. Western ways were emulated, and Eastern ways were looked down upon. This new juxtaposition in Beirut of two ways of life was but one of the many challenges to sectarian harmony." Leila Fawaz, *Merchants and Migrants in Nineteenth-Century Beirut* (Cambridge: Harvard University Press, 1983), 102.

[32] Arno Mayer, "The Lower Middle Class as Historical Problem," *The Journal of Modern History* 47:3 (September 1975): 411.

place of the lower middle class . . . among the majority of the human race."[33] Nevertheless, in the thirty years since that article appeared, few in non-Western historiography have accepted Mayer's challenge. Brian Owensby's discussion of Brazil's white-collar middle class and a growing awareness of the need to situate the indigenous middle class in South Asian historiography like Sanjay Joshi's recent history of Lucknow's middle class are notable exceptions that still serve only to test the rule.[34] Crucially, Owensby and Joshi have also emphasized the cultural links among the members of the middle class and overarching questions of modernity and anxieties about being sufficiently modern in the practice of "middle classness."

A middle stratum of Western and Western-style educated state bureaucrats and indigenous colonial officials, medical doctors, lawyers, military officers, middle-man agents, bankers, journalists, state high school teachers, college students, and similar professionals and white-collar employees is a fact of late-Ottoman and interwar Eastern Mediterranean urban society. This stratum was drawn primarily from previous generations of the urban merchant class, absentee landowners, the corps of dragomans, Muslim and non-Muslim clerics and scholars, and, in disproportionate numbers, the region's ethnic, religious, and linguistic minorities. As will be explored further in subsequent chapters, the social roles and expectations, forms of cultural capital and wealth, and training and education that made one a constituent element of this stratum were novel to the region and can be traced to individual ambition, reform efforts of the Ottoman state, and the growing presence of the West in multiple manifestations from missionary education to economic penetration and outright military occupation.

Critically my conceptualization of this stratum as the middle class builds upon a consensus that "middle class" is more than a neutral economic category, but rather constitutes an intellectual, social, and cultural construct linked to a set of historical and material circumstances; class is more than just one's relationship to the means of production or the accumulation of wealth (which is also a reason why I have avoided the potential confusion that might ensue were I to characterize this stratum as merely an Eastern Mediterranean petit bourgeoisie). Therefore, organizing this stratum as a coherent category carries with it significance that far exceeds

---

[33] Ibid., 409–410.

[34] Brian P. Owensby, *Intimate Ironies: Modernity and the Making of Middle-Class Lives in Brazil* (Stanford: Stanford University Press, 1999); Ranajit Guha, *Dominance without Hegemony: History and Power in Colonial India* (Cambridge: Harvard University Press, 1997); Sanjay Joshi, *Fractured Modernity: Making of a Middle Class in Colonial North India* (New Delhi: Oxford University Press, 2001).

a simple statement of economic status or profession.[35] Moreover, identifying it as a class is based on the conclusion that the middle class is not just a byproduct of industrialization, but that its appearance can be understood in the context of new kinds of communicative technology, transportation, and urban forms as well as high capitalism; and while classes emerge, they are also made and remade. Consequently this is less a work of traditional class history than an exploration of cultural and social change, using class as both a methodological tool and a basis for historical and transnational comparison. Nevertheless, class, similar to other analytical constructs like ethnicity and gender, elides a large body of experience and tends to flatten history. What might be lost in terms of diversity in this case is balanced, however, by making visible an otherwise ignored feature of contemporary Eastern Mediterranean history.

Indeed, many of those in the Eastern Mediterranean who would be considered middle class were they living in the West by virtue of vocation, education, or standard of living asserted their own cultural and moral distance from the poor and their distinctiveness from the customary patrician oligarchy of the region's cities in the language of class. This is evidence not just of the degree to which Western historical thought had entered into use very early in the colonial encounter, but also of how members of this stratum, recognizing the unique nature of their role in their society, sought to explain themselves to themselves using available means. By the early 1900s terms like "bourgeoisie" and "middle class" had been translated into Arabic, Ottoman Turkish, and Armenian and were used as descriptive categories in journalism, official documents, and scholarly and popular writing. For example, in 1925 Edmond Rabbath, a Sorbonne-educated, liberal-nationalist Aleppine lawyer writing in *al-Hadith*, could address the historical role of *al-tabaqa al-wusta* (the middle class) in European *and* Ottoman history and argue that its existence was linked to the emergence of a modern Syrian national community.[36]

Toward the beginning of the twentieth century, the definitive elaboration of "middle classness" in Western Europe that Rabbath drew upon for his article revolved less around objective standards of wealth than

---

[35] Dror Wahrman's writing on the dominant perception of the middle class in the period immediately before the British Reform Bill of 1832 echoes the transformation of the meaning of middle class when he contends that "it [the middle class] was rendered a natural and self-evidently visible part of social reality; it was seen as an uncontested and unproblematic statement of fact; it was provided with a cogent storyline that explained its origins and justified its existence; it was given the simplicity and power of an essence." Dror Wahrman, *Imagining the Middle Class: The Political Representation of Class in Britain, c. 1780–1840* (Cambridge: Cambridge University Press, 1995), 18.

[36] Idmun al-Rabbat (Edmond Rabbath), "The Decline of Democracy," *al-Hadith* 2 (February 1927): 100–101.

upon the desire of those in the putative middle class to distinguish themselves from the lower classes. As Christophe Charle contends, "the expression 'middle class' was synonymous with bourgeoisie in the first half of
the nineteenth century [in France], but took on quite a different meaning,
by acquiring a plural, at the end of the century. It was used to embrace
everyone who tried to escape from the masses (workers and peasants)
without being sure they would attain undisputed bourgeois status."[37]
Critically, this French middle class, and that of much of Europe—linked
to the political developments of the early 1800s—found itself defined primarily by what it was not. Peter Gay echoes Charle and argues further
that this process of definition lacked precision:

> It had something to do with respectability, though not that alone, since it was
> the standard that upper segments of the working classes also hoped to achieve.
> Other ideals were more distinctly bourgeois: probity in commercial dealings,
> fidelity to one's spouse, self-control in expenditure, the need for privacy, the
> gospel of work, the love of beauty. Good taste was a badge craved by those
> who could, and often by those who could not afford it.[38]

Jürgen Kocka shares this emphasis on the sense of probity in public behavior and extends those features into the political and cultural spheres:

> By stressing the principles of achievement and education, work and self-reli-
> ance, a vision of a modern, secularized, self-regulating, enlightened "civil soci-
> ety" emerged that was supported by many middle-class persons, in opposition
> to the privileges and autocracy of the *ancien régime*. . . . While developing cohe-
> sion in opposition to people above and below, the middle class defined itself by
> its culture.[39]

And Eric Hobsbawm adds that the very imprecision of the definition of
middle class required the creation of a distinctly middle-class "hierarchy
of exclusiveness." This hierarchy authorized criteria for mobility into and
within the middle class: "a middle-class lifestyle and culture was one such
criterion, leisure activity, and especially the new invention of sport, was
another; but the chief indicator of actual membership increasingly became, and has remained, formal education."[40] To situate the middle class

---

[37] Christophe Charle, *Social History of France in the Nineteenth Century*, trans. Miriam
Kochan (Oxford: Berg, 1994), 278.

[38] Peter Gay, *The Bourgeois Experience: Victoria to Freud*, vol. 3, *The Cultivation of
Hatred* (New York: W. W. Norton, 1993), 18. On Gay's discussion of the cultural dimensions of middle-class life, see his *Schnitzler's Century: The Making of Middle-Class Culture
1815–1914* (New York: W. W. Norton, 2001).

[39] Jürgen Kocka, *Industrial Culture and Bourgeois Society: Business, Labor, and Bureaucracy in Modern Germany* (New York: Berghan Books, 1999), 233.

[40] Eric Hobsbawn, *The Age of Empire: 1875–1914* (New York: Vintage Books, 1989),
174. Also see Kocka, *Industrial Culture*, 234, "Families from various middle-class catego-

in modern history, a focus on the hierarchy of exclusiveness provides a means to conceptualize this class both in terms of its relationship to other classes and on the basis of its internal dynamics of distinction.[41]

The linking of the ideational and epistemological foundations of modernity with definitive middle-class cultural and political praxis is a phenomenon that I term "middle-class modernity." As previously noted, middle-class modernity describes a mutually reinforced calculus by which to be modern meant to be not like, but again *just as modern* as, the imagined, idealized middle class and, in a transitive sense, the bourgeoisie of Europe. By the same token, being middle class—here almost exclusively in a cultural sense—was the best evidence of being modern. Middle-class modernity suggests a specific kind of experiential phenomenon of modernity distinguished in part by the fact that its "surface momentum conceals its inner sameness, its increasing reproduction of the safe limits of the bourgeois world."[42] And while that sameness is precisely what led Charles Baudelaire and others like Karl Marx to label this modernity "false modernity," its association with Europe and its dominant class exercised an immense magnetic attraction on aspiring middle classes throughout the non-West. The open question is, how safe do these limits actually remain as aspects of the "bourgeois world" are introduced and adopted outside of the West?

As a consequence of technological changes in communication and transportation, the growth of print capitalism, and the introduction of modernist literary forms, a consensual language of social practice that used the perceived behavior of the Western middle class as a standard was available in the Eastern Mediterranean and could serve to make distinctions within that society by the second half of the nineteenth century. When examples of middle-class modernity gained currency in the Ottoman Eastern Mediterranean through media, literature (novels and self-help books), and later film and radio, education, bureaucratization, travel, and colonial encounters, it contributed both to the emergence and to definitive aspects of the middle class. Middle-class modernity provided at once a ladder and an objective for indigenous middle-class aspirations,

---

ries shared a respect for individual achievement, on which they based their claims for rewards, recognition, and influence. They shared a positive attitude toward regular work, a propensity for rationality and emotional control, and a fundamental striving for independence, either individually or through associations. The middle class emphasized education. General education (Bildung) served as a basis on which they communicated with one another, one that distinguished them from others who did not share this type of (usually classical) education. Scholarly pursuits were respected, as were music, literature, and the arts."

[41] Distinction is used here in the sense suggested by Pierre Bourdieu, *Distinction: A Social Critique of the Judgment of Taste* (Cambridge: Harvard University Press, 1984).

[42] Peter Nicolls, *Modernisms: A Literary Guide* (London: Macmillan, 1995), 7.

while the underlying motives for wanting to incorporate that praxis and those ideas remain as complex as the class itself. Variables including education, wealth, and religion controlled the manner in which middle-class modernity was understood and employed at any given moment; nevertheless, it formed a stable matrix of ineffable specificity that had the power to shape this stratum politically and socially and provide its members, in turn, with a warrant and a guide with which to seek to shape their own society. To paraphrase Potter Stewart, one knew middle-class modernity when one saw it without necessarily being able to explain exactly why. Likewise, the adoption of middle-class manners, patterns of consumption, and ways of thought perceived as inherently modern was by definition a cultural necessity and their implementation a social imperative.

Equally important is the recognition that the adoption of middle-class modernity did not necessarily efface all pre-existing forms of social and political interaction; rather, at moments, the actual praxis of the middle class took on the quality of a palimpsest, where the pre-existing practices and modern ones often operated simultaneously and not always exclusively. A salient example of this phenomenon is the grafting by middle-class intellectuals of the key middle-class concepts of respectability, mannered behavior, and probity in public and business dealings to the core "traditional" concept of *adab*, loosely defined as manners, good taste, and humaneness.[43] Adab, and other terms like *husn al-mukafa᾽a* (social grace) and *maslaha* (common good), which have extensive genealogies in Ottoman and Arab-Islamic thought, figure prominently in historical and political writing of the period. However, as used in those modern contexts, these concepts bore less resemblance to their historical antecedents and more, in practice, to calques of French and English words; in the lexical sleight-of-hand peculiar to modernism, concepts and ideas could be rendered more palatable to, or incur less resistance from, a conservative audience when repackaged in antique garb; and conversely, the residual power of certain key words, especially those linked to identity, ethnicity, and religion, would be harnessed by a modernizing elite for its own purposes.

It is crucial to note that thus conceived, middle-class modernity is not a phenomenon unique to the non-West, and echoes of it resound throughout the social history of contemporary Europe and the Americas.[44] By

---

[43] *EI*[2], 175–176.

[44] An instructive comparison can be drawn between the emergent middle class in the Ottoman Eastern Mediterranean and the class of white-collar, salaried wage earners of contemporary Western Europe. Like the office workers of Berlin, *die Angestellten*, that Siegfried Kracauer used to mark the links between modernity, culture, consumption, and class, the emergent middle class of the Eastern Mediterranean "quite unequivocally signal[ed] their will to climb socially in the aspirations symbolized by their trappings. They [did] their best

thinking about the Eastern Mediterranean's middle class in terms of a globalized middle-class modernity, this work places the regional experiences of class dynamics and struggle into a larger transnational frame; at the same time it underscores the hegemonic power of high capitalism and colonialism to shape social and communal relations on the most local and intimate levels.

Fatma Müge Göçek's, *Rise of Bourgeoisie, Demise of Empire* locates formative moments of this class in the "unintended consequences" of the elite-sponsored reforms of the Tanzimat period, which "transformed three Ottoman social groups—merchants, officials, and intellectuals—into an emergent bourgeoisie segmented along religious and ethnic lines."[45] The segmentation along religious lines evolved from the basic terms of the customary relationship between the Muslim ruling majority of the empire and its non-Muslim minorities. Already encapsulated into quasi-autonomous administrative units, *millets*, the form of religious distinction in Ottoman society served as a template for the formation of separate classes.[46] The higher degree of access to Western education and forms of socialization and organization transformed the movement of some in these already self-contained groups into the middle class.[47] The cultural origins of this part of the middle class support the argument that the notion of "middle class" hinges less on objective standards of wealth than on a systematic adherence to patterns of behavior and presentations of self.

Crucial to this sectarian bifurcation of the class was the Ottoman Land Law of 1858 (Arazi Kanunnamesi). Before the midcentury, real property was not owned per se, but rather held by individuals for use, often in perpetuity, the land itself belonging to the state. As a feature of economic liberalization, the Ottoman state promulgated a series of land registration and purchasing laws. Used primarily by the urban notability to secure its position by recording vast amounts of land in its names, it also opened the door for smaller agricultural entrepreneurs and land speculators. Growing wealth among these smaller landholders created an economic basis for their movement into the middle class, primarily through the vehicle of state education and white-collar bureaucratic jobs. Legally, non-

---

to enter the middle class by means of mere semblance, by mimicry of the existing systems of rule." Gertrud Koch, *Siegfried Kracauer, an Introduction*, trans. Jeremy Gaines (Princeton: Princeton University Press, 2000), 69.

[45] Fatma Müge Göçek, *Rise of the Bourgeoisie, Demise of Empire: Ottoman Westernization and Social Change* (Oxford: Oxford University Press, 1996), 109–110.

[46] On the millet system in the nineteenth century, see Roderic Davison, "Millets as Agents of Change in the Nineteenth-Century Ottoman Empire," in B. Braude and B. Lewis, eds., *Christians and Jews in the Ottoman Empire* (New York: Holmes and Meir, 1982), 1:71–84.

[47] Göçek, *Rise*, 110.

Muslims could own land; in practice, however, state bureaucrats tended to obstruct the purchase of real estate by Christians and Jews in favor of Muslims.[48] On the one hand, this solidified the position of non-Muslims in the retail and banking sectors and resulting forms of cultural capital; on the other, it strengthened their sense of alienation from the larger Ottoman community.

Göçek's work represents a fundamental departure from previous studies of nineteenth-century Ottoman intellectual and social history in that she includes evidence from bourgeois intellectual productions and material culture, thus allowing this group to speak for itself, as it were. However, by her almost exclusive focus on the capital of the Ottoman Empire, Istanbul, she neglects to study the formation of the middle class in the periphery of that vast state. The process of fragmentation and bifurcation described in her work certainly occurred in other parts of the empire.

Such a process took on a specific character in cosmopolitan provincial cities like Aleppo, Beirut, Baghdad, Salonica, and Alexandria. One of the pertinent questions raised in the periphery is, to which grand world city (*métropole*) does the middle class look as its ideal? Some Constantinopolitans may have sought to re-create themselves in the image of their imagined Parisian cognate. They would never have considered Aleppines proper exemplars. In Aleppo, however, the fashions, manners, mores, and practices of the idealized class cognate in Istanbul, Cairo, Paris, or London—or any combination thereof—would have been considered exemplary by the middle class, though perhaps not equally so. Thus one not only behaved outwardly modern but also shared thereby in a middle-class anxiety about being as modern as European and central Ottoman archetypes. The Aleppine experience, similar to that in the remainder of the colonial world, confirms that both the desideratum of middle-class modernity and actual examples of it drawn from several métropoles were in a constant and fluid process of juxtaposition and informed possible choices and patterns of behavior.[49] The major distinction revolved around not just an abstract idea of modernity, but rather the degree to which the individuals or groups actively identify with a specific metropolitan practice of modernity. For the Aleppo of the nineteenth and early twentieth

---

[48] Kemal Karpat, *The Politicization of Islam: Reconstructing Identity, State, Faith and Community in the Late-Ottoman State* (Oxford: Oxford University Press, 2001), 93–98; Peter Sluglett and Marion Farouk-Sluglett, "The Application of the 1858 Land Code in Greater Syria: Some Preliminary Observations," in Tarif Khalidi, ed., *Land Tenure and Social Transformation in the Middle East* (Beirut: American University Beirut 1984), 409–424.

[49] "The specific categories and constellations of categories used by individuals within these groupings to organize their world and order their society naturally cohered with, and in some cases even duplicated, those enjoined by the dominant culture with the *métropole*." Gelvin, *Divided*, 16.

centuries, the exemplary métropoles were Paris, London, and Istanbul; later, in the 1930s, Berlin, Moscow, and Cairo were incorporated, and certainly now that list must include Hollywood and New York.

TOWARD AN ARCHITECTURE OF EASTERN MEDITERRANEAN COMMUNITY

By the end of the nineteenth century, the middle class had become a palpable public and social presence in the Ottoman Empire. And while increasingly substantial, it still represented a small portion of the total population. The middle class's growing role was determined less by numbers and more by its unique control of critical aspects of a modernizing society and increasing amounts of liquid wealth. From expertise in new military and communication technology, journalism, banking, espionage, and secular education, to a greater ability to interact with the West through knowledge of foreign languages, dual nationality as agents of foreign companies and governments, and legal and commercial acumen, this class occupied a position of power and influence in society disproportionate to its size. However, despite the large-scale political reforms of the Tanzimat period, the Eastern Mediterranean middle class never attained juridical legitimacy in the complex political theory of the Ottoman state. In other words, where the nineteenth-century political orders in France and England began to reckon with the demands of an increasingly substantial middle class, in the Ottoman Empire, no special political rights accrued to members of this stratum.[50] Not until the Young Turk Revolution did discussions arise about the actual position of a middle class in the new political order. While Aykut Kansu's insistence that the Revolution of 1908 was "one of the last examples of bourgeois revolutions to have taken place before the First World War" is overstated, it does reflect the fact that several Young Turk ideologues, most notably Yusuf Akçura, argued that the formation of a national middle class was fundamental to institutionalizing the revolution.[51] Indeed, aspects of Young Turk economic policy in the period after 1908 and later those of the Kemalists were dedicated to creating this class through the implementation of a *millî iktisat*, a national economy. This policy often resulted in the marginalization of Jewish, Armenian, Greek, Arab Muslim, and Christian middle-class merchants and bureaucrats and, in a few cases, the attempted violent elimination or the

---

[50] Selim Deringil's *The Well-Protected Domains: Ideology and the Legitimation of Power in the Ottoman Empire, 1876–1909* (London: I. B. Tauris, 1998) describes the political formulas and political structures Ottoman society in the prerevolutionary period, and the lack of the middle class in those formulas.

[51] Aykut Kansu, *The Revolution of 1908 in Turkey* (Leiden: Brill, 1997), 27.

mass extra-judicial killing of entire ethnic and religious communities, to facilitate the creation of a Turkish-speaking Muslim middle class.[52]

In Aleppo and in provincial cosmopolitan cities like Izmir,[53] Beirut,[54] or Alexandria,[55] this commercial or entrepreneurial middle class was dominated by non-Muslims. Why the middle class segmented so thoroughly along sectarian lines and persistently conceptualized politics in this vein is a question central to this book. Consequently, my analysis reflects the fact that historically contingent sect and communal conflict conditioned both inter- and intraclass relations, and as questions unfolded about the middle class in Eastern Mediterranean urban society, religious affiliation took on a significance it may not have acquired in the West. Nevertheless, this recognition points to a larger need to acknowledge how the question of modernity in the Eastern Mediterranean must be formulated against Muslim-Christian subordination, difference, and conflict. In prewar Aleppo the problematic sectarian element of Young Turk economic policy, the full dimensions of which had yet to be realized, caused some anxiety, but on balance the "bourgeois" nature of the Revolution of 1908 resonated positively with the local middle-class community.

More important than the economic policy was the premium Young Turk liberalism placed on elevating the middle class into a position of authority, over and against the empire's ruling elite and palace bureaucracy. Countering the customary political and legal restrictions placed on non-Muslims in Ottoman society, the idea of an increased role for the middle class filtered into provincial locations like Aleppo and introduced members of this class into the "politics of notables." In late-Ottoman provincial urban society, the calculus of power was the "politics of notables," in which the traditional Sunni Muslim urban oligarchy, in local parlance the a'yan (literally, "those in the public eye"), held power by virtue of both secular and divine sanction.[56] The middle class, especially

[52] Feroz Ahmad, *The Making of Modern Turkey* (London: Routledge, 1993), 42–46; Erik J. Zürcher, *Turkey: A Modern History* (London: I. B. Tauris, 1993), 129; Zafer Toprak, *Türkiye'de "Millî İktisat," 1908–1918* (Istanbul: Yurt, 1982).

[53] Daniel Goffman, *Izmir and the Levantine World, 1550–1650* (Seattle: University of Washington Press, 1990); Edhem Eldem, Daniel Goffman, and Bruce Masters, *The Ottoman City between East and West: Aleppo, Izmir and Istanbul* (London: Cambridge University Press, 1999).

[54] Fawaz, *Merchants.*

[55] Malak Zaalouk, *Power, Class and Foreign Capital in Egypt: The Rise of a New Bourgeoisie* (London: Zed, 1989); Robert Ilbert, *Alexandrie, 1830–1930: Histoire d'une communauté citadine* (Cairo: Institut Français d'Archéologie Orientale, 1996).

[56] "A relatively high degree of social and religious uniformity and cohesion in urban society itself allowed the urban upper class to pose successfully as a 'natural' leadership. In a sense, its domination of urban society was 'legitimized' because a high proportion of the population in each town—a population that, despite the dramatic changes of the era, was

its non-Muslim component, is likewise a silent element in studies of the "politics."[57] In the revolutionary period, the Eastern Mediterranean's middle class grew increasingly disconnected from the hegemonic social group of a'yan, but it nevertheless maintained an ambivalent relationship with it. More important, many members of the middle class—Muslim and non-Muslim—had grown dissatisfied with the form of political control it legitimized and sought self-consciously modern alternatives. If the idea of class can be built on a group's "sense of an overriding collective struggle for independence or hegemony," as Charles Maier has suggested, the many merchants, doctors, lawyers, bankers, and teachers who exhibited antipathy to the illiberal politics of notables in their everyday political practice clearly qualified as a class.[58]

The collision between the "politics of notables" and the notions of citizenship and representational politics authorized by middle-class modernity demands a more robust connection between state, society, religion, and culture in the writing of the contemporary history of the Eastern Mediterranean. Rather than a mere supplanting of old styles of leadership and the effacement of customary modes of legitimacy, the transformation of society linked to the emergence of the middle class transcended the political and entered social and cultural history in unprecedented ways.

What happened was something larger than the displacement of the "traditional" by the modern. For the middle class and the society that encompassed it, relationships with colonialism, emigration, forms of mass violence including genocide, new uses of space and kinds of technology, the draw of nationalism, the artifice of historicism, and the persistence

---

still very much attached to its traditional religious beliefs, cultural practices, and customs— identified the defenders of the faith and guardians of culture as well as the providers of vital goods and services with the local upper class." Khoury, *Mandate*, 13. The term "natural" leadership in this passage is drawn from the seminal work of Albert Hourani in his "Ottoman Reform and the Politics of Notables," in William R. Polk and Richard L. Chambers, eds., *Beginnings of Modernization in the Middle East* (Chicago: University of Chicago Press, 1968), 41–68. On the rise of the a'yan in the Ottoman period, see Halil Inalcik, "Centralization and Decentralization in Ottoman Administration," in Thomas Naff and Roger Owen, eds., *Studies in Eighteenth Century Islamic History* (Carbondale: Southern Illinois University Press, 1977), 27–52.

[57] Khoury notes, albeit viewing the question from the top down, "Our understanding of their [the notables'] connection to Christian merchants and moneylenders, and their relations with the urban religious minorities in general, remains grossly inadequate. . . . Indeed we need more information on the ways individual notables or their families were able both to mobilize and contain popular forces. . . . And greater attention must be paid to their role of notables in the cultural life of the towns, in particular their role in education and literary activities in this period of profound intellectual change." Philip Khoury, "The Urban Notables Paradigm Revisited," *REMMM* 55–56 (January and February 1990): 226.

[58] Charles Maier, *Recasting Bourgeois Europe: Stabilization in France, Germany, and Italy in the Decade after World War I* (Princeton: Princeton University Press, 1975), 19.

of sectarianism created a form of historical experience more fluid and dynamic than discretely constructed social or political history can describe. Understanding that history requires instead a recognition that "experience," in the words of Ronald Grigor Suny and Geoff Eley, is "always itself discursively framed and understood [and] creates identities of 'interest,' textures of identification and architectures of community"; at issue for the historian "is the way in which experiences are handled in cultural terms, embodied in traditions, value systems, ideas, and institutional forms."[59]

By forging a link between being modern and the emergence of the middle class, my work creates a template for locating the historical experience of modernity in the history of the Eastern Mediterranean that captures those "textures of identification and architectures of community." Moreover, by combining the cultural-intellectual dimensions of modernity with the radical alteration of urban political and social structures in the cosmopolitan cities of the Eastern Mediterranean, my approach offers a critical-theoretical and comparative means by which to describe the humanity, sophistication, and urbanity of a community and its members in an era of anxiety and rapid change that at once secures the uniqueness of their experience and confirms its familiarity.

Following an introductory discussion of the political and urban history of Aleppo in the late nineteenth century, the book traces in a roughly chronological fashion the middle class's historical experience of modernity in the three fields of revolutionary politics, historicism and nationalism, and colonialism. Preceding each of the three sections are short discussions of the theoretical implications of what follows, as well as the broader historical context, which may be unfamiliar to nonspecialists.

Qastun's New Year's address not only highlights the manifestation of the middle class in the political and social history of Aleppo but also serves as the point of departure for the first of these sections, "Being Modern in a Time of Revolution." This section locates the middle class in the political history of the city and follows the process by which it created and contested the civil society in the late-Ottoman period and into the early postwar years. Qastun's words also confirm the internalization of a specifically modern and middle-class view of history. Embracing a Hegelian notion that History is the unfolding of human freedom, this style of imagining the past derived from a general incorporation of modernist forms of history writing and narrative. The second part of the book, "Being Modern in a Moment of Anxiety," examines the way middle-class Alep-

---

[59] Geoff Eley and Ronald Grigor Suny, "Introduction," in Geoff Eley and Ronald Grigor Suny, eds., *Becoming National: A Reader* (Oxford: Oxford University Press, 1996), 10.

pines wrote their own history, reacted to the introduction of an official Arab nationalism, and dealt with the aftermath of the tumultuous period of the Great War. The final section, "Being Modern in an Era of Colonialism," follows several of these innovations in Aleppo as Ottoman suzerainty gave way to the French colonial presence, an occupation welcomed, at least initially, by Qastun.

TWO

An Eastern Mediterranean City on the Eve of Revolution

> I do not know Aleppo—an Oriental city will not admit you
> into the circle of its intimates unless you spend months within
> its walls—but I did not leave without having perceived dimly
> that there was something to be known.
> —Getrude Bell, 1905

Gertrude Bell's wistful recollection of her visit shares with the three previous centuries of travelers' accounts of Aleppo an emphasis on the city's architectural elegance, ethnic diversity, and obsession with trade and commerce. Arriving just a few years into the twentieth century, Bell was well placed to observe the cumulative effects of the transformations of the preceding decades on Eastern Mediterranean urban society. The most pertinent of these observations followed a chance meeting at the Baron Hotel with the prominent middle-class Arab Christian banker Nicola Homsy. While noting that Homsy was "representative of the best educated and enterprising classes in Syria," she concluded that he still suffers "at the hands of the Turk . . . because his interests call aloud for progress, and progress is what the Turk will never understand." Her Edwardian prejudices against "the Turk" (Muslims) of the day aside, Bell's conclusion would nevertheless be reflected in later public discourse, as would her valediction: "There must be some native vitality that corresponds to these signs of past greatness, but the town has fallen on evil days."[1]

Aleppines echoed this ambivalent view of their city in their writings and later memoirs, yet they still identified with Halab al-Shahba' (Aleppo the Gray)—the popular appellation for the city and a reflection of the use of gray stone in much of its architecture—much more than with any other geographical or political construct and took great pride in the fact that they lived there. Fierce identification of groups and individuals with cities was common throughout the Eastern Mediterranean, thereby marking the city, rather than the region or later the nation, as a crucial space from which to begin to ask questions about social and cultural change and

---

[1] Getrude Bell, *The Desert and the Sown* (London: W. Heinemann, 1907), 260, 266–267, 261.

modernity, more broadly.[2] Likewise, the city was a venue within which many of the bureaucratic and social reforms of the modernizing Tanzimat, notably urban renewal, including tearing down city walls and building wide thoroughfares in their place, the establishment of bureaucratically complex municipalities, and public health measures, were implemented, and it was in trading cities like Aleppo that ties with Europe and Europeans were the strongest. Over the course of the nineteenth century, these features of urban life helped shape the region's middle class and contributed to the kinds of deep cultural and political cleavages that would appear most distinctly after the Revolution of 1908 and into the interwar period.

Like other cities of the Mediterranean, including Trieste, Salonica, Izmir, and Alexandria, Aleppo fit uncomfortably into modernist structures of nation and ethnicity. A tremendous ethnic, religious, and linguistic diversity marked the life of these cities. From the perspective of the twenty-first century, such difference is remarkable, but before World War I inhabitants of places like Aleppo would have expected such diversity to exist, perhaps considering it proof of their city's prominence. Like these other cities, Aleppo sat astride global trade routes and served in the early modern period as a center of long-distance commerce in luxury goods, attracting merchants from all around the Mediterranean, northern Europe, and South and Central Asia.[3] Jewish traders, the Sassoon family in particular, came to the city from India,[4] augmenting an already large indigenous community. Armenian silk merchants and weavers arrived from Anatolia or Shah Abbas's imperial capital, Isfahan.[5] Europeans dis-

---

[2] Recent work on the profound changes in urban cultures of individual Eastern Mediterranean cities includes Fawaz, *Merchants and Migrants*; May Seikaly, *Haifa, Transformation of an Arab City 1918–1939* (London: I. B. Tauris, 1995); Leila Fawaz and C. A. Bayly, *Modernity and Culture from the Mediterranean to the Indian Ocean, 1890–1920* (New York: Columbia University Press, 2001); Jens Hanssen, Thomas Philipp, and Stefan Weber, eds. *The Empire in the City: Arab Provincial Capitals in the Late Ottoman Empire* (Würzburg: Ergon in Kommission, 2002); Mark Levine, *Overthrowing Geography: Jaffa, Tel Aviv, and the Struggle for Palestine, 1880–1948* (Berkeley: University of California Press, 2005); Jens Hanssen, *Fin de Siècle Beirut: The Making of an Ottoman Provincial Capital* (Oxford: Clarendon Press, 2005).

[3] On Aleppo's geopolitical links with global trade routes, see Heinz Gaube and Eugen Wirth, *Aleppo. Historische und geographische Beiträge zur baulichen Gestaltung, zur sozialen Organisation und zur wirtschaftlichen Dynamik einer vorderasiatischen Fernhandelsmetropole. Tübinger Atlas des Vorderen Orients*, Beihefte, Reihe B, no. 58 (Wiesbaden: L. Reichert, 1984).

[4] See Walter P. Zenner, *A Global Community: The Jews from Aleppo, Syria* (Detroit: Wayne State University Press, 2000).

[5] On the lives of Aleppine Armenians before the Armenian Genocide of 1915, see Artawazd Siwrmeian, *Patmut'iwn Halepi Hayots'* (Paris: Imprimerie Araxes, 1950), 3:1355–1908; Ina Baghdiantz McCabe, *The Shah's Silk for Europe's Silver: The Eurasian Trade of the Julfa Armenians in Safavid Iran and India* (Atlanta: Scholars Press, 1999).

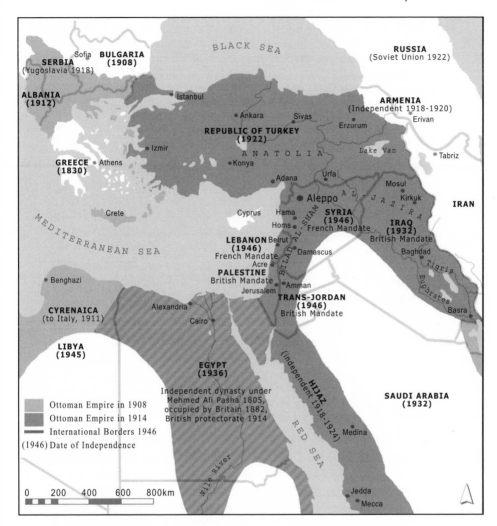

MAP 2.1. Aleppo in the Eastern Mediterranean, 1908–1946.

patched merchant adventurers to the city. Once there, they established trading houses in any one of the grand urban caravansaries located in and around Aleppo's massive central business district. The Venetians called theirs *fondaco*s; the French, *échelles*; and the English, factories.[6]

The basic modalities of this Western economic penetration of the region both exploited and enhanced the diverse nature of the city. Each of the

---

[6] Bruce Masters, *Christians and Jews in the Ottoman Arab World: The Roots of Sectarianism* (Cambridge: Cambridge University Press, 2001), and *The Origins of Western Eco-*

foreign merchant groups, known in the parlance of the day as "trading nations," maintained privileged relations with its preferred local religious community. The French favored the Uniate sects; the English, the Jews. These relationships created deep bonds between Europeans and local people—primarily non-Sunni Muslims—that transcended culture and language.[7] These relationships persisted even as Aleppo's international economic importance waned in the nineteenth century. Nevertheless, Aleppo remained a vibrant and cosmopolitan crossroads of the Old World well into the 1900s.

While Ottoman demographers did not enumerate people using notions of race or ethnicity, and instead counted people on the basis of their religious affiliation, the population description from the 1903 edition of Aleppo's *Sâlnâme*, the provincial almanac, provides a hint of this continuing cosmopolitanism. "Now there are in [Aleppo] Muslim Turks, Arabs, Turcomans, Circassians, Kurds; and from the Christians there are Greek Orthodox, Greek Catholics, Armenians . . . Syriacs . . . Maronites, Protestants, Chaldeans, and Latin Catholics. . . . And there are Jews. All the people," proudly concluded the anonymous Ottoman functionary, "are generous, intelligent, hospitable and hardworking."[8] The comfort the author had with mixing religious affiliation and seemingly ethnic terms like Arab, Turk, Armenian, and Kurd is an intriguing moment of hybridization and suggests that as these ideas acquired new shades of meaning in the region, they were simply grafted onto preexisting concepts of difference.

Muslims in the city, and in the rest of the empire, tended to cooperate in international commerce as superior legal partners. Unlike their non-Muslim counterparts, they enjoyed positions in the military, government, and religious establishment. As the Ottoman state expanded the bureaucratic, military, and educational systems along European lines over the course of the nineteenth century, knowledge of foreign languages and new technologies and forms of political and social organization penetrated into the Muslim community of the city and facilitated a transition to modern middle-class "ways of knowing" for Muslims. Significantly, for the Muslims in Aleppine society, their comprehension of things

---

nomic Dominance in the Middle East: Mercantilism and the Islamic Economy in Aleppo, 1600–1750 (New York: New York University Press, 1988). See especially chapter 3, "Merchant Diasporas and Trading 'Nations,' " 72–109.

[7] Ibid. On the *échelles* and their local connections and interlocutors, or *Beratlı lar*, see François Charles-Roux, *Les Échelles de Syrie et de Palestine au XVIIIe siècle* (Paris: Librarie Orientaliste Paul Geuthner, 1928). See also Ralph Davis, *Aleppo in Devonshire Square* (London: Macmillan, 1967); and Alexander Russell, *The Natural History of Aleppo* (London: Robinson, 1794), 2 vols.

[8] *Sâlnâme* (Aleppo, 1321 [1903]), 219.

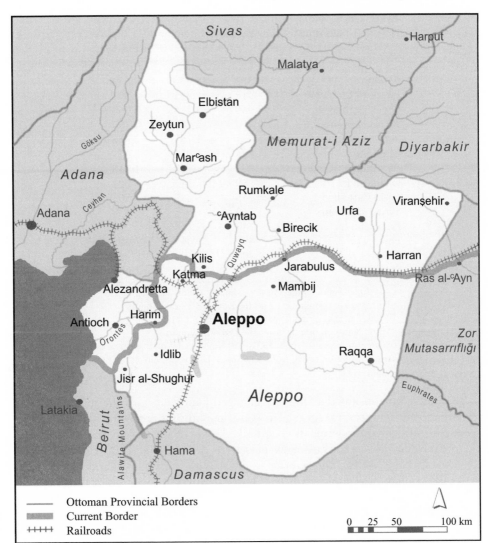

MAP 2.2. The Ottoman province of Aleppo, ca. 1908–1918.

modern derived less from direct contact with Westerners or their métropoles and instead passed through the lens of the imperial capital of
Istanbul.

At the outset of the nineteenth century, battles between the local Janissaries and the resident *eşraf*—the syndicate of descendants of the Prophet
Muhammad—for control of the city and an empirewide struggle for dominance between Mehmed Ali Pasha, the viceroy of Egypt, and the Otto-

TABLE 2.1
Aleppo Adult Population by Religious Community

Sect	Female	Male	Total
Muslim*	40,398	38,235	78,633
Greek Orthodox	418	461	879
Greek Catholic†	3,980	3,728	7,708
Armenian Catholic†	2,050	2,148	4,197
Syrian Catholic†	1,331	1,357	2,688
Maronite†	1,035	982	2,017
Armenian Orthodox	931	787	1,718
Chaldean†	89	113	202
Latin Catholic†	256	250	506
Syrian Orthodox	60	75	135
Protestant	42	55	97
Foreign‡	499	1,063	2,062
Jewish	4,405	4,506	8,911
Stranger§	553	1,028	2,081

* Includes Sunni, Shiite, Alawite, Ismaili, Yezidi, and Druze
† Uniate—in communion with the Roman Catholic Church
‡ Resident with origins outside the Ottoman Empire
§ Resident with origins inside the Ottoman Empire
Source: Sâlnâme (Aleppo, 1321 [1903]), "Population Figures of the City of Aleppo Extracted from the Census Data of the Ministry of Population," 241.

man sultans meant that the city changed hands on both the local and national levels several times. The sometimes abrupt process of state centralization and modernization embarked upon by the Ottoman state, the Tanzimat, linked the city more closely to the Ottoman central government. Nevertheless, the reforms, a devastating earthquake, and successive epidemics of cholera all contributed to novel forms of social dislocation within the city.[9] Intense communal violence at midcentury during which an angry mob attacked the extramural Christian neighborhood of Judayda, still remembered by the euphemism the "Events," provides evidence of sectarian atomization and growing economic differences in the city. Writing on the underlying causes of the Events, Bruce Masters notes that,

> In Aleppo, [the] change in commercial fortunes led to a rise of a Christian, usually Catholic, entrepreneurial class that no longer looked to partnerships with local Muslim merchants, as they had in the seventeenth and early eighteenth centuries, but rather to Europeans. Additionally, competition in the

[9] Herbert Bodman, *Political Factions in Aleppo, 1760–1826* (Chapel Hill: University of North Carolina Press, 1963), 144.

trades led to greater religious segregation in the remaining guilds than had previously been the case. Christian and Muslims were less frequently neighbors and coworkers in nineteenth century Aleppo than they had been in the past.[10]

As Masters has emphasized, conflict of this type in Aleppo should not be characterized as simply a question of sectarian tension. To explain the conflict as either an essential "ancient" problem of Muslim—non-Muslim animus or a result of growing economic inequalities is a failure to recognize the impact of political transformations and the growing colonial pressures of the period.[11]

Also absent from these conclusions is a consideration of the power modernist idealism within the city and the manner in which these ideas shaped the way various groups were perceived or perceived themselves, each other, and their surroundings. In her assessment of the 1860s' conflicts in Damascus and Mount Lebanon, Leila Fawaz has suggested that the violence of this time was a result of a growing gap between haves and have nots.[12] It is necessary to take her conclusion one step further and contend that during the late nineteenth century the very nature of who was a "have" also changed. The legalization of private property and the resulting accumulation of land and wealth in the hands of Christian businessmen and bankers certainly aided the creation of this new class of "haves."[13]

VISIBLE AND INVISIBLE HIERARCHIES: SOCIAL DISTINCTION AND SYSTEMS OF EXCLUSION

This new social category "had" something else as well: knowledge of *modern* forms of organization, commercial law, banking, and investment tools, and access—in the broadest sense of the term—to an ascendant

[10] Bruce Masters, "The 1850 Events in Aleppo: An Aftershock of Syria's Incorporation into the Capitalist World System," *IJMES* 22 (1990): 16.

[11] For a similar moment, see Ussama Makdisi's discussion of the links between the processes of bureaucratic and economic modernization, imperialism, and the creation of Eastern Mediterranean sectarianism, *The Culture of Sectarianism: Community, History, and Violence in Nineteenth-Century Ottoman Lebanon* (Berkeley: University of California Press, 2000).

[12] Leila Tarazi Fawaz, *An Occasion for War: Civil Conflict in Lebanon and Damascus in 1860* (Berkeley: University of California Press, 1994), 100.

[13] See Peter Sluglett's description of economic change in Aleppo during the later-Ottoman and early interwar period, "Aspects of Economy and Society in the Syrian Provinces: Aleppo in Transition, 1880–1925," in Fawaz and Bayly, eds., *Modernity and Culture*, 144–157. Also Kemal Karpat, "The Land Regime, Social Structure, and Modernization in the Ottoman Empire," in William R. Polk and Richard L. Chambers, eds., *Beginnings of Modernization in the Middle East* (Chicago: University of Chicago Press, 1968), 69–90.

world beyond Aleppo. This knowledge could be capitalized upon in the commercial sphere, but also more generally in civic life. While this knowledge and capital was by no means exclusive to the non-Muslim minority of the city, it nevertheless contributed to the growing distance between the emergent middle class and traditional Aleppo over the course of the century.

The Bureaucracy

This distancing had become apparent in the critical cleavages in the origin, training, and professional trajectory of the men occupying positions in the provincial bureaucracy. For the period 1876–1908 the basic text of provincial organization is the *Sâlnâme*. These volumes, published annually, are at once documentary evidence and a memorial to the universalizing and totalizing spirit of organization, which drove Ottoman reform during the Tanzimat period and later. The highly structured, impersonal, and uniform ordering of administration of power and authority in Aleppo as documented in the *Sâlnâme*s contrasts markedly with contemporary accounts of the period that portray a system driven by custom, personalities, venality, and nepotism.[14] According to the *Sâlnâme*, provincial organization followed the order at the center. At the core of the provincial administration was the "staff of the province" (*erkân-i vilâyet*), with the governor at the helm. The bulk of the almanac is dedicated to listing each and every state employee by department and position. Abbreviated notations indicating a rank, date attained, and awards follow each entry. The ranking and awards established a standardized pay scale and resembled civil services rankings in Europe.

Local organization in the later Tanzimat period, following the Provincial Administration Law of 1867, asserted Ottoman central control while recognizing the resilience of customary lines of authority. Hourani and others argue that the central authorities could not control provincial society effectively without the cooperation of local notables. Thus Ottoman officials sent from Istanbul were most numerous in executive positions, the military, and what could be termed technical-administrative roles. In contrast, representatives of established notable families appeared regularly in three areas of the bureaucracy: the local administrative councils, Muslim educational facilities, and the Islamic law courts.

While imperial parliamentary representation had ceased with the abrogation of the constitution, municipal and provincial councils, peopled by

[14] Hasan Duman, *Osmanl Yıllıklar (Salnameler ve Nevsaller)* [Ottoman Year-Books] (Istanbul: Renkler, 1982), 17–26.

locally selected representatives, continued to exist.[15] In principle an openly elected panel, the provincial council of Aleppo continued to be dominated by two families throughout the last decades of the nineteenth and first years of the twentieth century. These two families, the Jâbirî zâde and the Mudarris zâde, alternated control of the council as presidents and members. Jâbirî zâde ʿAbd al-Qadir, the father of Ottoman deputy Nafʿi Pasha and the elite-nationalist Saʿdallah al-Jabiri of the interwar period, occupied a seat on the panel until his appointment as the provincial *müftü* at the turn of the century. Jâbirî zâde Muhammad Asʿad Pasha served as president of the council for sixteen years and held that position at the time of the Revolution of 1908.[16] While governors rotated in and out of office every three years or so, the authority of the notables increased as they possessed a much deeper comprehension of the local situation and a much greater ability to control it.[17] Mastering this information distinguished those notable clans who survived the Tanzimat intact.[18]

Far from merely surviving the period 1876–1908, under the leadership of Nafiʿ Pasha, the Jâbirî zâde manipulated the bureaucratic system and landownership rules to such a degree and with such alacrity that they thrived.[19] Indeed, Nafiʿ Pasha defined the evolution of notable behavior necessitated by the Tanzimat. Trading on family prestige and control of an electoral district, he was elected to the first Ottoman parliament at the age of twenty-nine in 1876. Continued political activity moved his younger brother Ihsân into the Yildiz Palace as a chamberlain, thus guaranteeing the family's access at the highest levels. Locally, sixteen relatives served in various positions in the Aleppo bureaucracy. Writing about the local political scene in the months before the revolution, the British consul observed that:

> Four of his sons are in the correspondence department and one in the Dragomanate. His brother Hadji Murat effendi is not only a member of the Civil Court of Appeal but president of the Examining Court upon the decision of which the committal of an accused depends greatly. The rest are first cousins serving as clerks, the eldest of whom, Beha effendi, is chief scribe in the Public Prosecutor's office.[20]

[15] On the councils see, Ruth Roded, "Tradition and Change in Syria during the Last Decades of Ottoman Rule: The Urban Elite of Damascus, Aleppo, Homs and Hama, 1876–1918" (Ph.D. diss., University of Denver, 1984); and Elizabeth Thompson, "Ottoman Political Reform in the Provinces: The Damascus Advisory Council in 1844–45," *IJMES* 25:3 (1993): 457–475.

[16] *Sâlnâme* 1326 (1908), 126; *Notables*, 7:539.

[17] Khoury, *Damascus*, 46–48.

[18] Roded, "Tradition," 330.

[19] PRO FO 195/2272 Longworth (Aleppo) to O'Connor (Constantinople), 17 January 1908.

[20] Ibid.

The *Sâlnâme* confirms that a Hac Murat effendi served as a member of the court of appeals and as president of the examining court. Similarly, the secretary of the *Shariʿa* law court is listed as Beha'ettin effendi.[21]

By the early decades of the twentieth century, additional functions had been added to local governance: the provincial administration controlled the post, telegraph, and a portion of the banking sector. It also ran the local printing press—which printed the *Sâlnâme*—and organized a local chamber of commerce, industry, and agriculture, the directors of which were paid state employees.[22] The Régie du Tabac—the local tobacco purchasing monopoly—was also administered by the provincial government. Bureaucrats in the latter departments have names that lack the addition of titles or the suffix *zâde*, which usually marked notable status.[23] Names of notables—indicated most commonly by the addition of zâde—do not appear in the positions that required technical skills, like the post and telegraph. The names of employees in the agricultural bank, the Ziraat Bankası, and the educational inspectorate also lack appellations. Similarly, such name forms do not occur in the lists of the medical corps, dragomans, and gendarmerie.[24]

Hence, in the years before the revolution, the promise of a rational, incorruptible, and transparent system had been recast through notable cronyism to the point that one family in Aleppo controlled much of the administration. The salaries attached to these positions did not lead to great wealth in themselves; rather, these positions provided social prestige and multiple opportunities for socially accepted forms of venality. The notables kept to certain kinds of positions certainly determined by inheritance and access to sources of wealth, or limited by training and

[21] *Sâlnâme* 1326 (1908), 147, 148.

[22] Ibid., 144.

[23] The use of *zâde* to signify notable status in Ottoman Aleppo is an aspect of social practice of longstanding. Explaining the use of the term in eighteenth-century Aleppo, Abraham Marcus contends, "They adopted the trappings of the high Ottoman life-style as passports to advancement.... Their names rang proudly with Turkish titles of honor and rank—*agha, effendi, chalabi*. Their familial patronyms, borne like pedigrees, were sounded with the Turkish-Persian extension Zadeh (son) in keeping with Ottoman practice." Marcus, *The Middle East on the Eve of Modernity: Aleppo in the Eighteenth Century* (New York: Columbia University Press, 1989), 20. As the ties between the Aleppine elite and Istanbul grew stronger, the tendency to use such names and titles continued to expand. While not all men who used *zâde* were notables, all notables in Aleppo used the term to describe themselves and their families. More significant is the fact that many members of the middle class consciously rejected its use and used no honorific whatsoever; by customary practice, Christians could claim the title *khawaja*, yet with striking consistency moderns employed instead the convention of the last name.

[24] On the transformation of the Ottoman bureaucracy in the nineteenth century, see Carter Findley's definitive *Ottoman Civil Officialdom: A Social History* (Princeton: Princeton University Press, 1989).

custom. The ferocity with which the Jâbirî zâde and other notable families defended their access to these positions in subsequent years conveys a sense of the value they placed on them. Uniformly excluded from the opportunities that accompanied the inclusion in the lists, retail merchants, those in the liberal professions, and teachers constituted a wing of the middle class who found a voice in the period after the Revolution of 1908 and expressed their disapproval of what they saw as the systemic corruption that existed between the lines of the *Sâlnâme*'s text and at the root their society.[25]

Journalism

The system of exclusion also extended to the right to speak and participate in public discourse. Aleppo's experience with prerevolutionary journalism, while limited by late-Hamidian censorship, was not insignificant.[26] The oldest Arabic-type printing press in the Levant is Aleppo's Maronite Press (1701). The earliest journal did not appear, however, until 1864. Founded by Ahmet Cevdet Pasha, *Gadîr-i Fırat* [Source of the Euphrates]—known locally as *al-Furat/Fırat*—served as the province's official gazette. Like similar papers in the empire and Europe, this journal published local laws, proclamations, and official pronouncements. The few remaining copies of the paper rarely reveal news about events in Aleppo.[27] In addition to its heavily censored news of the empire

[25] It would be inaccurate to suggest that Ottoman administration was any more or less corrupt than the bureaucracies of Western Europe or North America. Underpaid state employees, lack of oversight, and greed were not limited to the Ottoman Empire. However, Findley has noted that "The fact that systemic corruption was still a reality of official life after a century of reform [the Tanzimat] marks one of the greatest failures of the reform movement." He has argued further that the administrative policies of the Hamidian period actually hurt non-Muslim and what he calls "modernist" bureaucrats, meaning those educated in a Western style and conversant in French. However, at the same time, inequities and inequalities in the system tended to benefit "traditionalist" Muslim bureaucrats, presumably including the Jâbirî zâde. He also speculates that "fuller documentation from the Young Turk period would probably show that non-Muslims were not the last minority officials to face growing insecurity as feelings about egalitarianism continued to evolve." Ibid., 332–333.

[26] Donald J. Cioeta, "Ottoman Censorship in Lebanon and Syria, 1876–1908," *IJMES* 10:2 (May 1979): 167–186. In the Hamidian period, the use of consular post offices to disseminate foreign-published Ottoman Turkish, Arabic, Armenian, English, French, and Greek language journals allowed a portion of the empire's population to consume unsanctioned ideas. See Orhan Kologlu, "La formation des intellectuels à la culture journalistique dans l'Empire ottoman et l'influence de la presse étrangère," in Nathalie Clayer, Alexandre Popovic, and Thierry Zarcone, eds., *Presse Turque et Presse de Turquie* (Istanbul: Isis, 1992), 123–142.

[27] A handful of editions of the paper are preserved in the Istanbul University library. No copies exist in modern Aleppo. Hasan Duman, ed., *Istanbul Arap Harfli Süreli Yayınlar*

and the world, it also provided a discursive and didactic platform for Cevdet, the preeminent Ottoman reformist bureaucrat of his era. Many of Aleppo's literary luminaries, including the legal scholar and Islamic modernist 'Abd al-Rahman al-Kawakibi and the jurist-historian Kamil al-Ghazzi, served on the editorial staff of the paper. *Fırat* also set a precedent that other Aleppine newspapers later followed, notably, bi-, or trilingualism. During its first few months of publication, the paper appeared in Ottoman Turkish, Arabic, and Armenian. Within a few issues, the Armenian disappeared. Perhaps reflecting an anxiety about the use of Armenian in a state organ, such a change confirms that literacy in Ottoman Turkish was widespread among educated Armenians and thus redundant in the paper, or local Armenians were content to read Armenian-language newspapers produced in Istanbul or elsewhere.

In the brief window of opportunity produced by the establishment of the Ottoman Constitution of 1876 and its provision for press freedom, members of the editorial staff of *Fırat*, including al-Kawakibi,[28] left to found the first independent newspaper in the region, *al-Shahba'* [The Gray]. The seven issues of *al-Shahba'*, which was closed by state order less than a month after it began publication in December 1877, paint a picture of a group of intellectuals—Muslim and non-Muslim—experimenting with novel literary forms and technologies. Beneath the newspaper's title, which appeared only in Arabic, in contrast to later offerings from the city that were transliterated into Latin letters, the editors informed their readers that "this paper contains all kinds of news (*al-hawadith*)." Conveying the sense that potential consumers of the paper, whose yearly subscription cost the princely sum of 2.5 silver *mecidiyes*, were being exposed to a new literary form, several of the first issues explained what newspapers did and clarified the value of purchasing a long-term subscription—even publishing the names of prominent subscribers. The opening paragraph of the first edition provides an example of this didactic position the paper took toward a formative reading public:

> Our paper has permission from the Sublime Porte to produce this literary paper so as to disseminate political news and local occurrences in a timely fashion [;

Toplu Katalogu 1828–1928 [Union Catalog of the Periodicals in the Arabic Script in the Libraries of Istanbul] (Istanbul: Islam Tarih, Sanat, ve Kültür Araştirma Merkezi, 1986), 111, 113.

[28] Al-Kawakibi would found a more explicitly Islamic modernist paper, *al-I'tidal* (Balance, 1878), after the closing of *al-shaba'*. This paper served as his *minbar* (pulpit), where he began to explore ideas about the centrality of the Arab identity to the practice of Islam. Raghib al-Tabbakh, *Notables*, 7:473; Filib di Tarazi (Philippe de Tarazi) *Tarikh al-Sahafa al-'arabiyya* [History of the Arab Press] (Beirut: American Press, 1933), 4:221–223. See also Hourani, *Thought*, 271–273.

it will include] as well a word or two about politics and also scientific and literary articles[.] Beyond this it will have investigations and studies to expand the public circle of knowledge and civilized literary exchanges[. It will] discover the secrets behind matters, enliven the thinking of the community, assist the state in local political actions and cry out when the local authorities infringe on the rights of society.[29]

Generally, the first page of the paper included a lengthy discussion of a contemporary issue, followed by a commentary on current events. The increasingly disastrous Russo-Ottoman War was the singular event that gripped the authors of the paper. As news from the front grew worse, the editors of the paper explored not just the tactical reasons for the failure of the Ottoman military, but also the very nature of Ottoman society. In the context of that analysis, a consciousness of the ideas of egalitarianism, transparency, and political participation first appeared that would become widely apparent in the period after 1908. Explicit in the paper's self-description are also the first hints of the creation of a kind of social space where newspaper criticism would play a role in politics and, presumably, newspaper editors with humble bureaucratic origins would have a voice. Ultimately, the authors were evolving the vocabulary needed to describe and define elements of civil society and civic life.

Illustrative of the currency of these ideas was a free-ranging article under the heading "A Political Piece" that blended emergent forms of criticism with a historicist reading of the medieval Crusades to illustrate the superiority of the Ottoman way of life over the European.[30] In a format that would be repeated in the revolutionary period and later, history was mobilized to point the way to a solution, in this case to fully extend the right to political participation and military service to non-Muslims. For the author such a development promised "internal improvement," could be justified on the basis of utility (*maslaha*) to the state, and was, furthermore, consistent with Islamic and Ottoman practice. This form of reasoning points to the lack, in the pages of *al-Shahba's* hesitant entrance into the public discourse, of references to Europe and the West as archetypes to be followed. It was not as though the editors of the paper lived in isolation from the West. References were often made to international affairs, including the publication of an address by Queen Victoria.

Its readership, topics, and editorial staff situate *al-Shahba'* firmly within the idiom of Tanzimat-era bureaucratic reform. Likewise, the form of criticism and style of writing is consistent with the bureaucratic ethos

[29] *al-Shahba'*, Aleppo, 28 November 1877.
[30] Ibid., 15 December 1877.

of the time: efficient technological reform, elimination of corruption, and the limited incorporation of Western forms alongside a cultural conservatism. Moreover, the fact that it was printed in Arabic tends to suggest that the authors came from reform-minded elements of the state religious establishment. Writing in Arabic was a conscious choice that, on the one hand, anticipates the later Arabocentrism of al-Kawakibi, and, on the other, a recognition that the potential readership in the city had greater facility in Arabic. The style of writing in the front page think pieces was never quite that of an article; it more resembled a *khutba* or sermon delivered from the pulpit. Each piece begins with a generic headline: "a note on politics," for example; it then proceeds without benefit of punctuation or paragraphs—both innovations that would distinguish fin-de-siècle journalism—in an argumentative and rhetorical form and concludes with the word "Amen."

A paper like *al-Shahba'* is less emblematic of the success of the project of middle-class modernity. It represents instead the historical phenomenon described by Dyala Hamzah as the movement from "*'ilm* to *sahafa*": the process by which Islamic knowledge as a form of practice was reshaped to fit the requirements of contemporary technological forms and growing social expectations of rational public discourse.[31] The kinds of questions asked in these articles and the way their authors sought to answer put the literary output of the paper beyond the intellectual reach of potential consumers, for whom many of the ideas must have seemed both alien and nonsensical. As such it resembles the literature of the so-called Nahda period, or Arab Renaissance, in Beirut and like movements in the Ottoman center, where an elite of reformers and foreign-educated intellectuals conducted their discourse within a closed fraternity. In the end, this was a paper for state bureaucrats by state bureaucrats; the ideas discussed therein would find little resonance within the middle class at large. Only in retrospect would these literary movements and their iconic figures be incorporated into standard nationalist awakening narratives.

Distinct from both *Furat* and *al-Shahba'* was 'Abd al-Masih al-Antaki's 1897 magazine, *al-Shudhur* [Selections]. Al-Antaki, the scion of a prominent Christian middle-class Aleppine family, established this Western-style periodical upon his return from university studies in France. *Al-Shudhur* anticipates the mimetic discourse so prevalent after the Revolution of 1908; its vision of the West, in contrast to *al-Shahba'*, highlights the growth of an internal sectarian division within the middle class of the

---

[31] Dyala Hamzah "From '*Ilm* to *Sahafa*: Negotiating the New Literary Field in Egypt at the Turn of the 20th century," paper presented at the fourth Mediterranean Social and Political Research Meeting, Mediterranean Programme of the Robert Schuman Centre for Advanced Studies at the European University Institute, Florence, 3 19–23 March 2003.

Eastern Mediterranean that would acquire even greater meaning in the interwar period. By virtue of its articles, style, and even illustrations, its intended constituency was not the elite of Aleppine society, but rather its emergent middle class and primarily the non-Muslim component of that class. While only twelve issues of the *al-Shudhur* remain in any available collection, they nevertheless offer a richly detailed image of the goals, aspirations, and self-image of the men and women who made up that class on the cusp of the twentieth century. And like *al-Shahba'* twenty years earlier, *al-Shudhur'* took a didactic approach toward its readership, yet in this case, it presented them with a template for proper middle-class manners and a how-to manual for a modern middle-class lifestyle. In this it anticipates other, more sophisticated quasi-instructional journals like *al-Hadith*.

The readers of this journal did not share the classical bureaucratic training and religious education of *al-Shahba*'s authors, nor their ground rules for social advancement, which, for the former, remained closely tied to the successful climbing of the Ottoman bureaucratic ladder; rather *al-Shudhur*'s readers were sober-minded entrepreneurs, petty capitalists, and professionals who were most at home when discussions of philosophy and poetry were followed by detailed accounts of the history of silk dyeing and new agricultural techniques. Indeed, in celebration of this juxtaposition, al-Antaki penned a poem on the unlikely topic of commercial law: "Knowledge for the poor is a path to wealth unbounded / And to the community of the prosperous a source untapped," and alongside arts and literature "Of the eternal virtues is law commercial / That flowers and blossoms and produces many a jewel."[32] He confirmed the nature of his audience in one of his frequent pleas for subscribers, again underscoring the precarious nature of print capitalism in the late Ottoman period.

> I decided to publish *al-Shudhur* with the clear purpose of community service in mind and it should be recalled that since its inception it has published exemplary pieces about literature, industry, agriculture, homemaking and health— all the things required by modern civilization; and I have done so in a way that is timely, easy in style and simple in presentation and I hope that the honorable inhabitants of the Gray City [Aleppo] will help me in this effort to educate and enrich society.[33]

This unself-conscious blending of idealized discussions of modernity and civilization with the more mundane realm of everyday practice—the hallmarks of middle-class modernity—was unprecedented and hints at the

---

[32] ʿAbd al-Masih al-Antaki, "Trade Law," *al-Shudhur* 1:5 (1897): 267.
[33] ʿAbd al-Masih al-Antaki, "Editor's Note," *al-Shudhur* 1:6 (1897): 278.

nature of the underlying changes in urban relations that would gain momentum in subsequent decades.

Moreover, it reflects the growing prominence of *being modern* in the conceptual horizons of the middle class. As presented in *al-Shudhur*, being modern was at once an understandable concept *and* an achievable condition, and one could imagine contemporary discussions about these issues taking place in urban settings in the West in very much the same way. Consider al-Antaki's disquisition into the social value of schools that he then reified into the constitutive elements of modernity:

> If we turn our attention to civilization, we see it is based on five elements without which it cannot exist: family, commerce, governance, religion, and science. . . . The family is the basis of human society. . . . Trade eases the lives of people and provides the necessities of life, governance protects the law and guarantees security, religion brings peace of mind and morality and science is the basis of everything.[34]

The unambiguous division of knowledge from practice (science and religion) evidences a profound demarcation at modernity's center; needless to say, separating religion from governance implies that the blending of these two—as was the case implicitly in the empire—would mark any such system as inherently uncivilized. Likewise, the mixing of the private realm of the family with being modern confirms the crucial nature of public probity to middle-class identity. In later essays al-Antaki advocated a "scientific" approach to household management and encouraged the systematic education of women and girls in home economics.[35] Commerce, too, acquires a certain dignity and prestige in his writing, not as a means by which to accumulate wealth alone, but rather as a kind of public-minded endeavor.

A recurrent theme in al-Antaki's essays and those he digested from other Arabic publications and European literature is the clear valuation of things Western as inherently superior. Yet al-Antaki sought to balance this stance by flattering members of the province's governing elite and the city's notability, going so far as to write a two-page panegyric poem to the local inspector of "Non-Muslim and Alien Affairs," who exercised control over the editor's ability to publish. Al-Antaki was no sycophant, and his was a survival strategy that sought to preserve intact his right to speak; nonetheless, it also made clear where he fit in the structures of discrimination present in the city at that moment and the chimerical nature of Hamidian-era secular citizenship. Thus, in contradistinction to his certainty of attaining a level of acculturation in things modern, middle

---

[34] ʿAbd al-Masih al-Antaki, "Schools," *al-Shudhur* 1:2 (1897): 81.
[35] Ibid., 89.

class, and Western, he found himself eulogizing petty bureaucrats and notables whose fluency in such things was much less certain. Being reminded at every turn that they were not quite equal emphasized for the non-Muslim middle class the increasingly encapsulated nature of their place in the city; simultaneously, it provided to the conservative Muslim elite another basis upon which to exclude them from access to power.

Any paper published in the Ottoman Empire between 1878 and 1908 easily fell victim to state concerns about criticism and sedition. All Aleppo's papers were censored and their presses locked. Al-Antaki, like al-Kawakibi and others before him, relocated to Cairo, where opportunities to ply one's trade as a journalist were less restrictive. And while state censorship stands as the most pertinent cause for the failure of these papers, that they folded so quickly and easily also suggests that a critical mass of readers, or rather readers sufficiently trained in the reading of newspapers and who had acquired a taste for such a commodity, did not yet exist in the city. Still, in the period before 1908, owing to a quirk of the Ottoman foreign capitulations régime, newspaper readers of cities like Aleppo and Beirut often could read French, English, and Greek publications sent via the independent consular postal service in addition to heavily censored domestic journals. Again, this augmented the cleavages present in other elements of the city's relations of power. The access was typical of connections to the outside world that were increasingly becoming the privileged possession of the city's middle class, and especially its non-Muslim middle class. It also highlights the fact that journalism and linguistic ability contributed to a middle-class transcendence of political and cultural barriers in new ways that were largely unavailable to other social strata or religious communities.

Urbanism

The most visible sign of a growing class of "haves" out of those who had been customarily excluded—and their increasing physical distance—was the creation of several extramural Aleppine "suburban" neighborhoods. These new neighborhoods were founded in the half-century after the communal violence in 1850 and laid out by Ottoman officials in a rectilinear plan in accordance with techniques of Western urbanism.[36] Modern homes, like the vast Bayt Antaki, which belonged to a relative of ʿAbd al-Masih al-Antaki, and multifamily apartment houses that resembled contemporary European domestic structures were built in these new neigh-

[36] Gaube and Wirth, *Aleppo*, 434.

borhoods.[37] The primarily Christian neighborhoods of ʿAziziyya, Hamidi-yya, and Sulaymaniyya and the predominantly Muslim and Jewish neighborhood of Jamiliyya each centered on modern institutions and civic organizations. By the beginning of the twentieth century, inhabitants of these neighborhoods had access to electricity, gas, fresh water, and indoor flush toilets. Very few of the city's established notability lived in these areas, perhaps preferring to remain in the city to be close to the people who made up the networks of patrons and clients that were the sources of their power.[38] By the early 1920s Kamil al-Ghazzi, Aleppo's premier annalist, could describe ʿAziziyya thus:

> This neighborhood is adjacent to some of the old districts of Aleppo and has become sort of an autonomous community [balda mustaqilla] and is regarded as one of the better places of Aleppo. It has wide streets and its beautiful houses . . . . combine the old style [of domestic architecture] with the modern style. In some parts there are gardens and the comforts of modern civilization [marafiq]. Many of the buildings have three levels and one whole family lives on each [floor]. Currently it is inhabited by Christians of distinction, businessmen and some Muslim families of quality.[39]

At the time of the Revolution of 1908, Jamiliyya housed the residence of the governor of the province of Aleppo and various municipal offices and, more important, the city's imperial high school, known locally in Arabic as the Thanawiyyat al-Maʾmun.[40]

Education

When the Thanawiyyat al-Maʾmun opened its doors in 1892, Fırat extolled the virtues of its modern architecture and sang the praises of Sultan

[37] On the urban transformation in Aleppo, see Charles Godard, *Alep: Essai de géographie urbaine et d'économie politique et sociale* (Aleppo: Aleppo Municipality, 1938); Jean-Claude David, "Les paysages urbains d'Alep" (Thèse de doctorat de troisième cycle, Université de Lyon II, 1972); Jean-Claude David and Dominique Hubert, "Maisons et immeubles du début du XXe siècle à Alep," *Les cahiers de la recherche architecturale* 10/11 (April 1982): 94–101; Jean Sauvaget, *Alep, essai sur le développement d'une grande ville syrienne, des origines au milieu du XIXe siècle* (Paris: P. Geuthner, 1941); and Abdul-Rahman Hamidé, *La région d'Alep: Etude de géographie urbaine* (Paris, 1959).

[38] Margaret Lee Meriwether, *The Kin Who Count: Family and Society in Ottoman Aleppo, 1770–1840* (Austin: University of Texas Press, 1999).

[39] *River,* 2:396–397. In this sense *al-marafiq* may quite simply be a euphemism for indoor plumbing.

[40] See *al-Dhikra al-miʾawi: al-Maʾmun* [Centennial Memorial: al-Maʾmun] (Aleppo: Ministry of Culture, 1994), especially Ihsan Shit, "Madaris al-fatra al-ʿuthmaniyya fi Halab" [Schools of the Ottoman Period in Aleppo], 31–35.

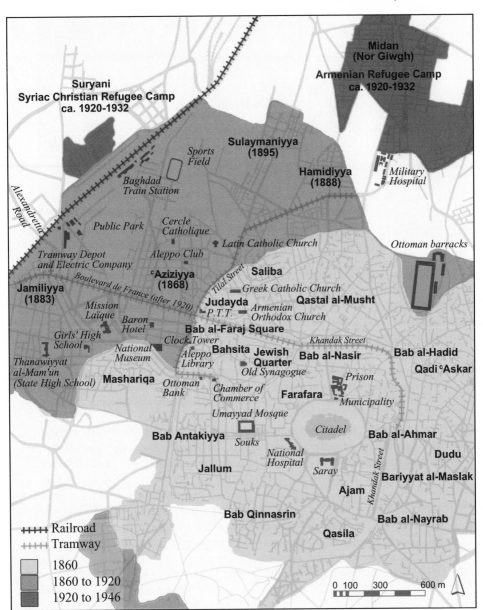

MAP 2.3. The city of Aleppo, 1860–1946.

FIGURE 2.1. Street scene in ʿAzziziyya, Aleppo (ca. 1890).
The photograph shows straight, broad avenues and multistory flats for single mid-dle-class family occupancy typical of Aleppo's modern suburban neighborhoods. Important civil society institutions like the Aleppo Club, the Aleppo Mutual Aid Society, and Cercle Catholique are located nearby. *Source*: G. Eric and Edith Mat-son Photograph Collection, Library of Congress Prints and Photographs Division.

Abdülhamid II for giving it to the city.[41] The form of the building itself differed little from other modern high schools in places like Konya, Er-zerum, Jerusalem, and the Istanbul Galatasaray Lisesi, perhaps signaling the uniformity and reproducibility of the instruction to take place within its walls. Empirewide, high schools like al-Ma'mun served as places wherein young men were trained for service in the rapidly expanding bu-reaucracy, but they were also places where these young men were systemati-cally disconnected from customary patterns of education. While the stu-dents did receive Islamic religious instruction, it was only one part of a curriculum, contained within the broader educational structure. Such cur-riculum is evidence of a key tenet of modernity: the conscious separation of knowledge from faith.[42] Although Islamic education was part of the Mus-lim students' course of study, far from solidifying Islam as a central compo-

---

[41] *al-Furat / Ghadîr-i Fırat* [Euphrates] (Aleppo), 29 September 1892.

[42] Jürgen Habermas, "Modernity's Consciousness of Time and Its Need for Self-Reassur-ance," in *The Philosophical Discourse of Modernity: Twelve Lectures*, trans. Fredrick Law-rence (Cambridge: MIT Press, 2000), 19.

nent in the production of knowledge, this act circumscribed it; significantly, the compartmentalization of Islam prefigures two of the fundamental trends of interwar discussions of the social role of the religion: the Kemalist drive toward laicism and the non-Muslim dominated Arab nationalist discourse of Michel 'Aflaq and others who argued that a positivist and historicized vision of Islam could serve as a shared component of Arab identity.

Using the lists of instructors in the *Sâlnâme*, it is possible to reconstruct this curriculum: It included physics, mechanical engineering, history, geography, chemistry, accounting, algebra, and trigonometry. In terms of language, all students were to take Ottoman Turkish and French, Muslim students could study Arabic and Persian as electives, while Armenian students had the opportunity to study the Armenian language with one Haçadur effendi.[43] In the same year that al-Ma'mun opened, a high school for girls accepted its first class. In 1906 the high school's 180 female students were instructed by Hüriye hanım and her colleagues in the arts, manners, sewing, needlepoint and language.[44] Alongside these imperial high schools, foreign missionaries—primarily Catholic religious orders—had earlier founded several high schools, most located in or around the Christian neighborhood of Saliba; the French-based Alliance Israélite Universelle had started a similar school for the resident Jews.[45] The expansion of secondary educational opportunities in the city was matched only by the growing tendency of young men to pursue higher learning at the imperial universities in Istanbul or at the Syrian Protestant College, the forerunner of the American University in Beirut. Many were also sent to schools in Europe and North America. Beyond the significant role these schools had in creating young men and women increasingly connected with modernity, the very act of sending one's children—both boys and girls—to school rather than the neighborhood imam or priest, in and of itself, fit squarely into the "hierarchy of exclusiveness" of turn-of-the-century European bourgeois social practice. Again, one of the keys to this hierarchy of exclusiveness, according to Hobsbawm, "was the demonstration that adolescents were able to postpone earning a living."[46]

[43] *Sâlnâme* (1321), 151. Also see Benjamin Fortna, *Imperial Classroom: Islam, the State, and Education in the Late Ottoman Empire* (London: Oxford University Press, 2002).

[44] *Sâlnâme*, 152.

[45] Ibid. Also CADN-MAE Consulat Alep Série "A" 46, Lorance (Aleppo) to Embassy (Constantinople), 15 April 1908, "Allocations to hospitals and schools." On the role that Alliance schools played in late Ottoman and Egyptian education, see Jacob Landau, "The Beginnings of Modernization in Egypt: The Jewish Community in Egypt as a Case Study," in William R. Polk and Richard L. Chambers, eds., *Beginnings of Modernization in the Middle East* (Chicago: University of Chicago Press, 1968), 299–312; Aaron Rodrigue, *French Jews, Turkish Jews: The Alliance Israélite Universelle and the Politics of Jewish Schooling in Turkey 1860–1927* (Bloomington: University of Indiana Press, 1990).

[46] Hobsbawm, *Empire*, 174.

Salon Society

A 1919 photograph of the members of the Cercle de la jeunesse Catholique, located in the heart of ʿAziziyya, indicates the fulfillment of other criteria in the "hierarchy" by documenting how members of the Aleppine middle class began to replicate and adapt modern forms of social organization and self-presentation. This photograph of the young men of the Cercle Catholique (fig. 2.2) still hangs in the club's Aleppo office. Attired in the starched white collars that became the universal emblem of the men of the middle class, the poses, styles of grooming, eyeglasses, and occasional smile all communicate a sense of self-confidence, of arrival, and of optimism. And the group photograph, unlike the individual portrait, makes concrete the lines of demarcation and the hierarchies of inclusion and exclusion critical to the formation of the middle class, its political ascendancy, and multigenerational reproduction. But the photograph also conveys a sense of standardization: with slight alteration, the image of young men in their Sunday best, arranged in ranks on the front steps, looking into the camera could be transposed to middle-class associations throughout the fin-de-sèicle and interwar worlds. Both a leisure and a sports club, the Cercle reinforced horizontal linkages of sociability and increased the "closeness" of the Europeans upon whom they modeled themselves by inviting visiting archeologists and educators into its social hall to give lectures, usually in French. The liberalization of rights to association following the Revolution of 1908 would transform and augment the role of these clubs had in the production of culture and the transformation of politics in the city.

The most-self conscious reproduction of these European, modern forms in the immediate prerevolutionary period was found in the literary salons that defined the city's middle-class cultural scene. Foremost of these was that of Marianna al-Marrash (1849–1919). Educated by the nuns of St. Joseph in Aleppo, she published poetry under the pen name of Bint Fikr, "a daughter of thought," and organized a salon in the home she shared with her husband. Habitués included the leading intellectuals of the city, most notably, al-Kawakibi, but also poets Victor Khayyat, Rizqallah Hassun, and Jibra'il al-Dallal. Wearing either all black or all white dresses ordered from Paris, Marrash hosted the mixed evening get-togethers in which literary topics as varied as the *Muʿallaqat*, a cycle of seven pre-Islamic poems or the work of Rabelais were discussed. Chess and card games were played, and complicated poetry competitions took place; wine and ʿaraq flowed freely; participants sang, danced, and listened to records played on a phonograph.[47]

---

[47] Antun Shaʿrawi, "Al al-Marrash waʾl-salunat al-adabiyya fi Halab fi al-nisf al-thani min al-qarn al-tasiʿ ʿashar" [The al-Marrash Family and the Literary Salons of Aleppo in

FIGURE 2.2. Members of the Cercle de la jeunesse Catholique, ca. 1919 (detail).

Festive social gatherings were nothing new in Aleppo; however, soirées
where unrelated men and women circulated with one another freely, and
where Christians and Muslims, who shared a similar educational background, drank and smoked cigarettes—rather than sharing a narghile—
together while they sat in straight back chairs around high tables, were
new.[48] Marrash's literary salon and similar milieux were places in which
Aleppo's doctors, lawyers, office workers, and clerks could congregate
and perform their "middle class-ness" in the eyes of one another. These
salons—like the more formal organizations and schools—acted as arbiters
of taste and sites wherein the middle class of Aleppo could be modern and
convey their middle-class modernity to one another. And in these forums
they behaved in ways to meet the criteria laid out for them in their chosen
métropole. They provided a place in which to create and maintain in-

the Second Half of the Nineteenth Century], *Majallat al-Dad* 9 (September 1995): 24–64.
See also *Notables*, 7:567–571.
[48] Jean-Claude David provides a valuable insight to the changing—and modern—use of
traditional domestic spaces in his "Alep, dégradation et tentative actuelle de réadaptation
des structures urbaines traditionelles," *BEO* 28 (1975): 19–56.

traclass networks of power and prestige; within each, they could replicate themselves and draw the boundaries of their class in the city.

These changes did not go unnoticed at the time. In despair at the fact that local Jewish families were going to clubs in which their daughters sang and danced with young men, Aleppo's Chief Sephardic Rabbi, Jacob Saul Dwek, lamented in a letter to a friend, "woe to eyes that see such things and to the ears that hear them."[49]

On the eve of the Revolution of 1908—and in the years before the global conflagration of World War I—the middle stratum of Aleppine society behaved in ways that suggested that they had incorporated many dimensions of the contemporary "hierarchy of exclusiveness" into their daily lives and had internalized middle-class modernity. But the structures of authoritarian rule in the empire at work during the reign of Abdülhamid II make it difficult to trace the way in which members of this middle class sought to transcend the spatial, intellectual, and political boundaries in which they were contained. Despite their exclusion from the political sphere, the middle class aggressively adopted the trappings of European urban culture (dress, literary forms, sociability, salons) as central features of their cultural practice and saw this practice as modern. Ultimately, this cultural practice created a template for future class-based solidarity and action in the revolutionary and interwar periods.

[49] Jacob Saul Dwek, *Derekh Emuna* (Aleppo, 1913/14) cited in Norman Stillman, *Sephardi Religious Responses to Modernity* (London: Routledge, 1995), 14.

Being Modern in a Time of Revolution

THE REVOLUTION OF 1908 AND THE BEGINNINGS OF
MIDDLE-CLASS POLITICS (1908–1918)

In July 1908 the diverse group of reform-minded military officers, bureaucrats, and intellectuals who formed the semisecret Ottoman Committee for Union and Progress (CUP) seized upon the opportunity presented by widespread discontent in the Ottoman Empire and, in particular, a season of bad harvests, tax revolts, and army mutinies in the Balkans to force Sultan Abdülhamid II to restore the constitution he had abrogated thirty years earlier in 1878. The return to constitutional rule was greeted with great popular enthusiasm and led to elections for the bicameral Ottoman parliament that overwhelmingly returned CUP delegates. However, in early 1909 a counterrevolution with clear Islamist undertones shook the foundations of the revolution. The Ottoman Army quickly restored order, but not before the massacre of tens of thousands of the empire's non-Muslim citizens, primarily in Central Anatolia. Following the suppression of the uprising, and in a moment emblematic of the secular impulses of the revolution, a four-member committee from the Ottoman parliament that included a Jew and an Armenian informed the sultan that he had been dismissed due to his alleged complicity in counterrevolutionary activities and replaced with his more pliant brother, Mehmet V. With the forces of reaction seemingly in check, the period 1909–1913 saw the concerted implementation of reform, including the reorganization and democratization of municipal and provincial governments and the systematic reinforcement of the constitution's liberal provisions for association and press freedom.

As the revolutionary Ottoman state dealt with internal threats, the principality of Bulgaria's unilateral declaration of independence and Austria's annexation of the province of Bosnia-Herzegovina shook public confi-

Portions of this introduction and the following two chapters were first explored at the Wissenschaftskolleg zu Berlin (2001) and Dartmouth College (2002) as part of the Alexander von Humbolt Foundation/Social Science Research Council/Institute for Advanced Study Summer Institute, "Muslim Identities and the Public Sphere." I thank Dale Eickleman, Dyala Hamzah, Geoff Eley, and Michael Becker for constructive comments and readings.

dence in the CUP. The Albanian revolt (1910–1912) and the Italian occupation of the empire's last North African provinces, Tripoli and Benghazi (1911), that followed led to a further loss of faith in the revolutionaries' ability to defend the homeland and translated into a poor showing by the CUP in 1911's by-elections, forcing the revolutionaries into a coalition government. The perceived weakness of this government precipitated the First Balkan War (1912), which witnessed not only former subject peoples defeating the Ottoman Army, but the empire's loss of almost all its remaining European possessions. And while the empire, under the leadership of Young Turk generals, regained a small portion of this lost territory in the Second Balkan War (1913), the territorial losses had tremendous implications for the religious and ethnic makeup of the state. No longer did a rough equality in numbers between the empire's Christian and Muslim subject-citizens exist; rather, the empire was now overwhelmingly Muslim. Likewise, its ethnic and linguistic diversity, while still present in its major cosmopolitan cities, was gone, and instead Arabic-speakers and Turkish-speakers constituted the majority. In the preceding decades, ethnic cleansing and territorial expansion by bordering European states, most especially imperial Russia, sent waves of Muslim, primarily Turkic, refugees into the empire, making a volatile demographic and ideological addition to preexisting ethnic tensions. The military humiliations of the revolutionary period were accompanied by widespread food and commodity shortages and inflation; the salaries of the empire's bureaucrats, including its high school teachers and police, were often in arrears.

Fearing that the coalition government would continue to make concessions to the European powers and their Balkan allies, and that domestic problems would erode support for the revolution, the military wing of the CUP manipulated elections, declared martial law, and returned to power in 1913 following what amounted to a coup d'état. Led by a junta of Ottoman officers of very middle-class origins, including Enver, Talat, and Cemal, the CUP continued to marginalize other political parties and executed or exiled their opponents, primarily those from the conservative Hürriyet ve Itilaf fırkası, the Liberal Entente Party. Through the beginning of World War I and until the empire's surrender in 1918, the junta, still committed to revolutionary elements of reform—indeed, considering itself the guardian of the revolution—administered the empire in a quasi-dictatorial and authoritarian fashion and increasingly drew on a reservoir of religious animus, xenophobia, and ethnic chauvinism to co-opt conservative opponents to their rule.

Mark Sykes, responsible for one of history's most cynical diplomatic accords, the Sykes-Picot Agreement of 1915, spent much of the early revolutionary period (1908–1909) in the Arabic-speaking provinces of the Ottoman Empire. He had been dispatched by the British Royal Geographic Society to map the territorial boundaries of ethnicities like Kurd, Arab, Turk, and Armenian, and his efforts resulted in a color-coded map that ultimately helped determine the division of the spoils envisioned in the diplomatic agreement itself, cloaking the imperialist land grab with a certain scientific legitimacy by basing it on the logic of ethnic homogeneity. Alongside that map, Sykes published a memoir, *The Caliph's Last Heritage* (1915), which included accounts of reactions in the Arab provinces of the empire to the reinstatement of the Ottoman Constitution after the Revolution of 1908.

Sykes's discussion of the events of 1908 in a chapter entitled "*Huriyeh*," after the word that signified political freedom or liberty (Arabic *hurriyya*, Ottoman-Turkish *hürriyet*), opens with a particularly sneering assessment of that revolution:

> *Huriyeh, Huriyeh!* again *Huriyeh!* Let us repeat it again with a Turkish accent, close our teeth, and staccato our delivery, saying once more "*Huriyeh*"—for in Arabic Huriyeh means liberty, and the Turks, being universal plunderers of an etymological kind, have seized upon the word to express that event which occurred in the Ottoman Empire last July. Huriyeh is a portmanteau expression of the greatest capacity; it at once describes an era, a historical incident, a mood, and a school of thought; also it has various interpretations besides: among other things it means "liberty."[1]

Contending that the meaning of "*Hurieyh*" was variously understood, he recalled a conversation with a villager on the outskirts of Jerusalem in the days following the imperial announcement of the reinstatement of the constitution: "Here I met an old comrade of mine; a Moslem Arab, with a strong dash of Turkish blood [*sic*] in his veins, stern, severe, laconic . . . 'Well,' said I, 'o father of Mahmud, what are these new things?' '*Hurieyh*, my lord?' he replied . . . [it means] 'That there is no law, and each can do as he likes.' "[2] Throughout the work he paints tableaux of gullible peasants, mendacious military men, corrupt bureaucrats, and delusional intellectuals for whom the complex issues of rights and law within the penumbra of the constitution were widely misunderstood or even misused, and he insinuates a cultural, perhaps even, in the parlance of the day, a racial inability of Muslims even to comprehend the concept of liberty. In the end, however, Sykes's account reveals his naïveté as he appears incapable

---

[1] Mark Sykes, *The Caliph's Last Heritage* (London: Macmillan, 1915), 464. See also Roger Adelson's biography of Sykes, *Mark Sykes: Portrait of an Amateur* (London: Cape, 1975).

[2] Sykes, *Caliph*, 464.

of comprehending Abu Mahmud's biting sense of irony with anything other than the utmost credulity.

Firmly within the genre of the Orientalist-traveler and certainly informed by the needs of wartime propaganda, Sykes's account is one of the earliest histories of the events of 1908 and among the first, but certainly not the last, to conclude that the Young Turk Revolution had been an abysmal failure. In the century since 1908 the historiography of the revolution has proved only marginally more charitable than Sykes. In the broadest of strokes, the historical literature on this moment argues that the revolution failed because it was a "revolution from above" and not a bourgeois "revolution from below." In line with the "failed" reform movements of late nineteenth and early twentieth centuries—Qing China's Self-Strengthening Movement, or Japan's Meiji Restoration, in particular—it did not alter appreciably the role of the nonelite in participation, power or the production of culture and knowledge. And like other early twentieth-century revolutions in Iran, China, and Mexico, it neither maintained the integrity of the state nor ushered in participatory, bourgeois, liberal constitutional rule. The ultimate culprits behind the failure of the Revolution of 1908, the argument is often made, were the Ottoman peoples and their unwillingness to embrace modernization and reject the antimodern impulses of religious chauvinism or the centrifugal attraction of nationalism.[3]

Specifically, the putative "failure" of 1908 hinges on the contention that the reestablishment of the Ottoman Constitution under duress by Sultan Abdülhamid II only superficially followed the path of the normative European bourgeois revolutions of the nineteenth century. Instead, the events of that year merely amounted to an intraelite struggle between reformers—primarily the members of the CUP and an older generation of reform-minded bureaucrats who had come of age in the post-Tanzimat era—at the pinnacle of the Ottoman civil and military bureaucracy. Accordingly, the insufficiently revolutionary nature of the revolution itself derived in part from the lack of or inchoate nature of a class that could adequately challenge and replace the Ottoman ancien régime.[4] Moreover,

---

[3] Prominent examples include Lewis, *Modern Turkey*; and Niyazi Berkes, *The Development of Secularism in Turkey* (Montréal: McGill University Press, 1961). Of note is Aykut Kansu's provocative discussion of the origins of this historiography, *The Revolution of 1908*, 1–28. See also my review of Kansu, *IJMES* 32 (2000): 168–171.

[4] Şerif Mardin argues, "But in Turkey [*sic*] the struggle was an intra-bureaucratic one of much narrower scope. Except for a small cone on top of the hierarchical pyramid, not much of an adjustment of class relations was involved. At most it was a new generation of bureaucrats who were replacing an older one. This dynamic is intelligible only in terms of 'class' for Turkish [*sic*] society. . . . social classes were very embryonic and scattered in Turkey. . . . groups shaped by market processes were unable to displace officials as those primarily re-

the ultimate failure of the revolution-that-was-not-a-revolution consisted in its inability to break the dual hold on society of Islam and Ottoman patriarchy; inasmuch as these two issues contributed to the persistence of sectarianism—or the failure of secularism—each was also a symptom and a cause of the failure to create cross-communal and interethnic, class-based solidarity.

Similarly, the revolution "failed" because of resistance to the modernizing and centralizing policies of the CUP. Evidence for this alleged resistance manifests in several ways, not the least of which was the migration of various national "revivals" from the purely literary realm into the political, giving voice to both elite and popular ethnic nationalist consciousness. The emergence of Arab, Greek, Armenian, and Turkish nationalisms is often cited as exemplary of the failure of the revolution and revolutionaries to articulate a successful Ottomanism upon which to build an coherent imaginable national community. Critical for the Gray City in this assessment is the rise of an ethnic Arab nationalist consciousness among the inhabitants of the major cities of the *Bilad al-Sham* (Beirut, Jerusalem, Damascus, and Aleppo) as a reaction to *Turkification*: understood as the oppressive centralizing linguistic policies of the Young Turks. This consciousness transcended class and religious interests and undermined support for the empire and its leadership, and, when allied with the centrality of the Arabic language to Muslim religious practice and law, it served as a rallying point for various interests committed to the establishment of an authentically Arab polity. A consistent trope in discussions of the revolution in the Arab provinces is that a stable Arab identity that constituted a definitive element of political legitimacy and a site of resistance to Ottoman and later European rule was formed during the period.[5]

Indeed, after 1913, as the Young Turks embraced policies and rhetoric that moved the revolution away from its secularism and pluralism toward

---

sponsible for the conduct of the affairs of the Empire, political or economic." Mardin, "Power, Civil Society and Culture in the Ottoman Empire," *CSSH* 11:3 (1969): 260. And while Mardin would concede that a middle class did indeed exist at the time, its participatory role in the postrevolutionary Ottoman Empire was limited by the revolutionaries' central concern in preserving the state rather than embracing bourgeois liberalism. The shadow of Kemalism creeps into Mardin's interpretation where he assesses as revolutionary the transformation of a belief in the preservation of the state into a secular Turkish nationalism, where equality is assured through national citizenship and participation in the national community.

[5] This argument has its origins in George Antonius, *The Arab Awakening: The Story of the Arab Nationalist Movement* (London: H. Hamilton, 1938). On Antonius, see William Cleveland, "The Arab Nationalism of George Antonius Reconsidered," in Israel Gershoni and James Jankowski, eds., *Rethinking Nationalism in the Arab Middle East* (New York: Columbia University Press, 1997), 65–86; and Zeine Zeine, *Arab-Turkish Relations and the Emergence of Arab Nationalism* (Beirut: Khayyats, 1958). I address the issue of postwar Arab nationalism and Aleppo's middle class more thoroughly in the subsequent section.

a position that emphasized the Islamic nature of the state and the preeminence of a Turkish national identity, the creation of such an Ottoman national community was less probable. The officially sanctioned and centrally organized wartime effort to rid Anatolia of its ethnically Armenian citizens through deportation and mass extrajudicial killings is perhaps the most acute manifestation of the destructive power of the combination of these forces. And while genocidal violence of such a degree is consistent with other revolutionary moments, it made irretrievable the cosmopolitan and pluralistic impulses at the heart of this revolution.[6]

Complicating the historical explanations of the presumed significance (or insignificance) of the Revolution of 1908 is the fact that it tends to be viewed backwards through the lens of the Ottoman Empire's collapse and the manifold ideological needs of the immediate post–World War I régimes—the Kemalists in what became Turkey, the Hashemites in Greater Syria, and, in the 1920s and 1930s, the British and French in the five successor states of the Levant and Mesopotamia (Palestine, Lebanon, Syria, Trans-Jordan, and Iraq)—to vilify and distance themselves from the political and religious structures of the Ottoman Empire. The animators of Republican Turkey, the Arab Kingdom, and the French and British Mandate states defined themselves as unambiguously modern and claimed legitimacy less from the form of their political institutions, many of which bore a striking resemblance to those of the Ottoman period, and more from the fact that they were not the failed, irrational, and unmodern polyglot empire. Likewise, the overarching emphasis on modernization theory that enjoyed a vogue in Middle Eastern studies a generation ago and its neoliberal typology of revolution places any assessment of this revolution and the late Ottoman period in a theoretical straitjacket borrowed from the trajectory of Western Europe's development.

Conceiving of the Revolution of 1908 as a failure also derives from an unacknowledged need to explain why indigenous Eastern Mediterranean society neither is liberal nor has seen the creation of viable civil society, an act that safely situates its history as exterior to Western history. The heightened focus on sectarianism, identity, and ethnicity (the irrational, savage, voluptuous, and Oriental) indicates that often for those writing

---

[6] Arno Mayer's conclusion that "conditions of decomposing sovereignty simultaneously favored the freeing of religious or ethnic minorities from bondage and the reawakening and incitement of chronic inter-religious or inter-ethnic animosities" seems borne out by the treatment of the Armenians in this context. Mayer, *The Furies: Violence and Terror in the French and Russian Revolutions* (Princeton: Princeton University Press, 2002), 485. On the Armenian Genocide, see Vahakn N. Dadrian, *The History of the Armenian Genocide: Ethnic Conflict from the Balkans to Anatolia to the Caucasus* (Providence: Berghahn Books, 1995); and Richard G. Hovannisian, ed., *The Armenian Genocide in Perspective* (New Brunswick: Transaction Books, 1986).

about this moment, the causes of failure resulted from conditions inherent to Eastern Mediterranean society as a whole and absent from Western revolutionary (the rational, objective, developed, and Occidental) domains. In centering these preconditions and ignoring discussion of liberalism and the formation of institutions of civil society and complex forms of political participation, the peoples of the Eastern Mediterranean are placed on a separate "not quite/not white" path that takes them not toward fully modern society but rather into an imperfect copy thereof. Consequently, such explanations are less removed from Sykes's initial appraisal than their proponents would hope and insinuate that, for the inhabitants of the Eastern Mediterranean, ethnic (or nationalist) interest and a narrow sectarianism (or Islamism) will *always* trump the forms of solidarity most fundamental to the formation of liberal civil society. In the end, among those most complicit in this "failure" to become liberal are the middle classes—military, commercial, and bureaucratic—the members of which did not behave rationally and reject these other identities and ways of thought to coalesce around their own best interests: a class in itself, but not for itself, to paraphrase a familiar formulation from Western European history.

However, the very condemnation of the middle class despite its clear role in the history of the period 1908–1918 highlights the significance of this moment and the need for a broader revision of the history of the Revolution of 1908, particularly in the Arab provinces. After 1908 the middle class became a visible and potent actor in the political and social history of the Eastern Mediterranean, and the Ottoman variation of this element of modern society constitutes one of the first appearances of such a category outside of Europe or the Americas. It is important not to lose sight of the novelty of such a class and the position it held in Eastern Mediterranean society in terms of both Ottoman political theory and urban demographics *at that moment.*

As I have previously noted, my focus on the historical experience of modernity in the crucible of class is intended to counteract a broad avoidance in Eastern Mediterranean historiography of the entire question of class itself, and in particular the urban middle class as a viable analytical category, this in the face of the fact that at the time of the Revolution of 1908 class and class identity played a central role in the public discourse of the Young Turks.[7] Focusing on the emergent middle class in this revolutionary moment also counters a trend in interwar Eastern Mediterranean historiography to link modernity exclusively to (as indeed a consequence of) the Western European presence—French, British, Zionist—in the region. While that conclusion is mirrored in the discourse of European im-

---

[7] Berkes, *Secularism*, 423–427.

perialists and the manner in which they produced knowledge about their colonial possessions or conquests, the French *mission civilizatrice* being the obvious example, more often than not neither the function nor the forms of modern political structures and institutions generally associated with the post–World War I period were the result of colonial intervention in the Eastern Mediterranean but had their origins instead in the Tanzimat, Hamidian, and revolutionary periods.

More to the point, at the moment of the Revolution of 1908, the members of the middle class confidently saw themselves on the cusp of great changes that were a portent of their full membership as modern people in the modern world—although the shape of this modern world appeared through the lens of idealized metropolitan middle-class society. Unlike the broader society, members of this middle class were the most adept at understanding the meaning of the new order, confident that it embodied their shared values and expectations and cognizant of how it could benefit them. It is the very agency of the middle class, its own widely broadcast belief in its membership and participation in the project of modernity, though denied in contemporary historiography, and denied as well to Middle Eastern society as whole, that an understanding of the full measure of urban social and political change in the revolutionary era restores.

The following chapters explore the manifestations of middle-class political, intellectual, and organizational activity during the period 1908–1918 in an attempt to understand how the Revolution of 1908 transcended an intraelite power struggle at the Ottoman center and constituted a moment of significant class conflict and social change throughout the provincial periphery. Moreover, each chapter examines how aspects of the Revolution of 1908 reached the vibrant social interstices of cities throughout the empire, especially in the Arab provinces, in a way that persisted into the interwar period, although in some ways aided by the imposition of the British and French colonial mandates on the region. This period saw not only the revolution, but also extraordinary violence and civil disturbances, the bloodiest of which occurred near the city of Aleppo only after the armistice of October 1918. It was a time of world-historical change when the peoples of the region would experience the crumbling of deep social structures and lines of authority culminating in the collapse of the six-hundred-year-old Ottoman Sultanate. Simultaneously, the introduction of new forms of political legitimacy, definitions of citizenship, and styles of violence was met with varying degrees of acceptance and ambivalence by the middle class. In sum, focusing on issues of middle-class civil society and tracing elements of identity, class conflict, religious authority, and political legitimacy across these years, it is possible to refine our understanding of the revolution in a way not clouded by what happened later in the interwar period either in Turkey or in the successor states of Syria, Iraq, Lebanon, and Palestine.

In this time of revolution, the Eastern Mediterranean middle class first defined its sense of itself and its position in the architectures of community by means of the social space created by voluntary organizations; it employed journalism and operated as a group-cum-party in formal and informal politics, using new communicative technologies to bypass the traditional elite in the exercise of power; and in the months before World War I, it faced its most serious challenge as forces in the center, bowing to the political demands of the customary notability of the region, altered the functional definition of the citizen, and adapted the tools of modernism to center Islam in political discourse. A majority of the middle class who sought to articulate a substantive role for themselves in the politics of their society originated in the region's large commercial middle class; as a class dominated by religious minorities, particularly Greek Catholics, Armenians, and Jews, their exclusion and their activism add an inescapable dimension to the form of conflict and change: the traditional patterns of hegemony had at their most fundamental basis Sunni Muslim religious authority and legally upheld superiority; Sunni Muslims were the *millet-i hakime*, the ideologically sanctioned dominant group. The mere act of being modern in this time of revolution challenged this sanction and rendered the bases of power of the old social elite unintelligible in the idiom of emergent middle-class society.[8] These moments of class conflict, which were reflected in journalistic exchanges, critical-rational discourse, and forms of public participation and structured sociability, were commonplace occurrences in the cities of the empire during the revolutionary period.[9] When taken as a whole, the interrogation of these local prosaic "engagements" with the politics of the time constitutes a way to theorize the larger significance of the Revolution of 1908 without recourse to the problematic topos of "failure."

Implicit also in the following chapters is an exploration of the uses and limitations of the analytical concepts of "public sphere"—a space of critical-rational discourse dominated by members of the middle class—and the linked notion of "civil society" in writing the history of the Eastern Mediterranean in the twentieth century. The public sphere seems inextricably linked to the urban political cultures of eighteenth- and nineteenth-century Europe with its coffeehouses, newspapers, and debating societies.

---

[8] Bruce Masters traces the origins of this non-Muslim entrepreneurial class to the internal and external political changes in the province of Aleppo, primarily the growing role of European merchants in the region and the interlocutory position taken primarily by non-Muslims. Masters, "The 1850 Events in Aleppo," 16.

[9] See Khoury, *Damascus*.

Moreover, the analytical boundaries and the incomplete nature of the "public" of the public sphere in Europe has been addressed by leading theorists, including Carole Pateman. However, forgoing the use of both Habermas's original concept and the subsequent critique of it as a comparative tool for theorizing middle-class politics against the backdrop of a revolutionary state simply because of its European origin strikes me as a limiting act of auto-essentialism.[10] The feminist critique of the public sphere, especially as it underscores the relationship between gendered difference and the evolution of citizenship, can certainly be applied in the Eastern Mediterranean. Equally resonate is Pateman's conclusion that "in a world presented as conventional, contractual and universal, women's civil position is ascriptive, defined by the natural particularity of being women; patriarchal subordination is socially and legally upheld throughout civil life, in production and citizenship as well as family. Thus to explore the subjection of women is also to explore the fraternity of men."[11] Her identification of the public sphere as a space of intense exclusion, despite the rhetoric of equality suffusing it, suggests as well a template for understanding the persistence of prevailing structures of religious distinction and limitations on the participation of ethnic, religious, and linguistic minorities and women in the face of aggressive projects of liberal and secular reform. Free-born Sunni Muslim adult men of property were the definitive figures of society—the absolute subject—and they were the raw material for the creation of the aʿyan, those in the public eye; however, rarely did those in the public eye participate in the institutional features of the public sphere, primarily eschewing participation because doing so would constitute a recognition of their equality to subordinate non-Sunni Muslim males. In part, the following chapters interrogate the larger significance of their absence from critical components of middle-class politics.

Similarly, "civil society," a term that in current usage is less a descriptive category of that space between the family, the state, and the market occupied by benevolent and civic organizations and institutions, and more an ill-defined rhetorical cudgel in debates over democratization, development, and globalization, is equally problematic when transposed to the

[10] For recent discussions of the limitations and utility of this framework, see Armando Salvatore and Dale F. Eickelman, eds., *Public Islam and the Common Good* (Leiden: Brill, 2004).

[11] Carole Pateman, "The Fraternal Social Contract," in John Keane, ed., *Civil Society and the State* (New York: W. W. Norton, 1988), 121, as cited in Geoff Eley, "Nations, Publics and Political Cultures: Placing Habermas in the Nineteenth Century" in Craig Calhoun, ed., *Habermas and the Public Sphere* (Cambridge: M.I.T. Press, 1994), 311. See also Pateman, "Equality, Difference, Subordination: The Politics of Motherhood and Women's Citizenship," in Gisela Bock and Susan James, eds., *Beyond Equality and Difference: Citizenship, Feminist Politics and Female Subjectivity* (London: Routledge, 1992).

Eastern Mediterranean. Where does the historian place the constellations of Sufi *tariqas* and their lodges—brotherhoods of practicing mystics who often promoted large-scale charitable and educational projects—in the firmament of civil society? Likewise, do the Chambers of Commerce and Industry of the cities of the region, modeled on the consummate organs of European collaborative capitalist civil society, but organized by the Ottoman government as part of its modernizing reforms, still constitute civil society despite their state origins?

Rather than merely measuring institutions against an abstract normative definition, this section uses as a point of departure the observation that institutional *forms* of civil society (voluntary civic organizations, political parties, sports clubs), the *technologies* of the public sphere (rational discourse, mass media, public opinion), and prototypical middle-class political *expectations* (fraternal equality, secularism, accountability) had become omnipresent and were linked in the imagination of the Eastern Mediterranean's middle class to the ascendance and dominance of Europe and by extension, its middle classes by the first decades of the twentieth century. The Eastern Mediterranean middle class's understanding of how its counterpart operated in civil society in Europe's cities, regardless of the objective accuracy of that understanding, became a guide for how it should operate in its own environment.

In no way should this be interpreted as a suggestion that the Eastern Mediterranean middle class merely passed through an identical stage of political development a hundred years after Europe's middle classes did. Instead, the civil society that took shape in cities like Aleppo reflected a novel pragmatic process of local adaptation to concrete economic, political, and technological realities. Or, as Geoff Eley argues,

> Conscious and programmatic political impulses emerged most strongly where such underlying processes were reshaping the overall context of social communication. [It] presupposed this larger accumulation of socio-cultural change. It was linked to the growth of urban culture—metropolitan and provincial—as the novel arena of locally organized public life (meeting houses, concert halls, theaters, opera houses, lecture halls, museums), to a new infrastructure of social communication (the press, publishing companies, and other literary media; the rise of reading public via reading and language societies; subscription publishing and lending libraries; improved transportation; and adapted centers of sociability like coffeehouses, taverns and clubs), and to a new universe of voluntary associations.[12]

This urban culture that reshaped the cities and societies of Europe and North America in the nineteenth century had become by the first years of

---

[12] Eley, "Nations," 290–291.

the twentieth century part of the shared reservoir of possible structures and institutions that non-Western middle classes employed as they encountered the realities of European colonialism and high capitalism. Like the middle class of Paris, London, New York, and Berlin, the "second-wave" middle class of Shanghai, Aleppo, São Paulo, and Lucknow self-consciously and purposefully manifested similar organizational forms and styles of communicative and political action. In the end, the middle class would "own" these forms and styles in a manner disproportionate to its numbers and append to them tremendous expectations as vehicles for self-interested reform and increased power in its society.

The following chapters blend articles and editorials from the few remaining copies of newspapers published in Aleppo before World War I and saved in local libraries and private collections, dispatches from the resident British, French, and American consuls, and the detailed reports from the Ottoman Interior Ministry's domestic secret police archive in Istanbul to explore four consummate moments at the very beginning of middle-class politics in this time of revolution. Combined, they reveal that the middle class used a "new infrastructure of social communication" in the fields of journalism, voluntary association, discursive political activism, and electoral politics to contest the hegemony of the old social classes, assert its right to political participation, and claim the modernity of its society. Nevertheless, bringing into relief middle-class thought and the way its members reacted to revolutionary change and conceived of their own role in society has required a certain degree of extrapolation from the modest literary sample that has survived the intervening century of wars, fires, and haphazard library centralization; often the most evocative evidence is also the most ephemeral and fragile: newspapers printed on what is now brittle, yellowing paper that crumbles at the touch, and random telegrams and pamphlets preserved in police dossiers or as enclosures in diplomats' reports.[13]

What happened in Aleppo was part of a larger process in which members of the Eastern Mediterranean's middle class formed clubs, founded newspapers, and entered into complex critical-rational discourse with one another and governmental and revolutionary authorities. Liberalism in

---

[13] When necessary, the Aleppine experience is contrasted with that described in studies of other parts of the empire, primarily Palmira Brummett's *Image and Imperialism in the Ottoman Revolutionary Press, 1908–1911* (Albany: State University of New York Press, 2001); and Rashid Khalidi's *Palestinian Identity: The Construction of Modern Nationalist Consciousness* (New York: Columbia University Press, 1998), which, despite its provocative title, paints a portrait of the vigorous middle-class intellectual and cultural life of pre–World War I Jerusalem. For a comparable account at the Ottoman center and in Eastern Europe, see Sarah Stein's *Making Jews Modern: The Yiddish and Ladino Press in the Russian and Ottoman Empires* (Bloomington: Indiana University Press, 2003).

its multiple forms was a recurrent theme of the discourse and appears in standard contexts including newspaper editorials, journal articles, and public speeches, but also in less expected places like poetry and transcripts of police interrogations. And in a telling parallel with bourgeois Western Europe, accompanying that emergence of civil society was the transformation of liberalism into a fetish of middle-class political interaction, where the adoption of its forms did not necessarily presuppose an adherence to a consistent program for implementing its underlying ideology of emancipation and social equality, contributing thus to the incompleteness of the project of modernity itself.

The middle-class adoption of these tools and the commitment to modernity, despite its clearly contingent nature and, at times, mawkish hypocrisy, transcended the constantly shifting position of reformers and revolutionaries at the political center and would continue after World War I as that center moved from Istanbul to Damascus, Baghdad, Cairo, Paris, London, and other cities. In other words, what is most revolutionary about the Revolution of 1908 is not the success or failure of individual reform-minded politicians, military-bureaucrats, or political parties, but rather how it made indelible and permanent the politics of middle-class modernity in the Eastern Mediterranean.

THREE

Ottoman Precedents (I): Journalism, Voluntary Association, and the "True Civilization" of the Middle Class

> It is beyond doubt that journalism is a token of the condition of the nation and it proves the degree of its progress or the decadence of its peoples . . . Journalism is the thing that we can be most proud of in our society, but at the same time the journalist can be the lowest in intelligence and manners, and he can be the greatest cause of evil on the planet.
> —Wadiᶜ al-Qastun, 1910

Excitement, enthusiasm, and optimism among the bureaucratic, military, and civilian middle class courses through diplomatic and journalistic accounts of the first months of renewed constitutional rule in 1908. Had Mark Sykes posed his question about the definition of *Hürriyet* to Hüseyin Saᶜd, an Istanbul-educated medical doctor and the inspector of health for the province of Damascus, he would have received a different, and certainly less humorous, answer. Saᶜd expressed his sense of the new period in a poem published in the bilingual Ottoman and Arabic Aleppine newspaper *Sedâ-yı Şehbâ/ Sadaʾ al-Shahbaʾ* (Echo of the Gray [City]). In the poem, "The Melody of Freedom," written in Ottoman Turkish, he expresses not skepticism or weariness but rather a very modern embrace of change and an optimistic belief in Progress:

> A new world, a new heaven
> A drunken dream of a new land just over the horizon
> We people of the nation resemble a new man of
> Noah's Ark touching land
> O the joy for our nation's youth[1]

The local diplomatic community echoed the spirit of Saᶜd's poem and his assertion of the essential "newness" of the period. Writing to his ambassador in Istanbul, Longworth, the long-time British consul in Aleppo, explained,

---

[1] *Sedâ-yı Şehbâ / Sadaʾ al-Shahbaʾ* (Aleppo), 16 December 1908.

The vizerial telegram announcing the revival of the Constitution was received here with astonishment bordering on incredulity. *Such a sudden break with the past* was wholly unexpected at Aleppo. . . . It was only when detailed news of the movement and its progress poured in from Salonica, Andrianople and Constantinople, that a burst of joy broke out in all directions. Staff officers were the first to throw off the mask and give vent to their suppressed feelings. They boldly and publicly advocated the cause of liberty and justice and they led the whole divisional army, from the commanding general to the last recruit, to swear on the Koran to defend the Constitution with the last drop of blood.[2]

The new American consul concurred and reported how members of the city's middle class organized themselves to inform and explain the meaning of this change in public, complete with the most advanced media device of the day:

The announcement of [the constitution] at first stupefied the people, and when they gradually came to a partial understanding of the situation, their joy knew no bounds. Great crowds collected in the streets, and soon the glad news was spread throughout the city. Owing to the illiteracy prevailing among the common people, in order to fully disseminate the information, it was decided to hold a great fête. . . . Stands were erected in four of the principal public gardens, and cineometegraph [*sic*] exhibitions, theatres, and refreshments were provided gratuitously to all by public subscription. Addresses were delivered by different Military officers, by the Director of Public Instruction and several prominent local men, the speeches being in Turkish, Arabic, and French. Children also delivered declamations. Frequent references were made to liberty, justice, and equal rights, each time receiving vociferous applause, mingled with cries of "long live liberty," "long live freedom." . . . Moslems, Christians and Jews mingled together, with brotherly feeling, and strong men of all sects wept with joy.[3]

Hikmet Nâzim, the editor of *Sedâ-yı Şehbâ*, noted the class-based nature of support for the constitution and openly worried that the only men supporting the new order were from the "military and civilian ranks";[4] Longworth called them the "strong body of men [who] thus stepped forward, with tact and zeal . . . [and] harangued the people on the true meaning of liberty."[5] Origin, education, class affiliation, and personal history contributed to the position individuals took toward the revolution. Those who supported it paralleled in terms of class and origin the military, bu-

---

[2] PRO FO 195/2272 Longworth (Aleppo) to Lowther (Constantinople), 10 August 1908 [emphasis mine].

[3] USNA II 10044/56 Jackson (Aleppo) to Asst. Secretary of State (Washington), 5 August 1908.

[4] *Sedâ-yı Şehbâ / Sada' al-Shahba'* (Aleppo), 16 December 1908.

[5] PRO FO 195/2272 Longworth (Aleppo) to Lowther (Constantinople), 10 August 1908.

reaucratic, and commercial middle class at the imperial capital who had forced the sultan to reinstate the constitution.[6] This class was also defined by what it was not. Arrayed against it at the local level were the leading figures of old social classes, preeminent among them the Sunni-Muslim landed notability, those whom diplomatic accounts identified as the "men whose interests are bound up with the late corrupt system."[7]

In sum, the juxtaposition of "old" and "new" and the consistent recourse to a generic vocabulary of liberalism in the descriptions of this moment is striking. Likewise, as these accounts confirm, a middle class of bureaucrats, intellectuals, military officers, and others had begun to employ openly and fluently novel and modern techniques of sociability, communication, and political organization. However, as they intervened in Aleppo's architectures of community they would encounter resistance from the old social classes, who would, at once, draw on their own customary reserve of tools and techniques of social control and mobilization, and experiment collectively with new social forms, technologies, and rhetoric. This chapter examines two significant components of this intervention as each emerged in the face of that conflict: journalism and voluntary associations.

THE "MALICIOUS JOURNALIST" AND THE "WHORISH PAPER": JOURNALISM AND THE PUBLIC SPHERE IN A TIME OF REVOLUTION

To the readers in cities like Aleppo, the most visible manifestation of change caused by the Young Turk Revolution was the immense volume of new newspapers printed and distributed in the city.[8] While in the period 1864–1908 only four journals began publication, and only one, the state's provincial official gazette, *Fırat* [Euphrates], published for any significant length of time (1864–1912), twenty-three new newspapers and journals appeared in the period 1908–1912 (tables 3.1 and 3.2). Although many of these papers constituted *journaux d'auteur* and reflected the personal

---

[6] "In July 1908 those elements in the Arab provinces who had been critical of Hamidian rule . . . were ready supporters of the CUP. The Arab opponents of Abdülhamid shared with the Unionists the same social values; they were products of modern professional schools, were exposed to secular European ideas and ideologies, and accepted a representative constitutional order as the prerequisite to strengthen the Ottoman state and to preserve its integrity. They represented families with no particular prestige, and thus resented the elitism of Istanbul as well as the social esteem and political authority that the traditional leaders enjoyed in the countryside." Hasan Kayalı, *Arabs and Young Turks: Ottomanism, Arabism, and Islamism in the Ottoman Empire* (Los Angeles: University of California Press, 1997), 78–79.

[7] PRO FO 195/2272 Longworth (Aleppo) to Lowther (Constantinople), 10 August 1908.

[8] Brummett, *Image and Imperialism*, 25–50.

political and ethical opinions of the papers' individual publishers, others served as organs for various emergent political groups.

What have not been preserved are any of Aleppo's satirical papers. With tantalizing names like *Maskhara* [Masquerade], *Ifrit* [Demon], *Hoppala* [Uppsy-Daisy], and *al-Ghul* [Ghost], these papers would have provided a welcome corrective to the dour and sometimes colorless political prose of Aleppo's "serious" press. The satirical press of the Ottoman Empire that emerged in the wake of the revolution, the *mizah mecmuaları*, blended a local aesthetic tradition of punning, burlesque, and the *karagöz* (shadow puppet play), with contemporary European styles of cartooning and caricature as seen in gazettes like *Punch* to create an elaborate and multilayered discourse; the satirical press was the "jaundiced eye, which saw in the revolution not solely the ideal-induced euphoria of freedom but the reality-induced skepticism of imperialist innovation and bureaucratic paralysis."[9]

Aleppo's serious press adopted the aesthetics and formulas of contemporary bourgeois journalism as well, even though the line between "news" and "opinion" would rarely prove to be clear. News was subdivided along local, national, and international lines, while opinion generally appeared on the front page along with leading stories. In another aspect of their format, these papers represented a significant departure from their pre-1908 predecessors in that they ran advertisements. The city's newspapers had, to some degree, attained the status of a commercially viable commodity; a commodity, produced and consumed by segments of society outside of the traditional elite. Contemporary French journalism influenced both the format of the papers and the practice of journalism. A visual marker of this influence appears in the bilingual mastheads of many of the Arabic-script papers. Most non-Muslim and many Muslim journalists in Aleppo had been educated in one of the city's several French Catholic missionary schools and, in keeping with established practice, had finished their training with a sojourn in Paris. The salient moments of French journalism and the emergence of activist intellectuals at the time of the Dreyfus Affair would have been part of the educational background of many of these journalists.[10]

While clearly influenced by both the styles of contemporary French journalism and the idealism of the profession, the self-assigned role of

[9] Ibid., 18.

[10] Charles Kurzman, "Intellectuals and Constitutionalism in the Late Ottoman Empire," paper presented at the Conference on Religion and Society in the Late Ottoman Empire, University of California, Los Angeles, 13 April 2002. Rashid Khalidi notes that the library of the author and journalist Ruhi al-Khalidi, who studied in Paris (1893–1908), included Emile Zola's *Humanité-Verité-Justice: L'Affair Dreyfus* (Paris: Eugene Fasquelle, 1897); Khalidi, *Palestinian Identity*, 238.

TABLE 3.1
Newspapers and Magazines of Aleppo, 1908–1918

Name	Type	Publisher	Language(s)	Date Begun	Life Span	Frequency	Sub-vention
Newspapers							
1. *Halab al-Shahba'* (Aleppo the Gray)	political Islamist	M. Nafi' Talas	Arabic	19/9/ 1908	short	weekly	
2. *al-Taqaddum* (Progress)	political	Kanaydir Bros.	Arabic	15/10/ 1908	1/6/ 1914*	3/week	French
3. *Sada' al-Shahba'* / *Sedâ-yı Şehbâ* (Echo of Aleppo)	political Islamist	Hikmet Nâzim &† Kamil al-Ghazzi	Arabic/ Ottoman	1/10/ 1908	1910	3/week	British
4. *al-Khatib* / *Hatip* (The Preacher)	political	Ibrahim Mu'thin	Arabic/ Ottoman	5/7/ 1909	9/1909	3/week	
5. *al-Sha'b* (The People)	political/ literary	Léon Homsy & Fathallah Qastun	Arabic	5/8/ 1909	1913	3/week	
6. *Maskhara* (Masquerade)	humor/ satire	Manu'il & Muhammad Nuri	Arabic	2/1910	9/1910	monthly	
7. *al-Kashkul* (The Scrapbook)	humor	Fatih 'Amri	Arabic	28/3/ 1910	8/1910	monthly	
8. *al-Ahali* / *Ahâlî* (The People)	political	Manu'il Mustafâ Âsım	Arabic/ Ottoman	12/5/ 1910	1 year‡	weekly	
9. *Lisan al-Ahali* / *Lisân-ı Ahâlî* (Voice of the People)	political	Ardashis Bughikyan Mustafâ Âsım	Arabic Turkish	28/6/ 1910	4 years	3/week	Ottoman Democratic Party
10. *al-'Ilan* (La Publicité)	political/ literary	Fathallah Qastun	Arabic/ French	2/7/ 1910	short	weekly	
11. *Tanwir al-Afkar* *Tenvîr-i Efkâr* (Enlightenment)	political	'Isa Muhammad Hashim	Arabic/ Ottoman	8/4/ 1911	6 mos.	2/week	CUP
12. *Mektepli* (The Pupil)	literary	Fethi Emrî	Arabic/ Ottoman	8/4/ 1911	short	infrequent	

journalist-as-crusader is a persistent feature of other reform and revolutionary era public spheres. Consider Joan Judge's description of journalists writing for Shanghai's premier early twentieth-century Cantonese-language paper, *Shibao* [Eastern Star]:

> These *Shibao* journalists and editors thus became the representatives, leaders and galvanizers of a newly defined Chinese "public." No longer passive and obsequious . . . this new public gave voice to an opinion that was, in the journalists' view, the agent of history and the motor of the new politics of contestation. Deriving its authority from both within the Chinese cultural tradition

TABLE 3.1
Newspapers and Magazines of Aleppo, 1908–1918 (cont'd)

Name	Type	Publisher	Language(s)	Date Begun	Life Span	Frequency	Sub-vention
Newspapers							
13. al-Masrah (The Stage)	humor	Mahmud Duhni	Arabic	18/4/ 1911	short	weekly	
14. al-Nahar / Nahâr (The Day)	political	Hüseyin Hâzim	Arabic/ Ottoman	18/5/ 1911	short	3/week	CUP
15. al-Sidq (The Truth)	literary	Mustafa Rushdi al-Himsi	Arabic	28/6/ 1911	1 year	weekly	
16. al-ʿIfrit / Ifrit (The Demon)	humor	Sami Ghalbi Mehmed Misri	Arabic/ Ottoman	1/7/ 1911	short	weekly	
17. Hubbla / Hoppala (Upsy-Daisy)	humor	Manuʾil	Arabic	5/7/ 1911	short	weekly	
18. al-Ghul (The Ghost)	humor	Musfafa Rashwani	Arabic	16/9/ 1911	short	weekly	
19. Tashabbath / Tesebbüs (Fidelity)	literary/ political	Manuʾil Sami Ghalbi	Arabic/ Ottoman	29/11/ 1911	short	weekly	
20. Aghbiwr (The Source)	literary/ political	Sargis Tʾicharian	Armenian	1912	1914	randomly	
Magazines							
1. Fawaʾid / Fevâid (Exemplars)	illustrated/ literary	Halil Kamil Cerrah	Arabic/ Ottoman	26/2/ 1909	1910	2/month	
2. al-Warqaʾ (The Leaves)	literary/ women's	Jirjis Shalhat	Arabic	1/11/ 1910	one year	monthly	French/ Maronite

* Resumed publication at the end of 1922 and published until 1949
† Ownership turned over to Khalil Ishaq and Mustafâ Fehmî
‡ Absorbed after a year by Lisan al-Ahali / Lisân-ı Ahâlî

Sources: ʿAʾisha al-Dabbagh, al-Haraka al-fikriyya fi Halab [The Intellectual Movement in Aleppo] (Beirut, 1972), 84–86; Suhayl al-Malathi, al-Tibaʿa wa al-sahafa fi Halab [Printing and Journalism in Aleppo] (Damascus, 1996), 42–50; Filib di Tarazi (Phillippe de Tarazi) Tarikh al-sahafa al-ʿarabiyya [History of Arabic Journalism], 4 vols. (Beirut, 1933), 4:2:55, 135.

and without, from the experience of the "advanced" constitutional nations, the *Shibao* editorialist regarded *yulun* [public opinion] as the embodiment of reason and progress.[11]

Like their contemporary Chinese counterparts, Eastern Mediterranean editors went to great lengths to provide and justify what they termed useful knowledge and social responsibility. For example, Fathallah Qas-

[11] Joan Judge, "Public Opinion in the New Politics of Contestation in the Late Qing, 1904–1911," *Modern China* 20:1 (1994): 65.

tun explained in the inaugural edition of *al-Sha'b* [The People] that "The newspaper *al-Sha'b* was established to strive for the people and to become a place of service, trust, and defense of the people; indeed! it is against the concealment of knowledge and the distortion of rationality . . . and we are ready to present our ideas in any way to serve the homeland."[12] They would be the protectors of the people, the shapers of opinion, and the ones who would speak "truth" to both the government and their peers. The very titles of the city's papers reflect the Jacobin spirit of the moment: *Voice of the People, The People, Enlightenment,* and *Progress.* In addition to the titles, Ottoman Turkish and Arabic words like *al-hada-tha* (modern), *vatan* (the nation), *al-dustur* (the constitution), *medeniyet* (civilization), and formulations like *al-hukuma al-hamidiyya* (the Hamidian government) were meant to demarcate the current era from previous ones and became the working vocabulary of revolutionary journalists. Their use of this vocabulary was akin to the alteration of political discourse in postrevolutionary France, where "certain key words," according to Lynn Hunt, "served as revolutionary incantations. Nation was perhaps the most universally sacred, but there were also patrie, constitution, law. . . . Uttered in a certain context or included in soon-familiar formulaic expressions, such words bespoke nothing less than adherence to the revolutionary community."[13] In the local context, the use of this vocabulary functioned also as a shibboleth for the broader fraternity of enlightened, modern young men.

Addressing the social role of journalism directly in an article entitled "Journalism," Artashes Bughikyan, the twenty-year-old co-editor of *Lisân-ı Ahâlî,* explained the purpose of his craft and its value: "what makes the practice of journalism special is its relationship to its place." He argued, further, that if journalism is only the exchange of work for pay, then it merely resembles "the creation of curio sellers or the trade of cloth merchants." For Bughikyan, journalism had other "virtues" (*maziy-yat*), those of "truth" (*al-sidq*) and "probity" (*al-istiqama*). "Newspapers have two duties," he continued, to convey "knowledge" (*al-ma'rifa*) and "guidance" (*al-irshad*).[14] The use of these words is a not simple act of translation of French calques; rather, each had connotations in mainstream Islamic thought as well as in Sufism. The motive behind investing these words with meaning in a modern context is similar in intent to the use of Confucian ethics by *Shibao*'s editors; with them, Bughikyan signaled that in this era, "New Men" like him would play the definitive role

---

[12] *al-Sha'b* (Aleppo), 5 August 1910.

[13] Lynn Hunt, *Politics, Culture and Class in the French Revolution* (Berkeley: University of California Press, 1984), 21.

[14] *Lisân-ı Ahâlî / Lisan al-Ahali* (Aleppo), 5 June 1910.

in the production of knowledge and the promotion of social good. The 'ulama' or those educated in a traditional manner would no longer play this part; instead, modern intellectuals, which included journalists, would take on this social function:

> The most important responsibility of journalism and journalists is to accustom the body politic—all of it—to the search for facts and the quest for reform through reading and analysis. This is the service which public opinion demands of journalism, this is the duty which legitimizes it. We continue to need general cooperation with this effort and it is incumbent upon all of us for the success of the nation and the happiness of the community.[15]

The city's journalists were not beyond chastising one another for imagined or real departures from these professional standards, however. In a front page editorial, Wadi' Qastun bemoaned the uncouth behavior of some journalists but defended their role and the need for unfettered access to the public: "It is beyond doubt that journalism is a token of the condition of the nation and it proves the degree of its progress or the decadence of its peoples. . . . Journalism is the thing that we can be most proud of in our society, but at the same time the journalist can be the lowest in intelligence and manners, and he can be the greatest cause of evil on the planet."[16] Without naming names, Wadi' Qastun's piece was more than an abstract disquisition into the social role of journalism or an effort to engage the assistance of the public in its support. He was attacking the other editor of *Lisân-ı Ahâlî*, Mustafâ Âsım, who had become involved in a conflict that had all the makings of an Eastern Mediterranean version of the Dreyfus Affair—writ much smaller and without a sympathetic central character. As a result of a series of muckraking articles, Âsım had been summarily arrested and sent in chains to the capital on the orders of the irate local governor, Fahri Pasha. As such, Bughikyan's discussion of the role of journalism in a modern society was also motivated by an effort to gain support for his colleague, Âsım. Indeed, within a few weeks of his arrest, a storm of organized protest emerged from the ranks of the journalistic community throughout the Levant that exposed the local hegemonic elite to a different group of political actors. As the conflict unfolded and played out in direct or oblique journalistic exchanges in the city's papers, it revealed the full dimensions of Aleppo's "public sphere" and how its members related to it. Nevertheless, this public was restricted, resembling a self-regulated "republic of letters," in which training, the use of written languages, and political and class affiliation determined membership.

[15] Ibid.
[16] *al-Sha'b* (Aleppo), 20 June 1910.

Âsım and Bughikyan, both young, upwardly mobile men and relative newcomers to the city, founded their newspaper in 1910. Âsım had served as the *kaymakam* (district governor) of the provincial backwater of Raqqa. Located southeast of Aleppo, Raqqa served as a frontier post between the settled regions of the Euphrates valley and the Kurdish and Arab tribal regions of the high steppe of the Jazira. During his tenure, and according to his own account, he sought to bring to the "backward" common people of the district the "blessings of constitutional administration."[17] Indeed these activities, he asserted later, were misunderstood or misconstrued by his enemies and served as the basis for the accusation of incitement. Bughikyan, born in 1890 in the region of Kharput, had moved with his family to Aleppo shortly thereafter. Attending both al-Ma'mun and the Franciscan high school, Collège de Terre Sainte, he graduated in 1908, fluent in Ottoman, Arabic, French, Italian, and Armenian.[18]

Published twice weekly in Arabic and Ottoman Turkish, the paper embraced the "newness" of the period and served as the organ of the short-lived Osmanlı Demokrat Fırkası (Ottoman Democrat Party), publishing the party's manifesto in full.[19] It did not shy away from controversy, and its favorite target was Fahri Pasha. No copies of the first four editions exist in available collections, but by the fifth, Âsim had been arrested and sent to Istanbul via Alexandretta. In the version of events passed to the diplomatic community by the governor, he had dismissed Âsim from his post in Raqqa for accepting bribes. Upon this dismissal, Âsım had gravitated to Aleppo and begun the paper. Several articles attacked the governor, who, according to Âsim's own account, offered him the position of *kaymakam* of Rumkale, another subprovince of Aleppo, as an incentive to desist. He rebuffed this offer, demanding nothing less than an executive position in Aleppo's municipal government, which the governor refused. In response, Âsim published another article that accused the governor of drunkenness and gambling.[20] More significantly, he insinuated that the governor "took his orders" from the local consular corps—an accusation tantamount to treason.[21] In anger, the governor arrested the journalist but failed to first secure an indictment from the local public prosecutor.

Accounts in various newspapers and archives differ somewhat from the governor's version of events. What is clear is that on orders from the governor, police commissioner Şevki bey searched Mustafâ Âsım's home

[17] BBA DH-MTV 1331.R.28 19/7.

[18] Robert Jebedjian, "Armenian Syrian Deputies," *Geghard* 5 (1996): 546–547.

[19] Tarık Zafer Tunaya, *Türkiyede Siyasi Partiler 1859–1952* [Political Parties of Turkey 1859–1952] (Istanbul: Arba Press, 1952), 254–261.

[20] PRO FO 861/59 Fontana (Aleppo) to Lowther (Constantinople), 15 November 1910.

[21] *Lisân-ı Ahâlî / Lisan al-Ahali* (Aleppo), 1 June 1910.

and arrested him. Âsım's wife told Bughikyan—who then reported it in the paper—that the police had rummaged throughout her husband's private papers and had found an edition of the newspaper *Meşrutiyet*. Bughikyan's account does not explain why the discovery of this newspaper was so damning, although it may have been a copy of an Ottoman journal published in Paris by the same name that had radical egalitarian leanings.[22] That the account did not pause to explain the reason the discovery of the paper was so objectionable shows that the readers of *Lisân-ı Ahâlî* probably knew of it by reputation. In subsequent newspaper accounts, primarily from *al-Taqaddum*, and in an autograph court document Âsım filed in February 1911, it appears that the governor had accused him of being a reactionary and having incited the *urbân* and *aşair* (tribes and nomads) during and after his tenure as the kaymakam of Raqqa.[23]

Âsım languished in Istanbul for much of July and August, yet by the end of the month, a telegram was received in Aleppo announcing that he had been freed. On 2 September, claiming illness, Fahri Pasha departed for Beirut, and he tendered his resignation shortly thereafter.[24] A week later, his erstwhile nemesis returned to Aleppo, only to be denounced once again by the interim governor, the *kadı*, Recep Hilmi, an ally of the notability, for allegedly being a member of a banned secret organization.[25] After this last accusation, of which he was later exonerated, the Ottoman archives give no information about Âsım's activities. The paper continued to publish for the next four years, and his name remained on the masthead as editor-in-chief, rehabilitated thoroughly by the young, reform-minded, CUP-appointed governor who succeeded Fahri, Hüseyin Kâzım.

Regardless of the actual facts of the case, in the minds of many the arrest of Âsım, the departure of the old governor, and the appointment of the new governor were causally linked. Fontana, the British consul of the time, interpreted the events no differently: "General Fahkri Pasha, who was on friendly terms with most of the eshraf . . . was dismissed for arbitrarily arresting and deporting Mustafa Âsim effendi, the corrupt ex-Caimakam and malicious journalist."[26] The French consul provided a similar interpretation. Assuming that the governor had orders to proceed against Mustafa Âsım, he was shocked when the government suspended Fahri's authority. The consul later discovered that Fahri Pasha "had acted on his own initiative" and had not shown the proper respect for constitutional liberties. He concluded, "the imprisonment of Assim Bey was only

[22] Duman, *Süreli*, 256.
[23] BBA DH-MTV 1331.R.28 19/7 and *Lisân-ı Ahâlî / Lisan al-Ahali* (Aleppo), 29 August 1910.
[24] BBA DH-MIU 1328.Ca.26 100–1 Telegraf.
[25] BBA DH-MIU 1328.N.8 129/23 Tahrirat.
[26] PRO FO 861/59 Fontana (Aleppo) to Lowther (Constantinople), 3 December 1910.

a pretext to get rid of a man [Fahri Pasha] who was detaching himself from the [CUP] in order to pass into the camp of the reactionaries."[27] The governor's persecution of Âsım had also proved unpopular with members of the middle class, led by the newspapermen of the city, who, with one telling exception, had rushed to support the editor and condemn the governor in print and with telegrams.

The men who rallied to support Âsım against the governor and his allies, including the notable families of the northern Levant, used the medium of modern media—newspapers and telegrams—to tap into the power of public opinion. With their words, they showed a consciousness of their membership in a distinct class; they were also aware that their class was in competition with the notable families for actual power within the city and, implicitly, Ottoman society as a whole. Specifically, local observers interpreted the editor's original attack on the governor and the subsequent agitation in his favor as a polemic not only against the governor, but also against "the great landowners who under a liberal appearance continued to use the worst procedures of yesteryear."[28] The British consul added to this assertion of a class-based support of Âsım: "During his stay in Aleppo Assim Effendi worked his way into the good graces of the local Committee of Union and Progress, the members of which are mostly subordinate military officers and tradesmen of small ability and reputation."[29] While Âsım and Bughikyan would not have agreed with Fontana's dismissive characterization of their and their supporters' social status, they had, nonetheless, acted in such a way as to shake the very foundations of traditional notable power in the city and had successfully formed, albeit briefly, an alliance with forces in Istanbul to threaten the dominance of old notable families such as the Jâbirî zâde and the Mudarris zâde.

Following Âsım's arrest, Bughikiyan had begun an ongoing effort to keep his case in the public eye and mold public opinion in his support. On 13 June 1910 he began the Ottoman Turkish section of the paper with a lengthy defense. Calling Âsım a "vatanperver" (patriot) who "desires nothing but the advancement and elevation of the nation and our state" and who did not lie in any of his writings, Lisân-ı Ahâlî asked, "Why was he imprisoned?"[30] Support for the editor also manifested itself in planned street protests and an attempt by junior officers to question Fahri about

---

[27] MAE CADN Consulat Alep Série "A" 47 Lorance (Aleppo) to Embassy Constantinople, Levant 115 / Ambassade 145, 29 August 1910.

[28] Ibid., citing an article in *al-Taqaddum*.

[29] PRO FO 195/2337 Fontana (Aleppo) to Lowther (Constantinople), 15 November 1910.

[30] *Lisân-ı Ahâlî / Lisan al-Ahali* (Aleppo), 13 June 1910.

his behavior during a meeting of the local CUP.[31] After four more editions containing strident attacks, the paper was finally closed, but not before it had successfully generated support for Âsım in the other newspapers not just of Aleppo, but of Damascus, Beirut, and Istanbul as well, confirming ✳ the emergence of a trans-Levantine "republic of letters."[32] Only al-Sha'b failed to mobilize its editors in defense of Âsım, perhaps because one of its animators, the leading intellectual Qustaki al-Homsy, was a personal friend of Fahri's.[33]

The significance of this kind of concerted, organized, and self-conscious action on the part of the journalists connected with the papers should not be underestimated. The very boundaries of a public sphere can be read in the journalistic support of Âsım: the organized nature of the journalists' activities, the vocabulary they employed, and the way those reading these words described their underlying meaning reveal its very topography. Likewise, their interaction within the public sphere provides a glimpse of what it meant to be modern in terms of public, political culture at that moment, and how closely that vision of modernity resembled its metropolitan cognate.

The vocabulary employed in support of Âsım shows a coherent statement of both the individual's subjectivity and the objective applicability of law and rights to the person. As Jürgen Habermas explains, "The bourgeois public's critical public debate took place in principle without regard to all pre-existing social and political rank and in accord with universal rules, [this debate] became universally valid [and] secured a space for what was most subjective; because they were abstract, for what was most concrete."[34] An example of this is seen in the headline above the exultant article heralding Âsım's release: "Intisar al-haqq wa li-sahib al-imza'" (Victory for the truth and the editor). The lead articles produced in the days following his departure define him in similar ways. It is important to remember that Âsım was a virtual stranger in Aleppo. He fit nowhere in the customary structure of power, he had no patron, nor was he a client

---

[31] PRO FO 195/2337 Fontana (Aleppo) to Lowther (Constantinople), 15 November 1910. Before the actual meeting took place, Fahri had left the city.

[32] These papers included al-Taqaddum, al-Muqtabas, al-Ittihad al-Uthmani, Lisan al-Sharq, Lisan al-Hal, al-Ahwal, al-Mufid, al-Ra'y al-'Am, and the intriguingly named Al-Jawab al-Kurdi. Lisân-ı Ahâlî / Lisan al-Ahali (Aleppo), 18 September 1910.

[33] Qustaki al-Homsy's intellectual output puts him firmly within the ranks of Arab authors of the Nahda period, having written one of the first books on Arabic belles lettres, Udaba' Halab dhu al-athar fi al-qarn al-tasi' 'ashar [Aleppo's Men of Letters in the 19th Century] (Aleppo: Maronite Press, 1925); PRO FO 195/2366 Fontana (Aleppo) to Lowther (Constantinople), 16 April 1911.

[34] Jürgen Habermas, The Structural Transformation of the Public Sphere: An Inquiry into a Category of Bourgeois Society, trans. Thomas Burger with Fredrick Lawrence (Cambridge: MIT Press, 1989), 54.

in any established urban networks. The vocabulary of protest defined him as a modern citizen and brother journalist who had been denied his rights *as an individual*. Thus *al-Taqaddum* could conclude that his release was a "demonstration of will to support the individual in the face of oppression."[35] In this way, Âsim operated as a metaphor for the subjective individuality of the private person in the public sphere.

The polemical structure of the articles was designed to intervene directly in public opinion; it argued that the new-found liberties were at stake *for all* in the case against {{Acircumflex}}sim, thereby linking Âsim's case directly with a concrete set of rights and liberties. Such was true, in Habermas's interpretation, of the emergence of public opinion in seventeenth-century England. "Public opinion," he writes, "was formed in the conflict of argument concerning a substantive issue, not uncritically based on common sense in either the naive or plebiscitarily manipulated assent to or vote about a person."[36] Likewise, the middle class sought to define the rules of "just executive authority" through the shaping of public opinion on a specific issue. Only in the real world of injudicious governors could the meaning of law be tested. The journalist had been denied his right to due process as the governor bypassed the local prosecutor. This fact was at the core of the outrage. The governor had contravened the letter of the law as well as its spirit. The willingness of the Eastern Mediterranean journalists to contest what they saw as an encroachment upon the sphere by an arbitrary irrational actor reinforces the vital nature of such debates and the internalization of modernity.

Finally, the articles, and the joy expressed at the replacement of a pronotable governor with a reformist like Hüseyin Kâzım, suggest that the release of Âsim was interpreted as proof that the rational basis of authority had taken root in the empire. It is also proof that the middle class understood that what they saw as the traditional sources of authority were incompatible with their desire to participate actively in and dominate the architectures of community. Thus the Âsim affair resembles historically the behavior of the Western middle classes whose "political consciousness developed in the public sphere of civil society which, in opposition to absolute sovereignty, articulated the concept of and demand for general and abstract laws and which ultimately came to assert itself (i.e., public opinion) as the only legitimate source of this law."[37] More distinctly, in Âsim's Aleppo, the conflict replayed itself as an attempt to assert middle-class power in the face of the politics of notables.

[35] *Lisân-ı Ahâlî / Lisan al-Ahali* (Aleppo), 26 September 1910.
[36] Habermas, *Structural Transformation*, 66.
[37] Ibid., 52.

Fahri was one of the notables' own; as Fontana had observed, he was on "good terms with most of the eshraf" and had created bonds with the local notability through marriages and commercial dealings. Conversely, when those who supported Âsım spoke out, they did so not just for themselves, but as members of a public; a public that was in opposition to the governor, the notables, and the system they embodied. Homsy, by not supporting the embattled journalist, actively opposed this public and came under attack from his fellow journalists. Bughikyan's denunciation of him in *Lisan al-Ahali* illustrates as well the vigor of political discourse in Aleppo:

> all of the newspapers have condemned this heinous event and defended the editor-in-chief [Âsım] except for a whorish paper, which never should have been called *al-Sha'b* in that it is incapable of understanding the trials and tribulations of the people. It did try to play a role: apologist for the governor. It approved of his dastardly deed and agreed that Âsım was a reactionary who was stirring up the tribes against the government. Manifest in this act . . . is contempt and baseness.[38]

His pun on the word "people" suggests the larger historical dimension of conflicts like the one involving Âsım in this time of revolution. Âsım's victory and return to the city represented the failure of the local, customary notability to phrase their hold on some of the structures of power in a language more appropriate to the middle class, which signified the loss of their "consent" to rule them. At that moment, it seemed that people like Âsım were in the ascendancy with the support of the middle class. Their incorporation of elemental components of the public sphere into their political practice, as well as the "victory" against the old governor, confirmed the power to be had in using key modes of modern political forms. Sensing the danger of that power, the notables' efforts to regain or retain their historical hegemony dominated their political activity in the city for the remainder of the prewar period and subsequently during the French Mandate.

THE ALEPPO MUTUAL AID SOCIETY: EMULATION AND THE BOUNDARIES OF MIDDLE-CLASS CIVIL SOCIETY

In a development that paralleled the explosion of journalism and the often ferocious journalistic exchanges of the "Âsım affair," political, literary and social clubs became a prominent feature of public life in the cities of the Eastern Mediterranean in the revolutionary period. Similar to the ti-

---

[38] *Lisân-ı Ahâlî / Lisan al-Ahali* (Aleppo), 29 September 1910.

tles of newspapers, the names of these clubs reflected the revolutionary spirit of the moment and the form of political change. Alongside overtly political parties like the local chapter of the Committee of Union and Progress were Masons, the Ottoman Brotherhood Society, and sporting clubs including the Armenian HoMenEtMen.[39] These associations evolved on a terrain that included preexisting organizations like the quasi-official Chamber of Commerce and Industry, and syndicates of the liberal professions, including those of Western-trained doctors and lawyers.[40] As a consequence of mid-nineteenth-century Tanzimat-era reforms of the millet system, lay committees had come to control many of the resources of non-Muslim religious communities. The Armenian orthodox millet, especially, had created an elected lay assembly system at both the empirewide and local levels that resembled a cross between a corporate board of directors and contemporary European municipal councils. Madeup of prominent Armenian businessmen, liberal professionals, and doctors, the committees monitored the use of church resources and investments and funded college scholarship programs, schools, and hospitals. More important, the representational and "civic" quality of these assemblies is often identified as a template for larger-scale political governance. As noted previously, less understood, and requiring further research, is the role of customary voluntary associations like Sufi orders or *esnaf* (customary guilds) in shaping middle-class civil society.

Despite the long history of these kinds of organizations, the exponential growth of the European-style voluntary associations in the revolutionary period bespoke a fundamental shift in civil society and the form of political and cultural activities within it. Critically, these voluntary associations sought to cut across professional and sectarian lines, to become sites of proper, urbane middle-class social interaction, and to provide a blueprint for the broader participation of the middle class in all elements of society. As in nineteenth-century Germany, "Such associational initiatives were fundamental to the formation of bourgeois civil society. . . . Put simply, voluntary association was in principle the logical form of bourgeois emancipation and bourgeois self-affirmation."[41] The populist, egalitarian, and benevolent motives in the rhetorical pronouncements of the clubs resulted

---

[39] The study of voluntary organizations in the Ottoman Eastern Mediterranean, especially in those areas that become part of the successor states of Syria and Lebanon, suffers from an almost exclusive focus on "secret" political parties or literary clubs linked however tenuously to the emergence of Arab and Turkish nationalism.

[40] See listing in the *Halep Vilâyeti Sâlnâmesi 1321* [Yearbook of the Province of Aleppo] (Aleppo, 1905). See also Geoffrey D. Schad, "Colonialists, Industrialists, and Politicians: The Political Economy of Industrialization in Syria, 1920–1954" (Ph.D. Diss., University of Pennsylvania, 2001).

[41] Eley, "Nations," 298.

in charitable work and to some extent laid the foundation for the possible broader liberalization of the Eastern Mediterranean itself. But most of all, they provided the middle class with a venue within which to maintain its distinction from other social classes, resituate gender difference along modern lines, and otherwise create models of embourgeoisement.

The quintessential voluntary association from this era is Aleppo's Nadi al-ta'addud, the Aleppo Mutual Aid Society. The association of the leadership of the club with the editorial board of the newspaper *al-Sha'b*, uniquely reveals the club's inner workings and presents a method to trace its members' collective vision of modernity. Founded in January 1910, the club clearly borrowed its name from contemporary French General Associations for Mutual Aid. The Second Republic version of these French clubs sought to diffuse the potentially explosive relationship between the working class and the bourgeoisie by virtue of the fiction of *mutualité*. In other words, directed by bourgeois sponsors, the working class would be initiated into the ways of thinking and behaving of the middle class and thereby enjoy the possibility of social advancement without challenging the established order. Seemingly beneficent, the opening of reading rooms, group investment funds, and night schools constituted, in the words of Carol Harrison, "the tacit recognition of the superiority of the abstract, intellectual labour—the kind of work that bourgeois men did and that the worker-pupils aspired to."[42]

While the Eastern Mediterranean did not feature the same critical mass of workers, the value of *mutualité* nonetheless motivated the leadership of Aleppo's Mutual Aid Society to extend assistance to the urban poor. Like comparable associations in France, the Mutual Aid Society assured the universality and legitimacy of middle-class modernity by the conceit of teaching its key concepts and practices to the lower classes, while at the same time assuming the elite practice of patronage. Unlike customary forms of patronage in Eastern Mediterranean society, this kind of social intervention in the lives of the poor took place beyond the realm of religious injunction, state efforts, or the provision of cash or employment. Aiding the poor is a key feature of religious practice of all the traditions of the Eastern Mediterranean, but this aid often took the form of communal charity, usually through the Muslim legal device of *waqf* (holy endowment), and never sought to change the pre-existing class status or social behavior of the poor themselves. The mediating figures in the customary forms were the leaders or functionaries of the various communities, priests and rabbis or *waqf* executors. Though the entire edifice of relief, charity, and elite patronage was undergoing a rapid transformation in

---

[42] Carol Harrison, *The Bourgeois Citizen in the 19th Century: Gender, Sociability, and the Uses of Emulation* (London: Oxford University Press, 1999), 140.

the late Ottoman period, the intensely middle-class form of assistance envisaged by the leaders of the Mutual Aid Society marked it as a distinctive and novel feature of the transforming architecture of community, focusing as it did on cultural pursuits, education, and urban behavior as much as on economic improvement.[43]

Introducing the Mutual Aid Society to the readership of al-Sha'b, the editor explicitly linked the task of the association to the domains of culture and sociability, noting, "There is no doubt that the establishment of a Society with the purpose of improving culture, arts and letters, raising the intelligence, manners and social skills of the youth of the nation, and aiding the less fortunate to help them reach the level of those who are improving themselves will require a great deal of effort and a long-term commitment." Nevertheless, the difficult work was justified because

> it is a project that brings together the various classes of society and aids the cause of overcoming individual differences and social disintegration. The essence of it [the Society] is mutual aid (ta'addud), which binds heart and hope and enjoins patience. For its end result will be the progress of wisdom and knowledge and the refinement of custom [and law] on the basis of the good of all mankind.[44]

The overall prescriptive definition of the association's activities reinforces the conclusion that, like its French cognate, mutual aid would serve to buttress the ideological underpinnings of middle-class distinction, shape the participation of various classes, and even introduce a more rational basis to the formulation of law.

In a two-part article under the simple headline "Mutual Aid," the Society's central purpose was elaborated by one of its members, the poet 'Isa al-Alabawi. Stating that "mutual aid is the natural foundation of society and the thing which separates animals and humanity," the author argued that it was the fundamental component of civil society: "when people study this natural state of animal affairs, they reject it and employ mutual aid to establish corporations, literary clubs, scientific colleges and political assemblies." Based on unity in the belief in humanity, love, and compassion, al-Alabawi argued that mutual aid required a unity of faith in industriousness, as well. "Industry," the author continued, "leads to the growth of wealth, which helps all to further aid each other."[45] The group's intention of establishing industry to employ the poor, and presumably

---

[43] See especially the work of the late Mine Ener, *Poverty and Charity in Middle Eastern Contexts*, with co-editors Michael Bonner and Amy Singer (New York: SUNY Press, 2004), and her *Managing Egypt's Poor and the Politics of Benevolence, 1800–1952* (Princeton: Princeton University Press, 2003).

[44] al-Sha'b (Aleppo), 16 March 1910.

[45] Ibid., 15 April 1910.

turning them into a working class, is a marked departure from the style of mutual aid associated with the clubs in France. The emphasis on industry as a mechanism for the alleviation of the plight of the poor hints at a need to deflect the motivation for industrialization away from the accumulation of wealth, replacing it with the belief that it constituted either a national imperative or a social good. Thinking about industrialization and wealth in such a way provided middle-class men with a tool to deal with the more uncomfortable vagaries of capitalism. Perhaps the best example of this anxiety is a panegyric to the Scottish-American robber baron-cum-philanthropist Andrew Carnegie by the Aleppine banker Antoine ʿUbaji. Describing Carnegie's "Gospel of Wealth," he enjoined his audience to learn from it and recognize the social good of the accumulation of wealth *and* the patronage of the arts and poor.[46]

Elsewhere in *al-Shaʿb*, al-Alabawi outlined the social benefits of mutual aid. Not only would it provide the basis of "economic cooperation between industry and workers . . . it conjoins wealth and the arts. . . . Therefore," the article concludes, "we must move from mere thought to action in this new age in which we are blessed by the light of freedom."[47] In addition to mutual aid, the socialization of the poor into urban bourgeois etiquette and polite cultural expression was a major goal, and thus the Mutual Aid Society would "seek to awaken knowledge, improve physical fitness and encourage choral singing." The "awakening of knowledge" was promoted through informal education with the opening of a reading room in the club's basement, and local and visiting intellectuals periodically made presentations in the Society's lecture hall. Indeed, in the pre–World War I period, these well-attended public lectures became a primary function of the group, eclipsing its other activities. "Physical fitness"— both team and individual sports—was desirable for its ability to "improve the quality of life and prepare young men for vigorous service to their nation."[48] Finally, members and their charges would enjoy singing and choral music, which was, like team sports, an innovation in the Eastern Mediterranean milieu. Despite their novelty in Aleppo, all of these middle-class forms of social interaction, leisure, and expression were central functions of the kinds of European groups upon which the members modeled themselves.[49]

The embrace of middle-class styles of leisure, charity, and education by the Mutual Aid Society betokened the adoption by its members of the archetypal category of nineteenth-century middle-class behavior in the

---

[46] Ibid., 22 April 1910.
[47] Ibid., 15 April 1910.
[48] Ibid.
[49] Ibid.

social realm, *emulation*. Used in this sense, emulation is more than copying or mimicry; rather, emulation is "honorable competition," and it provided the basis for group association and the building blocks of *al-haya al-ijtimaʿiyya* (social life)—a neologism that appeared often in the paper and the Society's discourse.[50] Ultimately, emulation could allow for both cooperation and collaboration within a framework for self and social improvement. And as this phenomenon manifested itself outside Europe, it took on an added dimension. Beyond simply emulating their peers in Eastern Mediterranean society, members of the Mutual Aid Society also emulated an imagined European cognate at a distance. This phenomenon constitutes the double anxiety of the non-Western middle classes: not only did they compete to preserve their status in their own immediate society, they also measured themselves against images in the media, primarily that of the middle class in metropolitan Europe.

This act of measuring against metropolitan exemplars became the chief organizational theme of the dozens of lectures given at the Mutual Aid Society for the purpose of improving "social life." Published in *al-Shaʿb*, each followed a strikingly consistent formula of pragmatism, a historicist reading of the past, a "rational" assessment of the present situation, and the centering of the (middle-class) individual as a heroic engine in the claiming of modernity. Common to both the historicist reading and assessment of the contemporary situation was an ambivalence about the West, but never about institutions of civil society, education, wealth, and fashion that originated in contemporary Western Europe. Western Europe was perceived as acquisitive, avaricious, and the greatest danger to the nation and its development. But "true civilization," in this context a cognate of modernity, existed outside of any geographically specified area and took the shape of a normative condition. The question asked by the Society's sundry presenters was how to embrace "true civilization" without a concomitant surrender of authenticity, hegemony, and status to the West. Previously seen in Fatallah Qastun's inquiry into how to become civilized, this anxiety was at the heart of the lengthiest speeches delivered at the Mutual Aid Society. Under titles such as "The Causes of Our Retardation," "Civilization," "The West Fears the East," and "Airplanes," speakers assessed the position of the Ottoman Empire within a world-

---

[50] " 'Emulation' resonated widely in the nineteenth century, and it referred to a relationship far more complex than that of model and copyist. A simple measurement of column inches dedicated to the term in the Larousse *Grand Dictionnaire universel* confirms the importance of emulation to nineteenth-century thought. To quote only the beginning of the definition, emulation is a 'a sentiment of rivalry that leads us to equal or better our peers; ordinarily with a positive connotation: to excite emulation, to lack emulation. Emulation is the stimulus of virtue.' " Harrison, *Bourgeois Citizen*, 2.

historical schematic.[51] The notion of Ottoman backwardness and the hierarchy of civilized nations employed the metaphorical language of class and emulation. The Ottomans were in the "middle" of a great international ladder of distinction, on a level with the other modernizing "Asiatic" power, Japan, and drew comfort from the fact that they were not at the "bottom." Regardless of the answer, the middle class expressed its confidence that it would be the group in society most capable of navigating this treacherous course toward complete modernity. Taken as a whole, these speeches in Aleppo and the hundreds like them with variations on the theme, "Osmanlı devleti nasil kurtabılır?" (How Can the Ottoman State Be Saved?)—delivered throughout the empire in the years before World War I—constituted a coherent body of thought and a self-composed coming-of-age narrative for the middle class. The shifting of the middle class from the margins of power to the center in the unfolding of modernity constitutes what I call the *critique of true civilization*. The critique diffracts into three broad areas that expand Hobsbawm's "hierarchy of exclusiveness" beyond inter- and intraclass dynamics to questions of international politics and gender.

Batriki Khayyat's February 1910 lecture entitled "The Causes of Our Retardation" incorporated all the elements of the critique. The editor of *al-Shaʿb* printed the speech in full and noted for added effect that he had received the text via telephone. The honorific *al-shabb al-adib* (young littérateur) appended to the author's name exemplifies the spread of the belief in the centrality of youth and youth culture in the rejuvenation of society and the claiming of modernity. "Experience teaches us that in every situation we are behind," Khayyat argued. "The farmer tills the earth and does not realize even a portion of what is needed to live . . . the merchant works hard and his efforts go up in smoke . . . as for the industrialist he cannot compete in the marketplace with western producers."[52] Two historical conditions caused the current state of affairs. The first was the prerevolutionary government: "The former government was a hindrance to the development of the Ottoman nation unlike any other, and because of the Hamidian régime we are far behind many countries in the struggle of thought and the attainment of civilization." The second reason took the form of self-criticism of the uncritical acceptance of Western commodities and manners—despite the fact that Khayyat must have appeared before his audience dressed in the current French style—and drew an intriguing analogy with colonialism in the Americas: "The Europeans offer us baubles and shiny clothes just like they did to the aboriginal

[51] Brummett, *Image and Imperialism*, 14–15.

[52] This and the other lectures discussed in the next few pages all appeared in *al-Shaʿb* (Aleppo), 2 March 1910.

inhabitants of America in the past and we accept them." This created a condition Khayyat labeled *al-futur*, a word that signifies lassitude, laxity, listlessness, and stagnation; and its root verb, *fatara*, carries the sense of cooling off and lacking heat. Khayyat attributed to stagnation, al-futur, the fact that in the twenty months since the reestablishment of the consti-tution, few if any grand undertakings had been mounted in education, commerce, or society, and that most people were still "stumbling around in the dark, enclosed in the cave of ignorance and beset by the gloom of oppression." "Stagnation," he concluded, "has caused our blood to stop flowing in our veins . . . and our hearts to stop beating in our chests."

Speeches like Khayyat's invariably included a road map for curing the ills of Ottoman society. To save the empire and fulfill the promise of the revolution, the youthful writer prescribed two remedies for the Ottoman peoples, *al-dhabiha* (sacrifice) and *al-hamiyya* (action, zeal, vigor and in particular the opposite of al-futur):

> We can look to examples from history wherein the conditions of nations were affected by the lack or abundance of zeal. For example, what is it that filled Esther with the courage to appear before King Ahasuerus without being sum-moned? And what was it that emboldened Judith to cut of the head of Holofer-nes? It was national zeal [*al-hamiyya al-wataniyya*] and nothing else! Ask the French about the zeal of Joan of Arc. And the English and the Arabs to tell us about the Lion Heart and Saladin and the Ottomans to explain Niyazi and Enver [heroes of the Young Turk Revolution].

In a telling moment of irony, and perhaps in recognition of the training and religious affiliation of most of his audience, the arc of the Khayyat's argument traces a version of history that does not include—with the ex-ception of Saladin, who appears only in the context of the Crusades—examples from an Islamic past but instead takes from European historiog-raphy, current events, and the Bible. The speech culminates in the present, where the heroes of the age are not noble rulers or touched by God, but the bureaucrat-officers at the center of the Revolution of 1908. The Revo-lution of 1908 *meant* that the men listening to Khayyat were now capable of influencing society and claiming modernity for it. The victory of ratio-nality and the implementation of constitutionalism ushered in a new con-dition in which "There is no need to fight the enemy with swords of steel, rather we fight stagnation and ignorance with the blade of zeal and knowl-edge." Sacrifice, al-dhabiha, functions in much the same way as zeal in the civilization critique. Like action, it had a new meaning in the postrevo-lutionary world. While traditional "blood sacrifice" (*al-dhabiha al-da-mawiyya*) was still possible, the moment also required intellectual sacri-fice (*al-dhabiha al-fikriyya*). Blood sacrifice was the burden of citizenship, "and people find it easy to make any effort either simple or hard to defend the nation." However, he continued, "intellectual sacrifice is when one uses one's intellectual ability to discover what is needed by the nation for its improvement."

Critical in this transformation of middle-class men into potential heroic actors at the core of modern society is the realization that such men hitherto had lived at the very margins of power. As nonnotables and in most cases non-Muslims, they had few opportunities to influence the "course of history," and even the military remained statutorily barred to them until 1912. The critique wrote middle-class men, and especially middle-class intellectuals, into history. Implicit in the lectures delivered by Khayyat and others at the time was that the middle class was uniquely suited for this task, and hence it was vital to protect, expand, and confirm its place in society. This critique, however, excluded other forms of knowledge and other classes from the betterment of society in anything more than a subordinate role. Thus, while Khayyat sought to show how action enjoined "all the classes" to cooperate, "mutual aid" and presumably the middle class "would light the fire of action in the hearts of the sons of the nation."

Beyond making a place for the middle class in the politics of the Eastern Mediterranean, the emphasis on styles of "action" and "sacrifice" particular to the *habitus* of middle-class men links the *critique of true civilization* to new concepts of the gendered self, primarily a middle-class and modern masculinity. Fleshing out this connection is complicated by the fact that the history of male-gendered identity is in its infancy in the historiography of the Middle East. Likewise, the social conditions that caused the so-called crisis of masculinity in Western Europe and North America in the nineteenth century were, in a prima facie sense, lacking in cities like Aleppo, Beirut, and Izmir.[53] Nevertheless, the alteration of the definition of masculinity and the shape of this "new man" is a diffraction of contemporary European men's crises through the lens of the texts Khayyat and Qastun were reading. They had merely grafted these ideas onto the political demands of the collapse of certainty in the structures of Ottoman patriarchy. The modern man, in the view of Khayyat and others, employed not physical action but intellectual action; ultimately he would be measured by political, social, and commercial achievement in the public sphere rather than by considerations of birth or religious affiliation. In the end, the activities of the Mutual Aid Society created a space in which middle-class men could be both masculine *and* modern before an audience of those similarly inclined and trained to recognize and reinforce their

---

[53] A possible exception to this is Akram Khater's study of gender dynamics in Mount Lebanon during a period of marginal industrialization and large-scale emigration of men to the West. See Khater, *Inventing Home.*

mutual modernity. These were not dueling clubs; rather, they promoted choral music, team sports, and other leisurely pursuits: attending lectures, writing poetry for the newspaper, and aiding the poor defined an urban modern middle-class masculinity and provided a refined homosociability that translated into possible male solidarity in commerce and politics.

This form of male solidarity dovetailed with the class-based conflict is evidenced in the Mustafâ Âsım affair as well as in the Hüseyin Kâzım controversy, which is detailed in the subsequent chapter. While much of their opposition can be explained as a jockeying for hegemony in the politics of the city, both moments reveal a clash in contrasting visions of what it meant to be a man, and more particularly a man in the public eye. In contrast to the middle-class "new man," the men of the notability were in practice, as freeborn Muslim males of real property, the definitive human being and absolute subject in the Ottoman context, and women and non-Muslims of both genders were, despite legal reforms, imperfect versions thereof. The notables exerted political power as patriarchal authority figures through a complex network of patrons and clients, and their authority mirrored on a smaller scale that of the sultan himself. Conversely, middle-class men, who would certainly have embraced the notions of domestic patriarchy at home, were excluded from the larger patriarchal authority of the notability in the prevailing structures of urban power; instead, they operated in the politics of the moment by mobilizing horizontal linkages of power defined by class and gendered solidarity. More to the point, the desideratum of middle-class political activism was not an alteration of the politics of notables so as to admit its members into the ranks of the aʿyan. Rather, as evidenced by the form of political conflict at work during the revolutionary period, the style of notable politics, indeed the customary Ottoman social order, was judged arbitrary, irrational, and antimodern; or, as seen from the perspective of the members of the Mutual Aid Society, modern men did not behave in such a way in a truly civilized society.

Alongside these evolving definitions of masculinity, middle-class men and women wrestled with the elaboration of a new, modern femininity as evidenced in discussions of women's education, membership in voluntary organizations, and emancipation in the context of social relations *within* the middle class. Likewise, women were located hierarchically within the *critique of true civilization.* Lecturing at the Society in June 1910, Antoine ʿUbaji quoted from Lamartine and Rousseau to call upon fellow members to support the education of girls. "Eastern woman has a long way to go in the sphere of knowledge. With guidance, assistance and rights it will be possible for girls to march alongside boys in learning and culture and become society's thinkers, writers and beneficiaries of liberated thought." Similarly, with training and education "women will be able to raise themselves up the ladder of thought, advance in knowledge, elevate the self and obtain perfect manners."[54]

While the Society may have outlined a project of cultural and social improvement for young women, it stopped short of advocating equality between the sexes, making aspects of gendered difference secure though transitory. Joseph Tawtil, in a presentation delivered on the occasion of "family night" at the Society, elaborated on these ideas for the women in the audience, asserting the importance of their role in "social life." But for Tawtil their role was qualified as "feminine." Women have "individual rights and liberties" and also serve as the link between the spiritual and the material, and moreover provide the emotional underpinning of the modern domestic household. Clearly, advocating the education of women reflected a local variant of Republican motherhood; it located femininity within domesticity, rather than the public sphere—which would remain the privileged domain of the new middle-class man. Again, such ideas have parallels throughout the Eastern Mediterranean at the time. Or as Nilüfer Göle observes of Celal Nuri Ileri's prewar book *Kadınlarımız* [Our Women]: "[It] demonstrates the extent to which the themes of social progress, civilized life, and the education and liberation of women corresponded to their attainment of the status of human being . . . women would not reach the status of human being for their own sakes but would be serving society in its attempt to rise to the level of 'civilized.' "[55] Similarly, the Egyptian writer Qasim Amin (1863–1908) first articulated these ideas in his *al-Mar'a al-jadida* [the Modern Woman] (Cairo, 1900). In this manner, Eastern Mediterranean middle-class discourse on women and gendered difference did not assert equality, but rather marked an attempt to negotiate the entrance of women into the project of modernity while maintaining the distinctive nature of middle-class masculinity. Women would be modern, but never quite as modern as men; their modernity would always be contingent on their utility to the modern man. Clearly, the partial emancipation of women was a key tenet of what it meant to be modern: the truly modern man must have an educated, socially graceful, and publicly presentable wife and mother to his children, rather than a secluded, customary one. Likewise, the affirmation of feminine emotionality and spirituality—both handicaps in the public sphere of rational secular discourse—would make modern woman especially suited to nurturing roles in that modern society.

Left unsaid in the speeches was the role of religious difference and categories of religious distinction in "social life." Critically, the speeches and

---

[54] *al-Sha'b* (Aleppo), 20 June 1910.

[55] Nilüfer Göle, *The Forbidden Modern: Civilization and Veiling* (Ann Arbor: University of Michigan Press, 1996), 39.

other activities of the Society lack any clear evidence of Muslim participation: there were no Muslims in its leadership, nor did any speak at its podium. The only recorded evidence of Muslim involvement with the Society appears in an account of a reception for the embattled governor Fahri in the presence of prominent politicians and bureaucrats. This was despite the fact that the members scrupulously avoided any reference to religion in the present, whereas they often did so in historical allusions, although these references invariably came from the Hebrew Bible or the New Testament. Of note is that this religious universe was more in keeping with Western European exemplars, as the more exotic and local attributes of Eastern Christianity seem equally absent. The members of the Society identified modernity with nonsectarianism, but an insistence on equality and cooperation bereft of religious distinction held little appeal for members of the Muslim elite or even portions of its middle class, as for them it represented the surrender of privileges and customary patriarchy; secularism held out the promise of empowerment only for non-Muslims. Moreover, the physical location of the Society—a majority Christian middle-class neighborhood, ʿAziziyya—the date and time of the clubs meetings—Sunday evening after supper—the occasional use of alcohol during social gatherings, and the public attendance of chaperoned women at the meetings coded the Society as non-Muslim and in particular Christian. For a middle-class Muslim to cooperate fully with the society, he would have been required to move into a social environment in which Christians and Jews no longer occupied inferior positions; rather, it were a space in which fluency in bourgeois styles of sociability and horizontal egalitarianism in the universe of voluntary associations was the price of admission. Participation in these clubs hinged on an acknowledgment of the superiority of Western forms of cultural capital acquired by the minority middle class over the preceding generation. In many cases, access to those forms was predicated upon their Catholicism, foreign contacts, and an ability to be modern with greater fluency than many of their Muslim counterparts. And further, the challenge posed by the opening of public spaces of sociability to women and minorities as part of the project of modernity hardened the intimate boundaries between, on the one hand, Christians and Jews, and, on the other, the Muslim community, writ large. While this time of revolution witnessed moments of intersectarian comity in the political and professional spheres, such connections were less evident or absent altogether in the more closed domains of education, sports, and leisure. This conclusion points to a need to incorporate discussions of informal fellowship, friendship, social gatherings like dances and musical performances, and the consumption of food and alcohol outside of the home in understanding the formation of viable civil society.

With the closure of *al-Sha'b* in 1913 by the state, there is little additional information about the Mutual Aid Society. However, it did survive
World War I and reemerged as the Aleppo Club. The transformation of
the Mutual Aid Society of Aleppo into the Aleppo Club accompanied the
maturation of its constituency and also foreshadowed a conscious retreat
from overt political activism by the middle class of the city. While the
Aleppo Club has survived into the twenty-first century and still hosts lectures, sponsors sports teams, and aids the poor, its chief function is as a
middle-class social club that self-consciously mirrors styles of European
bourgeois sociability; it has no overt political presence in the politics of
contemporary Syria. In the 1940s and 1950s it was the site of debutante
balls and bridge tournaments, and it now hosts gala wedding receptions,
karaoke nights, and cocktail parties. On paper, the Aleppo Club has maintained a strict nonsectarianism, but in practice it is still the domain of
the city's francophone Catholic middle class. The interwar Sunni-notable
politician Sa'dallah al-Jabiri frequented the Aleppo Club with his political
ally, Edmond Rabbath, a Greek Catholic. Attending the club without the
female members of his family, Jabiri recorded in his diary how appealing
the single, young Jewish and Catholic women dining in it were and
thereby stipulating the novelty of the setting.[56] Several of its prominent
members, including the Qastuns, 'Ubaji, and Léon Homsy, were active in
the postwar Aleppine literary and political scene. Fathallah Qastun
founded the short-lived weekly journal *al-Shu'ala* [The Flame], which,
according to its masthead, was a "political, literary, and economic periodical." Among its earliest series was an essay by Qastun bemoaning the
effects of the war on economy and society, and in particular on the morals
of young people. Like his work a decade earlier, those articles maintained
the optimism and certainty of the previous essays and lectures, though
only as a consequence of the French occupation of Syria.

In its brief lifetime, the very existence of the Mutual Aid Society, the Sunday night lectures, and the links with *al-Sha'b* provide evidence of a gener-
alization of once unorthodox ideas about who should and should not
exercise power, modern styles of masculinity, and patronage. What seems
to have been missing, but only from a teleological perspective, is any kind
of ethnic nationalism; rather, the membership of the Society, while often
addressing the needs of the "nation," rarely qualified what that nation
was, thus leading to the conclusion that the readers and the audience
implicitly knew what was meant. For the middle-class listeners and readers, an *Ottomanism*, and support for the integrity of the Ottoman state,
constituted a coherent and understandable formula and an imaginable

---

[56] MWT-Qkh. Folder 95: "Private Papers of Sa'dallah al-Jabiri," entry for 12 May 1929.

community that could also include middle-class Arab Christians, whose connection to the Ottoman state was not negotiable in the language of Islamic solidarity but was secured instead by the implicit and explicit promises of the Revolution of 1908. Youth could be prepared to defend it, women could be educated to better serve it by raising better citizens, and society could be mobilized to withstand the pressures of its enemies. This was an optimistic, successful progressive ideology. For the members of the club and the broader Eastern Mediterranean middle stratum, it evidenced a *possible* means for cross-sectarian, class-based solidarity built on the evolving sense of Ottoman citizenship and middle-class modernity—and, more to the point, in a way that transcended religious and ethnic difference.

FOUR

Ottoman Precedents (II): The Technologies of the Public Sphere and the Multiple Deaths of the Ottoman Citizen

> He is not a fanatic believer, he might even be a Freemason.
> —Aleppo's French consul, Lorance, on Aleppo's governor,
> Hüseyin Kâzım, 1910

The precipitous departure of Fahri Pasha in the wake of the Mustafâ Âsım affair constituted a tremendous blow to the local notability, which had supported Fahri. Their ferocious opposition to his successor, Hüseyin Kâzım, shows that these families understood the threat to their hegemonic position in the city posed by the new politics of the revolutionary period. Furthermore, the swift and concerted efforts of the notables reveal a degree of solidarity and group interest sufficient to suggest that they too viewed themselves as a class. Over the following months, the strife foreshadowed in the events surrounding Mustafâ Âsım culminated in an intense campaign by the aggrieved notability to oust the new governor. This campaign played out not only in the local press, but also at the highest levels of the Ottoman state. Like that of the middle class, the notable reaction employed new technologies and access to the state bureaucracy. Unlike the middle class, the notables' reaction invoked Islam and custom as a countermeasure to change. In the Âsım affair, much of the antagonism toward the old governor, Fahri Pasha, arose from non-Muslim circles. As this chapter documents, the alliance of the notables' political agenda with an Islamic idiom of Muslim dominance had the potential to reconfigure the conflict in the city as one of religious prerogative over foreign and non-Muslim subversion, rather than just a conservative reaction against a modernist recreation of society. Situating the debate in such a fashion maximized the notables' authority in religious interpretation as "defenders of the faith and guardians of culture."[1] It also rendered precarious the secularist bases of Ottoman citizenship and the promise of emancipation for non-Muslims in the region's middle class.

---

[1] Khoury, *Mandate*, 13.

When the news of Fahri Pasha's dismissal came, the *kadı* of Aleppo, Recep Hilmi bey, served as the interim chief of the province's civilian bureaucracy. Originally appointed at a time when Abdülhamid still ruled, Hilmi had seen not just his patron, Fahri, but his patron's patron fall from power through forces over which he had little control. Perhaps loath to see the process continue, he tapped into heightened tensions during Ramadan 1328 (August–September 1910) and used his position to try to redress the damage caused by the success of the upstart Âsım and others.

Aleppo had escaped the communal strife that had engulfed the Tarsus region and Antioch in 1909, though local observers felt religious tensions palpably in the postrevolutionary period. The freeing of notables arrested for incitement or failing to suppress a massacre of Antioch's Armenians by Muslims of the city troubled several Christian writers in Aleppo. They feared that the exoneration of these notables by the authorities in Istanbul would be interpreted as license to kill non-Muslims with impunity, or a retreat from the rule of law and egalitarian and secularizing reforms.[2] As Ramadan, the month of daytime fasting and stepped-up religious observance, approached, Hilmi took steps to enforce public morality through the dissemination of circulars and a threat to punish those who transgressed the public observance of the fast.[3] While the fast—and the circulars—applied only to Muslims, some interpreted the announcement as an interdiction on the public consumption of food and drink by Christians and Jews as well. Several non-Muslims were viciously attacked in the suq and other public places, among them the brother of Adolphe Sola, the Italian consul, who was beaten severely when a group of young religious students observed him eating near the offices of the consulate.[4]

Emboldened by the apparent popular enthusiasm for the enforcement of the fast, the *kadı* moved against the highest-ranking Unionist in Aleppo, the public prosecutor, Said Zeineddin. At the height of Ramadan, Hilmi burst into the office of Zeineddin, who was in conversation with the local judicial inspector, Ismail Hakki bey, both of whom were smoking cigarettes in contravention to his prior orders. He announced their infraction publicly as he rushed into the halls of the government house shouting that it would "be lawful to kill such a Free-Mason."[5] Subsequently, Hilmi

---

[2] *al-Taqaddum* (Aleppo), 6 August 1910.

[3] CADN-MAE Consulat Alep Série "A" 47 Lorance (Aleppo) to Embassy Constantinople, Levant 117/Ambassade 147, 7 September 1910.

[4] Ibid.

[5] PRO FO 861/59 Fontana (Aleppo) to Lowther (Constantinople), 2 October 1910. It was not uncommon then or since to equate Free Masonry with all Young Turks. See, for example, Husayn ʿUmar Himada, *Al-Masuniyya wa al-masuniyun fi al-watan al-ʿarabi* [Masonry and Masons in the Arab Nation] (Damascus: 1995), especially chapter 4, "al-masuniyun fi Suriyya" [The Masons in Syria], 99–172. In many accounts, including this

called a meeting of the notables of the city and demanded they sign a telegram calling for the dismissal of Zeineddin. In the minds of those notables who associated themselves with Hilmi, the smoking incident was more broadly representative of the religiously transgressive nature of the Young Turks and constituted yet another threat to their role as protectors of religious piety—a role from which they drew tremendous power and prestige. The telegrams that the a'yan would dispatch to Istanbul and the closing of ranks that they document epitomized notable solidarity and their corporate assessment that their position in the city's structures of power was under threat from new forces.[6] That they employed telegrams, a recent innovation in the Levant, to forward their cause speaks to the local notability's willingness to use all technical tools to their advantage. While telegrams were a technological innovation and an instance of modernization, their use does not imply an acceptance of the ideological structures of modernity. Rather, it reveals the notables' willingness to do what was needed to maintain hegemony, even if it meant employing techniques and ideas that could, when played out, contradict their own sources of authority; they did not associate certain modern technologies with the forms of political and social organization of modernity itself.

The *kadı* also acted to defend the notable presence in the Aleppine religious bureaucracy. Throughout the last third of the nineteenth century, his allies, the Jâbirî family, had dominated the law courts, which were the primary target of the reform impulses of the public prosecutor Zeineddin. He had enlarged the secular court offices and relegated Hilmi to a backroom. Shortly after the renovations were completed, arson destroyed many of the court records and two court rooms. Suspicion fell on Hilmi.[7] Nonetheless, he was not arrested; Zeineddin, on the other hand, along with two other Unionist bureaucrats, the *defterdar* (provincial finance director) and the *mektupçu* (chief administrative secretary of the province), were transferred by the authorities in Istanbul to attractive postings in Konya. The flurry of telegrams received by the Interior Ministry led to the temporary transfer of authority in the province to the military commander of the local garrison, who served until the arrival of Hüseyin Kâzım. Upon the young governor's arrival he dismissed Hilmi, recalled Zeineddin, and appointed him *kadı*.[8]

---

one, Young Turks and Zionists cooperated in a conspiracy against the Arabs. Of note is Himada's conclusion that Masons were also behind the Arab revolt.

[6] PRO FO 861/59 Fontana (Aleppo) to Lowther (Constantinople), 3 December 1910.

[7] PRO FO 195/2337 Fontana (Aleppo) to Lowther (Constantinople), 15 November 1910.

[8] *River*, 1:242.

CLASS CONFLICT BY TELEGRAM

Hüseyin Kâzım's bold move showed the notables of the city that he shared with his Young Turk allies a commitment to reform what they considered retrograde elements of Ottoman society. Moreover, Hüseyin Kâzım's tenure in the Gray City documents the full measure of social change taking shape throughout the empire in this time revolution, but also concrete transformations in the more pedestrian structures and mundane operations of provincial bureaucracies. Born in Trabzon in 1870 to that province's governor at the time, Kadri Pasha, this epitome of a young Ottoman middle-class bureaucrat intellectual spent his school years at Istanbul's Soğuk Çesme military academy and the Mülkiye, the imperial administrative college. Later he enrolled at the British polytechnic in Izmir, completing his studies at the Ecole d'Agronomie in Paris. Returning to the capital, he took positions in the Finance and Foreign ministries and taught at various high schools. Following the reinstatement of the constitution, he founded the Unionist newspaper *Tanin* [The Clarion] with two other Ottoman journalists, Tevfik Fikret and Hüseyin Cahid Yalcın. His association with the CUP led to his appointment as mayor of Samsun (1909) and later that year of Serez in the province of Salonica, where he oversaw Young Turk electoral victories. The untimely departure of Fahri accelerated his appointment to the governorship of Aleppo, clearly signaling the CUP's drive to dominate the politics of the most important city in the Levant.[9]

A key tenet of Hüseyin Kâzım's policies in Aleppo was a commitment to eliminate what he and his colleagues at *Tanin*, like the journalist Ahmet Şerif, labeled *derebeylik*—feudalism. Hüseyin Kâzım probably shared the views Şerif had expressed in several articles written in mid-1910 about the abusive practices of the large landholders in inner Anatolia. For these journalist-bureaucrats, a causal connection existed between the culture of land tenure in the empire and the continuing dominance of the notability. In a larger sense, the use of a neologism borrowed from Western European political economy to describe an entire class of Ottoman society marked a fundamental departure in thinking about the old notability. Far from viewing the notables as a crucial link in the structures of Ottoman governance, the notables were now living reminders of the unmodern in the midst of a new society. In other words, they were not just an obstacle to reform, but the very institutional form that the new society was marking as obsolete in the claiming of modernity. Consequently, integrating the notability into modernity would have contradicted the dialectical terms used by Hüseyin Kâzım and others as they imagined a modern Ottoman state. Any

---

[9] *Türk Ansiklopedisi* (Istanbul, Milli Eğitim Bakanlığı, 1943), 19:420–421.

privilege, any authority or power that derived from notable status was quite simply fruit from a forbidden tree. Thus, beginning with the transformation of the local legal structures, he struck out against the landed elite of the vast province of Aleppo with unprecedented vigor. While playing to an Istanbul audience, his actions reverberated in the local milieu, where his decision to undermine the invented traditions, as well as the cultural, intellectual, and fiscal bases of notable authority, drew the middle class of the city into an unprecedented form of political discourse.

The attack on the landed elite took the form of a proclamation/editorial carried by the local press in both Ottoman Turkish and Arabic.[10] The text reflects similar discussions about rights and the individual that had arisen at the time of the Mustafâ Âsım affair and should be read as a précis of the larger political and social agenda of the revolution's vanguard. While its rhetoric translated various Quranic passages into a liberal constitutionalism for its modern cosmopolitan readers, God's words could continue to elicit consent and support from a customary audience. This conscious choice had the potential to use a facet of notable power against that class by appropriating the right to control religious interpretation and to invoke the Quran to justify political action. The announcement began:

> O you notables, oppressive notables, since I have arrived in this province, I only hear everyone bemoaning your tyranny and misdeeds. . . . I cannot see rights ignored, the property of the orphans and of the wretched wasted or confiscated by the wealthy whose strength is based on the work of the poor. I know very well that you do not fear the demands of those whom you oppress. The government . . . has not yet succeeded in reforming jurisdiction of the empire to the point of making it morally capable to guarantee equity and the rights of all the classes of society. But know that this situation can no longer last because the people have changed and demand justice.[11]

Citing other verses, he outlined a definition of justice that differed little from the standard conception of Ottoman political theory on the subject.[12] Continuing to hector the notables, he warned,

---

[10] A version of the proclamation was reprinted at the center of the empire in the journal *Avam*. "He used strong language about the notables and the agas and announced that an end would be put to their oppression. There was a reaction to this proclamation from all sides. Because the Istanbul paper *Avam* printed this proclamation, it received letters of congratulations from many of its readers in Anatolia and Rumelia." Hüseyin Avni Şanda, *Reaya ve Köylü* [Common People and Villagers] (Istanbul: Habora Kitabevi, 1970), 10, cited in Feroz Ahmad, "The Agrarian Policy of the Young Turks, 1908–1918," in Jean-Louis Bacqué-Grammont and Paul Dumont, eds., *Économie et sociétés dans l'Empire Ottoman* (Paris: CNRS, 1983), 275–288.

[11] *al-Taqaddum* (Aleppo), 1 October 1910.

[12] See Findley's discussion of the concepts of *adil ve ihsan* (justice and goodwill) in the thought of the postrevolutionary Grand Vezir, Ibrahim Hakkı Pasha. *Ottoman Civil*, 195–209.

I advise these people [the notables] to fear the effects of their actions in this world and the next. Note well that honor and prestige is acquired only by services rendered to your compatriots. If you pretend to be honorable, and if you want prestige, show me the good that you have done for your city. . . . if you speak the truth I will be forced to give you the titles of honor by which you flatter yourselves, but if these titles are the consequence of your tyranny, know that you have no right to live in this city and be certain that the government is committed to executing this threat. Hear my warning well!

However, as the proclamation began its crescendo, it acknowledged the place of other groups and classes within a broader Ottoman polity and adopted a topos of revolutionary parlance, the existence of a fatherland or *vatan*. By linking people directly to the fatherland, rather than to the sultan, it redefined the relationship of the individual to the ultimate terrestrial authority.

This city is not only composed of you [notables], but those who form this city, and in general the holy fatherland, are the persons that you desire to keep under the weight of your tyranny. . . . The time has finally come when your poor victims, deprived for centuries . . . find a little bit of rest and taste the pleasure of living thanks to the constitution. . . .

You will see from now on that the first duty of the authorities will be to guarantee everyone his rights. I, myself, will try to conform to the precepts of God by "giving each person his due and not commit evil in this world."

Other formulations of revolutionary language emerged as the governor closed his statement, identifying the local civil servants, *memurlar*, as agents of the planned reform of the province,

Know well that I have the power to fulfill the functions the constitutional government has given me. My first duty and that of all the civil servants is to crush the oppressors.

The functionaries who have honor and who fear only God and who only seek to consolidate in this city the basis of constitutional administration which is founded on the will of the nation; these civil servants . . . will never consent to allow you to control and encourage venality.

They will put an end to your tyranny and your pride.

. . . Know that I am one of those who seek the tranquility of the empire and the prosperity of the people. Therefore I am ready to seize by the neck the oppressing notables . . . [and remove them from] the province like God prescribes. . . . By acting this way, I merely fulfill the duties of my function for the people. . . . I warn you: woe to the person who closes his ears in order not to hear. I advise you to think about what God said, "any kind of punishment is appropriate for tyrants."

The tone of the new governor's pronouncement led the local French consul to write that "like all his predecessors, he has felt the opposition of the great land owners to any attempt at serious reform, and that no serious result is possible as long as the administration has not crushed this reactionary and oppressive aristocracy."[13] Noting the Quranic passages in the attack on the notables, the same consul doubted Hüseyin Kâzım's religiosity, saying, "he is not a fanatic believer, he might even be a Freemason."[14] Yet the combination of passages from the Quran, the invocation of the divine, and abstract secular concepts of earthly justice had the potential to rework modern terms of equality and rights into words comprehensible in customary religious practice.[15]

Critically, the cocktail of familiar passages from the Quran and neologisms seen in the widely disseminated proclamation constituted at the time a second wave in the project of Islamic modernism. The leading intellectual figures of that school of thought from a previous generation, Muhammad ʿAbduh and ʿAbd al-Rahman al-Kawakibi in particular, would have been comfortable with many of the efforts of the CUP governor, which paralleled their own attempts to translate concepts crucial to modern forms of governance, education, democracy, and thought into what they considered an Islamic idiom.[16] Further, the careful deployment of terms with stable meanings in the Ottoman-Islamic context in the more mercurial setting of revolutionary politics suggests that the boundary between Islamic learning/practice and secularizing, modern intellectuals at this moment was less discrete than it became in the interwar period.

The extent to which this projected land reform was ever implemented is unclear. Feroz Ahmad argues that CUP land reform policies, though intended to distribute land to the peasantry, were subverted by the large

---

[13] CADN-MAE Consulat Alep Série "A" 47 Lorance (Aleppo) to Embassy (Constantinople) Levant 134 / Ambassade 174, 5 November 1910.

[14] Ibid. Halide Edip remembers meeting Hüseyin Kâzım in Beirut during the war. Having fallen out with the Young Turk leadership, he took up residence in the city and opened an orphanage. "I had several talks with him," recalled Halide, "which impressed me very much. He spoke Arabic well and had broad ideas about the treatment of Arabs and the other minorities. A convinced Muslim, he cited the Koran and prophesied that all rule based on tyranny was doomed to fail." Halide Edip, *Memoirs of Halide Edip* (London: The Century Co., 1928), 400–401.

[15] Hüseyin Kâzım's later literary activity suggests that he continued this process of modernizing religious concepts and sought a fusion of trends in Islamic modernism and evolving Turkish nationalism. In 1915, under the pen name of Şeyh Muhsin Fani, he advocated the abolition of the sufi orders and defended the translation of the Koran into Turkish. Şeyh Muhsin Fani, *Istikbale Doğru* [Straight toward the Future] (Istanbul, 1915). By 1924 he had completed "the first relatively successful full-length translation" of the Koran. Berkes, *Secularism*, 487.

[16] Hourani, *Arabic Thought*, 130–160, 271–272.

landholders and fell prey to the revenue needs of the state.[17] In Aleppo some notables were dispossessed of their land. However, as local land disputes tended to be adjudicated by the notable-dominated administrative council, peasants rarely prevailed.[18] In a lengthy article on this process in *Lisân-i Ahâlî*, Mustafâ Âsım observed that legal structures had been subverted by notable control of state institution. Accusing Jâbirî zade Nafiᶜ Pasha of conspiring with his brother Fakhr and the kaymakam of the kaza of Jabal al-Samᶜan to the west of Aleppo—the fief of the "al Jabiri" (the Jâbirî clan), as Bughikiyan called them—to register state land illegally in their name, the journalist noted that the only legal recourse was to petition the administrative council, which Asᶜad Pasha, another brother of Nafiᶜ, chaired and upon which yet another brother, Haj Murat, sat ex officio as the defterdar of the kaza, thereby underlining the futility of such action.[19]

Nevertheless, the rhetoric and the limited actions of the governor did strike at the roots of notable power: an invented tradition of legal and religious structures to defend the acquisition and maintenance of large landholdings and the near-feudal control of the lives of the people living on them. Taken to its logical extent, the governor's actions would have vitiated their sources of wealth. The notables initially responded to the governor's proclamation with a couplet penned by Ibrahim effendi al-Kayyali and published by *Lisân-i Ahâlî*, which Âsım dismissed as "mere doggerel":

> O governor of the Gray City verily with a letter,
> In which you warn those who consume the tithe

> You have brought forth a miraculous bit of knowledge
> I see that you have disgraced the liberals[20]

In other words, the governor had behaved dishonorably by attacking those in a position of honor; and consequently the notables seemed to have missed the governor's point entirely.

However, as the reality of the governor's actions sank in, the notable reaction crystallized in the province and the capital. Nafiᶜ Pasha, also the senior legislator from Aleppo and speaker of the Meclis-i Mebusan (House of Representatives), wrote an article criticizing the governor in the conservative Istanbul paper *Ikdâm*.[21] With this article and the use of

---

[17] Ahmad, "Agrarian Policy," 281–284.

[18] PRO FO 195/2336 Fontana (Aleppo) to Lowther (Constantinople), 20 March 1911.

[19] *Lisân-i Ahâlî / Lisan al-Ahali* (Aleppo), 16 October 1910.

[20] In ibid., 6 November 1910. The last word, "al-ahrar," has multiple meanings. It may be pun on the word in Arabic signifying liberal, but it also can mean "high-born."

[21] FO PRO 861/59 Fontana (Aleppo) to Lowther (Constantinople), 3 December 1910.

telegrams sent directly to the minister of the interior—aided by the presence of powerful Aleppines in the capital[22]—the notables communicated directly with the center, bypassing the local authority. Such a strategy was reproduced in center-periphery encounters between other Anatolian and Eastern Mediterranean provinces and Istanbul at the time.[23]

The most decisive aspect of the notable reaction emerged following a meeting in the last weeks of 1910 during which representatives of all the major notable families pledged 500 Turkish pounds to underwrite a telegram campaign against Hüseyin Kâzım. From the outset, the conflict played out in public; upon learning of the amount pledged, the governor announced that he would gladly resign if only the notables were to donate these funds to the poor.[24] Yet as the telegram campaign developed over the following weeks, the notables co-opted the rhetoric and vocabulary of the public sphere, caricaturing the very language of liberalism and reform that was the stock-in-trade of the middle class. Written in the traditional form of a *mazbata* (petition), the telegrams included lists of signatories, so that from the perspective of reconstructing the boundaries of the social groups engaged with the corpus of ideas in the penumbra of the public sphere, they provide an invaluable source.[25]

In the first telegrams received at the Interior Ministry in mid-February 1911, a leading member of the Aleppine notability, Marʿaş zâde Fatih, writing in Ottoman Turkish and using two familiar themes from customary Ottoman political theory, accused the governor of disrupting "social cohesion" and spreading "disunity" by attacking the *eşrâf* and the *erbâb* (descendants of the Prophet and large landowners). This telegram coincided with the publication of Nafiʿ's article in Istanbul. It was followed by a telegram bearing the signatures of thirty prominent Sunni Muslim Aleppines, including Jâbirî zâde Murad and Jâbirî zâde Mehmet Asʿad Pasha, Kathüda zâde Rashid, Ibrahim Pasha zâde Said, and Mudarris zâde Fuad—the established representatives of their families in the city.[26] The second telegram explained that the governor had violated property rights in the province. Two days later the governor responded by sending a telegram depicting his actions in the province as a response to the needs

---

[22] Primarily Nafiʿ's brother Ihsân, who served as a chamberlain to the sultan.

[23] Ahmad notes, "The landlords operated on two fronts: locally where they had economic and political power they obstructed reform; and in parliament where they used their majority to either halt measures directed against them, or to introduce measures designed to further their interests." "Agrarian Policy," 282.

[24] FO PRO 861/59 Fontana (Aleppo) to Lowther (Constantinople), 3 December 1910.

[25] The traditional mazbata usually bore the seals of the signatories; the telegrams simply showed their names beneath the text.

[26] BBA DH-MTV 1329.Ca.30: 18/20. Telegram to the Ministry of Interior from Jâbirî zâde Esʿad Pasha et al., dated 1 Şubat 1327.

of the people and consistent with his role as a revolutionary reformer: "Finding the people of the [countryside of] Aleppo very poor and in the greatest of need," he was forced to act against the oppressive notables because of his commitment to constitutionalism and the application of the rule of law "without distinction of rank."[27] No doubt aware that Minister of the Interior Talat Pasha was an ally of Hüseyin Kâzım, the notable coalition sent other telegrams to the offices of Ibrahim Hakkı Pasha, the grand vizier, and the minister of justice in the hopes of finding a more sympathetic reception.[28] Such petitions were part of the role of the notability as understood at the time; a manifestation of their social hegemony was the obligation to speak for or represent the local community to the imperial center. Prior to the Revolution of 1908, the governor represented the ultimate authority in the provinces. However, with the advent of constitutional rule—and the compression of space and time following the introduction of telegraphy, telephony, and rail and steamships transportation—the lines of authority grew cloudy and the notability were forced to deal with a large number of officials. More important, they no longer had unique access to those officials.

As that week in 1911 progressed, other social groups in Aleppo started to send telegrams, claiming thereby a voice and right to speak for the city as a whole. Muslim and Christian ecclesiastical leaders, including the Maronite Bishop Yusuf Diyab, the Greek Catholic Metropolitan Dimitrius, the Armenian Bishop Shahi, the Syriac Catholic Bishop Ephraim Dionysius, the Armenian Catholic Bishop, and the Müftü, Muhammad al-'Ubaysi, signed a telegram defending the governor. And in the phrase that would come to signify the class and religious distinction of those who supported the governor, they referred to the him as *walina* in Arabic and *valimiz* in Ottoman Turkish: *our governor*.[29] In contrast, the notable-generated telegrams open with the impersonal "Aleppo governor, Hüseyin Kâzım bey."

As leaders within the millet structure, these religious officials had responsibilities that included the prerogative to speak for their respective religious communities, yet over the next month the bureaucratic and professional middle class who had found a voice during the Mustafâ Âsım controversy seized upon the telegrams to express their support for the governor. As such, they entered into a new form of critical-rational discourse that, in a crucial sense, *denied* the notability the prerogative to speak for them and society as a whole—the technology of the telegraph

---

[27] Ibid. Telegram to the Ministry of Interior from Hüseyin Kâzım dated 3 Şubat 1327.

[28] PRO FO 195/2336 Fontana (Aleppo) to Lowther (Constantinople), 20 March 1911.

[29] BBA DH-MTV 1329.Ca.30: 18/20. Telegram to the Minister of Interior from Yusuf Diyab et al., dated 3 Şubat 1327.

gave them equal access to the center; the new politics of revolution provided the idiom.

Ten days after the telegram of support from the religious leaders, fifty-one Muslim, Christian, and Jewish businessmen, bankers, and liberal professionals authored a similar message: "Our governor," the telegram insisted, had defended constitutional rights and aided the poor and had not stolen lands; rather, he had merely given some tribes grazing access. More important, it argued that the governor had been motivated by "thoughtful action," and, ultimately, this action would promote the peace of the nation.[30] In a subsequent telegram from a group of local bureaucrats, the governor's actions were contrasted with those of the notables themselves. "*Our governor*, His Excellency, Hüseyin Kâzım bey, is the soul of constitutionalism, the true protector of justice, the genuine servant of the oppressed and the single sincere enemy of tyranny," while the notables commit injustice and terrorize the state.[31] On 2 March 1911 (18 Şubat 1327), many notables who had signed the initial telegram added their names to a missive that also included those of religious teachers and the leader of the local Rifa'i Sufi brotherhood.[32] The addition of these names calls attention to the fact that the position of the notables was supported by Islamic religious institutions beyond the direct control of the secular bureaucracy. Still, the notable campaign was relentless: another telegram arrived in the capital two weeks later, this time signed by more Aleppines from notable families. All Muslim, and representing a half-dozen clans, the list of names is a comprehensive inventory of the city's notability.

Textually the telegrams crystallize the terms of class conflict in the city and the region. The first telegrams sent by the notables used an idiom of social equilibrium and conservatism and insisted that the governor's actions contravened established political norms. In his defense the governor had portrayed his activities as falling within the structure of secular justice, pragmatism, and rationality, suggesting a commitment to a definition of civil rights and equality that ignored the traditional prerogatives of notable hegemony. The telegrams from the middle-class cadre in his support also stressed such ideas and castigated his opponents for exercising what may have appeared to the latter as the divinely determined natural order of things. Later telegrams from the notables, however, evidence a significant rhetorical shift by embracing the terms of debate prevailing in the time of revolution and invoke references to constitutionality, law and

---

[30] Ibid. Telegram to the Grand Vezir Ibrahim Hakki Pasha from Fathallah Antaki et. al., dated 11 Şubat 1327.

[31] Ibid. Telegram to the Ministry of the Interior from 'Aqqa 'Abdu Najib et al., dated 7 Mart 1327.

[32] Ibid. Telegram to the Justice Ministry from the hadith specialist of the al-Hurfa Mosque, Muati', dated 18 Şubat 1327.

order, and rights. Like the earliest telegram, the last group, sent simultaneously to the Interior Ministry, the grand vizier, and Nafiʿ Pasha, begin with the accusation that the "the administration of the governor is spreading dissent," then moved to a different tact: "his actions were "destroying the *constitutional order*. He is a man who seeks to advance his career through lies and deceit. He has taken tithe-lands, state lands and liens. . . . *We are concerned with the basic law and with the preservation of personal rights and national sovereignty.* Because of this we feel the need to speak out."[33] In other words, unlike the governor, the notables themselves were the protectors of the new liberal order, while at the same time the addition of names from the Muslim religious establishment to the list of signatories signaled the broadening of their base of support among the most conservative, traditional elements of society. As shown in later chapters, the co-optation of the rhetoric of modernity, as such a passage shows, does not necessarily constitute a commitment to it; rather, it reveals the notable class's extraordinary flexibility and ability to use tools both intellectual and technological to defend its hegemony. That the notability were forced to adapt their discourse in such a fashion likewise suggests the extent to which these aesthetics and concepts had currency within Ottoman society in both central and provincial contexts.

The telegrams had been matched within the city by an active campaign in the press against the notability. In line with the other papers of the city, *al-Shaʿb* published a lengthy poem praising the governor, earning its author, "Siwasi," a death threat from the Jâbirîs.[34] Mustafâ Âsım and Artashes Bughikyan supported the governor in their pages, publishing an Ottoman Turkish version of his declaration in *Lisân-ı Ahâlî*, and an article about the true meaning of *al-Sharaf* (honor) in the Arabic portion of the paper—a reference to the eşrâf (lit. the "men of honor") that implied that those in an honored social position behaved dishonorably.[35] Ultimately, the intensity of the growing class conflict—and the clear shadows of sectarianism that accompanied it—led the local British consul to conclude, "the town of Aleppo has been divided into two camps, on the one side the Moslem land-owners, Notables and Eshraf, and on the other the Moslem people of the poorer classes, the leading officials and the Christians."[36]

Why did members of the Aleppine middle class support Hüseyin Kâzım to such a degree? It is unlikely that the governor's modest land reform

---

[33] Ibid. Telegram to the Grand Vezir from Marʿas zâde Hüseyin, 30 Şubat 1327.

[34] PRO FO 195/2366 Fontana (Aleppo) to Lowther (Istanbul), 15 April 1911.

[35] *Lisân-i Ahâlî / Lisan al-Ahali* (Aleppo), 6 November 1910. The article was a reprint of a lengthy piece that had appeared originally in Jamal al-Din al-Afghani's seminal newspaper *al-ʿUrwa al-Wuthqa* [The Unbreakable Bond] in the 1890s. See Hourani, *Arabic Thought*, 226.

[36] *Lisân-i Ahâlî / Lisan al-Ahali* (Aleppo), 6 November 1910.

program, which provoked the uproar in the first place, could have benefited them directly. The underlying cause of the support of the governor
most probably lay in the phrase "*valimiz/walina*," our governor. The middle class of the city had recognized that any possible augmentation of their
power in Ottoman society through social mobility and modern political
practice was predicated upon the supplanting of notable hegemony. The
Mustafâ Âsım controversy had shown that the CUP central authorities
embraced modernity and supported it through a centrifugal exertion of
their power. For many in the middle class, Hüseyin Kâzım epitomized this
force: they identified with him. Unlike his predecessor, he appeared willing
to enforce the notion of secular equality and the rule of law; and he most
closely embodied the ideal of a rational basis of authority. By the same
token, as a journalist and liberally educated middle-aged man, he resembled them. An overview of the professions of those who expressed support
for the governor highlights the profile of the men who made up the middle
class (tables 4.1 and 4.2) Among the signatories of the progovernor telegrams appeared the names of many persons involved in international
commerce, banking, and the liberal professions. Salim Janbart served as
president of the Aleppo Chamber of Commerce from 1921 to 1950, and
Albert Homsy, a prominent banker, was active in Syrian politics in the
postwar period.[37] Others were those of scions of local Greek Catholic and
Jewish entrepreneurial families such as Magarbana, Antaki, and Kubaʿi.
They also dealt most directly with Europeans: Rizqallah Ghazala served
as the dragoman for the French consulate; Albert Homsy and his brother
Nasrallah were the dragomen of the Italian representative; their relative
Naum Homsy served in the Belgian consulate; and Dr. Yusuf Aswad was
the Spanish consul's physician.[38]

Yet the most arresting feature of the series of telegrams is the cleavage
in religious affiliation. With the exception of Habib Tuma, a licorice root
dealer in nearby Antioch, all the signatories of the antigovernor telegrams
were Muslims. In fact, the leading Muslim religious officials of the city—
with the important exception of the müftü—aligned themselves with the
notability. Many of these officials also held large amounts of land or controlled them as *waqf* executors. That is not to say that only minorities
exhibited support for the governor or identified with him. Rather, it meant
that the Jews and Christians, who had a greater interest in and easier
access to Western-style education, and had more consistent exposure
through trade and occupation to explicitly modern idealism, had come to
expect from their postrevolutionary politics representation, equality, and
rationality. They had come to see themselves as representatives of a type

[37] Jurj Faris, ed., *Man huwa fi Suriyya* (Damascus: Arab Syrian Research Office, 1951), 168.
[38] *Sâlnâme* 1326: 194–196.

TABLE 4.1
Religious and Social Distinction of Telegram Signatories

Religion:	Muslim	Christian	Jewish	Unknown	Total
11 Şubat 1327 Progovernor	21/41%	23/45%	7/14%	1/1%	52
17 Şubat 1327 Antigovernor	49/98%	1/2%	0/0%	0/0%	50
Honorific:	Zâde	Tüccardan	Other	None	Total
11 Şubat 1327 Progovernor	0/0%	1/1%	0/0%	51/99%	52
17 Şubat 1327 Antigovernor	30/60%	7/14%	12/24%	1/2%	50

Other includes hadith scholars, religious teachers, and ʿulamaʾ.
Zâde: an honorific which tended to convey notable status; *Tüccardan*: Muslim traders and merchants.
Source: BBA DH-MTV 1329.Ca.30: 18/20.

of modern *Weltanschauung* that contrasted with that of those who opposed the governor. That the majority of those supporting the governor were non-Muslims reaffirms the need to revise the role of Muslim–non-Muslim difference in the political arena of the revolutionary period, where minority support for revolutionary reform is often unacknowledged.[39] When this support is considered in light of the governor's use of Islam to sanction his attack on the notability and the vigor of the elite Muslim dissent, it calls into question how viable or popular his particular way of thinking about Islam, and moreover, the whole project of Islamic modernism, was outside of a very narrow band of liberal professionals and bureaucrats. Clearly, non-Muslims drew comfort from his interpretation of the Quran, while the leading Muslim religious officials of the city did not. Moreover, the governor asserted that being modern meant a commitment to laicization—something later enshrined in the Kemalist agenda and interwar forms of Arabism. However, the shift of religion from the realm of public to private—perhaps even from the community to the individual—that predicated the kind of support Hüseyin Kâzim enjoyed would have been received differently by the more religiously inclined or

[39] See Rashid Khalidi, "Ottomanism and Arabism in Syria before 1914: A Reassessment," in *Origins of Arab Nationalism* (New York: Columbia University Press, 1991), 50–69.

TABLE 4.2
Profession or Occupation of 11 Şubat 1327 Progovernor Telegram Signatories

Banking	Liberal	Retail	Exp./Imp.	Unknown
6/11%	2/3%	22/40%	19/35%	3/6%

Banking: bank employees, mortgage brokers, currency traders
Liberal: doctors, dentists, lawyers, journalists
Retail: retailers of groceries, hardware, jewelry, cotton thread, and general merchandise
Export/Import: exporters and importers of oil seed, petroleum, licorice root, automobiles, bicycles, machine tools, sewing machines, and electric motors

Total entries exceeds the number of signatories as several individuals were involved in more than one commercial activity.
Source: USNA State, Record Group 84 Aleppo Consulate, Jackson [Aleppo] to Secretary of State, 3 January 1911, corrections to *World Trade Directory*. This document list trade categories and the names of firms and individuals involved.

those who made their living in Islamic institutions. For them, it would have seemed a most profound abandonment of first principles; in other words, the middle class's attempt to mitigate the position of Islam in political and cultural structures of legitimacy and normative social and political behavior, and to modify or eliminate its primary role in the architectures of community, would have been perceived as sectarian and socially disruptive by those observing the process from the outside. The unintended religious dimensions of this conflict frightened many in Aleppo's Christian community. Noting that serious religious conflict had bypassed Aleppo in the postrevolutionary period, the editor of *al-Taqaddum*, Shukri Kanaydir, worried that "the dispute between the governor and some people has now transformed into a religious one and it threatens to become the cause of discord between Christians and Muslims."[40]

A month after the flurry of telegrams, the Interior Ministry received one last antigovernor missive signed by many, but not all, of the Muslim parliamentarians of the Arab provinces.[41] This prompted the governor to travel to Istanbul in April 1911 in an effort to defend his position. On his return a month later, a large crowd greeted him at the train station. Troops in formation and a band made up of students from the Collège

---

[40] *Al-Taqaddum* (Aleppo), 4 April 1911.
[41] BBA DH-MTV 1329.Ca.30: 18/20. Telegram to Grand Vezir from Aleppo Deputy Nafiʿ et. al. dated 18 Nisan 1327. The telegram was signed by deputies from Aleppo, Hama, Yemen, Kerak, Mosul, Jerusalem, Beirut, Damascus, Hawran, Basra, Baghdad, Asir, and Tripoli.

de la Terre Sainte serenaded his arrival. Refusing to board a carriage, Hüseyin Kâzım walked to the governorate building with this procession, stopping to deliver two speeches on the way. In contravention of established protocol, "no Moslem Notable attended the station to welcome his arrival."[42] Nonetheless, the governor's position in Aleppo had been severely compromised. He requested a transfer from the city and departed in June 1911.[43] The Aleppine annalist, Kamil al-Ghazzi, who had supported the embattled governor at the time, encapsulated Hüseyin Kâzım's tenure thus: "He was a brilliant writer though he denounced the notables of Aleppo; because of their arbitrary treatment and oppression of the poor and the peasant farmers he coined the phrase the 'tyrannical honored and the honorable tyrannized' [al-ashraf al-mutaghaliba wa al-mutaghalib al-ashraf]"[44]

The departure of the governor points to some of the major barriers faced by the Eastern Mediterranean middle class as they sought to carve out a place for their interests in structures of urban power in this time of revolution. Among the most debilitating factors was the constantly uncertain nature of administrative leadership in the provinces as governors and other officials were so frequently moved in and out of office and transferred to other postings in the empire. Both a manifestation of the ambition of the various governors to move to Istanbul and a strategy employed by the central state to preclude the possibility of governors becoming corrupt or independent actors, it nonetheless meant that the local notability could manipulate this situation to its advantage through its permanent relationships with both the center and the periphery. The best example of this was that, when opposed locally, the Aleppine notability had some of its own members present in the capital who could press their case. An even greater problem was the middle class's inability to translate the activism evidenced in the telegram campaign into any permanent political structures; middle-class sociability seemed more attentive to creating intraclass formations and temporary cohesion across ethnic and religious boundaries than to founding of parties and movements.

RENEGOTIATING OTTOMAN CITIZENSHIP: THE "BIG STICK" ELECTIONS
OF 1912 AND THE IDEOLOGICAL RETREAT OF THE YOUNG TURKS

Hüseyin Kâzım's brief period in office saw few tangible results as far as local land reform was concerned. Nevertheless, it did bring into relief a

---

[42] PRO FO 195/2366 Fontana (Aleppo) to Lowther (Istanbul), 3 June 1911.

[43] CADN-MAE Consulat Alep Série "A" 48 Malpertuy (Aleppo) to Embassy (Constantinople), Levant 33 / Ambassade 55, 21 July 1911

[44] River, 3:413.

growing class conflict in the city colored in part by sectarian difference. Much of the conflict revolved around the question of who had the legitimate right to speak for the community. An insistence on representational democracy had defined the modern reformulation of this concept for the early years of this time of revolution; however, the 27 April 1911 telegram sent by deputies to the Ottoman Parliament from Arabic-speaking regions points to the challenges faced by reformist elements in the empire as a whole as they sought to fulfill the promise of representation. Hence, while elections certainly took place, they often functioned to elect what moderns like Hüseyin Kâzım would have labeled the feudal elite,[45] who then used their position in parliament to oppose reforms.[46] Many, including Nafiʿ Pasha, had allied themselves to the newly formed Liberal Entente. The ideological basis of the party appealed to notables since it emphasized a decentralist policy; once implemented, it would act to secure their local hegemony from further erosion. Yet, at the most basic level, the opposition to Young Turk reforms motivated its members. It won a surprise victory in the Istanbul by-elections of 1911, forcing the CUP to change tactics as the empire went to the polls later that year. The Italian invasion of Libya at the end of 1911 also called into question the ability of the reformers to keep the empire intact and undermined their overt legitimacy.

On the dissolution of parliament in January 1912, the last significant elections in the prewar period were held against the backdrop of the Ottoman Empire's worsening diplomatic and political position in the Balkans and the growing inability of Young Turk politicians to effect reform. These are known as the "Big Stick Elections" because of the heavy-handed tactics of the CUP—the Unionists—and their civilian and military supporters. However, Hasan Kayalı has observed that this moniker "does justice neither to the spirited contestation nor to [the] significant implications" of the contests.[47] Throughout the empire, the elections occasioned an often-fierce exchange of ideas, the use of public forums, and the formation and reformation of constellations of religious, class-based, and even "ethnic" alliances. In the course of these elections as well, Aleppo's Unionists sought to marginalize those notables associated with the Liberal Entente, while appropriating many of the latter's positions on religion, education, and decentralization. While the Young Turks would ultimately fix the elections, an ideological shift took place at the time that distanced them from ideological bases upon which much middle-class support had be based. At that moment, the CUP sought to recast its claim to power

[45] Kayalı, "Elections and the Electoral Process in the Ottoman Empire, 1876–1919," *IJMES* 27 (1995): 270.

[46] Ahmad, "Agrarian," 282.

[47] Kayalı, "Elections," 273.

on a religious and ethnic basis, in part reflecting a rapidly transforming demographic situation in which Turkish and Arabic-speaking Muslims had become the vast bulk of the empire's citizenry. The use of an ethnic dimension in public discourse was unprecedented in Aleppo.

During the 1912 elections the Aleppine notability, like that in Damascus and the cities of Anatolia, altered its tactics in an attempt to win votes. As they had used telegrams before, the notables used the technologies of the public sphere—in this case public rallies and a political party—to attempt the recovery of their hegemony. Simultaneously they sought to translate their role as protectors of the Muslim community in a manner that undermined Unionist legitimacy. In other words, as Christian powers ate away at the periphery of the empire, they, as Muslim leaders, would act to *ensure* the Muslim nature of the state. The CUP had abandoned this role, they could argue; the fervent support of the Unionists by leading Christians and Jews aided this argument.

The Liberal Entente began its campaign in February 1912 with the arrival at Aleppo's Baghdad railway station of Lûtfi Fikri bey, the deputy of Dersim in the Ottoman Parliament. Echoing the return of Hüseyin Kâzım bey less than a year before, a small crowd of Liberal Entente supporters, primarily Jâbirîs and their retainers, welcomed him at the station. This reception committee was dwarfed by the sudden appearance of a group of approximately two thousand people led by the chairman of the local CUP, Shaykh Riza effendi Rifaʿi. The Rifaʿis, another Aleppine family of note, had allied themselves with the CUP. Significantly, such an alliance had brought together the family of the premiere religious figure in Aleppo (if not the empire), Shaykh Abu al-Huda al-Rifaʿi, and the Unionists. As recently as a few months previously, the Rifaʿis had opposed the Young Turks; however, their co-optation showed both a flexibility on the family's part and the party's willingness to take positions that would appeal to such a group. The alliance was no doubt calculated to quiet questions about the Muslim credentials of the party. Arriving at the station, the mob pelted Lûtfi with eggs; the crowd also chanted insults against the Jâbirîs. The two groups were kept from blows by the arrival of troops. Lûtfi, who had intended to stay at the home of Jâbirî zâde Haj Murad effendi, was ushered to the Baron Hotel for his own safety.[48] More than an unsavory manifestation of street politics, the untoward reception afforded the Entente delegate is an example of the way notables could direct popular political action in a public arena and presaged the kind of violent

---

[48] PRO FO 861/61 Fontana (Aleppo) to Lowther (Constantinople), 19 February 1912; CADN-MAE Consulat Alep Série "A" 50 La Porte (Aleppo) to Embassy (Constantinople) Levant 5/ Ambassade 11; 19 February 1912; *Lisân-i Ahâlî / Lisan al-Ahali* (Aleppo), 12 March 1912.

street politics that would increasingly be used by the notability in the interwar period to control the middle class.

Three days later Lûtfi delivered a speech at the hotel, outlining the Liberal Entente's program. The CUP was obsolete, he maintained, and it was time for a change. The Entente was better prepared to protect the *vatan*, the fatherland.[49] Later that week, Félix Faris, a multitalented Greek Catholic writer and educator from Beirut, formulated the CUP's response in a speech that observers noted differed little from that given by the Ententist.[50] For the people of Aleppo, the ideological differences between the parties must have been difficult to fathom. Nevertheless, the CUP put many of the men who had signed the telegram in support of Hüseyin Kâzım on the ballot for the province's administrative council. These included Salim Janbart and Nasrallah Homsy. Yet they continued to maintain alliances with the other notables of the province, with the exception of those most publicly aligned with the Liberal Entente. As planned, the elections returned a parliament overwhelmingly Unionist in composition. With the elections completed, the CUP in Aleppo sought to consolidate its hold by tying into several of the issues raised by their erstwhile opponents, namely, those issues that reflected an empirewide shift on the part of the CUP away from a secularist, modernist vision of reform toward one that emphasized, at least publically, a religious dimension to authority and sectarian chauvinism. The day following the elections, a CUP-generated pamphlet appeared in the city:

> Protest tomorrow at 8:30 . . . at Suq al-Juma, the meeting will take place to protest against the Italian naval attack [on Beirut]. We will encourage the government to continue the war, promising to sacrifice everything, including our lives, for the defense of the vatan. . . . Thus we will make the powers and the whole world understand that not a single Ottoman will accept a shameful peace that would taint the honor of Ottomans in general and Muslims in particular.[51]

Defense of the *vatan* was now once more the unique prerogative of the Muslims. During the protest, the new deputies, state employees, and various religious functionaries made speeches to the largely Muslim crowd. Among the speakers was a mosque preacher who attacked both Europeans and local Christians. The Armenian archbishop, Nerses Davidiyan, followed him to the podium. The crowd booed him as he spoke and threw

[49] *Lisân-i Ahâlî / Lisan al-Ahali* (Aleppo), 12 March 1912.

[50] PRO FO 861/61 Fontana (Aleppo) to Lowther (Constantinople), 19 February 1912. Faris was an editor of the Beiruti journal *Lisan al-Ittihad*, a teacher in Aleppo, and author of *Confidences aux femmes de Syrie*. See K. T. Khairallah, *La Syrie: territoire, origines ethnique et politiques* (Paris: E. Leroux, 1912), 121–127.

[51] CADN-MAE Consulat Alep Série "A" 50, La Porte (Aleppo) to Embassy (Constantinople): Levant 21 Ambassade 43, 30 April 1912.

stones at him; he escaped only with the aid of the police. The new CUP-tolerated abuse of local Christians did not escape the French consul's notice: "This event caused great emotion in the city where everyone blames the CUP which continues to excite Muslim fanaticism in certain quarters. [The CUP's] attitude vis à vis Christians has changed a great deal lately."[52] Growing sectarian violence in the province's outlying cities, like Zeitun, ʿUrfa, and Marash, reflected this change of attitude. While British Consul Fontana's claim that "the CUP is intent on fomenting anti-Christian disturbances to avert the public attention from themselves at the close of this disastrous [Tripolitanian] war"[53] may exaggerate the extent of this modification of the CUP's stance, it indicates that some elements of Ottoman society that had aligned themselves with a modernist sensibility and expressed that sensibility through an adherence to a "rational basis of authority" in the past were now willing to abandon this commitment as a political expediency.

Moreover, the demographic transformation of the empire over the course of the previous century—a process accelerated in the years after the revolution—from a multireligious, multiethnic polity to a primarily Muslim state dominated by Turkish and Arabic speakers forced a deeper reappraisal of the usefulness of the more secular and modern ideals of Ottomanism.[54] This reappraisal manifested itself most visibly in the various language and administrative reforms made by the CUP in the spring of 1913. Arabic was reinstated as an official language; similarly, the CUP, in and out of power over the course of 1912–1913, reformed some of the provincial structures of administration. However, these attempts to co-opt the opposition and to mitigate the appeal of the decentralist impulses, especially those that revolved around Arab religious prestige, bespoke a significant polarization in the region's middle class. "Muslim patriots," Göçek concludes, "envisioned sharing equality with all, but only under the rules they themselves determined. The minorities wanted equality to erase all social differences among them and the Muslims and were frustrated when this did not occur."[55] Unable to solve *Göçek's Dilemma*, the region's middle class, primarily its Christians, was forced to rethink the Young Turk commitment to liberalism and secular citizenship. Elements of this dilemma have continued to haunt minority non-Muslim–majority Muslim relations, especially in those officially secular societies like Egypt,

---

[52] Ibid.

[53] PRO FO 861/61 Fontana (Aleppo) to Lowther (Constantinople), 18 November 1912.

[54] C. Ernst Dawn's discussion of this transformation remains among the most persuasive on this topic; see his *From Ottomanism to Arabism: Essays on the Origins of Arab Nationalism* (Urbana: University of Illinois Press, 1973).

[55] Göçek, *Rise*, 136.

Syria, Iraq, and Lebanon where Christians and non-Sunni Muslims constitute significant portions of the population.

The political discourse of the 1912 election suggested to some in Aleppo an alternative to the sectarian polarization within the city's middle class. This alternative focused on the special nature of Aleppo, spawning a kind of localism that emphasized the antiquity of the city, its putative tradition of tolerance, and its alleged status as an Arab city. Not expressed as a form of nationalism or even protonationalism, it did attempt to create a linguistic bond among the city's disparate elements. In late 1911 Shukri Kanaydir of *al-Taqaddum* told his readers, "Aleppo is an ancient city of Arabia . . . the first literary, racial awakening took place in it. From the seventeenth century to the middle of the nineteenth century various poets, writers, and scholars have served this [Arabic] language." Despite this past,

> Between Frankification and Turkification, Aleppo is on the verge of losing its Arabic. Most Christians and Jews study foreign languages like French, English, and German because they are involved in trade and banking, trading houses and the occupations which require the knowledge of foreign languages. And the Muslims choose to study Turkish in order to receive positions in the government.[56]

Nostalgic in tone, the article expresses a certain pride in learning one's mother tongue well, while it nowhere advocates anything more than an enhanced dedication to the learning of Arabic. Kanaydir held up the city's Armenians as an example of a people that made an effort to learn both a "native" language and other languages.

Within a year, however, the Arab nature of the town became a divisive issue and split former allies in the local middle class. On the question of whether the city should use Arabic rather than Ottoman in the courts, as was the case in Beirut and Damascus, Mustafâ Âsım had written in *Lisân-ı Ahâlî* that Aleppo was not an Arab city but rather an Ottoman city. In an article entitled "Are We Turks Despite Ourselves?" Kanaydir responded that *his* Aleppo was indeed Arab, that state employees were the only Turks in the city, and that no more than 1 percent of the total population spoke Turkish. In a strange turn, this paper that had tended to oppose the notables embraced them as Arabs as well: "While we could say that the Mudarris, Jabiri, 'Adli, Mar'ash and the other ancient Aleppine families are Turks . . . most of them have lived a long time in the Arab lands and today their language is Arabic." The article launched into a personal attack on Âsım, suggesting that he change the name of his paper from

---

[56] *al-Taqaddum* (Aleppo), 26 September 1911.

"*al-Ahali* to *al-ghuraba'*," that is, from the "people" to the "strangers."[57] Kanaydir's response to Âsım reflects a reaction to the conflation of an Islamic prerogative with an ethnic basis of the state that had emerged in the immediate prewar period. The rules for social inclusion, and the construct of a postrevolutionary Ottoman citizen, had ceased to include unambiguously men like Kanaydir, a Greek Catholic Arab-speaking and writing intellectual. Increasingly alienated from professionals and intellectuals in the Muslim middle class, he and his peers sought a new definition for themselves. While a linguistic basis had the potential to accomplish this task, at that moment, it is unlikely that the "ancient Aleppine families" would have conceded such a definition; for them, religion and religious difference still played the preeminent role, and Ottoman Turkish still functioned as a language of customary prestige and proof of their links to the Ottoman ruling elite. However, the asserted link between modernity, ethnicity, power, and the notability presages the postwar strategy of the old social classes of Syria to employ nationalism and the services of middle-class intellectuals like Kanaydir to alter the definition of their hegemony to fit more closely the demands of nationalism.

The resurrection of the Ottoman Constitution in 1908 had encouraged the formation of a complex public sphere, a place of critical rational discourse, where businessmen, bureaucrats, and liberal professionals behaved as a group and engaged in a form of political discourse reminiscent of similar activities in Europe. The use of newspapers, telegrams, "public opinion," and voluntary associations distinguished this discourse from previous patterns of behavior, thus revealing support for the ideology of modernity. This concatenation of post-Enlightenment ideas carried with it a commitment to rights, equality, and the subjective individuality of the person. The middle class's belief in the rational basis of authority—a rationality known self-referentially—dismissed as irrational the pervasive influence of the old social classes of Eastern Mediterranean society. Under threat, the local landed notability, who maintained authority through wealth, the monopoly over interpretation of Islamic knowledge and law, and the control of the bureaucracy, acted to defend its role using all means available.

As external pressures and internal demographics forced the central government to reconsider its commitment to a secular Ottoman citizenship, the stability of the definition of middle-class citizen also came under intense strain. Seeing a diminution of the center's support for these ideas, and its rethinking of the role of religion and social distinction in a manner at odds with their definition of modernity, members of the middle

---

[57] Ibid., 13 February 1913.

class of the city, primarily the non-Muslims, were caught on the horns of a dilemma. On one hand, the alliances they had forged in the previous years with seemingly modernist elements in the center that spoke to a desire to recast their society on the basis of a perception of the political dimensions of European middle-class social practice seemed to be crumbling; on the other hand, such alliances had alienated them from local structures of authority and power. As the CUP seemed less and less distinct from the local notability, the middle class retreated and turned inward. A cosmopolitan vision of society having been rejected by those in power, some found themselves considering the use of definitions of self and community that emphasized the religious, the ethnic, and the linguistic rather than class or social distinction. The ethnic definition—the Arab and Turk—had at that moment little appeal beyond those few individuals in the ranks of the Arabic-speaking Christians of the city conversant with a similar discourse in Damascus or Beirut and proved immediately moribund. Nevertheless, locating the origins of an Arab nationalism in the failure of the state to safeguard Ottoman citizenship can provide a more plausible origin for that movement than recourse to the romanticized trope of awakenings.

The abrupt movement of the Ottoman state to a military dictatorship removed even the technologies of the public sphere from the hands of the middle class. State censorship, fixed elections, and domestic espionage continued after the empire entered the First World War in late 1914. The months between the closing of the newspapers, clubs, and other associations in 1913 and the outbreak of hostilities saw the collapse of middle-class civil society altogether. The failure to protect the integrity of these institutions and forms, alongside the extension of conscription to Christians and Jews for the first time in Ottoman history, accelerated the middle-class's disenchantment with the revolution, and with the revolutionaries themselves. Young Turk and opposition political rhetoric of the time increasingly associated the non-Muslims of the middle class with Europeans, finding them a convenient local scapegoat for Ottoman military and diplomatic failures. Initiating what would become a recurrent theme in the story of the middle class in the Middle East, as policies and hardening attitudes closed down avenues for expression, economic advancement, and political participation, or placed its members beyond the pale of citizenship and denied them protection from the violence of nonstate actors, middle-class people "opted out" and departed for the West, their fluency in things Western and modern that had brought them into conflict at home facilitating the transition to life in the Americas or Europe. The diplomatic files of the French, British, and United States consulates are replete with requests for visas, applications from dual nationals for passports, and, where a son, father, or brother had already emigrated, petitions for family reunification. And distinct from the emigrants of Mount Lebanon from the previous generation, as described by Akram Khater in his *Inventing Home: Emigration, Gender, and the Middle Class in Lebanon, 1870–1920*, who traveled to the West and worked as itinerant peddlers, saved their money, and returned to their ancestral villages to live lives as rich peasant-gentry, many of those who left in the years immediately before the war did so because they could no longer see themselves and their future in their own communities and had no intention of ever returning. The option, even necessity, of leaving, especially for non-Muslim members of the middle class, had become by 1914 an omnipresent and painful reality; during and after the war, it would be a matter of basic survival for refugees and displaced persons. Elia Kazan's 1963 film *America, America*; many of the short stories and plays of William Saroyan; and the paintings of the New York abstract artist Vosdanik Adoian, otherwise know as Arshile Gorky, whose haunting *The Artist and His Mother* (1926) is based on a photograph his mother, Shushanik—who would starve to death in 1919—had intended to send on to his father in America as they fled Anatolia during World War I, collectively capture the middle-class immigrants' and their children's sense of profound betrayal in the Ottoman homeland. At the same time, their work encapsulates the alienation of exile in a West that would never quite accept them.[58]

One of the few remaining primary sources of what Aleppo looked like on the eve of global conflagration is a lengthy and bitter dispatch from British Consul Fontana, dated 31 August 1914. Writing on the occasion of Germany's declaration of war on Britain, he described how Aleppo had been placed under martial law, wages and prices frozen, and mass mobilization and the requisition of matériel begun in a brutal and wasteful manner. In his characteristically jaundiced appraisal, the preparations for war had inflamed divisions of class, religion, and origin in the city, marking the complete abandonment of the revolution's promise of intersectarian comity, rule of law, and rational exercise of authority. Although perhaps most worried about the property rights of His Britannic Majes-

---

[58] Elia Kazan (1909–2003), born in Istanbul, based this film on the story of his uncle Joe Kazan's journey to the United States in the first decade of the twentieth century. Kazan's own immediate family would take this same path immediately prior to the outbreak of the World War I. See his autobiography, *Elia Kazan: A Life* (New York: Random House, 1988). William Saroyan (1908–1983) was the only member of his family to have been born in the United States. His father, Armenak Saroyan, was an American-educated Protestant minister who left Bitlis in Anatolia ahead of his family to work with the growing Armenian immigrant community in California's Central Valley. Especially evocative of this experience is his cycle of plays, *The Armenian Trilogy* (Fresno: California State University Press, 1986). On Adoian (1904–1948), born near Lake Van, see Hayden Herrera's recent *Arshile Gorky: His Life and Works* (London: Bloomsbury Publishing, 2003).

ty's subjects, whose goods and livestock were being impounded without proper compensation, he observed

the calling out of the reserves of all classes up to the age of 45 years produced general misery and distress. Authorities made no secret that they merely aimed at wringing exemption money from such of the Christians as could pay, and did not need them as soldiers. The payment of this money has fallen terribly hard on almost all those who have managed to effect it there being hardly any gold in circulation and the authorities insisting on payment in hard cash. Thus merchants and shopkeepers whose resources are paralysed by the moratorium and whose merchandise is requisitioned by the military commission have to scrape together beg or borrow sufficient cash to pay exemption money for themselves, their sons or their employees, meanwhile what is left of their merchandise lies in depot or even at the custom house with no possibility of sale or withdrawal the customs, nevertheless exacting the ordering cadre housing dues. Taxes are levied continually and even with armed force. Venality is as strong as ever, and certain food commodities requisitioned by the authorities are being sold in the Moslem quarters at less than half the original price. Even horses requisitioned are being dispersed the same way. If the Military requisition continues much longer and the moratorium is prolonged for another two months there will be famine general bankruptcy and ruin. The country is being devoured by human locusts.[59]

Looking back from 1921, Fathallah Qastun collapsed the last days of Hamidian rule, the time of the Revolution of 1908, and the Great War into "a nightmare of unprecedented horror."[60]

[59] PRO FO 861/63 Fontana (Aleppo) Fontana to Mallet (Constantinople), 31 August 1914.
[60] Fathallah Qastun, "Aleppo: Yesterday, Today and Tomorrow," *al-Shu'la* 2:5 (August 1921): 5–7.

Being Modern in a Moment of Anxiety

THE MIDDLE CLASS MAKES SENSE OF A "POSTWAR" WORLD
(1918–1924)—HISTORICISM, NATIONALISM, AND VIOLENCE

> To articulate the past historically does not mean to recognize
> it "the way it really was" (Ranke). It means to seize hold of a
> memory as it flashes up at a moment of danger.
> —Walter Benjamin, "Theses on the Philosophy of History,"
> 1939

The Ottoman Empire entered World War I on the side of the German
and Austrian empires in November 1914. Aleppo's civilian bureaucracy
fell under military control, and a member of the CUP's ruling junta,
Cemal Pasha, administered the province, along with the other provinces
of the Eastern Mediterranean from Damascus. While he faced no substantive opposition in the period 1914–1918, Cemal is remembered as al-
saffah, the "blood letter" in the collective historical consciousness of the
successor states of Syria and Lebanon, for his serial executions of a group
of notables, journalists, and politicians from Damascus and Beirut (August 1915, May 1916). While Cemal accused these men of treason and
collaboration with the French, most had merely been active in prewar
politics as members of parties opposed to the CUP, including the pronotable Liberal Entente, or had expressed pro-French attitudes in print or
public speeches. They were certainly not Arab nationalists or separatists,
although they are now remembered as the first martyrs to the Arab
Nation's cause.

Far from engendering opposition, Cemal Pasha's wartime policies were
accepted by the populace, the notability, and the bureaucracy, high-
lighting the fact that the majority of the region's inhabitants tended to
identify with the Ottoman side in the war without question. Much like
the public political rhetoric of the immediate prewar period, throughout
World War I, the CUP continued to link the defense of the *vatan*, the
homeland, with the protection of the Islamic community, the *umma*,
thereby securing this support.

Unconnected with the executions in Beirut and Damascus, the British,
who controlled Egypt, sought to co-opt the emir of Mecca, Husayn bin

Ali, to the Allied side in the war. His position as the protector of the holiest sites in Islam, for which he bore the honorific "*sharif*," was imbued with a great deal of symbolism, but relatively little power, as most administrative and budgetary responsibilities lay with the Ottoman governor of the Hejaz. Appointed to the post by Abdülhamid II in 1908, Sharif Husayn, like other figures on the periphery of the Ottoman Empire, used the disorder of the revolutionary period to try to carve out a higher degree of local autonomy *in* the Ottoman system for himself and his family, the Hashemites. The advent of the war and British overtures convinced the sharif that he could acquire actual independence and create a dynasty, akin to that established by Mehmet Ali Pasha in Egypt during the previous century. The British, assured by their staff of Orientalists of the wisdom of putting forward an Arab counterweight to the sultan-caliph, also hoped to undermine transnational Muslim loyalty to the Ottoman state, while at the same time generating an Arab guerilla force to aid the war effort. In the first of a series of overlapping promises bearing on the postwar settlement, the British assured Husayn he would become king of the Arabs, though the boundaries of his kingdom were left unspecified and remain a heated topic of debate to this day. Much, if not all, of that territory had been or would be promised to Zionists, the French, or reserved by the British themselves. While Husayn's Arab Revolt (1916–1918) attracted defectors from the Ottoman officer corps, prisoners of war, and a number of returned exiles, it was ignored for the most part, or, when acknowledged, greeted with a great deal of skepticism by the Arabic-speaking inhabitants of the empire. He received no real popular support as his forces, under the command of his son Faysal, moved along the right flank of the British advance into the Levant in 1918.

Earlier in the war Ottoman forces had defeated the British and their colonial troops from India, Australia, and New Zealand at Gallipoli (1915) and checked their advance into Mesopotamia (1915–1916), in many ways providing a measure of the success of the modernizing project of the preceding decades, as well as the competence of the Ottoman officer corps. Likewise, initial losses to Russia in eastern Anatolia were reversed after the Bolshevik Revolution by the terms of the Treaty of Brest-Litovsk. Without a substantial industrial base, however, the Ottomans were dependent on German matériel. As German support dried up in 1917, Baghdad was captured and the Ottoman Army in the Eastern Mediterranean could not withstand General Edmund Allenby's "big push" of 1918; the army made an orderly retreat under the command of Cemal's replacement, Mustafa Kemal, into the Taurus Mountains of southern Anatolia. Ensconced in Anatolia, Mustafa Kemal prepared his forces to fend off the anticipated Anglo-French invasion and mount a counteroffensive to reclaim lost territory in the Eastern Mediterranean. British and

Arab troops occupied Damascus and Aleppo in October 1918, just days before an armistice brought a temporary end to hostilities and led to the Allied occupation of Istanbul. Ottoman military casualties were approximately 300,000; however, more than a million civilians had perished as a consequence of starvation, ethnic cleansing, genocide, and disease.

In December 1918, and at the behest of the foreign occupiers of his capital, Sultan Mehmet VI prorogued the Ottoman Parliament and began to rule by decree, seeing close cooperation with the British and French as a possible way for his house to survive. The leaders of the Young Turk junta had been executed or had fled into exile, and others awaited trial for war crimes; over the next two years, the occupied Ottoman state accepted the treaties of San Remo and Sèvres (1920), which separated Anatolia from the Arab provinces of the Ottoman Empire and subdivided both parts among the victors and their local allies. According to the terms of the treaties, France would play a dominant role in the newly created state of Cilicia, Greece was given control of the port city of Izmir and its hinterland, and the Republic of Armenia was established in eastern Anatolia.

Bound together by opposition to these treaties, CUP bureaucrats and officers, like Mustafa Kemal, tribal leaders, Islamists, and Communists, forged a viable political and military mass movement in the relatively isolated regions of central Anatolia (1920). The movement first defeated the nascent Republic of Armenia, whereupon a small residual portion of that state was absorbed into the new Soviet Union. Victory in a series of brief but brutal wars against France in Cilicia and Greece in western Anatolia followed shortly thereafter. Faced with mounting losses and with their own populations exhausted by the cost of war in Europe, the Powers agreed in 1923 to the Treaty of Lausanne. This final treaty abrogated many of the provisions of the previous agreements, recognized those areas under the movement's control as Turkey, and confirmed the boundaries between it and Syria, and later Iraq. Following the international recognition of this new state, Mustafa Kemal, whose charisma and leadership skills had helped to knit together the movement, and who had eliminated the leftist and Islamist elements of it to secure power, was elected Turkey's first president. Taking the name Atatürk (Father of the Turks), he and his government embarked upon a program of rapid Westernization that resembled the early program of the Revolution of 1908. Atatürk's version was much more aggressively secularizing and nationalist, however, and included moving the capital from Istanbul—and its associations with the cosmopolitan, "Oriental" past—to Ankara, adoption of the Latin alphabet and rejection of the Arabic script, and the eventual abolition of the Ottoman sultan-caliphate itself (1924). The state Atatürk inherited had less of the ethnic and religious heterogeneity of the prewar period as a consequence of the Armenian Genocide of 1915, postwar campaigns of ethnic cleansing, and exchanges of populations between Greece and Turkey. Thus the project of making Turkey Turkish on the basis of shared language and religion, with the exception of the difficulties that would be encountered in assimilating the significant population of Kurds in eastern Anatolia, was more feasible and imaginable than it had ever been for the Young Turks.

In accordance with their prewar promises, the British turned over control of inland Bilad al-Sham to a puppet state led by Faysal in 1918. His government, the Kingdom of Syria, would last only a few months, enjoy little domestic legitimacy, lose British support, and fall victim in July 1920 to French imperialist claims on his territory deriving from the Sykes-Picot Agreement of 1915. Under the guise of a League of Nations' mandate, the French established a colonial presence in Syria and would remain for a generation, leaving only in 1946.

While Aleppo did not share the postwar fate of Izmir, which burned in September 1922,[1] or Mount Lebanon, whose inhabitants faced mass starvation as a consequence of Allied sanctions and Ottoman mismanagement during the war,[2] it could not escape the horrors of World War I entirely: most notably, Aleppo served as the chief transfer point for hundreds of thousands of Armenian deportees, primarily women and children, from Anatolia en route to their eventual extermination along the Euphrates River Valley in 1915.[3] In an overlooked moment of moral courage, Aleppo's civilian governor at the time, Celal Pasha, traveled to Istanbul to petition for an end to the Young Turk's genocidal plan on both administrative and ethical grounds, only to be rebuffed and forced from office. Celal was not alone in this act; for patriotic and humanitarian reasons, other Ottoman bureaucrat-intellectuals objected to the mass murder of the empire's Ottoman-Armenian citizens. Hüseyin Kâzım, for example, told a German diplomat in April 1916 of his disillusionment and intention to resign his position as the director of a program to resettle refugees along the Orontes River, adding "This atrocious policy

---

[1] Reşat Kasaba, "Izmir 1922: A Port City Unravels," in Fawaz, ed., *Modernity and Culture*, 204–229; Marjorie Housepian Dobkin, *The Smyrna Affair* (New York: Harcourt Brace Jovanovich, 1971); and Dora Sakaryan, *An Armenian Doctor in Turkey, Garabed Hatcherian: My Smyrna Ordeal of 1922* (Montreal: Arod Books, 1997) provide evocative first-person and autobiographical accounts of the destruction of the city.

[2] Much has been written on the famine and its origins in Lebanon. See Thompson, *Colonial*, 1–38 passim.

[3] Martin Niepage, *The Horrors of Aleppo, Seen by a German Eyewitness; a Word to Germany's Accredited Representatives* (London: T. F. Unwin, 1917). Niepage was a teacher at the German Technical School in Aleppo during the war.

of destruction . . . is the shame of Turkey and is going to harm Turkey very much after the war."[4]

Most devastating to all ranks of society in what had once been the province of Aleppo and has since become northern Syria and southern Turkey was the now-forgotten bloody fratricidal civil war and episodes of ethnic cleansing that had continued after the armistice—a conflict that at one point threatened to spread to the city and would eventually grow to a full-scale international conflagration. Following the allied occupation, roving bands of armed *çete*s and demobilized troops terrorized rural populations, and sectarian urban warfare brought complete civil collapse to the nearby cities of Marʿash, Adana, and ʿAyntab.[5] Fleeing the disorder, wave after wave of refugees—primarily Armenian and Assyrian Christians—swelled Aleppo's population to over 300,000 and in so doing inexorably altered its communal balance, social fabric, and civil society.

Aleppines watched with dismay as new borders were drawn around them by the Allied victors of the Great War, cutting their province in half and dividing them from their economic and cultural hinterland. Likewise, the city's merchants and entrepreneurs knew that this would drain their commercial life-blood, and its middle-class bureaucrats had to confront their city's demotion from a position of honor as a premier provincial capital of the Ottoman Empire to a subordinate of Damascus in a truncated new national/colonial construct, Syria, and the consequential loss of prestige and possibilities for professional advancement to Istanbul. Especially for those educated in the Ottoman system, this was more than just the redrawing of a line on a map; rather, it meant disconnection from the ideological and cultural networks binding them to the Ottoman center that had served as the bases for their identity and sense of self. It was a moment of extreme anxiety and intense uncertainty made even more so by the imposition of a novel and alien political leadership supported by foreign troops of occupation.

This section explores how Aleppo's middle class sought to make sense of these new realities by using modern intellectual, cultural, and social tools. Examining in turn an early experience with Arabism, nationalist historicism, and a prelude to ethnic cleansing; a violent indigenous rebellion that bound members of the Ottoman bureaucratic middle class to prominent representatives of the aʿyan; and a body of history writing by leading local intellectuals, it follows the way the middle class and others engaged this moment of world-historical change. Being modern in this

---

[4] Cited in Vahakn N. Dadrian, "The Naim-Andonian Documents on the World War I Destruction of Ottoman Armenians: The Anatomy of a Genocide," *IJMES* 18:3 (1986): 334–335.

[5] See Kerr, *Lions*.

moment of anxiety made unprecedented demands on the Eastern Mediterranean's middle class; characterizing the multiplicity of responses to those
challenges, especially as these responses often cleaved along religious and
ethnic lines, has significant implications for understanding the shape of
the contemporary Middle East.

Chapter 5 follows the attempt by functionaries of the short-lived government of Faysal to fill the ideological vacuum left by the Ottoman collapse to shape historical consciousness and impose an Arab nationalism
in the Levant, in part by using the new newspaper *Halab* (Aleppo), a
process that was especially fraught in the diverse city of Aleppo. In so
doing they hoped to begin the process of cleansing the area of non-Arabs
and thus enhance their claim to rule in the language of Wilsonian "national self-determination." The next chapter analyzes the Ottoman bureaucratic and military middle class's rejection of the narrow ethnic nationalist vision of the future presented by the newspaper and the foreign
occupation of their country in the form of violent rebellion, allied to the
larger civil war in Anatolia, which led to the creation of the Republic of
Turkey. Focusing on the reception of the terms of that civil war in Aleppo
and Ibrahim Hananu's revolt against French forces, Chapter 6 seeks to
capture the confusing and ambiguous dilemmas of identity and citizenship facing the middle class in places like Aleppo as the old structures of
empire crumbled. Far from a simple bureaucratic act of renaming, the
process of turning Ottoman subjects into modern Syrian Arab citizens
raised significant questions about religiously sanctioned authority, the
persistence of Ottoman forms of legitimacy and political theory, the nature of citizenship, and the public role of Islam. And these questions were
not unique to Aleppo but were shared by other peoples of the Eastern
Mediterranean.

Chapter 7 continues to consider this process of "making sense" as it
appears in Muhammad Raghib al-Tabbakh's biography of the epitome of
the post-Tanzimat provincial Muslim Ottoman middle-class bureaucrat-
officer, Mahmud Kamil al-ʿAyntabi, in his *Iʿlam al-nubalaʾ bi-tarikh
Halab al-shahbaʾ* [Information about the Notables in the History of
Aleppo the Gray] (Aleppo, 1923), and Kamil al-Ghazzi's account of a
1919 massacre of Armenian refugees from his *Nahr al-dhahab fi tarikh
Halab* [The River of Gold in the History of Aleppo] (Aleppo, 1926). Tabbakh's book is both a biographical dictionary, in Arabic a *tabaqat*, and a
chronological narrative of local events by Islamic calendar years, approxi-
mating most closely to an Ottoman-era conception of the court chronicle,
the *vakayiname*. Kamil al-Ghazzi's book includes an historical topography, in Arabic *khitat*, and a chronicle similar in format to that of Tabbakh.

Though the works of Tabbakh and Ghazzi are self-conscious resurrec-
tions of the classical Arabic genres of the local chronicle and the biograph-

ical dictionary—both of which had remained dormant for two centuries—
each evidences the adoption of nineteenth-century historicist sensibilities
and a bourgeois aesthetic.[6] Nevertheless, their choice of style was clearly
anachronistic, a conclusion reinforced by the fact that European history
books were widely available in the city, and the authors and their contemporaries make reference to these kinds of works. Their mutual friend and
colleague, Qustaki al-Homsy, had even published a recognizably modern
literary history, *Udaba' Halab dhu al-athar fi al-qarn al-tasi' 'ashar*
[Aleppo's Men of Letters in the Nineteenth Century] in 1925. First serialized in 1922 in the Fathallah Qastun's postwar magazine *al-Shu'la* [The
Flame], the book places Aleppine authors of Arabic belles lettres within
the context of the broader Arabic literary renaissance of Beirut, Istanbul,
and Cairo.

The very titles of the books and the agnomens of the authors reveal the
contested nature of civic identity at play in Aleppo. Tabbakh and Ghazzi
adopted the atavistic title of *al-Halabi*, the "Aleppine," as a formal part
of their names, and each book seeks to tell the history of Aleppo as a
distinct entity enmeshed in world history. In a parallel development,
Ghazzi, Homsy, and other intellectuals supported the founding of the region's only amateur archeological society in 1925, Jam'iyyat 'Adiyat
Halab, which was concerned with the scientific study of the province's
rich archeological remains from Paleolithic times until the early Ottoman
period, and was especially interested in the Byzantine Dead Cities and the
old city's Mamluk-era walls and gates. Krikor Mazloumian, whose family
owned the city's vaunted Baron Hotel, also sponsored the new society as
an act of civic patronage and with the pragmatic understanding that the
preservation and promotion of Aleppo's past translated into tourists and
clients for his hotel. Each project privileged a definition of Aleppo as an
autonomous whole. In the case of Tabbakh, it was a whole that persisted
in an Ottoman form. Neither Tabbakh nor Ghazzi accepted that they had
been liberated by Faysal and his Arab Army in 1918; the assertion that
Aleppo was an "Arab city" did not play for them the pivotal role that
this concept did in the journal *Halab*. Nevertheless, as the following also
shows, history, or rather an Orientalist-informed national history of the
Arabs, courses through the pages of that paper and constitutes yet another
answer to the postwar search for meaning.

In a larger sense, those middle-class bureaucrats, educators, and journalists searching for the meaning of the Great War were embroiled in a

[6] Muhammad ibn 'Umar al-'Urdi's seventeenth-century *Ma'adin al-dhahab fi al-a'yan
al-musharrafah bi-him Halab* and Muhammad Amin al-Muhbbi's (1651–1699) *Khulasat
al-athar fi a'yan al-qarn al-hadi 'ashar* were the most recent Aleppo-centered works in these
genres.

protean ideological and social crisis. The complex nature of their search confirms that Jay Winter's conclusion, "Even to pose that question [what did World War I mean?] was bound to be appallingly difficult; full of ambivalence and confusion, charged with tentativeness and more than a fragment of futility," applies equally in the cities of the Eastern Mediterranean.[7] There, however, the contours of the crisis were shaped not just by the war, but also by the broader moral and economic dislocations of the Revolution of 1908, the Arab Kingdom, and the French colonial occupation.[8] Ibrahim Hananu's decision to take to the field to defend his status as an Ottoman bureaucrat-officer was one of many social and political choices available as a response to that crisis. Other options took a more personal character but still intersected the spheres of identity, ethnicity, and thought.

Crucially, a significant portion of the historical discourse that emerged in this moment of anxiety resembles its European cognate in its articulation of the prewar period as a backward, old-fashioned "then" characterized by an irrational and unnatural world of polyglot empires, opposed to a modern, forward-looking "now" epitomized by a rational system of nations and nation-states. In between the "then" and "now" was the war and its world-shattering violence, which demarcated the two eras in an indelible manner. In these histories, the war and its violence are consigned to the past—it ended, and with it ended an old and decrepit world. However, another discourse—still coherent in the idiom of modernity—existed simultaneously that dissented from these accounts of what was "past." These other histories denied the very "pastness" of the war, asserting its persistence into a continuing present. For the historians of these accounts, the social and political dislocations of the antebellum and interwar period caused by revolutionary, nationalist, and colonial regimes alike constituted an uninterrupted assault on the legitimate order. Put simply, the violence had not ended; it had merely moved from the sanguinary into other dimensions of human interaction.[9]

---

[7] Jay Winter, *Sites of Memory, Sites of Mourning: The Great War in European Cultural History* (Cambridge: Cambridge University Press, 1985), 2. See also Daniel J. Sherman, *The Construction of Memory in Interwar France* (Chicago: University of Chicago Press, 1999).

[8] Thompson notes in the Lebanese context that "collective memories" of the war diffracted along gender, class, and religious lines: "These war and famine memories evoke a wrenching, nightmarish experience of a world gone awry, of families not simply abandoned and split apart, but actually turned against each other. Men who had prided themselves on protecting their families could no longer do so. Mothers and wives, soldiers' inspiration or life and love of country, were selling themselves to strangers and devouring their children. Women habituated to social norms of seclusion howled in the streets, naked, or were attacked in their homes by strange men. All social and familial norms seemed suspended." *Colonial*, 25.

[9] Acknowledging that narratives of the war unfolded in distinct ways is seen by Sherman as crucial for any understanding of broader social and intellectual transformations of the

Moreover, those who chose to write about their past, to paraphrase Hayden White, had taken upon themselves the responsibility to explain why things are what they appear to be in accounts that reveal the way things really were.[10] Significantly, the modalities of representation employed in all of these accounts were marked departures from older ways of writing about the past and reflected what Roland Barthes identified as nineteenth-century bourgeois conceptions of realism.[11] Embracing a Hegelian notion that History is the unfolding of human freedom, this style of imagining the past constituted a more general incorporation of bourgeois styles of inscribing history on memory and the insinuation of the intellectual tools of modernism on ways of remembering.[12]

Ironically, the apotheosis of the city implicit in much of that history occurred as the nation-state itself was becoming ascendant. Syria as a formal political unit or a meaningful construct would not become part of Aleppine historical discourse until late 1925, and then only at the linguistic and educational margins. With the publication of Edmond Rabbath's polemical *Les états unis de Syrie!* (Aleppo, 1925), Syria and Aleppo as a part of that whole gained some intellectual currency. Significantly, Rabbath, born in 1901, was a quarter century younger than the above-mentioned writers and had been educated entirely in foreign schools or abroad; by contrast, much of Aleppo's venerable literati attended the Ottoman school system. In addition, he wrote primarily in French, rather than Arabic or Ottoman Turkish. As such he belongs to a later generation of thinkers.

Moreover, the contentious and fluid boundaries of the *Nation* (Arab, Turkish, Syrian, Ottoman) at this moment tend not to be acknowledged in the prevailing etiology of nationalism in the Middle East. Rather, discussions bifurcate along primordialists and modernists lines, which elide class-based uses of nationalism, or the more intriguing possibility of middle- or subaltern-class ambivalence about the ideology and its local man-

interwar period: "But the emphasis on unitary meanings, whether republican, consolatory, or Christian, risks distracting attention from a deeper dynamic at work in the commemorative process after the Great War, one that arguably constitutes its most lasting legacy to the twentieth century." Sherman, *Construction of Memory*, 6.

[10] Hayden White, *Tropics of Discourse: Essays in Cultural Criticism* (Baltimore: Johns Hopkins University Press, 1978), 114.

[11] Hayden White, *The Content of the Form: Narrative Discourse and Historical Representation* (Baltimore: Johns Hopkins University Press, 1987), 80.

[12] Though failing to historicize or localize his understanding of these processes, Pierre Nora reinforces this conclusion by arguing that "The passage from memory to history has required every social group to redefine its identity through the revitalization of its own history. The task of remembering makes everyone his own historian. . . . Following the example of ethnic groups and social minorities, every established group, intellectual or not, learned or not, has felt the need to go in search of its own origins and identity." Pierre Nora, "Between Memory and History: *Les Lieux de Memoire*," *Representations* 26 (Spring 1989): 15.

ifestations entirely. Ultimately it is crucial to keep in mind that an exclusive focus on the rise of Arabism or Turkism in the immediate postwar period is misplaced and obscures the fact that what is now conceptualized as nationalism, especially so-called popular nationalism, were forms of consciousness—political, class-based, religious, or otherwise—that operated within their own universe of meaning and language of symbols and signs, and possessed dimensionality for which nationalism cannot always account.

That history writing would play a crucial role in the lives of the middle class reveals the way a particular manner of understanding the past fulfills the emotional, ideological, and practical needs of middle-class modernity. At its most basic, the act of being modern requires historical thinking; just as the modern seeks out contemporaneous "unmodern" spaces against which to gauge its secure possession of its own modernity, it also must secure itself as the historical moment that follows a period of definitive premodernity.[13] Thinking historically, as seen in the prewar period, was a consummate middle-class act. History—of both Europe and the "East"—was mobilized to serve a didactic and pragmatic function in the discourse of the Aleppo Mutual Aid Society and newspapers like *al-Sha'b*. In the interwar period, especially as questions of political legitimacy hinged on more distinctly historical constructs like ethnicity, nationality, and secular legal precedent, what Carl Schorske identifies as "thinking with history" held a much greater social and public value in the politics of the city and state. Moreover, it is no accident that this form of history tends to intersect with the city: the nineteenth-century historicist Johann Gottlieb Fichte—whose writing on the nation and education would strongly influence interwar nationalist thought[14]—responded to the "the chaos of his unfree and divided nation, . . . [by locating] in the late medieval and early modern city-states a German paradise lost that could serve as a moral-political model for constructing a modern national community."[15] Aleppine historians, faced with an even deeper moment of anxiety, and using similar forms and tools of historicist thought, would use their city's past to inform its present and shape its future. The Eastern Mediterranean city's architectures of community, broadly conceived—its institutional forms, its social networks, its middle class—would play a pivotal role as the moral center of an emergent modern order. And Aleppo, in particular, would serve as a unique exemplar for correct middle-class behavior, dignified cosmopolitanism, and socially responsible capitalism.

---

[13] Mitchell, *Questions*, 24.

[14] The interwar intellectual Zaki al-Arsuzi was especially influenced by Fichte. Watenpaugh, "'Creating Phantoms,'" 365.

[15] Carl E. Schorske, *Thinking with History: Explorations in the Passage to Modernism* (Princeton: Princeton University Press, 1998), 7.

The Eastern Mediterranean experience with history writing underscores the hegemonic power of historicist forms of thinking among all modernizing Western and non-Western middle-classes. It evidences as well the formation of a transnational middle-class style of historical memory—linked to colonialists' imaginings—that emerged in the historiography in the later nineteenth and early twentieth centuries, not just in the Eastern Mediterranean, but throughout East and South Asia. As Ranajit Guha notes of the internalization of this form of knowledge and the way it coalesced with the project of middle-class modernity, "It had a chronology, causality, comparability—indeed, it had all the method and craft of Western historiography for its equipment. What is equally significant is that it was modernist not in methodology alone but in concept as well. For to be world-historical was to catch up with modernity and its most advanced column, Europe itself on the road to progress."[16] Weaving these elements together, Fathallah Qastun had first placed Aleppines as exemplary Ottomans on that road in 1910. And as the empire now seemed to collapse around them, history would serve as a tool to return them to that path of *true civilization*.

However, when he and his colleagues sought to write their city's past in the mode of modern historians, it required that they assure it, and by extension themselves, a place within History's providential horizons. In conception and practice this act was tough. By dominant Eurocentrist definitions, the Orient was a realm exterior to History itself; in the Hegelian sense, it was a place with a past, but not History. This conclusion would have been apparent from the authoritative European texts upon which middle-class authors were modeling their histories. For Indian historians in the same period, the singular challenge of writing the often mythic and irrational pasts of India into history was met by "collapsing the past with its 'happenings, deeds, events' into the narrative present . . . thus India was rescued from Prehistory by her own historians and ushered by them across the border into World-history."[17] Faced with the identical dilemma, the noted early twentieth-century Japanese historian Kurakichi Shiratori instead embraced the mythic past of Japan to define "a pure character of Japan before its culture was altered or covered." This then eased a synthetic vision of Japan as "combining the best of *toyo* (Easternism) and Europe," back into a universal History, while simultaneously maintaining a Japanese authenticity.[18]

Unlike the environment enmeshing these other modernist historians, vestiges of the Hellenistic, Roman, and much earlier ancient pasts, which

---

[16] Ranajit Guha, *History at the Limit of World History* (New York: Columbia University Press, 2002), 53.

[17] Ibid., 54.

[18] Tanaka, *Japan's Orient*, 154, 155. On the difficulty in defining *toyo*, see "Introduction: The Discovery of History," 1–28, passim.

had been integrated into the story of the West's ascent, physically surrounded Eastern Mediterranean historians. The value of being part of this
past was continually reinforced by the eagerness with which American
and European archaeologists excavated in the environs of Aleppo. By the
last decade of the nineteenth century, local writers, basing their accounts
on Western Orientalists, had begun to claim for Aleppines descent from
similar ancestors.[19] When viewed from the West, the Middle East, though,
had left the path of civilization with the advent of Islam.[20] In a passage
that would have been readily available to Aleppines in both the original
German and French and English translations, Hegel had reduced in his
posthumously rendered *Vorlesungen über die Philosophie der Geschichte*
the East and West to a simple pair of opposites:

> On the one hand we see the European world forming itself anew—the nations
> taking form root there, to produce a world of free reality expanded and devel-
> oped in every direction. . . . But the East itself, when by degrees enthusiasm
> had vanished, sank into the grossest vice. The most hideous passions became
> dominant, and as sensual enjoyment was sanctioned in the first form which
> Mahometan [*sic*] doctrine assumed, and was exhibited as a reward of the faith-
> ful in Paradise, it the place of fanaticism. At present driven back into its Asiatic
> and African quarters, and tolerated only in one corner of Europe through the
> jealousy of Christian Powers, Islam has long vanished from the stage of history
> at large and has retreated into oriental ease and repose.[21]

Later writers, including Ernest Renan and, most recently, Bernard Lewis,
have contributed variations on this theme. As noted earlier, while leading
Muslim intellectuals of the nineteenth century like Jamal al-Din al-Afghani dismissed such an idea, for many of the historians of the Eastern
Mediterranean, it presented a seemingly insoluble paradox: To recognize
the trajectory of modernity meant accepting the modern derisive depic-
tion of Islam and the Islamic world.[22] For most in this milieu—in particular non-Muslim historians—it seemed easier and wiser to defer any attempt to solve the paradox, and they chose instead to retreat into the

[19] *Sâlnâme* (Aleppo, 1321 [1903]), 217.

[20] The literature on this topic is vast: Edward Said's *Orientalism* (New York: Pantheon
Books, 1978) is the canonical text in English; also see Hicham Djaït's thoughtful meditation
on the philosophical origins of this discourse, *L'Europe et L'Islam* (Paris: Éditions de Seuil,
1978).

[21] Georg Wilhelm Freidrich Hegel, *The Philosophy of History*, trans. J. Sibree (New York:
Colonial Press, 1900), 355–360.

[22] For an account of how contemporary Western Orientalists were constructing hegemonic notions of Islam and bringing racist science to the history of the region, see Susan
Bayly's "Racial Reading of Empire: Britain, France, and Colonial Modernity in the Mediterranean and Asia," in Fawaz and Bayly, eds., *Modernity and Culture*, 285–313.

modernist methodology of a positivist bourgeois historicism; in the case of Ghazzi, Tabbakh, and others, like the Damascene historian Muhammad Kurd Ali, the same task was accomplished by using the antique forms of *khitat* and *tabaqat* to make a careful camouflage of their innovation.[23] This deference had the effect of leaving the question of Islam and modernity to be answered by marginalized figures outside mainstream thought. Nevertheless, their direct avoidance of this issue speaks to the professional historians' consciousness of the role of history in the definition of their present and how any aberrant understanding of the past could upset the moral order of their society in the future.

Still, this decision did not prevent historians and critics, while not necessarily seeing themselves or their class in Hegel's or similar characterizations, from using their intrinsic moral standards to pass judgment on the lower classes and justify greater ethnic and religious distinction *within* their societies; thus, it was at once possible to defend the rectitude of Islam—even to cast Islamic practice as a form of definitive bourgeois probity—by vilifying "misbehaving" lower-class Muslims, rural people, and nomads, or those, primarily non-Muslim, refugees who by virtue of ethnic origin were alien to society and its ways. Despite the instability that this shift in the application of the role of Islam occasioned, the form of historical writing that emerged in this moment of anxiety reflected clearly the fluidity and dynamism in conceptions of Islamic practice, intercommunal relations, and notions of citizenship in the Eastern Mediterranean's middle-class consciousness.

---

[23] Muhammad Kurd Ali, *Khitat al-Sham* [The Topography of Damascus] (Dimshq: al-matba'a al-ahdath, 1925).

FIVE

Rescuing the Arab from History: *Halab*, Orientalist Imaginings, Wilsonianism, and Early Arabism

> [The imperialist's power] is based upon lies and is as fragile
> as if it were made from the thread of a spider's web.
> —*Halab*, 12 July 1920

The reading public of Aleppo opened the 18 April 1919 Arabic-language official gazette *Halab* (Aleppo) to read, under the headline of "al-Nahda al-ʿarabiyya al-jadida" [The Modern Arab Awakening], the initial article in a series that told the story of the Arab Revolt (1916–1918).[1] These articles, the first on the subject since the city had fallen to a British force six months earlier, would explain how and, more important, why Aleppo had ceased to be part of that empire and was now under the control of the son of a nobleman from the Arabian peninsula, Faysal ibn Husayn.

"Several centuries ago a great nation arose," the series began, "and historians have named it, 'the Arab [nation].' " Wherever these Arabs went, they brought with them enlightenment, the arts and sciences. However, the Arabs lost control "of their affairs, and had nothing left but their language . . . and [thus] were bereft of the tools of the nation and denuded of all the traditions of nationalism (al-wataniyya) and of the race (al-ʿunsuriyya). This was a great disaster," concluded the author.[2] Unlike later writers, primarily George Antonius, who located the resurrection of this nation in the midnineteenth-century Arabic literary renaissance of Beirut and linked it with American Christian missionaries,[3] the unnamed author of the newspaper's text found it instead in the period following the rein-

---

[1] The earliest account of the Arab Revolt I have been able to find in Aleppo is an Arab Bureau tract published in Cairo in 1916. Anonymous, *Thawrat al-ʿArab: muqadimatuha, asbabuha, nataiʾjuha* [The Arab Revolt: Its Origins, Causes, and Goals] (Cairo, 1916). The author is listed as a member of the "Arab Society." The condition of the paper and the name of a Hama publishing house, Abu al-Fidaʾ, on the binding suggest that it may be a reprint from the period of union with Egypt. Regardless, the text in some form may have shaped the version published in Aleppo.

[2] *Halab* (Aleppo), 18 April 1919.

[3] Antonius, *The Arab Awakening*. On Antonius, see William Cleveland, "The Arab Nationalism of George Antonius Reconsidered," in Israel Gershoni and James Jankowski, eds., *Rethinking Nationalism in the Arab Middle East* (New York: Columbia University Press, 1997), 65–86.

statement of the Ottoman Constitution in 1908, when "among the Turks, the idea of oppressing the sons of the Arabs in the peninsula" first appeared. Soon, groups of Turkish soldiers in the capitals of Syria and Iraq "practiced oppression and killed patriots."[4] Even though they had announced the complete equality under the law of all "races and peoples," such equality existed only on paper. Then, "in the period of the dreadful war [World War I] . . .the opportunity came for the Turk to leave the Arab and for the Arab to leave the Turk." This potential for an amicable parting dissipated when the "Turks fell under the tutelage of Germany and oppressed the people in a way too horrible to explain, and an atmosphere of despair spread among all the non-Turkish peoples [al-shu'ub al-ghayr turkiyya] like the Armenians, the Greeks, and, most of all, the Arabs."[5]

A few editions later, Aleppines learned of the root cause of this oppression. Conceding "that [while] the old Turks had been thoughtful, honorable, forbearing, and just men, the Unionists (CUP) and their followers are not the Turks we knew"; "the modern education" they received had "poisoned their minds and made them selfish and aspire to eradicate everyone but themselves."[6] The editor singled out the cruelty of Cemal Pasha, whose litany of crimes included the deportation of the heads of many notable families and the hanging of "Arab patriots" in Beirut and Damascus. "This was the infamous Cemal whom we know of as al-saffah (the Blood Letter)," the author reminded his audience. Driven to extremes by the cruelty of the Blood Letter, Faysal obtained the support of the British and began the "liberation of the nation." "Emir Faysal," a scion of the "loftiest house of Arabia—the Hashemites—who possessed from time immemorial all the blessings and honor of the race," led the movement in accordance with the wishes of his father, the Sharif of Mecca, Husayn. England, France, Russia, and Italy, the article explained, had recognized Husayn as king of the Hijaz. The next week's Halab narrated the opening campaign of the revolt and the capture of 'Aqaba.[7]

Since the end of World War 1, most popular and academic histories of the period before and during the Arab Revolt have resembled the account read by Aleppines in the spring of 1919. Its basic outline has remained virtually unchanged: Ottoman imperialist oppression, Turkification, a struggle of the Arabs to throw off the alien Turkish yoke. The story line fit neatly into pre-existing European literary genres, especially that of the noble savage pitted against an inveterate and decadent imperial power;

[4] Halab (Aleppo), 21 April 1919.

[5] Ibid., 24 April 1919.

[6] Ibid. This good Turk/bad Turk dichotomy appears most visibly in Zeine, Arab-Turkish Relations. Though dated, Zeine is still widely read.

[7] Halab (Aleppo), 3 June 1919.

and, in a curious sleight of hand, it employed the well-established literary devices of centuries of prejudice against "The Terrible Turk," which meant until the end of the nineteenth century Muslims in general rather than an ethnic category. The story has even become a permanent fixture of Western popular culture owing first to Lowell Thomas's postwar traveling multimedia show, "With Allenby in Palestine and Lawrence in Arabia"; T. E. Lawrence's own memoir, *The Seven Pillars of Wisdom*; and later David Lean's epic film *Lawrence of Arabia*.[8]

However, in the months immediately following the end of the war, an Aleppine reading these articles may have known only bits and pieces of that narrative, possibly including the fact that Cemal Pasha had hanged his political opponents, or even that the sharif of Mecca had concluded an alliance with the British to make war on the Ottoman state. Moreover, the sharif's son, Faysal, could just as easily have been perceived as an alien opportunist allied with a Christian power against the legitimate leader of the Muslim community, the Ottoman sultan; the image of Faysal as a traitor springing to mind more freely than that of an authentic leader whose authority rested on the linking of his status as a descendent of the Prophet with a right to lead a nationalist rebellion. For the majority of Aleppine newspaper readers, such an intellectual leap had no precedent.[9]

The didactic format of the serialized account of the Arab Revolt, its "textbookish" texture, confirms that from the perspective of the new rulers of the city, Aleppines were not remembering the past the way that they should. They lacked a *correct* understanding of recent events and had not organized these events into an appropriate narrative. This was to be "nation as pedagogy" in the sense suggested by Timothy Mithchell, where

the national community is understood as the history of a self that comes to awareness, or of a people that begins to imagine its peoplehood. History is written to describe the growing self-awareness of imagination of a collective

---

[8] See Lowell Thomas, *With Lawrence in Arabia* (New York: Grosset, 1924), a book that has been reprinted at least nine times and in several languages in the last eighty years. On the film's continuing impact on Middle East studies, see Steven C. Caton, *Lawrence of Arabia: A Film's Anthropology* (Los Angeles: University of California, 1999). Also see T. E. Lawrence's *Revolt in the Desert* (New York: George H. Doran, 1927), a best-seller of the late twenties, and his *Seven Pillars of Wisdom, a Triumph* (Garden City, N.Y: Doubleday, Doran, 1935); Elizabeth P. MacCallum, *The Nationalist Crusade in Syria* (New York: The Foreign Policy Association, 1928); and Stephen H. Longrigg, *Syria and Lebanon under French Mandate* (Oxford: Oxford University Press, 1958). The trope of Turkification has become a standard feature of most Arabic historiography of the period. Examples include ʿAli Sultan, *Tarikh Suriyya 1908–1918* [History of Syria: 1908–1918] (Damascus: DAR Talas, 1987); Tawfiq Birsu, *Al-ʿarab wa al-turk fi al-ahd al-dusturi al-ʿuthmani* [Arab and Turk in the Era of the Ottoman Constitution] (Cairo: Arab World University Press, 1960).

[9] Recent and persuasive revisions of this period are Kayalı, *Arabs and Young*, and Gelvin, *Divided*.

subject. This imagination takes the form of a gradual revealing of the collective subject to itself, a revelation shaped by those powers of communication, reason, and consciousness that define our understanding of an emergent self.[10]

And thus, with the printed words in the paper, the city's new rulers—a cadre of British-supported Arab nationalists, returned exiles, ex-Ottoman Army officers from Palestine, Iraq, and Arabia, and a few local allies—would seek to fix a version of the past in the popular consciousness, telling the readers and others how the nation had come into being and awareness by remembering the troubles, changes, and horrors of the preceding decade in an idiom of racial and linguistic purity and ethnic distinction that used a syntax—nationalism—novel, though not completely unknown, to the city and the region.[11]

Seen in this light, while the narrative of the awakening of the Arab nation in the newspaper was calculated to garner support for the immediate political aspirations of the British-imposed régime of Faysal and his lieutenants, it also operated as one element of a broader project for diffusing a specific vernacular of nationalism, in this case Arab nationalism.[12] Critically, they would make the appropriate substitutions, tie into linguistic and cultural preconditions, narrate a history, impose a meaning on the salient points of that narrative, and deny or obliterate divergent interpretations, alternative renderings of the past, and local knowledges. In so doing, the paper's editors would translate a metropolitan "high culture" ideal nationalism into a parochial version for use in the cosmopolitan city as a prelude to cleansing the city of its "un-Arab" components.

Wielding the paper as a discursive weapon in the Aleppine milieu, and elsewhere in the Allied-controlled regions of the Eastern Mediterranean, these nationalists sought to persuade the readers—despite obvious evidence to the contrary—that they belonged and had always belonged to a "Syrian" Arab whole by writing the city and its citizens into the Arab nation. The use of the paper as the medium for this project points to the utility of print media in the non-West, the potential power of a reading public, as well as the growing currency of discussions about history and the nation in public discourse.

Halab's lesson plan also provides telling evidence that as the newspaper was being published, people throughout the region were actively seeking

[10] Timothy Mitchell, *Rule of Experts: Egypt, Techno-politics, Modernity* (Berkeley: University of California Press, 2002), 183.

[11] See especially, Ranajit Guha, *Dominance*, 184–188, and Partha Chatterjee's reading of Tarinicharan Chattopadhay's mid-nineteenth-century history of "India," *Bharatbarser itihas*. Chatterjee sees in Tarinicharan's periodization an internalization of European historiographical technique. Chatterjee, *Nation*, 94–96.

[12] See Benedict Anderson's *Imagined Communities*, 2nd ed. (London: Verso, 1991), 4–81 passim.

to make sense of postwar realities by using available intellectual and cultural tools. The debates and public discourse occasioned by the collapse of Ottoman rule resolved into a series of deceptively simple questions: what did it—the war, the occupation—all mean, but also, who are we and where do we belong, or rather, of which whole are we now a part? The writing of history and the adoption of a version of nationalism would serve some as tools in answering those questions. An evolving Arabic historiography, which attempted to define the authentic and inauthentic in Aleppo's past—including, but not limited to, the history of the Arab Revolt—sits at the center of those questions in the city itself. Crucially, as these questions were answered, they were rendered in historicist typologies legible only in a modernist light, paralleling developments in the emergence of rationalist bourgeois historicism in other colonial domains.

This chapter reads the process of diffusion and cleansing in several episodes as each appeared in the newspaper during the years it was controlled by functionaries of the Arab Kingdom (1918–1920). Using the paper's serialized history of the Arab Revolt, its formation and vilification of an "other," and its creation of external and internal boundaries—the very nature of which were often mediated and defined by European colonial Orientalists—this chapter situates the journal's efforts within the confluence of the interwar spread of European nationalist idealism and historicist typologies. The text of the paper also brings into relief elements of profound postwar crisis in the city and the region. Defining the broader constituent elements of this conflict—a metonymy of antagonism—became a central feature of public discourse in the postwar Arab Middle East.[13] The definitions of these elements emerged through the 1920s in the ephemera of bourgeois cultural production: newspaper articles, museum displays, histories, amateur archaeology, biographical dictionaries, and literary criticism, and they were sharpened by mass organized and random violence, colonial intrigue, and regional military realities. Far from taking the form of a simple choice between "Syrianism," "Pan-Arabism," or loyalty to the new Republic of Turkey as the natural successor of Ottoman state, the form of the debate in places like Aleppo also signaled concerns about religiously sanctioned authority, the persistence of Ottoman forms of legitimization, and questions of citizenship that were shared by other peoples of the multilingual and multireligious Eastern Mediterranean. Those in Aleppo most adept at making meaning in historicist struc-

---

[13] The term is Homi Bhabha's: "The work of hegemony is itself the process of iteration and differentiation. It depends on the production of alternative or antagonistic images that are always produced side by side and in competition with each other. It is this side-by-side nature, this partial presence, or metonymy of antagonism, and its effective significations, that give meaning . . . to a politics of struggle *as the struggle of identifications.*" Homi Bhabha, *The Location of Culture* (London: Routledge, 2004), 29.

tures occupied a key position in the formulation of that discourse; namely, the Western-educated middle class, presumably the target of the paper's persuasion, which, far from uniformly supporting Faysal and his British allies, still sought to make sense of the ambiguities that epitomized Aleppo and what it meant to live there in the wake of the moral, social, and political tremors occasioned by the "war to end all wars" with intellectual tools particular to modernity.

Equally, the editors of *Halab* sought to "awaken" that class to what they considered the essential rightness and rationality of nationalism and to persuade them of the fallacy of their antediluvian belief that cosmopolitan society was the norm. The iteration of Wilsonian ideals as axiomatic features of the new world order in the journal highlighted this suasion and reflected the apotheosis of the nation, something the outcome of World War I, in which (legitimate) nations had won out against (illegitimate) empires, had verified for many. Yet the very insistence on the authority of the concept of the nation indicates that such recognition of the nation's godhead may not have been commonly understood by *Halab's* readers. The argument in favor of the Aleppines as Arabs and Aleppo as an Arab city, however, proceeded from the assumption that modernity itself teaches that the individual is of a nation *sui generis*. Ultimately, if the Arabs were to be modern, then they too, must have a nation. Nevertheless, Aleppo's heterogeneous nature—a quality shared by many other cosmopolitan cities in the Eastern Mediterranean and beyond—became an obstacle and a problem, something preternatural. The condition of prewar Aleppo, in which Arabs were largely unaware of their "Arabness," failed to measure up to *Halab's* version of modernity.

Moreover, beyond showing the conceptual links between nation, historicism, and modernity, a close reading of *Halab* is an exercise in the archaeology of an idea: while the specifics of Arab nationalism would change over the next generation, especially under the influence of fascism, in its broadest outlines the ideology has changed little from the version in the paper—especially the elaboration of an instrumentalized Arab history. This was the earliest instance of Arab nationalism operating as state dogma in the Eastern Mediterranean; it was also the first time a diverse urban population would be systematically exposed to that novel way of thinking about the past, ethnicity, and political legitimacy. Although the idea of the Arab nation had circulated throughout the salons and newspapers of Beirut and elsewhere, it had little resonance beyond a small circle of Christian intellectuals in the prewar period and was certainly not joined to state bureaucratic and educational institutions. Nevertheless, while the Arabism of *Halab* did articulate a formula for liberation from the Ottoman Empire, by its very nature, it also legitimized the European conquest of the region and the imposition of an alien ideology.

A striking feature of this early version is the insistence that the Arab is a nonsectarian designation and that Muslims, Christians, and Jews could be equally Arab and possess the same right to full citizenship; further, in this Arabism, Islam has no role whatsoever in governance or the bases of legitimate authority. Consequently, in the pages of *Halab* it is possible not just to begin to trace the origins of Arab nationalism and a nationalist historiography, but also to characterize the ideological terrain in which Islamist radicalism in the Arab world first takes root. Locating the roots of this radicalism in nationalism's heyday confronts the tendency to collapse Islamism into an undifferentiated, blanket antimodernism or anti-Westernism with origins in the last few decades; with the secular Arabism of *Halab* in mind, it should be recalled that Islamism in the Arab world in part emerged as a reaction against the imperialist division of Ottoman Muslims into separate states, as well as against the nonsectarian, emancipatory, and bourgeois dimensions of interwar liberal Arab nationalism.

FINDING THE ARAB; FINDING THE TURK

As the British military captured Ottoman territory in 1918, one of the first steps they took to consolidate their presence was the establishment and subsidy of sympathetic Arabic-language newspapers like *Halab*. Foremost among these was *al-ʿArab* [The Arab], begun in British-occupied Baghdad in early 1918. These papers were often associated with al-Nadi al-ʿArabi, the Arab Club, which British agents likewise aided. In the region, which shortly became Syria, two major papers began publication, *Halab* in Aleppo (9 December 1918) and *al-ʿAsima* [The Capital] in Damascus some weeks later.[14] The papers constituted the provinces' official gazettes. Like the previous official papers of the Ottoman period, such as *Fırat* [Euphrates], local announcements, train schedules, and official wages and prices filled much of the paper. When used alongside the clubs, these two elements created a politically sanctioned way to monopolize and condition an understanding of the historical construction of the city.

On the front page of the first edition of *Halab*, an article printed in a headline-size font informed Aleppines of what whole they were now a part. Thanking Shukri Pasha al-Ayyubi, a former Ottoman officer, Istanbul carpet importer, and, at that time, the military governor of Aleppo, for allowing the paper to publish, the editor explained that the paper's pages would serve "to explain the new condition, spread knowledge, en-

---

[14] On *al-ʿAsima*, see Saliha Fellache, "*al-ʿAsima*, organe politique-étude du journal officiel du gouvernement du Fayçal entre février 1919 et août 1920" (M.A. thesis, Bordeaux III, 1994).

liven trade, and lead the Arab nation along the path to prosperity." A central tenet of this new condition, and a more significant intervention in the definition of Aleppo, took the form of an official proclamation from the military administration in Damascus buried on the second page. "We have made known . . . a ruling concerning the Turks present in the city [Aleppo] and we have advised them to register their names as soon as possible." The article failed to explain how a "Turk" was to know he or she was a Turk; but the remainder of the proclamation made it abundantly clear who was to stay and who was to go.

1. The Turks born in Aleppo and married with Arabs are not to leave these relationships.
2. The Turks with proprietary or trade relationships who have maintained a good demeanor during their stay in Aleppo are exempt from deportation.
3. Turkish civil servants and others who have none of these relationships nor a livelihood are to depart immediately and the Arab government will assist them and guarantee their safety.[15]

Presumably, the announcement reflected a similar policy in Palestine and the Ottoman province of Damascus, areas also under British control. However, the heterogeneity of the city's population did not so easily lend itself to such national distinctions. With few exceptions, the question of who was an Arab and who was a Turk rarely arose in the city. Most urbane, literate Aleppines would have bristled at being designated mere "Arabs" or "Turks"—terms which in prenationalist consciousness connoted for them backward desert dwellers or rough country people. Certainly, however, if such a question did arise prior to the British capture of Aleppo, as it did increasingly in journalistic exchanges in the period after 1912, it would not have carried with it the possibility of social exclusion and political expulsion. The proclamation was much more than the implementation of a bureaucratic measure. Rather, expelling Turks was part of a drive to cleanse the city of now "unnatural" elements as defined by the "metonymy of antagonism." It was the first operation of a mechanism that sought to uncover the "Turk" by finding the "Arab"; this Turk was to be the "not-Arab" and, vice versa.

The "Turk" as he emerged from the pages of *Halab*, the "old Turks" of the Arab Revolt story notwithstanding, was an ill-mannered individual, replete with onerous character flaws, intent on defying modern civilization, intellectually deficient, and morally corrupt.[16] As the paper explained in a piece entitled "The Policy of Division": "the Turks controlled the provinces [of the Ottoman Empire] . . . by sowing enmity between

---

[15] Khoury, *Urban*, 147–148.
[16] *Halab* (Aleppo), 5 May 1919.

people of different religions and causing racial disunity (fitna al-'anasir)," and this policy had forced the allied powers to intervene in the region. This disunity harmed the Arabs most:

> The Young Turk government was gripped by the idea that Anatolian Turkey is the basic unit of the Turkish Kingdom . . . and they convinced themselves that they should establish in Anatolia a state for their nationals only—no strangers allowed. The question of the "Arab and Turk" moved from clubs to the cities and villages of Anatolia. They accused the Arabs of treason and hatred of the Turks, prejudicing them against them until the Turks' hearts turned against the Arabs.[17]

While the "Turk" causes disunity, the Arab government, the articles concluded, treats all people equally and unites the Arabs, regardless of religion.

The paper also put the issue of "Turkish" complicity in communal discord to good use while reporting on a brief but bloody massacre of Armenian refugees.[18] *Halab* apologized for the disturbance by making an oblique reference to the Armenian Genocide of 1915: "We and the Armenians are brothers, we suffered under the same tyranny," the edition of 27 February 1919 explained. On 7 March a much longer article addressed the same topic: "It is unfortunate that you soiled your whiteness with the red blood of innocents and the black stain of shame." It continued with three questions the individual must ask should a similar situation occur:

- Am I doing all I can for the nation?
- Am I behaving now like the Turks?
- Am I acting in the way an enemy of civilization would act?

The proper answers to these questions should prevent Aleppines-as-Arabs from committing such atrocities. As if to reinforce the notion that, recent events not withstanding, the commitment of atrocities against civilians was a national characteristic of Turks, rather than Arabs, the paper followed with scrupulous detail the war crime trials of various Young Turks in Allied-occupied Istanbul.[19] Arabs, then, were everything the Turk was not. An article entitled "Arab Tolerance" that appeared in the summer of

[17] Ibid., 12 December 1918.

[18] Early in the morning on 26 February 1919, a mob attacked several buildings and shanties housing Armenian refugees to the north and west of the city. Two hours later nearly 100 Armenians lay dead; British and Arab army troops wounded or killed about 50 of the attackers. The crowd's anger, European observers claimed, grew out of resentment against the French-supported Armenian Legionnaires whom the French had organized into armed military units. PRO FO 371/4179 E 39672/2117/44. General Headquarters Egypt to War Office, 3 March 1919.

[19] *Halab* (Aleppo), 31 July 1919.

1919 invited readers to "study the pages of history to see many examples of the tolerance the Arab nation had for those who lived in it," whereupon they would realize that "the Arabs are at the forefront of tolerant nations." The paper went on to explain that subject "Greeks" and "Christians" of the Middle Ages had achieved much in the sciences and medicine. "From this it is known," the article continued, "that the nature of the Arabs is not at all what some would call today 'bigoted' (ta'assub)." It concluded: "The history of the Arabs does not bring to mind the disgrace of bigotry toward the sons of their nation, unlike what is mentioned in the history of other nations. They [the Arabs] have followed the admonition 'religion is to God and the nation is to the people.' "[20]

In building this modern national identity, *Halab* tied the speaking of Arabic to being an Arab in a simple equation: the Arab speaks Arabic. As the paper assured its readers, reading in Arabic, "Arabic is our national language."[21] Yet defining Aleppines in such a way—reinforced by the fact that Faysal's administration declared Arabic the sole language of state— contradicted the traditional bilingualism, or even trilingualism, of the resident population and overturned six centuries of practice. It should be recalled that in the antebellum Ottoman Eastern Mediterranean, the use of literary Ottoman Turkish—which no one spoke as a native language—for affairs of state existed alongside the use of Quranic Arabic— also which no one spoke as a native language—for the purposes of religion and law. Nevertheless, the blueprint for the nation used by *Halab* insisted that the Arabic print-language that had begun to be employed in newspapers and literature during the last decades of the previous century in places like Istanbul, Cairo, and Beirut was the natural language of the Arabs. In a plebiscitory sense, Arabic did not suggest itself more readily than Turkish for the native language of the inhabitants of the Ottoman province of Aleppo. However, in the city of Aleppo, a dialect of Arabic was probably the most widely spoken language, especially among the resident Christian population.[22] Nevertheless, the large number of bilingual papers published in the prewar period suggests that print literacy existed equally not only in Arabic and Ottoman, but also in Ar-

[20] Ibid., 18 June 1919.

[21] Ibid., 29 October 1919.

[22] For a measure of the degree to which the patois of Aleppo had been interpenetrated by various languages, primarily Ottoman Turkish, Armenian, and Kurdish, see Khayr al-Din al-Asadi, *Masu'at Halab* [Encyclopedia of Aleppo], 8 vols. (Aleppo: Aleppo University Press, n.d). Both this work and the early nineteenth-century diary of Naum Bakhash, *Yawmiyyat Halab* [Aleppo Diary], 3 vols. (Aleppo: Maronite Press, 1990), detail the use of a vibrant and useful colloquial Aleppine Arabic that could convey complex ideas and concepts.

menian.[23] Knowledge of languages played a prosaic and functional role in the lives of the people of Aleppo, and such competence had not acquired the all-encompassing cultural and national determinative value it would have in the framework of nationalism.[24] A truism of the Ottoman system was that birth in an Arabic-speaking (or Kurdish or Armenian or Turkish, for that matter) household had never barred access to Ottoman sinecures. The political elite of the Arab nationalists who surrounded Faysal, and Faysal himself, knew Ottoman, Arabic, and various European languages. Despite this, the paper made clear the pivotal role Arabic had in defining the Arab and further embraced it as a central aspect of the individual constructed by modernity.[25]

Given the centrality of Arabic to this ideology, the editors of *Halab* advocated a systematic approach to its instruction and correct propagation. An article entitled "The Arabic Language and the Arab Club" (29 October 1919) outlined five measures to counter "the weakened condition in which we see the instruction of the Arabic language." The Arab Club, as a center for adult instruction in Arabic, French, and English, served as the locus for the Arabic language's revival. It would "spread the Arabic language and ease its instruction for the sons of the nation." The first measure of the five-measure plan made "the study of Arabic compulsory for anyone who comes to study a foreign language at the club. He cannot study another language until he has mastered Arabic." The remaining parts of the plan insisted "that it is important to study grammar, diction and declamation as well as the history of the Arabs and of the Arabic language." A hint to the populist impulses behind such a program appeared in the second item, which prioritized scholarships for those who wished to learn Arabic.

Both the insistence upon a language proper to the Arabs and the activism to spread and strengthen that language among Aleppines derive from

[23] See di Tarazi, *Sihafa*, and Malathi, *al-Tibaʿa*.

[24] Carter Findley adds a historical dimension to this question: "Deriving from the acute cultural cleavage of the period [late-nineteenth century] our first organizing principle contrasts a new cultural orientation responsive to—often dominated by—western ideas with a conservative, Islamic orientation. Many Ottoman Muslims responded to both orientations to some degree, so internalizing the conflict between them. In this sense, a given individual might not have a single cultural orientation. Contemporary Ottomans tended not to see things this way, however. Having historically identified erudition largely with the linguistic medium of its expression, they now tended to take the languages a person knew or used as indicative of that person's cultural tendencies." *Ottoman Civil Officialdom*, 144.

[25] See William Cleveland's biography of Faysal's minister of education in Syria and later in Iraq, Satiʿ al-Husri, *The Making of an Arab Nationalist: Ottomanism and Arabism in the Life and Thought of Satiʿ al-Husri* (Austin: University of Texas Press, 1971). Al-Husri, born to an Aleppine father in Yemen (1882), grew up speaking Turkish and learned Arabic only as an adult.

two of the basic requirements of nationalism itself. First, as understood at the time, nationalism's internationally recognized logic—at least in theory—demanded a one-to-one correspondence between sovereignty and the collectivity of the speakers of a given language. In conformity with this logic, *Halab* sought to establish that this collectivity was pre-existent; it was a necessary precursor to the assertion of the nation's sovereignty. And second, the exclusivity of Arabic as a defining quality of the Arab and the paper's insistence upon the language's systematic cultivation adhere most closely to an attempt to persuade the "reading-class" readers that the nation's dimensions included its nonreading class. Arabic may not have been the native language of Aleppines, but in this climate of ascendant nationalism, asserting that Arabic was the language of Aleppines-as-Arabs and creating structures and institutions that valorized it presented the reading class with a possible and novel modus vivendi for social cohesion or interclass and nonsectarian solidarity. It also served as a basis for creating a political unit that divided Aleppo from Istanbul and included it with Damascus, an innovation in borders not seen since the collapse of the Mamluk Empire in the fifteenth century. Such language-based solidarity promised to create, paraphrasing Benedict Anderson, a useful "fraternity" of Arabic-speakers.[26]

ORIENTALIST IMAGININGS: THE "TERRIBLE TURK" AND THE "OPPRESSED ARAB"

In addition to the seemingly objective use of a linguistic device to define Aleppines as Arabs and Aleppo as Arab, the paper used the words and authority of Western diplomats, politicians, and Orientalists to make its case and write the city into a stream of Arab history. Within the first month of its founding, the Arab Club of Aleppo hosted François Georges-Picot and Mark Sykes. The two diplomats toured Syria in late 1918 and early 1919 delivering speeches calculated to lower local expectations of complete independence, no doubt in anticipation of the implementation of the territorial arrangements outlined in the once-secret treaty between France and Britain that the pair had engineered. Despite this lowering of expectations, their presentations insisted on the existence of a separate Arab nation that, Picot maintained, had been oppressed "for four centuries by the government of Istanbul."[27] Both claimed that the liberation of the Arabs and other peoples from this oppression had been the major motive of the French, the British, and the Italians in their decision to make

[26] Anderson, *Imagined Communities*, 7.
[27] *Halab*, 2 January 1919.

war on the Turks. The two diplomat-historians depicted the Arabs as a nation among nations; nations that had joined together to "end Turkish despotism and return freedom to the people."[28]

Picot charged his audience with "the unification of all Arabs by your efforts, from Aleppo to the desert, whatever their origins or customs or particular beliefs." Similarly, Sykes, whom the Arab Club's agenda qualified as the "great Orientalist" (al-mustashriq al-kabir), assured the assembly, "everyone is enthusiastically supporting the Arab Awakening, we know how great it was in the past and will be in the future."[29] This speech may have been the last one he ever delivered, as Sykes died a month later in a Paris hotel room, a victim of the catastrophic influenza pandemic that followed the war. These speeches told the members of the club—and with their publication in *Halab*, the rest of the city—which boundaries the victors of the world war had drawn around them. Their authoritative and prescriptive tone must have appealed to an audience hungry for external recognition and reinforcement; it conveyed a sense that the Arab nation had arrived and had joined the exclusive club of nation-states, nations that had the right to be "free." While the definition of this freedom supplied by Picot and Sykes meant that Arabs should rule Arabs, neither had a commitment to anything other than complete European dominance of the region. Their speeches provide a striking reminder of the way colonialism dupes its colonized through the rhetoric of the nation.

Each history lesson shared an emphasis on the historical narrative of greatness followed by decline, oppression, and then a reawakening. The opening paragraphs of the paper's history of the Arab Revolt, "The Modern Arab Awakening" followed the same plot. The paper assured the readers, on the authority of Europeans, that an Arab nation did indeed exist; that the Arab, being the non-Turk, belongs to a people once oppressed and now liberated. Such a narrative structure is far from unique. "Borrowed" from European histories of the nineteenth century, primarily accounts of the Greek revolution or Italian unification, these historicist typologies were manifested clearly throughout non-Western nationalist histories. Consider the example of nationalist historiography in the Indian subcontinent:

For Indian nationalists in the late nineteenth century, the pattern of classical glory, medieval decline, and modern renaissance appeared as one that was not only proclaimed by the modern historiography of Europe but also approved for India by at least some sections of European scholarship. What was needed was to claim for the Indian nation the historical agency for completing the proj-

---

[28] Ibid.
[29] Ibid., 6 January 1919.

ect of modernity. To make that claim, ancient India had to become the night of medieval darkness. Contributing to that description would be all the prejudices of the European Enlightenment about Islam . . . . [in] the new nationalist history of India would be a stereotypical figure of "the Muslim," endowed with a "national character": fanatical, bigoted, warlike, dissolute, and cruel.[30]

The nationalist history that unfolded in the pages of *Halab* cast the stereotypical figure of the "Turk" in the role of the "Muslims"; the post-Enlightenment vilification of the "Terrible Turk" in such an effort proved an easy translation. Yet, beyond strengthening the definition of the Arab as the non-Turk, such a history functioned, at its very core, to obliterate the Islamist bases of Ottoman legitimacy. The persistence of this Islamic form of Ottoman legitimacy threatened the definition of "freedom" outlined above. Had the history depicted the Ottomans as ruling as just bad Muslims rather than brutal ethnic "Terrible Turk" oppressors, the ethnocentric argument put forward by Faysal and his European allies would have sounded hollow. To take full advantage of the modernist definition of Arab and Turk, the paper and its masters needed to obscure the religious bond between Arabic- and Turkish-speaking Muslims and thereby disengage the newly imagined ethnicities from a dependence on Islam and preclude the emergence of an anti-imperialist resistance movement phrased in the idiom of interethnic Islamic solidarity. Such a coincidence of both nationalist and imperialist interests presages the entire postcolonial ambivalence with Islam itself in Kemalist Turkey and Baathist Syria and Iraq, where Islam both is (or was) a definitive component of identity and operates as a marker of an unenlightened and unmodern past.

As the paper continued to create this past, this history of "we the Arabs," it resorted to European periodizations and extensive quotations from other Orientalist historians as a key discursive strategy. It was incumbent on the Arab nationalists to create a history for the Arab nation, a narrative in which the Arab "character" moves through a plot.[31] In addition to the earlier account of the Arab Revolt, the paper also presented the history of the Arabs in a serialized paraphrase of passages from Gustave le Bon's 1884 *La Civilisation des Arabes*.[32] In the 22 October 1919 edition of the paper, Rushdi Duhna justified this history lesson:

> In a French book, I stumbled across a page from the history of Arab civilization and I wanted to translate it so the readers could be informed about the extent

[30] Chatterjee, *Fragments*, 102.

[31] See Anderson, *Imagined Communities*, especially chap. 2, "Cultural Roots," 9–36.

[32] Gustave Le Bon, *La Civilisation des Arabes* (Paris: Firmin-Didot, 1884). On Le Bon's broader influence in Egypt, especially, see Timothy Mitchell, *Colonising Egypt* (Los Angeles: University of California Press, 1991), 123–124.

of the efforts which our grandfathers had expended in the advancement of science and knowledge and of the great hand they had in the various arts and industry so that they could be an example to us in our modern life. And we should follow their example and their lead, and we should not be content only with taking pride in them.

The article enumerated a series of mathematical and medical innovations made in the medieval period by people the author classified as Arabs. Further installments charted advances in architecture, metallurgy, and agriculture. The last section dealt with commerce and highlighted the "Arab" role in the trade of ivory and gold across the Mediterranean, and of silk from China.

The editor's use of this Orientalist account conveyed to his readers that the West recognized something of value in the Arab past. The implication that this past "ended" in the medieval period, that is, the period before the "four centuries of Ottoman rule," added a causative element to the argument: Arab greatness had been extinguished in the morass of Ottoman decadence. On a functional level, the editor resorted to a French version of "Arab" history because he had no alternative. The dominant tradition of local historiography, written in Arabic and Ottoman, did not periodize history in such a manner. Rather, as preserved in such texts as the Ottoman almanac, the *Sâlnâme*, Aleppo's history was divided into divinely ordained periods, namely, before and after it became part of the Islamic world,[33] or, in the case of Christian Aleppine writers, before and after the birth of Christ.[34] Ottoman court histories periodized the past along dynastic lines or reigns, but national history as a genre originated in Europe in the early nineteenth century.[35] In other words, to find a history that separated a national or ethnic Arab history from a Muslim history, and which included Aleppo in a larger Arab whole, the editor had no choice but to use foreign sources. Ultimately, some in *Halab's* audience may have viewed the foreign, modern sources as inherently more authoritative.

The use of European periodization and historicist structures points to a more fundamental commitment to modernity and to the importation of

---

[33] See, for example, the entry in the last prerevolutionary *Sâlnâme* for Aleppo (1908), 17–21.

[34] The salient example of this phenomenon is Mikha'il b. Antun al-Saqqal al-Halabi's (1852–1938), nineteenth-century two-volume manuscript. The first volume, *Tara'if al-nadim fi tarikh Halab al-qadim* [Rare Pleasantries in the Ancient History of Aleppo] takes the city's history to the birth of Christ; the second volume, *Lata'if al-Hadith fi tarikh Halab al-Hadith* [Sweet Conversations in the Modern History of Aleppo], carries the story until his present in prewar Aleppo. The manuscript's current location is unknown.

[35] See Hobsbawn, *Nations and Nationalism since 1780: Programme, Myth, Reality* (Cambridge: Canto, 1990).

the logic of the nation itself. In the paper's various discussions of the progress of the King-Crane Commission through Palestine, Syria, and Cilicia, in panegyrics to President Woodrow Wilson, and most clearly in essays entitled "Humanity and the Nation" or "the Free Man," the mimesis of the rhetoric of nationalist thought is drawn into relief, reinforcing the observation that Aleppo in 1919 had become an ideological battleground in which questions about a political unit's coterminality with a cultural homogeneity took center stage. The argument hinged on the *fact* of the victory of nation-states in the war, and more deeply on the conclusion that a rational system of nations represented the best of all possible modern worlds. *Halab's* articles turned these ideas into a syllogism. The major premise was the existence of nations; the minor, that the Arabs constituted a nation. However, the subsidiary argument that Aleppines were, and had always been, Arabs begged the very question the journal sought to answer.

The articles also shed light on the way in which concepts that enshrined the rights of the nation, Wilson's "right to national self-determination" in particular, were understood at an early moment in their postwar diffusion. The paper's unabashed enthusiasm for Woodrow Wilson derived from the symbolic value the American president had placed upon the war and his unreserved endorsement of the rights of the nation. The article that first acquainted Aleppines with him, entitled "Rajul al-duniya Wilson" [Wilson, Man of the World], attributed Wilson's pivotal importance to "the role he has played in the recent war which changed it into something of great importance to the future of nations and peoples everywhere." Wilson "the Great," the paper continued,

> made plain the way to prevent war: each nation must be under the control of itself and must not remain under the unjust control of others. . . . Universal brotherhood prevents wars, as does the liberation of people from tyranny. If it is true that Noah is the second father of humanity, because he freed them from the flood, then Wilson is their third father, because he freed them from the flood of continuing oppression.[36]

This article told Aleppines not only that they had been unjustly oppressed, but that the key to peace lay in the alignment of nation and political control. The parallel with Noah is more than a picturesque hyperbole: the Quran presents Noah as the first prophet of punishment and as a man who ushered in a new epoch. Wilson, from his ennoblement in the press, had given an almost supernatural sanction to the construction of the nation in his own period of human history.

[36] *Halab* (Aleppo), 20 March 1919.

Such rhetoric was calculated to persuade the readers of the historical necessity of the nation. In addition to arguing that correct social order, peace, and justice flow from the establishment of ethnically homogenous states, this rhetoric implies that the individual could not reach his potential in anything less than the nation. "When he comes to believe in the nationalist cause," read a passage in "Humanity and the Nation," "he then defends his own life, because he sees that the nation is the basis of his individual life and being. He sees that all of what is called happiness in the world is based on the person living in his native nation. He becomes committed to making his nation free from unnatural rule, that is, rule that is non-nationalist." In the same vein, the article referred to the naturalness of the nation: "the fire of nationalism is a natural fire whose flame is inextinguishable."[37] The nation, then, far from being a novel innovation, actually represented the realization of the true state of man's being. Consequently, opposing it, and dissenting from the modernist nationalist paradigm articulated in *Halab*'s pages, would have denied both nature and rationality.

The paper's efforts at persuasion, while conceptually tied into the whole nationalist enterprise, had a more immediate rationale in early 1919: the dispatch of a fact-finding board to the Middle East. *Halab* greeted the news of the appointment of the King-Crane Commission with enthusiasm.[38] Beneath a headline that read, "The joy of the nation is tremendous thanks to the blessed delegation," the paper explained that the allies "have dispatched a Commission to Syria to study the spirit of the land and learn the needs of the people and their souls' desire." Dismissing concerns that the commission's results would be disregarded as " pure rumor-mongering," it portrayed its purpose in the region as a type of test: "If the delegation sees in the land the things which are needed by nations for independence and if it sees true nationalism, cooperation and desire for progress . . . then it will not doubt that the nation is worthy of inde-

---

[37] Ibid., 13 January 1919.

[38] The progress of the peace talks in Paris had become stalled as Lloyd George and Clemenceau locked horns over the settlement of conflicting British and French claims on the Middle East. Wilson, fearing that the conflict would pit Britain's ally, Faysal, against the small French presence in the region, proposed that a commission be sent to gauge local opinion in the contested areas, primarily inland Syria and Palestine. French and British diplomats bowed to Wilson because of the president's unparalleled prestige—though they objected, contending that public opinion did not exist in the region. France and Britain withdrew their delegates from the commission prior to its departure, signaling their support for the prewar arrangements of the Sykes-Picot agreement. However, the American commissioners—Charles Crane, a friend of President Wilson and a millionaire contributor to the Democratic Party whose family had made its money manufacturing toilet bowls, and Henry King, the president of Oberlin College—arrived in the region in June 1919. Longrigg, *Syria and Lebanon*, 89.

pendence and freedom. It will then gain all the blessings of freedom given by the nation and nationalism."[39] Subsequent articles outlined the measures the people of Syria in general and Aleppo in particular would need to take in order to meet such a challenge.

At the heart of this lesson plan lay the goal of teaching the people to speak a language of nations and nationalism intelligible in the intellectual framework that gripped the period. From the announcement of the commission's formation until its arrival in Aleppo, the paper spilled a great deal of ink to teach its audience this language. On its pages, the aspects of the imagined community were spelled out and reiterated in great detail for the readers. The history of the Arab revolt ranks among the earliest efforts in this regard; it appeared in the paper alongside the announcement of the formation of the commission itself, and it created a unified narrative of the war years that the people with whom the delegation spoke could reproduce for the commission. Similarly, articles such as "The United Country" (25 April 1919) introduced the even newer concept of the "natural boundaries of Syria," which figured prominently in the pseudo-populist rhetoric that greeted the members of the commission.

When the commission arrived in Palestine in June, *Halab* reprinted its standard questionnaire as it appeared in a Palestinian paper. This questionnaire asked the locals about the kind of government they wanted and whom they wished for their leaders. Alongside the questions, *Halab* published the *correct* answers. As the commission progressed through Palestine to Beirut and then Damascus, *Halab's* prescriptive efforts intensified, as did the official efforts of imposing ideological control on the local population. An article unabashedly entitled "Kayfiyyat istifta' al-wafd al-duwwali" [What to Tell the International Delegation] proved the most salient and explicit example of this effort. "The most important thing we can do in these times," it told its readers, "is follow the progress of the international delegation so that we can know how they gather together the opinions of the people . . . and then we can leave an impression on their consciences." The article explained that the commission had interviewed various notables, learned men, journalists, and members of religious and cultural organizations. During the interviews that would take place in Aleppo, the paper demanded, "we must work to be an unbroken chain of opinions and viewpoints." It is incumbent upon us, the sons of this land, to bring together [all of those the commission will interview] and inform them of the unity of beliefs and shared opinions. We must convince this group not to present the members of the committee with anything other than a single opinion."[40] Thus, by the time the commission

[39] *Halab* (Aleppo), 21 April 1919.
[40] Ibid., 23 June 1919.

arrived in Aleppo from Hama by train on 17 July 1919, Aleppines knew what they were supposed to say and how to say it before the first question was asked.[41]

"What is the ratio of Muslims to non-Muslims in Aleppo?" King and Crane asked the mayor of Aleppo, Ihsan al-Jabiri, in interview published in the 21 July 1919 edition of *Halab*. Stipulating that Jews and Christians made up three-tenths of the population and had representation according to these numbers, he moved quickly to assert that what the people of Aleppo wanted was in complete agreement with the program of the Syrian National Congress.[42] The Americans received a similar response when they questioned the representative of the Muslim women of Aleppo, the daughter of the late Jâbirî zâde Nafi' Pasha, Aleppo's senior delegate to the prewar Ottoman Parliament, and Ihsan's niece, Shukriyya al-Jabiri:

> *Question:* Are you representatives of the women of Aleppo?
>
> *Answer:* Yes. [Shukriyya then presented the chairman with a written statement.]
>
> *Question:* Are you aware of the activities of the women in Beirut and Damascus?
>
> *Answer:* Not at all!
>
> *Question:* Is this something [i.e., the written statement] you all want?

[41] Ibid., 18 July 1919. The day following the commission's arrival, *Halab* published the schedule of its planned meetings. In the early morning the commission members were to meet the administrative council, followed in half-hour time blocks by the qadi, the mufti, and leading 'ulama'. Delegations from the various non-Muslim religious communities of the city—Greek Catholic, and Protestant, Armenian, Syrian Catholic, and Chaldean—and, late in the afternoon, a group of Muslim women filled subsequent half-hour slots. The following day the commission received the mayor, the administrative council, notables, guildsmen, farmers, tribal shaykhs, sufis, and members of the Arab Club and its youth wing. Such a breakdown of society may represent an American comprehension of late-Ottoman social structure, possibly mediated by the commission's advisor, Howard Bliss, president of the American University of Beirut.

[42] The Syrian National Congress was a meeting of "delegates" from the cities of "Syria," which included several men from Aleppo. At a meeting held 15 June 1919, electors of the second degree from the last Ottoman election had met and chosen Sa'dallah al-Jabiri, the younger brother of the late Ottoman deputy, Jâbirî zâde Nafi' Pasha, Shaykh Riza Rifa'i, Muhammad effendi al-Mudarris (the son of Mudarris zâde Fuad), and two Christian delegates, Salim Janbart and Théodore al-Antaki, to represent Aleppo. Rural delegates included members of the large landholding families of Hananu, Kikhiya, Qudsi, and Mar'ashli. Meeting in Damascus, the delegates outlined a response to the King-Crane Commission that served as the basis for orthodox Syrian nationalism in the remainder of the interwar period. Animated by two concerns—first, that the region was slated for division according to the Sykes-Picot agreement, and second, that France would become the dominant power in some areas—the delegates articulated a series of resolutions only comprehensible in the dominant language of nationalism. The ten-part declaration that the congress issued (1 July 1919) embraced the Wilsonian definition of the postwar world. Khoury, *Urban Notables*, 88.

Answer: It is the only thing in our hearts and thus it is our only answer.

Question: Do you have political experience?

Answer: We do not. But our men have been oppressed and they work all the time to liberate the nation and we know this.[43]

On the following day, the delegation of notables, led by Murad effendi al-Jabiri, Shukriyya's uncle, met with the Americans and told them the same thing.[44] An arresting feature of the commission's visit to Aleppo is that despite the attempt to divide Aleppo along lines of civil society, one family, the Jabiris, both male and female, had arrogated to themselves much of the right to speak for Aleppo. The family's role in representing both the city and several *qadhas* at the Syrian Congress in Damascus and in the presence of the Americans signaled its ongoing dominance of local structures of authority. Allying themselves closely with Faysal, the Jabiri clan had successfully adapted the nationalist discourse deployed at the congress and in *Halab* to the "politics of notables" and then repackaged it for the Americans. In the end, it was as though the subaltern and middle classes of Aleppo could not be trusted to give the right answers.

Halab published some minor dissent from the position of the Jabiri clan on the part of the Greek Catholic and Maronite spokesmen and spokeswomen, who "demanded complete independence of Syria in her natural borders but also advocated for France's role as an assisting state" during their meeting with the commission. The same article revealed that some groups refused to voice their opinions: the Protestant delegation (representing primarily Syriac or Armenian converts who had taken refuge in Aleppo) and the Armenian delegation had demurred, "because we are guests in this country."[45] The memory of recent episodes of violence, like that of January 1919, had no doubt cowed this population into silence, and to have done otherwise might have been seen as an implicit expression of a belief that the refugees would not be able to return home. Underplayed in the press, this significant gap between the Muslim notability and the local powerful and business-oriented Greek Catholic community resembled a similar cleavage in antebellum Aleppo. It also represented a failure on the part of *Halab* to convey and confirm its version of the imagined community to all of its middle-class readers.

In the weeks following the King-Crane Commission's departure from the Middle East, *Halab's* tenor changed precipitously. The conciliatory and cooperative sentiments of the previous months, when the paper maintained that the world had recognized an Arab nation and had endowed it

[43] *al-Nahda* (The Awakening) (Aleppo), 24 July 1919.

[44] Fu'ad al-'Ayntabi with Najwa 'Uthman, *Halab fi mi't 'am* [One Hundred Years of Aleppo], 3 vols. (Aleppo: University of Aleppo Press, 1993), 2:203–204.

[45] *Halab* (Aleppo), 21 July 1919.

with the rights of all nations, gave way to desperation and an unremitting insistence not just on the legitimacy of the Arab government and the Faysali régime, but also on the existence of a "Syria" itself.[46] However, in a telling lacuna, *Halab*, whose articles reported in detail on events in Damascus, Beirut, and even Cairo, ignored the postarmistice undeclared war between reconstituted Ottoman forces and French and Armenian armies that were raging in the northern and western parts of the province of Aleppo, well within what Faysal's Arab nationalists had called "Syria's natural boundaries."[47]

The paper's fierce exposition of nationalist idealism was motivated by the growing consensus in Damascus that the Paris Peace Conference would not resolve in favor of Hashemite dominance of Syria, and from a realignment on the part of Faysal himself, who had grown distant from his British allies.[48] It came as no surprise to the paper's readers when the government in Damascus declared independence. When viewed from the West, this declaration claimed Syria's right to be fully independent and free from the mandate. Within Aleppo, however, a reader of the paper could easily have asked, independent from whom? Certainly the declaration could be characterized as a diplomatic tactic to preempt France's intention to exercise its "right" to a mandate. However, the paucity of attention paid to the conflict in the north shows that the declaration of independence also meant a formal separation from the Ottoman *Devlet-i Âliye*, the Sublime State, and from the Ottoman Sultan as well.

Word of the Syrian Congress's decision to declare independence and crown Faysal king of Syria reached the readers of *Halab* in the 18 March 1920 edition of the paper. "This is the day in which Syria is restored to the Arab community," began the lead article in the paper, "a community which possesses dignity . . . this is the day in which Syrians begin to move towards security, freedom, the recovery of strength and mastery; their guiding principle is the truth. Their motto is independence, unity and liberty." The subsequent paragraphs outlined the origins of the decision

---

[46] Before World War I, the term "Syria," a Latin word of classical origin, applied in late Ottoman parlance only to the province of Damascus, sometimes called Süriye Vilayeti. More commonly, it was known as Şam Vilayeti. In medieval Arabic geographies, there exists a region called Bilad al-Sham, the Land of Shem. For Aleppines, while they may have been in the Land of Shem, as defined by these geographers, it is highly unlikely that they ever identified as shami, "of Sham." Shami only meant Damascene, al-Asadi, 5:19. If proverbs can be considered evidence of commonly held beliefs, then for Aleppines, Damascenes, known in the local dialect as *shawwam*, were held in very low regard. See Yusuf Qushaqji, *al-Amthal al-shaʿbiyya al-Halabiyya* [Popular Aleppine Sayings], 2 vols. (Aleppo: Maronite Press, 1984).

[47] Zürcher, *Turkey*, 144; Ahmad, *Making*, 48.

[48] On the political transformation of Faysal upon his return from Paris see Khoury, *Damascus*, 89–91.

and recognized the central irony of the colonialist enterprise; namely, that while the definition and the imperative of the nation may proceed from the West, the West had little interest whatsoever in a universal realization of the national project in the non-West. "Rest assured," it continued, "that our dear allies, who certified our rights and told us that they would stick to their words . . . will want peace in the East. . . .There is no doubt that this promises the speedy advancement of the East and its further awakening." A few days later even this muted sarcasm gave way to a direct assault on what the paper saw as Western duplicity.

> Some of the covetous sons of the West have received news of the Eastern awak-enings with dissatisfaction and they are the very same ones who kept saying that such awakenings were necessary and supported them. . . . This East is awakened and does not lack support from those just men of the West who have raised their voices demanding that we "render unto Caesar that which is Caesar's."[49]

Under the banner headline of "That Blessed Day," the editors drew the boundaries of this new nation in greater detail. "Today is the day," the article began, "in which the nation is graced by the holy light of independence." Continuing with the motif of the new day, they wrote:

> Today the beloved Syria enters its new age; the age of freedom and independence; the age of happiness. . . . Today, Syria has announced to the heads of the [nations] assembled [at Versailles] that it [Syria] is a unified bloc from east to west, from the desert to the cities, from the north to the south. . . . Today the West and its sons see how the sons of Arab Syria have awakened to fulfill their nationalist aspirations and to recover their national honor. They will see this lofty spirit calling upon free nations to aid it. *They will see how Syria is unified and there is no difference between Muslims, Christians and Jews, rather all are Arab Syrians* demanding an independent life under the protection of the Arab national banner, streaming above this land for which they have sacrificed their blood and souls, and that they have taken with their own hands.[50]

Inasmuch as Faysal had sought remedies other than a unilateral declaration of independence, he had nevertheless become the " 'captive' of his [Arab] nationalist supporters,"[51] who honored him thus: "Syria has been brought together by its savior, Prince Faysal the Great, now crowned with the crown of a noble king. And Syria has become an independent kingdom liberated from the occupied enemy territory."[52]

---

[49] *Halab* (Aleppo), 25 March 1920.

[50] Ibid., 19 March 1920. Emphasis mine.

[51] Khoury, *Urban Notables*, 91.

[52] *Halab* (Aleppo), 19 March 1920. The phrase was itself part of the nomenclature of the British postwar government of the region, which they referred to as Occupied Enemy Territory Administration-Turkey (OETA-T).

The adoption of the phrase "occupied enemy territory" and the nonsectarian definition of Syrian citizenship consciously distanced the new entity, Syria, from Ottoman suzerainty and Muslim political dominance. Like the earlier historical "explanations" of Aleppo's true past as an Arab city in an Arab state, this declaration of independence also implied that basic political mechanisms in the city would be authorized by a European-style ethnicity rather than an Ottoman-style absolutism and a supraethnic caliphate. This new mechanism, while appealing to portions of Aleppine society, and clearly in line with elements of reform dating from the prewar revolutionary period, constituted an innovation in communal relations in the urban milieu. It would have had an uncomfortable presence in customary Aleppo as it signaled a division between "church and state" unprecedented in the city and is akin to the use of the rallying cry "religion is to God and the nation is to the people."[53]

Advocating socially transformative (though in the idiom of modernity, emancipatory) ideas like sectarian equality may have undermined the credibility of the paper with a traditionally minded audience, nonetheless, it still could have reflected the view of its modern readers. The willful obliviousness that gripped the paper in its drive to ignore what was becoming a viable opposition both to the imperialist drive of France to carve out a presence for itself in the region and to Faysal's attempt to create a nationalist, Arab state doubtless undermined its credibility as a "news" paper even with a sympathetic audience. Word of the conflict in the North came to Aleppo with successive waves of Christian refugees. News of the battles reached as far away as America within days of arriving in the city. Alongside an announcement of a potential strike by elevator operators and doormen, and below an article on the release of Irish volunteers from British prisons, a page one *New York Times* headline of 15 April 1920 exclaimed: "Americans Besieged in Two Turkish Towns; Their Flag Defied; French Move to Rescue." While the *Times* editors focused on the American element of the story, it certainly shows that information traveled regularly and with ease across the short distance from the front lines to Aleppo. Yet on the day information about the siege of the American compound in ʿAyntab reached the city, *Halab* chose to lead the edition with an exposition of postwar instability in Germany. The edition also contains a rare glimpse of Mustafa Kemal (later Atatürk), though the statement merely makes mention of his dismissal as inspector general by the Allied-controlled Ottoman government in Istanbul and the demand that he break off relations with a shadowy "nationalist movement."[54] No further references to this movement nor to Mustafa Kemal appeared in

---

[53] See Gelvin's discussion of the origins of this phrase, *Divided*, 181–186.
[54] *Halab* (Aleppo), 8 April 1920.

the paper in the additional three months during which it was still under the control of the Arab government. Only a strict censorship regime can account for the lack of coverage of the ongoing conflict in the North.

The Ottoman Anatolian resistance taking shape in the province of Aleppo's northern reaches presented itself as not only a military movement bent on the expulsion of Westerners and the suppression of their Christian allies, but also a drive to reestablish the Ottoman Empire and everything that it encompassed. The French may have posed the most immediate threat to the Hashemite dominance of the fledgling Arab state of Syria, though in the fiction of the mandatory system imposed by the League of Nations something like Syria would not necessarily be extinguished. The movement in Anatolia, in contrast, threatened to rob the nascent Syrian state—as it was built on the notion of sectarian equality and a linguistic collectivity's sovereignty—of its very being. If such a movement were successful in attaining its stated goal, no legitimacy whatsoever would adhere to this self-consciously ethnic nation-state. The conflict presented Aleppines with a possible alternative to the Arab nationalist government of Damascus, one that rejected the nationalist logic advocated in the pages of *Halab*. The decision to suppress information about the conflict, even an unwillingness to contrast the Arab government with the anti-imperialist Ottoman movement in Anatolia, is a tacit recognition of the extraordinary symbolic and actual power that movement had in Aleppo and other places that were considered Arab even at this early time.

The 152nd edition of *Halab* would prove to be the last one published while Faysal sat on the throne of Syria. A forlorn passage concludes this final day's front-page article and stands in stark contrast to Fathallah Qastun's sentiments a decade earlier:

> This is the new spirit of politics in the affairs of the Eastern peoples [a realization that the policies of the allies were imperialist in nature] and there is no doubt that they will win their rights and prove victorious against them; if they are committed to the idea of freedom they will become stronger than their enemies, those with the old spirit, because [their power] is based upon lies and is as fragile as if it were made from the thread of a spider's web.[55]

After a three-week hiatus that followed the relatively uneventful French occupation of the city on 23 July,[56] the paper resumed publication under

---

[55] *Halab* (Aleppo), 12 July 1920.

[56] Unlike the occupation of Damascus, which was preceded by a violent encounter between French, French colonial, and Arab troops, in the Battle of Maysalun, French troops were merely transferred from the cease-fire line in Cilicia to the precincts of Aleppo. While the countryside around Aleppo was far from quiet, "They [the French Troops] were received

new editors with the announcement of martial law in the city (August 4). Its new editors retooled this porte-parole of a Damascus-centered Arab nationalist ideology as a more traditional official gazette for the newly created and smaller state of Aleppo. Energetic front-page editorials gave way to dry renderings of administrative codes and official French proclamations.

In its brief lifetime, *Halab* had conditioned the reading class of Aleppo to an explanation of the Arab Revolt; more important, it situated cosmopolitan Aleppo—the city and its citizens—within the boundaries of an imagined Arab Nation. To facilitate this process, the paper adopted a didactic stance vis-à-vis its readers. At the core of this curriculum stood the need to teach Aleppines the postwar idiom of power: liberal nationalism, an idiom that would serve as the lingua franca of a new and thoroughly modern world order. As such, *Halab's* editors imported the order's programmatic foundations. Establishing a definition of self was a fundamental feature of the lesson plan; this definition arose primarily from the identification and vilification of an "other," in this case the "Turk." The definition also hinged on the use of a language—Arabic—as the definitive characteristic of the citizen in this state. By centering sovereignty on questions of ethnicity, "race," or language, the paper decentered the role of religion; by adopting a laicist definition of the Arab, the paper equated modernity with nonsectarianism. It insisted upon the equality of the customarily subordinate, though tolerated, Jews and Christians of Aleppo with the Muslim ruling group; not only was this something required by the Western victors of the war, it was demanded by the logic of nationalism itself. In so doing the papers underlying nationalist ideology made the persistence of the city's cosmopolitanism improbable, condemning Aleppo to second-class status behind the new capital of Syria, Damascus.

A dominant group rarely sees the broadening of rights as an edifying process. Rather than an act of awarding equality, it is often interpreted, as shown in the subsequent chapter, as humiliation and a diminishing of status, and it is often seen as theft.[57] The prescriptions that *Halab* advocated were not universally accepted in Aleppo or in the remainder of the post-Ottoman Eastern Mediterranean, for that matter, and may have seemed hollow to many. Throughout the period, a dissent from national-

---

with outward calm, and in places with expressions of welcome of which by no means all were insincere," Longrigg, *Syria and Lebanon*, 104; Gelvin, *Divided*, 135.

[57] An instructive analogy is the "Andalus syndrome," a sense of loss experienced by Muslims in postindependence India. Sudhir Kakar concludes, "for many sensitive members of the [Muslim] community—including some of its writers, scholars, and artists—this loss of Muslim power and glory is explicitly mourned." *The Colors of Violence: Cultural Identities, Religion, and Conflict* (Chicago: University of Chicago Press, 1996), 130.

ism and its corollaries of ethnic solidarity and sectarian equality emerged in the region, which insisted on speaking in an idiom less alien but still modern, and one that echoes in contemporary Islamists discourse. The choice of many to continue speaking in this idiom proves that *Halab* and other discursive nationalist efforts failed to accomplish their most basic goal to obliterate divergent visions of the past as a guide for the future. While the paper may not have succeeded in convincing all the city's readers, it nevertheless signaled the permanence in the city's public discourse of a Western and modernist nationalist alternative. The ambivalence toward nationalism evidenced in the counteridioms—as they often derived their vocabulary and concepts from it—could only partially reject the ideology as a consonant referent; this peripheral vernacular of nationalism had become an undeniable part of the modernity of the city's architectures of community.

SIX

The Persistence of Empire at the Moment of Its Collapse: Ottoman-Islamic Identity and "New Men" Rebels

Although the Ottoman Empire had reached an armistice with the Allies in October 1918, ending World War I in the Middle East, civil wars, communal violence, and large-scale brigandage continued unabated throughout Anatolia and northern Syria. Perhaps the most sanguinary of these conflicts—now remembered as the Greco-Turkish War—began after the formal conclusion of hostilities, when the army of the kingdom of Greece invaded western Anatolia. This war, which raged throughout much of 1921–1922, had been launched to fulfill a Greek nationalist dream of establishing a trans-Aegean Hellenic state. While the Greek Army enjoyed some early success, they were defeated by troops under the command of Mustafa Kemal Pasha and Ismet Pasha (Inönü) and forced to retreat to the coast.

Mustafa Kemal, later known as Atatürk, was one of the few Ottoman bureaucrat-officers to emerge from World War I with his reputation intact, largely because of his inspired leadership at the Battle of Gallipoli (1915). Along with other middle- and high-ranking members of the CUP, he rejected the Ottoman surrender of 1918 as well as the treaties that limited Ottoman sovereignty or dissected the country. In addition to their victory against the Greeks, this group of officers had also successfully coordinated resistance to the French occupation of Anatolia and had quashed an attempt to establish an Armenian state in eastern Anatolia. Official Turkish history and many Western historians of the Middle East collapse these episodes into the formative moments of the emergence of national state, the Republic of Turkey. The driving of the Greek a modern,army into the sea and the burning of Izmir in September 1922 is but the culminating event in this purely "Turkish" war for independence.

As these forces fought back the Greek advances, feelings ran high several hundred kilometers away in Aleppo, now, at least on paper, in another country, called "Syria," which the Allied victors of the war had placed under French colonial occupation. Many in Aleppo's Muslim community had celebrated the capture of Izmir with exuberant and triumphant prayer meetings in local mosques.[1] Such enthusiasm was not confined to Aleppo but was shared by the inhabitants of Damascus and Beirut as well. Committees in Beirut, for example, collected some £tqs. 10,000 for the troops fighting in Anatolia; and the Mufti of Damascus had read from his pulpit in the Umayyad Mosque a telegram from Mustafa Kemal confirming the conquest of Izmir and the defeat of the Greek Army. In the telegram the pasha asked the mufti to lead prayers of thanksgiving for the deliverance of the Muslims.[2]

The joy at the victory over the Greeks befuddled foreign observers and struck them as somehow mercurial. The British consul in Aleppo concluded, "the Turkish successes have made manifest the pro-Turk feelings of the Moslem populations. At the time of the Armistice this population pretended to be pro-Arab to escape the consequences of defeat. It subsequently became Syrian and has now come out as pro-Turk."[3] A few months later, American Consul Jackson, a resident of Aleppo for nearly fourteen years who had just taken up his post at the time of the Revolution of 1908, telegraphed the U.S. high commissioner in Istanbul asking for instructions if the victorious forces, fresh from their triumph in the west, were to turn south and try to capture the city. He noted, "if a serious attempt should be made to take Aleppo the forces at hand would be unable to prevent it. Local Turkish people boast Aleppo shall suffer the same fate as Smyrna [Izmir]. As this city has great stores [of] supplies sorely needed by the Turks, the project appears to be most logical."[4] The consul speculated that if these forces were to attack from the north, they would be aided by local irregulars and "thousands of the Mohammedan [*sic*] residents of the city."[5]

The attack never came. Still, the observations in these distraught dispatches call into question the utility of the modern vocabulary of nationalism, ethnicity, and race employed by these Westerners and since imposed on the region by colonial discourse and contemporary historians; likewise, the larger historical context suggests the need for a careful reconsideration of the use or even the relevance of ethnic or national designations like "Arab," "Syrian," and "Turk" in the immediate postwar period altogether. The patronizing sneer implicit in the British consul's comment obscures a situation in which the terms of his analysis proved insufficient; the conflation of Turks with Muslims in the American's description shows that such terms were not clear even in the minds of those using them.

[1] PRO FO 371/7848 E10963/274/89 Morgan (Aleppo) to Secretary of State, 27 September 1922.

[2] Ibid., Palmer (Damascus) to Secretary of State, 23 September 1922.

[3] Ibid., Morgan (Aleppo) to Secretary of State, 27 September 1922.

[4] USNA II 867.4016/771 Jackson (Aleppo) to Gray (Istanbul), 3 December 1922.

[5] USNA II 867.4016/809 Jackson (Aleppo) to Secretary of State, 4 December 1922.

Nevertheless, where these consuls may have been convinced that the behavior of their hosts was erratic, when viewed through the lens of patterns of authority, class distinction, legitimacy, and religious prerogative of prewar society, this seemingly capricious shifting of allegiances reappears as pragmatic and thoroughly consistent. More important, when decoded, these dispatches convey the sense that many in the Eastern Mediterranean continued to adhere to an imagined *Ottoman-Islamic* community formed in the prewar and in some cases prerevolutionary periods, and although most of the institutional structures buttressing it were no longer present, persisted in conceiving of this community as a palpable and vital presence in their lives. Such a persistence subverted colonial and local efforts to impose alternative national imaginings upon the region's inhabitants.

This behavior acquires further meaning when juxtaposed with the intense efforts mounted by the Hashemite allies of Great Britain—Faysal and his associates—who tried over the course of the nineteen months they controlled Aleppo to incorporate it as an Arab city into an Arab Syria. This Arab Syrian identity hinged upon a *modern* definition of the self and the citizen, where the seemingly rational concept of race and prosaic concerns like spoken language preference took precedence over religion, family, and rank. To this end, as seen in the previous chapter, they sought to impose an "official" Arab nationalism on the city through the establishment of Arab Clubs and with the control of the editorial content of several Arabic-language newspapers, including *Halab*. Ultimately, *Halab* represented only one side of a multifaceted dispute about Aleppo's role in the emerging postwar order. The argument it presented—the style in which it imagined Aleppo—derived from the contention that the city had always been Arab and thus should be a part of the realm of Faysal and his Arab Kingdom. However, such a contention assumed that the war had established certain incontrovertible "facts on the ground." The most important of these facts was that the conflict had ended and that Britain, France, and the Arabs of the Hijaz had won. Consequently, the victors held legitimate authority. *Halab* was used in part to assure the people of Aleppo and elsewhere of the facts of this victory. That such persuasion was necessary suggests the absence of a shared consensus. The polemical and didactic structure of *Halab* further confirms the existence of other vital, simultaneous arguments antithetical to its own ideology. The most fundamental of these counterarguments implied the rejection of the view that the well-established patterns of legitimacy, authority, and identity that bound all strata into the late Ottoman system had been made irrelevant at the stroke of a European diplomat's pen or by the fiat of a newly minted monarch. As James Gelvin shows in his detailed study of Damascene urban politics during the brief period Faysal ruled Syria, "By privileging 'Arab nationalism,' historians are privileging a select group of intellectuals and activists, political associations, and institutions that did not necessarily represent the aspirations of a majority of those involved in nationalist politics, much less a majority of Syrians."[6]

For those now labeled Syrians by the Arab nationalists and the European diplomat-Orientalists advising the Powers in Paris—and indeed many of whom would have found such a term nonsensical if not insulting—the ramifications of the Revolution of 1908, the Great War, the Arab Kingdom, and the French occupation had alienated them from the certitude of late Ottoman society. Though under great strain, the late Ottoman system had given each person a place by virtue of social rank, gender, and religion. The Revolution of 1908 had begun to alter that certainty. But it remained a *knowable* structure. At that moment, roughly 1918–1924, that structure seemed to have collapsed altogether under the weight of military defeat and foreign occupation.

This chapter follows three historical threads that began in the revolutionary period to interpret the broader meaning of this collapse and how it affected the architectures of community in Aleppo and by extension other Eastern Mediterranean cities: (1) the role of Islam—as both a cultural practice and historically contingent component of political theory—within larger postwar discussions of citizenship and social order; (2) efforts by post-Tanzimat middle-class Muslim bureaucrat-intellectuals, officers, and educators, the empire's "New Men," to resist European domination with political mobilization and violent organized rebellion in the hopes of rebuilding society in a way consistent with their conceptions of modernity *and* Muslim political preeminence; and (3) the local notability's continued infiltration of the public sphere in an effort to regain or retain local hegemony and co-opt opponents of its rule. Methodologically, the style of revolutionary politics that brought the non-Muslim middle-class into view did not do likewise for the Muslim wing of that class. However, after the war, imperial governments inimical to prewar styles of Ottoman-Islamic forms of dominance challenged the sense of self and corporate identity of Muslim members of that class to such a degree that their understanding of what being modern meant at the time comes more easily to light. What also emerges is the conclusion that ideas about ethnicity and interclass communal solidarity and conceptions of subordination that stood at the margins of middle-class discourse had moved to the heart of conflict in the city.

The resilience of these modern Ottoman "New Men," who had come of age in the prewar period, and who could turn to a repertoire of organizational techniques, styles, and genres of urban politics perfected in the late Ottoman period, reveals the complex nature of the city's politics in

---

[6] Gelvin, *Divided*, 143.

the years after the war. In the face of tremendous upheaval, this class of bureaucrats, officers, and white-collar professionals, at times in cooperation with and at other in competition against the city's elite, employed tools of popular mobilization, class solidarity, and prestige as representatives of a legitimate order to confront the foreign occupation. As the "New Men" of the late Ottoman period resisted the postwar European presence in their midst through the assertion of the civilized nature of antebellum society, many of their Christian neighbors, some of whom had been their most fervent allies in the prewar period, imagined themselves as having attained a new level of "true civilization" with the occupation/liberation of their city by the French and the departure of Faysal in 1920. This critical cleavage in the multiplicity of responses to colonialism and the simultaneity of imperial allegiances in populations that had tended to be much more uniform in the past requires disaggregating responses to both the war and the rapidly shifting political terrain of the postwar period along class and communal lines rather than ethnic or allegedly nationalist.

THE OTTOMAN-ANATOLIAN RESISTANCE AND THE ALEPPINE REACTION

As the Arab Kingdom of Faysal began to collapse in late 1919, in the face of both French demands that Britain live up to its wartime promises and local opposition, an article carried in the only newspaper to survive from the time of revolution, *al-Taqaddum*, indicated the contours of the possible alternative vision many could have had of Aleppo's position in the postwar Middle East. In this vision, the war did not constitute a rupture or a break with the past; the Ottoman Empire as a political entity had never ceased to exist, Aleppo had never stopped being a part of it, and the foreign occupation was merely temporary. As Ottoman officers and bureaucrats organized resistance to European forces and their local Christian allies in eastern and central Anatolia—a region much more closely linked to Aleppo historically than Damascus or Beirut—their stunning victories won them additional prestige and legitimacy. With their mounting success, the possible reestablishment of the status quo ante became more real.

Al-Taqaddum published a communiqué issued by a group of Ottoman soldiers, bureaucrats, and intellectuals at a meeting in the central Anatolian town of Sivas. The Sivas Conference, as this meeting has come to be known, sought to rally Ottoman society to resist the terms of the postwar peace settlements. It was a follow-up to an earlier meeting between Mustafa Kemal Pasha and Kâzım Pasha (Karabekir), an eastern Anatolian warlord in Erzerum. The earlier meeting had initiated the creation of a superstructure connecting various local ad hoc administrative military committees both in Allied-occupied and unoccupied parts of the empire. The Sivas Conference imbued the rather amorphous movement with an ideological dimension. The document it issued, the *Misâk-ı Millî*, translated today as the *National Pact*, is considered by modern Turks as the foundational document of the Republic of Turkey. However, in the context of 1919, describing the pact as a "Turkish" nationalist document belies its actual text and the intent of many of its framers. An exclusively nationalist reading of this document is quite simply anachronistic.[7]

Al-Taqaddum carried an edited Arabic version of the document on its front page on 17 October 1919, proving that readers in Aleppo learned of the growing resistance to the humiliating cease-fire of the previous year that had brought World War I to a close from its very beginning. In contrast to the political discourse suffusing the Arab Kingdom, the discursive terms that permeated this resistance were not of an apposite Turkish nation, but rather an Islamic *umma*,[8] conceived as being at least equal to— or superior to—the West. This intriguing hybridization has troubled historians, who have merely attributed it to the cynical motives of unreconstructed Unionists.[9] Regardless of motives, that the participants of the Sivas Conference chose to identify on the basis of religious distinction as the organizing principle their resistance points to the persistence of late Ottoman concepts of civilization and social equilibrium in the region after the Allied victory. Far from being a superannuated concept, Islam itself thus remained the most palpable and reliable social and political con-

---

[7] *Millî* (Arabic) or *Millî* (Ottoman Turkish) did not gain currency as "national" in the sense of an ethnic nation until the Kemalist period. In 1919 it could have meant "popular" or, in view of the intensely sectarian tone of the document, "communal" pact.

[8] The term *umma* is usually translated as "nation." However, it is important to recall that the "umma" in its meaning as the "community of Muslims" represents something much more than a nation, especially as the nation was defined in the late nineteenth century. The most basic difference between the two concepts concerns their respective linearity. The umma had the potential to possess no earthly limitations; the nation, conversely, had immutable and absolute boundaries. Internal limitations or hierarchies of ethnicity had little or no meaning in the nonethnic umma.

[9] See Ahmad, *Making*, 48: "The nationalists took great pains to counter this religious propaganda for they understood the powerful influence of Islam in Turkish society. Their task became easier when Istanbul was occupied by Anglo-French forces and they could describe the sultan-caliph as the captive of Christian powers waiting to be liberated. The nationalists understood the value of Islamic discourse as the means of providing maximum unity among a mixed population of Circassians, Lazes, Arabs, Kurds and Turks, communities they wanted to mobilise for their own cause. The terms they used to describe 'nation,' 'national,' and 'nationalism' were derived from millet, a word of Arabic origin which had come to mean a religious community in Turkish usage. Had the national movement desired to project a secular image, it could have easily adopted terms derived from *vatan* meaning fatherland or patria."

struct. Significantly, the Sivas Declaration could also translate this construct into a definition of nation intelligible in terms of the modernist language of nationalism, suggesting that for some the two concepts were not mutually exclusive.

The proposed national boundaries on the maps being prepared in Versailles sought to follow "scientifically" determined linguistic and "racial" lines drawn by Orientalists like Sykes in the prewar period. To some Muslims, however, the way the Allies seemed intent on dividing up the Ottoman Empire could just as easily appear as a division along religious lines. These religious lines had delineated new states for Armenian and Greek Orthodox Christians, who often spoke the same languages as their Muslim neighbors and were perhaps even indistinct from them "culturally" as well. In these new states, resident Muslims would constitute minorities and be divorced from legal structures that guaranteed their social and legal superiority. Zionist plans for Palestine struck a similar chord. Yet the mapmakers planned to separate the Arabic-speaking Muslims of the Eastern Mediterranean from the Muslim communities of Anatolia, Mesopotamia, and Egypt.[10]

The Sivas Declaration challenged such divisions and advocated an alternative community. According to "article one," as it appeared in Aleppo: "the Ottoman lands which remained within our boundaries the day of the armistice between the Ottoman state and the Allies . . . being regions in which the majority of the people are Muslim, it is impossible to separate them or divide them from the Ottoman community (al-jami'a al-'uthmaniyya)."[11] This unambiguous rejection of the proposed terms of settlement under consideration at Versailles denied the nation-state paradigm, which predicated the Wilsonian rhetoric of those discussions. Rather than being conceived on a linguistic or ethnic basis, such a community, according to article 5, constituted a "national whole" based upon "historical, ancient, religious and geographical rights."[12] The congress participants committed their lives and honor to defending this "national whole" and to resisting all occupations or invasions of it, especially those intent on creating independent Greek or Armenian states, and to defending the position of the institution of the Caliphate-Sultanate. The declaration's last article left no doubt as to the collectivity upon which sovereignty was based: in the words of the document, non-Muslims formed a subordinate group in soci-

---

[10] Egypt was still nominally part of the Ottoman Empire until the opening days of World War I.

[11] al-Taqaddum (Aleppo), 17 October 1919. The original text of the document included the additional line not present in the Aleppo version, "but the fate of the territories inhabited by an Arab majority which [are] under foreign occupation should be determined by plebiscite." See Zürcher, Turkey, 144.

[12] al-Taqaddum (Aleppo), 17 October 1919.

ety, who possessed—in a textual rendering of *Göçek's Dilemma*—"equality" as long as they "did not prejudice our [Muslim] political sovereignty or social equilibrium [*al-muwazana al-ijtimaʿiyya*]."[13]

Concern about this final point may have motivated the editors of *al-Taqaddum* to carry the declaration. The paper had become the organ of the Greek-Catholic community, and French agents had recently resumed the paper's subsidy.[14] Just as non-Muslims in Aleppo openly worried about the declaration, some Muslims were heartened by it. While the terms of the declaration excluded Aleppo, as it lay on the wrong side of the cease-fire line, one can surmise that this was a temporary political and military expedient. The only territorial features in the document consisted of opposition to the establishment of an Armenian state in the "six provinces" (i.e., the six Anatolian Ottoman provinces in which Armenians represented a plurality).[15] It did not draw the physical boundaries of a national homeland; rather, it left such a question open to interpretation and kept "the door open for the expression of Arab will in favor of cooperation with the Anatolian movement."[16]

The conference unified the Anatolian resistance into a coherent military movement by forming the Society for the Defense of Rights in Anatolia and Rumelia.[17] Following the British withdrawal from Aleppo in fall of 1919, the existence of an Aleppo chapter of the society became evident, along with loosely formed irregular military bands.[18] Putting aside prewar differences, a coalition of notables, former members of the CUP, and middle-class intellectuals formed Aleppo's branch of the society. Consistent with the other branches, and in a telling and marked departure from the spirit of intersectarian comity that distinguished the public discourse of *Halab*, it had no Christian or Jewish members. Its emergence signaled its members' recognition of the legitimacy of the emerging Ottoman-Anatolian resistance, but also a residual dissatisfaction with Faysal, whom many

---

[13] Ibid.

[14] PRO FO 861/68 "Report on Situation at Aleppo," 9 September 1920. The report claimed that the French had begun to provide subventions to several papers in the city, the largest subsidy of £40 going to *al-Taqaddum*.

[15] These provinces—Van, Bitlis, Diyarbekir, Elazığ, Sivas, and Erzerum—were slated to join the newly founded Republic of Armenia.

[16] Kayalı, *Arabs and Young Turks*, 204.

[17] In Ottoman Turkish, Anadolu ve Rumeli Müdafaa-i Hukûk Cemiyeti; in Arabic, Jamiʿ-iyyat al-difaʿ ʿan huquq al-Rumayli wa al-Anadul.

[18] Jamil Ibrahim-Pasha, *Nidal al-ahrar fi sabil al-istiqlal* [Struggle of the Freeborn on the Path of Independence] (Aleppo: Dad Publishing, 1959), 20; Shaw and Shaw, 2: 340; PRO FO 371/3657 E1922/512/58 General Headquarters (Egypt) to Director of Military Intelligence (Istanbul), 1 January 1919, describes a situation in which one General Nihat Pasha was organizing the local population throughout the province of Aleppo into an armed force called the "Islamic Union."

in Aleppo had concluded was more concerned with foreign interests than with upholding their authority. Several of the notables supporting the movement, or their family members, had lost their positions in a purge of the Aleppine bureaucracy in 1919 that had been prompted by the aforementioned massacre of Armenian refugees. Others, like Shaykh Rifaʿi, had been jailed for failing to stop the violence.[19] Consequently, many of the members of the old social classes were ill disposed toward Faysal.[20] However, their association with the movement was based on something more than just animosity toward the Hashemites: support for the Ottoman Anatolian resistance, as seen from the text of the Sivas Declaration, carried with it a profound desire to cleanse the Ottoman Empire of alien forces; it stood for the social, religious, and territorial integrity of the Ottoman state and the institutions it articulated, primarily the sultan-caliphate; and it called for the unmitigated Muslim sovereignty of that state. In their actions, it is possible to identify a coalition of Aleppines who persisted in imagining themselves as members of a larger community, the conditions of membership being linked to dominate Ottoman high culture and the practice of Sunni Islam. Likewise, membership in this community was predicated upon their moral and legal superiority to the resident non-Muslims and foreign interlopers. Such support for the perpetuation of the empire manifested itself in other, more visible and public ways. The first Friday after the French occupation of Aleppo, prayers were said in the name of the Ottoman sultan. While, the French certainly preferred that Faysal's or his father Husayn's name be omitted from the *salat*, the recourse to that of Mehmed VI constituted an affirmation of the Ottoman sultan's position as Aleppo's "Commander of the Faithful."[21]

[19] MAE-CADN: Fonds Beyrouth, Petit Fonds Political et Adminastratif, carton 2372, Pilley (Aleppo) to Georges Picot, 22 May 1919.

[20] James Gelvin has argued that the formation of such associations reflect the breakdown of Aleppines into Anatolia-oriented partisans of Mustafa Kemal—whom he calls Kemalists—on one hand, and Damascene-oriented supporters of Faysal on the other. Gelvin, *Divided*, 131–132. The historic setting of 1919 does not warrant the use of the term Kemalist to describe this movement; rather, Mustafa Kemal in 1919–1921 merely numbered among the leading Ottoman officers committed to resurrecting the Ottoman state. British diplomats coined the word "Kemalists" in a pejorative sense, and as a way of distinguishing the Anatolian-based resistance from the captive Ottoman government in Allied-occupied Istanbul. For an example of this British overestimation of Kemal's influence, see PRO FO 371/5036 E83226/2/44 Derby (Paris) to Secretary of State (London), 14 July 1920: "Aleppo is divided into two factions, a Turkish party supporting Mustapha Kemal and a Syrian party supporting the Emir Feisul. Of these the Turkish party is gaining ground with the consequence that sympathy between Aleppo and Damascus is weakening." While Mustafa Kemal had become military commander of the bulk of the Anatolian forces by that time, he had never, unlike Faysal, claimed royal independent sovereignty but rather continued to fight as a representative of the sultan himself.

[21] PRO FO 371/5040 E13874/2/44. Fontana (Beirut) to Secretary of State, 23 October 1920.

Beneath the surface of this attitude ran a subterranean suspicion on the part of the Muslim elite, religious leaders and educators, and even portions of its middle class, that many of the current failures of the Ottoman Empire—why it collapsed so readily in the face of the Western Allies—could be laid at the very openness and intercommunal comity that had been hallmarks of the prewar period. A cautious parallel, and one that recognizes that there is no equivalent to European anti-Semitism in the Eastern Mediterranean at this time, can be drawn between the old-social-class suspicion of liberal, emancipatory reforms and the postrevolutionary attitudes of the elite of other ancien régimes. As Arno Mayer writes of the situation in Russia at roughly the same time,

> reputable members of the old ruling and governing elites now embraced a Manichean worldview, foisted the responsibility for the crisis of Russian civil and political society, and their own endangered standing in it, upon the Jews, who best lent themselves as being portrayed as the incarnation of evil. Protestants and Freemasons of their day, all the more so now that the opposition increasingly denounced the persecution of Jews as symptomatic of the ancien régime's depravity. Every accusation, traditional and new-fashioned, was fastened upon them: they were charged with being not only modernizers, strangers, and infidels, but also . . . westernizers, as well as master revolutionaries.[22]

This cross-identification of modernity, non-Muslims, and the multiple humiliations of Western imperialism had a considerable impact on how Christians and Jews were integrated, or were not as the case might be, into the politics of the interwar period.

The support for this revived Ottomanism in the late 1919 formation of Aleppo's Society for the Defense of Rights, which led the primary local opposition to the French occupation in the early 1920s, demands a reconsideration of the ideological and political positions of those who led and fought in these movements. The guerrilla bands that rallied around the Antiochian notable Subhi bey Barakat and the "New Man" bureaucrat-officer Ibrahim Hananu against the French occupation were linked inextricably to the revivified Ottoman movement in Anatolia itself. While the ideological tendencies of those involved in this resistance acquired a different, "nationalist" texture retrospectively in the 1930s, at this juncture, however, and especially before the Treaty of Lausanne (1923) and until the abolition of the caliphate (1924)[23] and the creation of a Turkish

---

[22] Mayer, *Furies*, 508.

[23] The abolition of the Caliphate by Atatürk in 1924 occasioned a great deal of distress in Aleppo. A few local imams inserted the name of King Husayn of Arabia, the father of Faysal, as *amir al-mu'minin*, leader of the faithful. The majority concluded that even though the Caliph had been expelled from Turkey, he was still the caliph. A compromise was reached to the effect that the question of the caliph would be held in abeyance until the

nationalist Turkey, the self-consciously Ottoman-Islamic movement emanating from Anatolia held sway in the Gray City. It seemed as well to vitiate the clear distinctions between some notables and the upper echelon of what was left of the Ottoman middle-class provincial bureaucracy.

Stylistically, the formation of these committees and the organization of armed resistance marked the *reemergence* of forms of solidarity, organization, and efficiency characteristic of the political activity of the city's modernizing middle class: the bureaucratic reforms, clubs, and political parties of the prewar period had established the blueprint for these groups and movements. Identifying Aleppo's committee as evidence of an "alternative but previously inchoate consciousness of 'national' community," as Gelvin does, beyond the inherently problematic assertion that nations are somehow organic and can have inchoate natures, reproduces the nationalist periodization and paradigm he himself seeks to revise and disregards the clear Ottoman-era precedents for the formation of such committees and paramilitary movements, as well as their ideological contours.[24] Far from reflecting the formation of a popular Syrian nationalism, the armed resistance and committees drew from the shared values and textures of identity of the prewar period, especially a corporate identification with the Ottoman state as protector of Islam and Muslim prerogative. As noted above, many Aleppine members had been affiliated with the CUP in the prewar period, and one can hardly attribute involvement in the Young Turk movement as evidence of Syrian nationalism, but rather a profound sense of entitlement and membership in a larger Ottoman bureaucratic and high cultural whole. These were the hard-core members of Ottoman officialdom in the city, the allies of Hüseyin Kâzım, and in particular those bereft of an honorific like zâde or pasha by their name; they drew status from their association with the modernization programs of the Ottoman state and recognized the very real threat that the colonial occupation represented to their careers and sense of self. While seeking a degree of local autonomy as the price of cooperation, the notables had yet to seek full-blown independence and joined them in this effort. The notables too brought to the table financial resources and their extensive networks of clients to serve as foot soldiers in the guerrilla forces or as the raw material of street protests and demonstrations; they drew a great deal of status and distinction through cultural and family ties to the Ottoman center and royal court, ties that would dissipate were they merely "Syrians." What drew these histori-

---

Muslim world expressed its will. It was then decided merely to include the phrase "commander of the faithful" without mentioning a specific man. USNA II 867.404/85 Buhrman (Aleppo) to Secretary of State (Washington), 14 March 1924.

[24] Gelvin, *Divided*, 288.

cally opposing groups together was a not just a shared enemy, but rather a commitment to the *reestablishment* of what they considered "social equilibrium," and a turning back of the clock. However, the desire to reinstate such a condition should not be seen as reactionary proto-Islamic fundamentalism by all of its participants, but rather again as a manifestation of *Göçek's Dilemma*. Quite simply, in their own appraisal, it had fallen to them to repair the damage to the empire by foreigners and non-Muslim minorities alike. As modern "New Men," they alone had the skills and acumen to return the Ottoman Empire to its proper path of modernization and attain the goal of "true civilization."

Shortly after organizing resistance at the meetings in Sivas and Erzerum, Ottoman forces coordinated with irregular forces in the northern reaches of the province of Aleppo to fight against French troops and their local allies. Resistance arose first in the cities of Marash, ʿAyntab, ʿUrfa, and Kilis, where, unlike in Aleppo proper, Allied occupation had begun shortly after the armistice. The French authorities had lumped these cities together with Adana into another anachronistic territorial construct along the lines of "Syria" and "Palestine" (both of ancient Roman provenance) into "Cilicia," a territorial designation more or less coterminous with the Crusade-era Kingdom of Lesser Armenia. Clearly, the medieval origins of the territory itself played into the contemporary French colonial obsession with "France's" historical relationship with the Levant, a relationship that the French claimed dated back to the Crusades.

Following the armistice on 31 October 1918, British troops occupied the region and then, by January 1919, French troops arrived in nearby Adana, which they made the capital of the new territorial construct of Cilicia. As part of their program to organize the region, the French began to replace Ottoman officials, whom they saw as opposing them at every turn, with French civil servants and Western-educated Armenians.[25] The French program could not have been more insulting or humiliating to local Muslims. Far from creating "sympathy . . . between France and Cilicia," as the anonymous author of the secret report had hoped, the brief and understudied French presence in the region proved to be an excessively bloody moment in the province of Aleppo's history. The state of war in the North was interpreted in some circles as a herald of the reestablishment of Ottoman suzerainty in the city. That the conflict devolved into one phrased almost entirely in a sectarian rhetoric could not help but color the comprehension of the conflict in the Gray City.

The early phases of the conflict consisted of guerrilla war against the French occupiers. How coordinated these forces actually were in this period is open to debate, but writing from the perspective of 1922, the Alep-

[25] Ibid.

pine annalist Tabbakh explicitly linked the violence in the region as part of the broader Ottoman-Anatolian movement. At the time of the Sivas Conference,

> The war was in full swing in Cilicia between them [the resistance] and the French state, it was growing even stronger in Marash, ʿAyntab and Kilis . . . but this struggle was not an organized conflict between states, because the indigenous forces only had guerrilla bands to make war with the large numbers of organized soldiers, and ʿAyntab remained under siege for eight months, and its people defended it, until they had nothing left in the way of arms or provision, . . . because of this the city of ʿAyntab is now called Gaziantep [ʿAyntab the warrior].[26]

By the end of 1920, Ottoman-Anatolian forces reached the city of ʿAyntab and started to engage the French and their Armenian allies. By the middle of January 1921, the French had withdrawn from ʿAyntab and redeployed the bulk of their forces 40 kilometers northwest of Aleppo, near Kilis. In the battle of ʿAyntab, French forces had been confronted for the first time by a corps of soldiers known as the *Yeşil Ordu* (Green Army), who distinguished their uniforms with the addition of bright green sleeves and called themselves *mücahid* or soldiers for the faith. Mambij then fell. Earlier that fall, Ottoman-Anatolian forces had taken Marash.[27] Antioch was under attack from within and Kilis surrounded. Thus, by the end of the April 1921, Aleppo was the only major city of the province not restored to Ottoman control. In mid-December 1920 placards had been posted in the city calling on the populace to expel the French or remain neutral and leave things to the resistance "who would make blood flow plentifully later."[28]

The capture/liberation of Aleppo by the resistance that had seemed a foregone conclusion in the early months of 1921 was postponed indefinitely in the wake of the Greek invasion of Anatolia that year. At that moment, the forces fighting an offensive war against the French in Cilicia found themselves on the defensive in western Anatolia. In the autumn of 1921 the French took advantage of the situation and sent Senator Henri Franklin-Bouillon to Ankara to negotiate a French retreat from Cilicia in exchange for a cessation of hostilities and military supplies. This separate peace facilitated an almost immediate recall of forces from the Cilicia front—allowing them to be moved to the other theater of operations;

---

[26] Tabbakh, 7:614–615. Gazi (Ottoman Turkish) and ghazi (Arabic) is a word that denotes a warrior for the faith.

[27] On the battle for Marash, see E. Stanley Kerr, *The Lions of Marash* (Albany: State University of New York Press, 1973).

[28] PRO FO 371/6543 E854/117/89 Fontana (Aleppo) to Secretary of State, 26 December 1920.

more important, it recognized the Ottoman-Anatolian conquests north of Aleppo. The negotiated settlement led the high commissioner for the now truncated French Mandate of Syria and Lebanon, General Henri Gouraud, to announce during a visit to Aleppo, "In virtue of the strong pact between the two nations you can rest absolutely certain that France would never withdraw from Aleppo."[29] Such a statement must have been cold comfort to those who had supported Faysal, or those who identified their own fate with the Ottoman-Anatolian resistance. However, organized infiltration, continued low-grade guerrilla warfare, and even the publication of a newspaper in Ottoman Turkish, *Şefak* [Evening Twilight],[30] encouraged irredentist thinking among both the notability and the now "ex-Ottoman" bureaucratic middle class.[31]

An emerging consensus in Ankara that the regions of Anatolia and Thrace occupied by forces under Mustafa Kemal's command represented defensible frontiers—and the international recognition of those frontiers—led what could from 1923 correctly be called Kemalists to embrace the new borders. With the Treaty of Lausanne (24 July 1923), the newly minted nation state of Turkey ceased to be the Ottoman Empire and temporarily renounced claims to the remainder of the province of Aleppo and the province of Mosul. Thus, the hope of incorporating Aleppo into the "old" political order dissolved in the face of a modern Turkish rejection of that order.[32]

[29] In PRO FO 371/6455 E9105/117/89 Morgan (Aleppo) to Secretary of State, 23 July 1921.

[30] *Şefak* began publication 7 April 1921. The lead article began, "Today for the first time for nearly two and a half years in the Syrian region a Turkish language newspaper is being published."

[31] A British observer noted with unreserved glee that "None of the Christian [dignitaries] formulated any objection to the [Ankara accord], though the Armenian and other prelates no doubt do not approve of it. A Moslem of Aleppo, by name Shakir Nimat el-Shabani an Arab who was once a Turkish official made a tactless speech in French expressing the joy of the Moslems of Aleppo at the conclusion of the agreement and going on to say that he, and other Moslems of the town, felt that Turkey was their first motherland and Syria their second and that Turkey owed her present existence to her army. . . . Perhaps General de Lamothe was disconcerted to find that after France had ceded part of Syria to Turkey there were yet elements in the unceded [*sic*] part who hankered after Turkey and publicly eulogized it instead of expressing unbounded and undivided loyalty to France. . . . The eulogy of Turkey by Syrian Moslems also runs counter to the French theory that all disloyalty to France on the part of Syrian Moslems is due to British and Arab intrigue, as even the most anti-British Frenchman can hardly accuse the British of inciting Moslems to declare themselves in favour of Turkey." PRO FO 371/6457 E13739/117/89 Morgan (Aleppo) to Curzon, 24 Novemeber 1921.

[32] While Turkey may have at that moment renounced claims to the region south of the line agreed to at Ankara in 1922, it continued through other means to try to acquire territory in the province of Aleppo. In the 1930s it successfully took control of the Sanjak of Alexandretta and renamed it Hatay. After the fall of France in 1940, Turkey made overtures to

RESURECTING THE EMPIRE: THE LAST OTTOMAN, IBRAHIM HANANU

Ibrahim Hananu, one of the more charismatic and intriguing figures to emerge from the morass of war and inhumanity in post–1918 Aleppo, was an Istanbul-educated member of a large landholding family. Hananu's political and military career, spanning roughly three decades from the first years of the century until the 1930s, is emblematic of the ambiguous and contingent comprehension of postwar realities in the province, the way in which the persistence of empire shaped the early postwar architectures of community in what became Syria, and how notables and middle-class Ottoman bureaucrat-officers made the transition to citizens of the empire's successor states. Much recent Syrian nationalist historiography considers Hananu's rebellion as but the first of a broader series of coordinated revolts, including the Great Revolt of 1925, against the French occupation of the emerging nation state of Syria. Prominent in this genre is Adham Jundi's problematic *History of the Syrian Revolts*. Written in 1960 at the time of unity with Egypt and the very apex of Pan-Arabism, it is rife with hyperbole and sanitized by the distortion and erasure of facts for the purpose of creating a "useable" nationalist history, and consequently it is a highly compromised source.[33] These works seek to present an early and centrally organized "Syrian" resistance to the French occupation. Several American and European historians who base their accounts of Hananu's revolt on Jundi tend also to draw it into this same construct.[34] In the end, the later apotheosis of Hananu as a premier Syrian nationalist fulfills the political needs of a later period rather than the realities of the 1920s and has no basis in historical fact.

A closer look at Hananu's biography, archival documentation, the oral histories of some of his fighters, and evidence that emerged at his trial for sedition in 1922 calls these accounts into question. Rather than being a "Syrian" rebellion, Hananu's revolt tied into the larger trans-Eastern Mediterranean resistance against European imperialism and the broader struggle to rebuild the Ottoman Empire. Until the last decade of his life, Hananu acted in a definitively modern Ottoman way by exhibiting loyalty to the state, subordinating his linguistic and familial identity, in his case

Britain suggesting that Turkey occupy northern Syria to safeguard airfields against Axis use. Instead, Britain invaded Syria in 1941. See Longrigg, *Syria*, 296–298. Since the conclusion of the second Gulf War (1990), Turkey has occupied parts of the former Ottoman province of Mosul; and since the U.S. invasion of 2003, Turkey has threatened to invade northern Iraq, currently under autonomous Kurdish control.

[33] Two of his other works, equally hagiographic, a history of "martyrs" in the Great War and a compendium of artists and poets, suggest that Jundi had identified a fertile market for his work.

[34] Examples include, Gelvin, *Divided*, 133–134, and Khoury, *Mandate*, 105–108.

Kurdish, to a membership in an empirewide bureaucratic and military order, and by rejecting any limitation on Muslim political sovereignty and social preeminence.

Born in Kafr Tukharim near Harim (1879), the young Ibrahim attended the local Qur'an school until his family sent him to the imperial high school in Aleppo; like Hüseyin Kâzım, he continued his studies in administration and education at the Mülkiye in Istanbul. Upon graduation he briefly taught at the military academy. While still a student in the mid-1890s, he joined the CUP. Shortly before the outbreak of World War I, he left Istanbul and served as mayor of a subprovince of the province of Diyarbakir in south-central Anatolia.[35] There is no evidence—either in contemporary archival sources or in Aleppine newspapers or journals— that Hananu had any relationship with Faysal prior to the British occupation of Aleppo, or that he ever joined al-Fatat, the secret Arab nationalist organization; rather, his education and professional trajectory place him squarely in the empire's middle management of bureaucrats and officers—a consummate "New Man."

Returning to Aleppo at the time of the British occupation and the Arab Kingdom, he was Harim's representative at the Syrian Congress of 1919 and briefly served as secretary to the governor of Aleppo, though he resigned both positions upon renouncing his seat in the congress, for reasons that remain unclear. However, his actions coincide precisely with the arrival of information about the Sivas Conference. Hananu took up residence at the family's farm near Harim and quickly organized a regional Committee for Defense.[36] This committee, which had both administrative and military functions, resembled other, similarly named postwar Ottoman committees.[37] Moreover, the fact that Hananu's organization predates other forms of military mobilization in Damascus but was simultaneous to the formation of similar bodies in Cilicia and the Upper-Euphrates leads to the conclusion that he modeled his activities on those movements and saw his committee as one of several that emerged in areas territorially adjacent. Further, Hananu's later reestablishment of local municipal councils and the installation of military bureaucrats in positions of leadership in the areas conquered from the French again emphasize

[35] *al-Nida'* (Aleppo), 23 November 1945, in al-ʿAyntabi, *100 Years of Aleppo*, 3:220–221. The article commemorates the tenth anniversary of the death of Hananu.

[36] Walid Muallim, *Suriyya*, 181.

[37] See, for example, Kerr's description of the formation of a Committee for Defense in Marash. "At midnight on 27 November 1919 a group of Turkish patriots gathered secretly at the home of Vezir-oghlu Mehmet to organize resistance to the French occupation. They elected a committee of eight, and the members took" an oath. Eventually subcommittees were formed and fighting squads made up of civilian volunteers and former officers and enlisted men from the Ottoman military. *Lions*, 67.

how he drew from a prewar repertoire of Ottoman military-bureaucratic administration. Finally, the organizational framework he established took shape at a time when the Arab government existed in the region. It was thus not officially sanctioned and had evidently been created in opposition to the Faysali government's administration, which Hananu most likely dismissed as collaborationist. While no evidence exists to show an explicit link between the Sivas Conference and Hananu's new administrative body, that both occurred at roughly the same time is an arresting coincidence in the very least. Hananu cooperated with Faysal only until what he considered a viable—and more legitimate—alternative presented itself. The Ottoman-Anatolian resistance constituted such an alternative.

Furthermore, upon resigning, Hananu apparently resumed his contacts with members of the CUP in Aleppo and in Anatolia.[38] Mustafâ Âsım, the prewar newspaper editor who had been commissioned a captain in the Ottoman Army during the war, numbered among his associates in the field.[39] In a similar vein, much of the support of the Committees for Defense in Anatolia came from men who shared Hananu's class, religious affiliation, and educational background.[40] Thus, when viewed from Damascus, as Syrian nationalist historians and others have done, Hananu's early career seems an uncanny anticipation of the fall of Faysal's Arab Kingdom to the French. Yet when viewed from Anatolia, or even from Aleppo, Hananu's actions appear very much like those of other Ottoman bureaucrat-officers in places as nearby as Urfa, 'Ayntab, and Kilis—all of which lay across a frontier that existed only on maps at Versailles.

Hananu's revolt began as part of the coordinated Ottoman-Anatolian rebellions against the French and their Armenian allies in Urfa, 'Ayntab, and Mar'ash, which started in January 1920 and continued for several months. Closer to Hananu's home, in late 1919 the French forces in Cilicia had moved the headquarters of the 2nd Division from Adana to the town of Kilis. This move brought French forces into direct contact with Hananu. Taking advantage of the diversion of forces caused by the fierce battle for 'Ayntab in April, he attacked the small French garrison in the city of Harim, Hananu's "hometown," as it were. The "Battle of Harim" began on the morning of 18 April 1920 as 50 irregulars entered the city. As word of the attack spread to the surrounding villages, Hananu's forces grew to some 400.[41]

---

[38] *al-Nida'* (Aleppo), 23 November 1945.

[39] USNA II 891d.00/72 Jackson (Aleppo) to Secretary of State (Washington), 12 April 1921.

[40] Zürcher, *Turkey*, 154.

[41] Muallim, *Suriyya*, 182. PRO FO 371/5048 E5252/3/44 Wratislaw [Consul General Beirut] to Secretary of State London, 7 May 1920.

In September 1920 Hananu reached an accord with the commander of the 2nd Army of the Ottoman-Anatolian movement, Selahettin Âdil bey, for more supplies and aid.[42] Along with the aid, several Ottoman officers were dispatched to buttress Hananu.[43] By the end of winter, Hananu had made hit-and-run attacks in his sector of a semicircular front that extended east to west from Urfa to Antioch. Strategically, Hananu supported the main fronts by harassing the French left flank; meanwhile, a similar effort began in the East, where at Viranşehir, a Kurdish tribal force allied with the Istanbul-educated sons of Ibrahim Pasha Milli, and beyond Raqqa, a Bedouin force confederated with the Ottoman officer Ramadan Shalash, initiated guerrilla action against French divisions. At the time local diplomats considered Hananu's activities part of the broader conflict between French forces and the Anatolia resistance. Writing in December 1920, the British consul of the city explained,

> Turkish Tchetas [çetes], expected to be 5000 under the command of Ibrahim Hanano . . . have attacked Idlip. They have saccaded [*sic*] the town and murdered the Christians. The French for their part have burnt the city. Damages are reported to be serious. . . . Ibrahim Hanano has received from Marash 2 guns [light artillery] 9 machine guns, arms and ammunition, and, it is also reported, Turkish Officers arrived with these arms to direct the rebellion. . . . Owing to this disaster the French have withdrawn their force from Idlip, Harim, Jissir-Choghour [Jisr al-Shaghur] and Kafar Tcherim [Kafr Tukharim].

A French counterattack during Christmas week dislodged Hananu's forces from Harim and forced him to retreat to the mountainous region to the south of Idlib called the Alawite Mountains.[44]

Aid and ammunition continued to flow from the Anatolian lines to Hananu during the first months of 1921. In March the American consul reported "30 machine guns and 20 horse loads of ammunition were sent to [Hananu's forces] by the Turks, passing within two hours journey south of Aleppo and less than 10 days [before] a large supply of ammunition was sent to them from near Djerablous." Clearly Hananu's ability

[42] MWT-QK "Ibrahim Shaghuri's Memoirs of Hananu's Revolt," 10. He places Hananu with {{Acircumflex}}dil bey on 7 September 1920.

[43] While fleeing to Trans-Jordan in July 1921, some of his men were captured in the desert near Palmyra. Of those captured, six were identified in a French secret report as "Turkish Officers." MAE-CADN Fonds Beyrouth Cabinet Politique carton 744, Bulletin de Reseignements 229, 22 July 1921. One of this number was Halid Amıdık, an Ottoman officer who had defected to Faysal during the Arab Revolt and had since rejoined the Anatolian resistance. PRO FO 371/6455 E 9296/117/89 Palmer [Damascus] to Secretary of State, 29 July 1921. Also see MD-SHAT 4H43 Dossier 8. Telegram, Gouraud to Paris. 20 July 1921.

[44] FO PRO 861/68 Consul [Aleppo] to Consul General [Beirut], 11 December 1920, "Report on the situation in Aleppo and District."

to tie down several thousand French forces in the region corresponded with the arrival of this aid.[45] Similarly, Yusuf al-Saʿdun, one of Hananu's men, recalled in his oral history of the revolt that sometime in April he made contact with Ottoman-Anatolian forces and agreed to convey arms and ammunition to Salah al-ʿAli, an Alawite tribal leader who continued to engage French positions above Homs and Hama.[46]

With Salih al-ʿAli, Hananu sent a letter to the American and Spanish consuls of Aleppo in which they stated their political aims and defended themselves against French accusations that they were behaving as mere brigands (March 1920). More important, the document, unlike the much later oral histories, sheds credible light on the ideological basis of their actions and has the virtue of having been produced at the time. While positing the notion that "Suriyya," here meaning the province of Damascus, had a right to be independent from the French, the document nevertheless embraces the idea that the Syrian people—*shaʿb* and *ahali* being used interchangeably—is part of a broader whole associated with the Ottoman state. While this seeming contradiction represents a departure from received notions of Wilsonianism, the fact that Hananu and Salih called themselves commanders of the "general national movement in the region of Western Aleppo" in the text beneath their signatures connotes that they did not conceive of themselves in the ethnic terms that typified contemporary nationalist discourse.[47] Rather, in the words of the document, they demanded that the French should decamp

> because of the existence of the government of the paramount Islamic Caliphate [*hukumat al-khilafa al-islamiyya al-ʿuzma*] which is giving aid to it [the people], [this people] who consider themselves one part of the several parts of the general Islamic community [*al-jamiʿa al-islamiyya*], and fights under its flag in its lands as witnessed today in its dependent territories [*mulhaqat*] of Aleppo, Hama, Homs and parts of Syria.[48]

[45] USNA II 891d.00/72 Jackson (Aleppo) to Bristol (Constantinople), 12 April 1921. Jackson puts French forces around 20,000 (a division): "2000 at Aintab, 4500 in the Idlib district, 1000 at Katma, 1500 at Kilis, 2000 at Antioch, 3000 at Alexandretta and Beylan, some 5000 at Aleppo," with the remainder being spread out in the field.

[46] MWT-QKh "Hananu's Revolt," "Al-Shaykh Yusuf al-Saʿdun's Memoirs of Hananu's Revolt," 48.

[47] MWT-QKh "Hananu's Revolt," "To the honorable consul of [name blacked out]" 29 March 1921. The consul was J. Jackson of the United States. See USNA II 890d.00/76 Jackson (Aleppo) to Bristol (Constantinople), 13 May 1921.

[48] MWT-QKh "Hananu's Revolt," "To the honorable consul of [name blacked out]" 29 March 1921. On a more local nationalist reading of this rebellion, see Nadine Méouchy, "Les mobilisation urbaines et rurales à l'époque mandataire," in Nadine Méochy, ed., *France, Syrie et Liban 1918–1946: les ambiguïties et les dynmaiques de la relation mandataire* (Damascus: Institute Français d'Études Arabes de Damas Press, 2002), 315–324.

The document makes no mention of Arabs or Turks and seems to operate on two levels, one appealing to notions of Western ideological norms, for the benefit of European and American public opinion, and another embracing a vital Islamic community, although to a certain extent it did adopt terms consistent with late nineteenth-century Islamic modernism. The document also proves a valuable corrective in comprehending the motives of other forces opposing France; the absence of an objective nationalism and an overwhelming appeal to Ottoman persistence undermines both the Arab and Turkish nationalist claim that these conflicts represent seminal moments in their respective "national awakenings." Rather, the language employed in Hananu's declaration reveals not only an ambivalence about the type of nationalism ascendant in the postwar world, but also an attempt to recast prewar ideas about rights and religious prerogatives in a modernist mold in a way strikingly similar to Hüseyin Kâzım's efforts ten years earlier. Certainly, Salih at most desired a return to a decentralized Ottoman polity dominated by Muslims in which the state would protect his hegemony as a landowning rural chieftain. Hananu, on the other hand, would have been uncomfortable with anything that could be interpreted as separatist or in contravention of the idea of the Ottoman-Islamic whole. He wanted something more complex, underscoring the ambiguity of this moment in a way that recalls the contradictory anxieties of Qastun's 1910 speech. For Hananu, the Ottoman state, Islam, and modernity were not mutually exclusive, despite the West's implicit assertion to the contrary; like others of his class and educational background, as a "New Man," his *habitus* revolved around the successful unification and continued harmonization of these key concepts in his public and personal life. Like the transformations of society anticipated by the middle class in the revolutionary period, Hananu's efforts confirm what was at issue for him and others like him in the fight against the French: it was about political control and a profound sense of attachment to place, but also his professional dignity, personal ambition, and sense of modern self. Moreover, were the French not to be defeated, his status as the absolute subject and definitive human being of his society could be lost entirely and he would be forced to relinquish hegemony to foreign interlopers and their local allies, lose his and his family's landholdings, and become the equal of formerly subordinate non-Muslims.

Hananu's fortunes turned for the worse as a consequence of a power struggle in his ranks and the aforementioned rapprochement between France and the Ottoman forces in Cilicia. Yusuf Saʿdun recalls that sometime in April or May, Hananu had Mustafâ Âsım shot, though his recollection of this event might be cloudy, and shortly thereafter, several of Hananu's officers and men "went to Turkey," though the names of these men have been erased from the copy of the oral history transcript in the

Syrian state archives.[49] These officers may have been disgruntled over Hananu's execution of the editor-cum-guerrilla, or more likely commanders in Anatolia had recalled them to fight against the Greek invasion of western Anatolia. While the terms of the London Accord of March 1921 called for a cease-fire in Cilicia, they did not lead to a suspension of all aid to forces in the area.[50] The Ottoman-Anatolia forces continued to use the irregulars in the region to keep the French off balance and interested in further negotiations. Nevertheless, in June 1921 ammunition from Anatolia ceased to flow to Hananu. This final cut in aid could have resulted from a direct diplomatic request or from the Ottoman Anatolian forces' need to concentrate the bulk of their men and matériel on the Greek front. Regardless, Hananu must have seemed expendable to a pragmatic Ottoman Anatolian leadership preparing to fight a war for survival against the invading Greek Army. This abandonment, however, would have had a much deeper meaning to Aleppines in general, and to Hananu in particular. It said to them that some of those in Ankara were willing to sacrifice Muslim solidarity and a commitment to a revived Ottoman state in order to consolidate a much more limited territorial construct. It also confirmed that this construct did not include them. The Ankara Accord of October 1921, in which France recognized a boundary between a pair of states named "Syria" and "Turkey," and which gave an international legal sanction to the division of the province of Aleppo, reinforced this conclusion.

Fearing arrest by the French, Hananu fled to the newly created British mandated state of Trans-Jordan, whereupon the French authorities pressed the British to deport him to Aleppo to stand trial as a criminal.[51] Eventually, the British acquiesced. His four-day court martial on charges of sedition (15–18 March 1922) served as a focal point around which local urban opposition to the French occupation of Aleppo coalesced. His trial also revealed a degree of notable solidarity and showed to this class the potential power a charismatic figure like Hananu could have in gathering popular support and asserting their demands in the face of the French. The trial revolved around the question of whether Hananu's actions constituted brigandage or irregular warfare; in other words, was he a rebel (perhaps, in contemporary circumlocution, an enemy combatant) or a soldier? Fathallah Saqqal, a French-educated, Armenian-Catholic lawyer and littérateur from Aleppo, who had practiced in Egypt during World

[49] MWT-QKh "Hananu's Revolt," "Al-Shaykh Yusuf al-Saʿdun's Memoirs of Hananu's Revolt," 50.

[50] Aid continued to flow to Shaykh Salih and Hananu from forces led by Ahmet Şefik (Yüzdemir), who also mounted attacks French positions in and around Killis and Mambij after the London Accord. See MAE-CADN Fonds Beyrouth Cabinet Politique carton 744, "Bulletin de Reseignements 229, 22 July 1921.

[51] MD-SHAT 6N190 Etat Major de l'Armee to Beirut 157/8, 26 March 1922.

War I, defended his client by presenting the court with documents from Ankara to establish that the now-recognized Turkish government had deputized Hananu to prosecute legal warfare against French forces. Saqqal placed several notables and religious men on the stand who reiterated that Hananu was no brigand and acted out of patriotic motives. Simultaneously, notables circulated petitions to the French Mandate authorities demanding his release. Signed by members of the Jabiri, Kayyali, Mudarris, and other clans, the petitions repeated the claims made in court.[52] His acquittal on a three-to-two vote led to several days of parades and organized demonstrations. Banners eulogizing him were placed along the road to his home in Aleppo; bands and processions coursed through the streets chanting slogans that made references to the figure at the center of Egyptian opposition to the British, Sa'd Zaghlul.[53] While Zaghlul enjoyed brief acclaim in Aleppo, a few months later, at the capture of Izmir by the Ottoman forces, Mustafa Kemal was back in favor, and his pictures were for sale in the souk.

The underlying sectarian tenor of the demonstrations led some in Aleppo to worry openly that the city would be plunged into a round of violence like that that had descended upon the cities in the North. However, upon a request from the American consul and various non-Muslim religious leaders, Hananu prevailed upon the crowds to return peacefully home.[54] Hananu derived power and prestige from this moment and in an ideological volte-face quickly became the unquestioned leader of the notable-led elite nationalist movement in Aleppo. The forging of alliances between the notable families, especially those who had supported the reunification of the empire—Mudarris—with partisans of the Hashemites—Jabiri—reveals their pragmatic recognition of the moribund nature of the Ottoman Empire. From this moment, many in the Aleppine notability, with the aid of middle-class intellectuals, turned to the language of nationalism to legitimate calls for a resumption of their hegemonic illiberal position in the city.[55]

Hananu's revolt had been a sideshow in the larger strategy of the Ottoman bureaucrat-officers who led a resistance against the division of the

---

[52] MAE-CADN Fonds Beyrouth 548 Renseignements. "Situation Report Aleppo," March 1922.

[53] USNA II 890d.00/105 Jackson (Aleppo) to Secretary of State (Washington), 22 March 1922. On Saqqal's defense, see his *Min Dhikrayati fi al-muhama fi Misr wa Suriyya* [My Memoirs of the Courts in Egypt and Syria] (Aleppo, Maronite Press: 1963).

[54] USNA II 890d.00/105 Jackson (Aleppo) to Secretary of State (Washington), 22 March 1922.

[55] For a discussion of the "nationalist turn" among the notability of immediate postwar Aleppo, see Peter Sluglett, "Will the Real Nationalists Stand Up? The Political Activities of the Notables of Aleppo, 1918–1946," in Méouchy, ed., *France, Syrie et Liban*, 273–290.

Ottoman state. The movement presented to Ottomans like himself an opportunity to reconstruct their world on the basis of what they considered legitimate principles. Those principles, while powerful and persuasive, could not survive the modernist paradigm of *Volk* and state that the Allied victory in the First World War imposed on the region. Embittered by the *Realpolitik* of the Kemalists, Hananu turned to a Syrian nationalism that grew more defined over the next decade. Nevertheless, the struggle for the expulsion of the French and the reassertion of Muslim political dominance—and not secular Arabism—remained a central tenet of this ideology.

The historical literature on the years between the Revolution of 1908 and the abolition of the Caliphate (1924) tends to regard World War I as an irretrievable break in the history of the Eastern Mediterranean, thereby adopting crucial turning points in nationalist and European imperialist narratives as axiomatic markers. Left uncorrected, this narrative structure conveys a sense that much of what happened after the war was discretely disconnected from what had happened before and during; and it reifies the Franklin-Bouillon Line between Republican Turkey and French Mandate Syria—the path of which merely traces a ceasefire line determined by a railroad bed—into a relevant cultural and ideological boundary.[56] This has contributed to narratives that take recourse to awkward constructions like "popular Syrian/Arab nationalism" to explain complex, deep social and political movements that are neither nationalist nor Syrian nor Arab. Situated in a narrow field of view, these explanations make the mistake of ascribing to violent opposition to British and French colonialism a preeminent role in the "awakening" of identity—nationalist, Syrian, Arab, Turkish, or otherwise—ignoring the continuing place of complex transformations of class, forms of thought, and styles of politics in late nineteenth- and early twentieth-century Ottoman society. In so doing, advocates of this position deny the very agency of their subjects, reducing them to one-dimensional, exotic, and vaguely romantic figures who exist only insofar as they oppose Western imperialism and whose ideologies, worldviews, and textures of identity appear *ex nihilo* in the interwar period fully formed and in a way that can be easily placed within normative social and political categories sometimes uncritically borrowed from the study of Europe or South Asia. Functionally, popular nationalism is an effort to assert that a "national consciousness" can take root in the absence of, or perhaps prior to, the introduction of nationalism itself and

---

[56] Exemplary in this genre are James Gelvin, *Divided*; M. Provence, "A Nationalist Rebellion without Nationalists? Popular Mobilizations in Mandatory Syria," in Méouchy et al., eds., *Comparative*, 673–692; and his recent, *The Great Syrian Revolt and the Rise of Arab Nationalism* (Austin: University of Texas Press, 2005).

has the kind of emotive appeal of "alternative modernity." Thus, nationalism and/or national consciousness becomes an essence rather than an ideology with clear historical roots in nineteenth-century Western Europe and the Americas. Conceived in such a vein, various rebellions against state and imperial authorities, and other similar movements in the Ottoman Eastern Mediterranean, can be construed as evidence of national consciousness, giving an "authentic," "real," and subaltern genealogy to contemporary nationalist movements, rather than one that is "derived," "imagined," and elite in the ways described by a diverse cadre of theoreticians of nationalism from Partha Chatterjee to Ernest Gellner and Benedict Anderson. Hence one can have nationalism without nationalists. From the perspective of writing the history of this period, the singular danger in such formulations is that any rebellion or moment of civil disorder—the early modern Celali Revolts in Anatolia or the communal violence of 1850, for example—or oblique references in late Medieval Mamluk-era Arabic geographies to territorial constructs that bear some resemblance to modern states (Bilad al-Sham, Suriyya, Syria) can become evidence of a prenationalism nationalist consciousness or a formless protonationalism. More critically, these efforts strike me as an attempt to repackage the core nationalist myths of "folk," "national/racial character," "national memory," and the organic nation—myths that have been inherited by Baʿthism and other radicalized and racist postcolonial ideologies in the region and elsewhere—in a more palatable idiom by linking them to subaltern histories.

Recognizing nationalism as a *unique* corollary of modernity, affirming the limited historicity and contingency of the nation, and understanding how nationalism cannot exist without specific institutions, forms of media, and a body of thought—and moreover that nationalism has its *origins* in the West and has *spread* to the non-West—preserves the significance of what were indeed distinct and new mass Arab nationalist movements in the 1950s and 1960s primarily in Egypt, Syria, and Iraq. These nationalist movements were linked to individuals schooled in the ideology, as well as to innovations in communicative technology like radio and cinema, radical populist politics, land reform, national compulsory education, and rising literacy rates. And at the same time the recognition and the rejection of the way nationalists nationalize history is the first step in accurately and humanely writing the history of the nonelite at moments of profound change in the early twentieth century in a way unencumbered by the anachronistic noise of improbable popular nationalism—a noise that drowns out what is complex and unique about its historical experience.

Only by painting this period on a larger canvas and using the vast reservoir of archival and literary documentation in Ottoman Turkish, and other languages, about the period 1908–1924 is it possible to critically revise the history of the immediate postwar era in a way that eschews Arab and Turkish nationalist and neonationalist dogma. Likewise, in extending the analysis to cover this longer period, the prejudice, which derives from a need to assert a lengthier authentic national past to the fierce struggles that gripped the region in the 1930s and 1940s, can be avoided. In this revision, 1924 and the passing away of any hope of revivifying the Ottoman Empire and returning to its antebellum structures becomes the breaking point; and, as following chapters show, this realization forced many to reinvent themselves and their politics in new and significant ways, creating a deep crisis in middle-class identity that manifested most notably in a burst of writing about the past. Ultimately, the movement of the peoples of the Eastern Mediterranean from subjects of a world empire to citizens of limited national constructs would be far from smooth and continually beset with ruptures, false starts and cul-de-sacs. That credible discussions could take place about the breakup of Iraq in the early twenty-first century is evidence that this process is far from complete.

Nonetheless, it is equally important to stress the magnitude of 23 July 1920—the day the French occupied the city—in the lives of the middle class of Aleppo. The French conquest and administration of the city altered forms of middle-class distinction: their policies accentuated class and religious cleavages by undermining preexisting forms of hierarchy, inverting social privilege, and institutionalizing ethnic and religious conflict through the manipulation of electoral systems, military recruitment of Christians and non-Sunni Muslims, and the staffing of the bureaucracy with foreign-educated local members of the middle class. And while the Ottomans had used sectarian-based formulas in revolutionary era politics, the arrival of the French signaled a new level of sectarianism in Eastern Mediterranean politics and culture.

The multiplicity of ways in which the middle class of Aleppo responded to the occupation of their city by the French in 1920 reveals that being invaded and occupied does not always occasion resistance and instead can engender the reverse. Many of those in Aleppo's middle class who had celebrated alongside their neighbors the departure of Faysal, his Arab Kingdom, and his Bedouin troops welcomed the French on the following day. The French occupation altered the equations of power and distinction to such a degree that two competing visions of empire and the promise of imperial citizenship existed simultaneously for a moment in city. In those first months of France's occupation of what would become Syria, the modern Islamic-Ottomanism that motivated Hananu and others persisted as a viable basis for governance and path to the future. Simultaneously, for still others, the arrival of the French and their empire offered the possibility of formal admission to the inner sanctum of modernity.

SEVEN

Remembering the Great War: Allegory, Civic Virtue, and Conservative Reaction

> [The Great War] made orphans of their children and widows of their wives.
> —Raghib Tabbakh, 1973

Fathallah Qastun introduced a special edition of *al-Shuʿla* on the history of Aleppo by narrating the city's past, present, and future in a plot line of Progress. Accordingly, Aleppo, whose history had begun in the "recesses of time," had been ruled by the Assyrians and called Halbun, and then later, Seleucus renamed it Berea; it had enjoyed prominence in the Middle Ages under Sayf al-Dawla as the Kingdom of Aleppo and had been a first-tier provincial capital of the Ottoman Empire since the sixteenth century, second in importance only to Izmir or Konya. Of late, the city had passed through dark times including the era of Abdülhamid II, the Young Turks, and World War I.[1] However, in 1921, Aleppo, enjoying a brief interlude again as a capital of a quasi-autonomous rump state in French Mandate Syria,

> is awakening from its nightmare, raising itself up from its slumber by following the example of the traces of its noble past and great scholarly tradition and returning quickly to glory and efflorescence. It is guided by the dawn of independence and freedom. And the Aleppo of tomorrow is grown great by its science and trade, industry and agriculture, and the energy of its inhabitants.[2]

In acquiring this plot line of Progress, Aleppo itself was anthropomorphized as an ideal middle-class individual that was perfecting itself by hard work and bourgeois ingenuity. Moreover, what made Aleppo "great" was that it had sloughed off the irrational and desultory parts of its past—as Qastun noted, "we must look to the past lest we return to it"—and had embraced a future built on rationality, modernity, and liberalism. The things that made the city virtuous were those things particular to the middle class: commerce, science, and rational thought. Qastun had

---

[1] Fathallah Qastun, "Aleppo: Yesterday, Today and Tomorrow," *al-Shuʿla* 2:5 (August 1921): 5–7.

[2] Jirjis Manash, "The Aleppo of Yesteryear," *al-Shuʿla* 2:5 (August 1921): 8–23.

come to believe, partially perhaps as a consequence of his heavily French-influenced education, Voltaire's maxim that "the city stimulates progress in reason and taste and thus perfects the arts of civilization."[3]

The lengthy and footnoted text by the historian-priest Jirjis Manash, which follows Qastun's essay, extends Aleppo's past back to the very origins of secular human history, to the ancient Arameans, noting they are mentioned both in the Bible and in Egyptian hieroglyphs. Manash's history adopts a clearly historicist view of the city's past, distinguishing between myth and fact, and documenting each passage with references to European Orientalists and Arabic texts. By bringing a bourgeois historicity to Aleppo, Qastun and others in the journal gave the city an ancient, pre-Islamic, and pre-Christian past on which, according to the rules of positivist historicism, they did not have to pass judgment. For non-Muslims like Qastun and Manash, building a history that emphasized the shared heritage of the city's Muslims and non-Muslims was an act of self-preservation and was calculated to lay the basis for intercommunal cooperation—an anxiety that persisted from the prewar era. This thread of a shared, consensual, intersectarian past would figure prominently in later nationalist thought in Turkey, Syria, and Iraq.[4] However, the clearly class-based dimensions of the discourse and its inextricable links to the city distinguished this moment. The anxiety, moreover, points to how the past was also being constructed in ways that denied their shared heritage, or at least the right of all to participate equally in Aleppo's present.

The Great War as Moral Test: Tabbakh's Biographical Entry for Mahmud Kamil al-ʿAyntabi

A text fundamental to understanding the way middle-class Aleppines comprehended the shared past of the city as well the multiple meanings and narratives of the war years is Raghib Tabbakh's *Information about the Notables in the History of Aleppo the Gray*.[5] The annals section of the published work covers the history of the city from ancient times until the Revolution of 1908, and while Tabbakh intended to extend his survey until his present (1922), a period "fraught with grave and consequential events," he never completed this task.[6] Instead, he chose to explain the

---

[3] Schorske, *Thinking*, 39.

[4] Two recent texts on this subject are Stéphane Valter, *La construction nationale syrienne: Légitimation de la nature communautaire du pouvoir par le discours historique* (Paris: Éditions CNRS, 2002); and Étienne Copeaux, *Espaces et temps de la nation turque: analyse d'une historiographie nationaliste, 1931–1993* (Paris: Éditions CNRS, 1997).

[5] (Aleppo, 1923). This work is the source for the epigraph to this chapter.

[6] *Notables*, 1:26.

war in an innovative manner, by interlacing a narrative of the years 1908–
1922 with the biography of one of the most prominent Aleppines of the
period, Mahmud Kamil al-'Ayntabi, a highly decorated Ottoman bureaucrat-officer who died around the time of the chronicle's completion. Tabbakh cast Mahmud Kamil as an allegorical figure, representing the
broader Aleppine historical experience, and in so doing he asserted
Aleppo's membership in a broader Ottoman-Islamic community, which
more or less resembled the status quo ante. Given the origins and education of Tabbakh, this construction reflected the forming aesthetic historical sensibilities of the Aleppine Muslim bureaucratic and commercial middle class. This was how they chose to remember what had happened to
them, their city, and the empire in the war; Tabbakh's account both reflected and reinforced such an image. This narrative ran counter to that
presented in the Arab nationalist *Halab* and sought to integrate Aleppo
into a very different stream of history on terms that dissented from the
nationalist, egalitarian, and emancipatory rhetoric of the paper.

Born in 1877 into a family involved in trade, religious scholarship,
and Sufism, the young Raghib Tabbakh was torn between following his
father into business and living up to the example of his grandfather, Hashim, who had served as a kadı in Istanbul in the early part of the nineteenth century. The family's business, the weaving and dying of silk and
cotton textiles, remains one of Aleppo's trademark commercial occupations. The young Raghib often helped to sell these goods from the family's headquarters in Khan al-'Ulabiyya. As a teenager, and under the
influence of his paternal uncle, a librarian at one of the city's mosques,
he began to study Islamic jurisprudence. Active in the intellectual life of
the city, he published articles on various historical and legal subjects
in the region's newspapers, primarily the Unionist paper, *al-Ittihad al-
'Uthmani* [Ottoman Union].[7]

A gap appears in Tabbakh's biography for the war years. After the
armistice, and more important, after the fall of Faysal's Arab Kingdom
and the occupation of the city by the French, he took up a prestigious
position as a teacher of Arabic and religion at the *madrasa* of the al-
Khusrawiyya Mosque (1921). His tenure at the al-Khusrawiyya, located
at the base of the citadel, was marked by an active process of modernizing
the curriculum by introducing new disciplines and restoring the architecture of the mosque complex.[8] By 1937 he had attained the post of director
of Aleppo's religious schools, had been inducted into the Arab Academy
in Damascus, and had served on the founding board of directors of

---

[7] Ibid., Muhammad Kamal's introduction, 1:10–13 passim.
[8] Jean Gaulmier, "Notes sur l'état de l'enseignement traditionnel à Alep," *BEO* 9 (1942–
1943): 18–27.

Aleppo's national museum. His two biographers, his son Yahya Tabbakh and Muhammad Kamal, gloss over the years 1914–1920, perhaps because, when viewed from the late twentieth century, his wartime career could prove embarrassing.[9] Indeed, archival evidence suggest that he had accompanied the Ottoman forces as they withdrew to the Taurus Mountains in late 1918, and that he resurfaced in Cilicia where French intelligence identified him as a CUP sympathizer and implicated him in the organization of resistance to Britain and its ally Faysal.[10]

This brief foray into political action situates Tabbakh, forty-one years old at the time, as an opponent of the Allied presence in the region in general, and of Faysal in particular. The way he wrote about the Arab Revolt and the loud silences in his history confirm this animus.[11] It may have also colored his choice of the biography in which to elaborate his commentary on recent history. Jâbirî zâde Nafiʿ, a notable par excellence by any definition, had died in time to be included but is conspicuous by his absence. While he had included several members of the Jabiri clan from the previous century in his work, Tabbakh chose to exclude this notable, which may represent a slight against a family that had become inextricably and indelibly linked to the now compromised and alien Faysal. By contrast, in Mahmud Kamil, Tabbakh found the epitome of the post-Tanzimat provincial Muslim Ottoman *Bildungsbürgertum* and used him as a powerful didactic device.[12] And the historian narrated his life as a way to teach his readers the origins, causes, and meanings of the troubling transformations of state and society through which he and his fellow Aleppines had just lived; his work is a unique window on the way the Eastern Mediterranean middle class made sense of that recent and troubling past for themselves. The contours of this understanding, this process of "making sense," manifest in Tabbakh's account present evidence again of the profound persistence of a universal-imperialist Ottoman consciousness, a form of communal belonging that superseded one based on ethnicity or language, and one that maintained social hierarchies on the basis of religious affiliation while simultaneously imagining itself as *thoroughly* modern and civilized.

Tabbakh also created room in his text for a middle class, a class that was his audience as well. The best evidence of this opening of a new intellectual space is his expansive definition of "notable." While the entries in

[9] Muhammad Yahya Tabbakh, "Muhammad Raghib Tabbakh: hayatahu-atharahu" [Muhammad Raghib Tabbakh: His Life and His Works] (Ph. D. diss., Syrian University, 1951).

[10] PRO FO 371/3657 E1922/512/58 General Headquarters (Egypt) to Director of Military Intelligence (Istanbul), 1 January 1919.

[11] *Notables*, 7: 605–606.

[12] For a definition of this concept see Gay, *Pleasure Wars*, 5:60.

the dictionary pass through the centuries, who is considered important enough to be included changes. In his introduction he defined who would appear in his works: "the vizier and the great emir, the scholar of hadith criticism and the Islamic legal jurisprudent, the descendent of the prophet, the noteworthy, the preacher, the medical doctor, the poet, the writer, the trader, the military man and others of merit and those who have done great deeds."[13] Faithful to its genre, *Notables* is heavily intertextual as it includes material from earlier biographical dictionaries, primarily, the Ottoman-era work of Muhammad ibn al-Hanbali,[14] and other historical and archival texts. As Tabbakh moved beyond the entries derived from previous dictionaries produced in the city, and as the time frame moved into the nineteenth century, he included non-Muslims and, in one case, a woman: (the Christian writers Rizqallah Hassun and Antun Saqqal, and the poet and *salonniere* Marianna Marrash). These individuals, despite their prominence in Aleppine society, possessed neither the power nor the prestige of the landed notability. However, their importance becomes more readily apparent when measured against modernist tastes. It is a reminder of how the very nature of who was important changed as a consequence of modernization. On a more pragmatic level, as Tabbakh had written his work to be sold, the mechanism of print-capitalism no doubt encouraged him to broaden his definition of "notable" to include a wider base, therefore insuring that the middle-class relatives and colleagues of those mentioned in the dictionary, finding exemplars of themselves, would purchase the volumes.

His account of the life of Mahmud Kamil is similar in format to any entry in a biographical dictionary. The ʿAyntabi family, as the name suggests, originated in the city of ʿAyntab, to the north of Aleppo. Renamed Gaziaintep, and now an important regional center in the Republic of Turkey, it served as one of the most crucial links in Aleppo's trade network in the prewar period. At the beginning of the Tanzimat period, Mahmud Kamil's father, Nacî, received an appointment as the *müdür-i evkaf* (director of religious endowments) in the newly reorganized Aleppine provincial administration, a position he held until his death in 1895. Mahmud was born in 1877, the fourth of four sons. He learned the Qur'an in a local *mektep* and then acquired the rudiments of a modern education at the Aleppo imperial elementary school, *Şems-i Maarif*. At the age of thirteen he left Aleppo to be trained at the Damascus military preparatory academy. After completing the course of study in Damascus, he earned admission to the elite imperial war college at the heart of the empire in

[13] *Notables*, 1:28.
[14] Muhammad Ibn al-Hanbali, *Durr al-habab fi tarikh aʿyan Halab*, 4 vols. (Damascus: Ministry of Culture, 1972–1974).

Istanbul. There he became friends with Enver, a future member of the Young Turk triumvirate.

After graduating at the top of his class, the young Mahmud was commissioned a lieutenant in the Ottoman Army and returned to Aleppo with the 3rd Army, where he remained until the Yemen uprising took him away from his native city. In this province at the southern extreme of the empire, Mahmud Kamil participated in the Ottoman government's suppression of the Ibadi revolt. For Tabbakh's subject a kind of "awakening" took place in the Yemen. "Awakenings" are a standard trope in much of nationalist literature, especially in nationalist autobiography;[15] here, however, Mahmud Kamil had awoken to a consciousness that internal incompetence and venality and external interference threatened to rip apart the Ottoman whole. Tabbakh placed this awakening in the context of a mystical journey Mahmud Kamil took to the deserts of the Anis mountain range.

> An old man came to him and said, "come with me tonight so I can show you a cave of great interest." He thought that he meant to show him an old place of historical significance, so he went with him, and when he entered the cave, he did not see what he had expected to see, and then the old man said to him, "do you see the vastness of this cave. . . ? The liras which the people of this impoverished and oppressed province have paid could fill this cave a number of times. . . . How is it possible after all this not to rise up and rebel . . . and if you do not solve this problem and oppose tyranny and oppression, it will be impossible to keep the peace and return security to the region."[16]

In the prevailing repertoire of metaphorical language, the cave stood as a symbol of Ottoman oppression. The old man then informed him that a local official, Çerkesli Zakariyya, had absconded with thousands of gold liras and put them in the British bank in Aden, and "British officers and commanders had helped him in this endeavor."[17]

As a consequence of this newly found awareness of corruption, injustice, and tyranny, Mahmud Kamil began to study in earnest the local conditions, and the manners and customs of the people. "He associated with [the region's] important men as well as the people," studied Arabic, learned many prophetic sayings, and memorized poetry. More important, "he promised them [the people of the region] that the liberation from the evils of Sultan Abdülhamid, who was under the influence of men committed to the hypocrisy and chicanery which had caused these civil wars and those uprisings was near. By this he meant the declaration of the constitu-

---

[15] Chatterjee, *Fragments*, 138.
[16] *Notables*, 7:591.
[17] Ibid.

tion would happen soon."[18] Though disillusioned by the current leadership, he had not lost faith in the Ottoman system; it is interesting to note that in this frontier province of the empire, Mamud Kamil began a return to a pure and pietistic way of Islamic practice.

The themes of corrupt Hamidian rule, foreign intrigue, and selfless motivation of his subject appear more distinct in Tabbakh's account of the Revolution of 1908. Mahmud Kamil returned to Istanbul via Cairo and Aleppo, visiting several exiled Unionists incognito en route. He was in Edirne at the local war college when the revolt broke out:

> A fire was smoldering under the ashes in the Balkans. International conferences were held in European capitals with a view to use the matter of the Balkans to divide the Ottoman state, Turkish officers in the Ottoman military were also watching these conferences . . . and they understood [the potential] consequences, and thus they issued the constitution in spite of the will of Sultan Abdülhamid and his apparatus.[19]

As one of these revolutionary officers, Mahmud Kamil was appointed an inspector general for the War Ministry. Despite the promise of the revolution, the leitmotif of "international intrigue" reappeared and various "states openly distributed glittering gold to secret societies in Istanbul and the Balkans."[20] Within a year, the sultan and his men mounted a countercoup. The reason for the counterrevolt in Tabbakh's appraisal was the resentment felt by the sultan and his entourage at the humble, middle-class origins of the Young Turks. Mahmud Kamil escaped harm and aided in the suppression of the reactionary forces.

As Tabbakh continues his narration of the wars and rebellions that tore at the empire in the years preceding World War I, the themes of international involvement, corruption, and incompetence course through his descriptions. When Italy invaded Tripolitania, it "set fires of disunion [*fitna*] in the Balkans to divert the attention of the Ottoman state from Tripoli." Similarly, "a bloc of Bulgarians, Serbs, and Greeks seized this splendid opportunity [i.e., the Tripolitanian War] to unravel [the Ottoman state] from all sides and they began to act in detestable ways. The Western countries encouraged them and extended to them means and material."[21] These international conspiracies were compounded by local failures.[22]

---

[18] Ibid.

[19] Ibid., 7:592.

[20] Ibid.

[21] Ibid., 7:593.

[22] In a more expansive passage, Tabbakh catalogs the incompetence of Grand Vizier Gazi Ahmet Muhtar, who lead the government at the time of the war. In Tabbakh's estimation, he was "that senile old man who thought that it would be possible to solve these great problems by diplomatic means through an agreement with the Western states. He was beholden to them and dazzled by their empty promises." Ibid.

During one of these crises, Tabbakh's Mahmud Kamil rose to the occasion by delivering a eulogy at the Abide-i Hürriyet (Monument of Freedom) hill to the north of Istanbul. This space had become a memorial to officers killed during the counterrevolution and a kind of secular pulpit from which revolutionary officers gave speeches.[23] While memorializing his fallen comrades, Mahmud Kamil criticized the leadership of the empire as corrupt and inefficient. Reporters from several of the capital's papers attended the ceremony: "the Unionist papers applauded his speech and the Ententist complained of its emptiness and aloofness."[24] His complaint caught the eye of the new grand vizier, Mahmût Şevket, who dispatched him to Shkodra (Scutari in modern Albania) to defend one of the last Ottoman outposts in Europe during the First Balkan War. The war had disastrous results for the territorial integrity of the Ottoman state, and at its conclusion Ottoman holdings in Europe consisted roughly of Istanbul itself. Despite his heroic defense of the citadel, which earned him the title of the "hero of Shkodra" [batal Ushqudara], the Ottoman state surrendered the city. Nevertheless, as Mahmût Şevket says to a former governor in Tabbakh's account, Mahmud Kamil "was one of best commanders not just of Turkey, but also of Europe."[25] The implication was that this honorable soldier's defense would have been sufficient to defend Ottoman dignity, but foreign conspiracy, dishonorable Balkan rebels, and complacent leaders in the capital subverted his efforts.

Within a year of Mahmud Kamil's return to Istanbul, World War I began. In among the most stirring passages on the origins of the conflict in any language, Tabbakh exhibited a tone at odds with the exaltation expressed in *Halab*. Far from presenting an opportunity to remake society on the basis of Wilsonianism, the war consumed humanity in a conflict that nearly annihilated the Ottoman-Islamic order itself. Tabbakh described the days before the war:

> Its signs were clear; its lightning flashed and it smoldered beneath ashes. There is no need to mention what took place in the Western world and European capitals in the way of politics and intrigue, that world whose practice became little by little the basis of all evil and wickedness between states and peoples. . . . The rest of the world became the [West's] prey; it was cut off by it, starved by it, and desired by it.[26]

Tricked and manipulated by the West, the Ottoman people were dragged into the war against their will by their leaders and Germany. The war

[23] The space has since become a memorial to Young Turks and other reformers like Midhat Pasha.

[24] Ibid., 5:596.

[25] Ibid., 7:598.

[26] Ibid., 7:599.

"toppled the thrones of Earthly Caesars and tyrants, the jeweled crowns of kings fell to their feet, friend fell upon friend. . . . Of those who were industrious or those who were lowly, those who went to coffee-houses or dance halls, those who have nothing but hunger, those with no shelter, [the war] made orphans of their children and widows of their wives."[27]

In perhaps the most damning of all passages in his work, Tabbakh noted that the war had been waged to "satisfy the greed of a few individuals, no more than could be counted on both hands, whose souls are poisoned with the devil's politics . . . and gaze upon . . . all other classes of society with an eye of disdain. . . and they consider them mere livestock to be sold to the tyrannical butcher." All Ottoman peoples suffered at the hands of the Europeans in a war that benefited only a few. Nevertheless, Tabbakh assured his readers, in this war Mahmud Kamil did not waver in his duty. As he told Enver, "'I am a military man who follows orders and does not question them. Whatever state you make war upon, I am prepared to sacrifice the last drop of my blood to defend the sacred ground of the homeland [al-watan] and state [al-dawla], and to defend the faith [al-iman] of the Islamic community.' "[28] In depicting a good Ottoman but a bad war, Tabbakh exonerated those officers who remained loyal to the state despite the dubious origins of the conflict. He also elevated loyalty to the Ottoman state—defined by a willingness to put the homeland and the Islamic community, the boundaries between these two entities never being fully explained, above self. Thus Tabbakh adopts one of the major topoi of nationalism: a willingness to die for a limited imagining. Still, this topos operated in the absence of an internationally sanctioned nationality or a politically determined entity. This construction also allowed Tabbakh to use Mahmud Kamil as an ideal-type of Ottoman middle-class modern "New Man" against whom all others could be judged during the course of the war and after.

Initially, the Ottomans fared well in the war, despite supply problems and a lack of developed infrastructure. Soon, however, the "fingers of foreigners began to manipulate some staff officers, until they lost honor, and abandoned their religion and patriotism, others they [i.e., foreign agents] bought with glittering gold."[29] Tabbakh may have included in this number Ottoman officers who deserted to join the British and the forces of Faysal. As with Halab, Tabbakh locates much of the support for Faysal in the actions of Cemal himself. However, where Halab identified a systemic flaw in Ottoman control, Tabbakh attributed the resentment of the people of the region—Syrians and Iraqis—to the mismanagement of one incompetent officer and certainly not to Arab nationalism.

[27] Ibid., 7:600.
[28] Ibid.
[29] Ibid., 7:601.

He [Cemal] finally realized that all of the efforts which he expended in this region, from killing some of its leaders and exiling many of the rest to Anatolia, did not improve the situation, nor did they provide any benefit. Rather than producing the expected results, it left the people resentful and a few of the Syrian troops and their officers joined Emir Faysal . . . because he had taken the Arabs of the Hijaz to the Maʿan and Aqaba front to support the English Army which was making war on the Ottoman state at the Suez Canal. His [Cemal's] resignation had been demanded many times and finally he tendered it.[30]

Within this passage appears Tabbakh's one and only reference to the ethnonym *Arab*. In this context, the word applies solely to the tribesmen of the Arabian peninsula. He used limited territorial designations, "Syrian" (which did not include Aleppo in his usage) and "Iraqi," when he described the inhabitants of Mesopotamia (excluding the province of Mosul). In his discussion of the "Arab Revolt," a term he does not use, he takes great pains to explain the motivation of the soldiers who deserted the Ottoman Army. By the time Mustafa Kemal replaced Cemal in Syria, "Ottoman forces were not what they should have been . . . the soldiers had become demoralized, hungry, and desperate . . . the situation became impossible to bear and many had no choice but to go over to Emir Faysal." Tabbakh registered a certain inevitability to the Ottoman losses in Syria in his account. Indeed, when asked by the minister of war, Enver, to replace Cemal, Mahmud Kamil demurred, replying, "the situation is beyond repair in that region, and it is impossible to fix, regardless of the expertise of the people sent or the style of politics used."[31]

In Tabbakh's counternarrative of the war, the explanatory strategy decenters the conflict from the causative event in the formation of a new, Arab political order, depicting it instead as one of the many tragedies faced by the Ottoman peoples. The two paragraphs dedicated to the "Arab Revolt" pale in comparison to the several pages he dedicates to the battles on the Russian Front or the Dardanelles. That the narrative of the Hejazi cooperation on the Palestine front or even the "Arab Awakening" plays such a small part in the construction of the events of the previous years shows the relative unimportance or lack of relevance these events represented for Tabbakh, perhaps for his middle-class audience as well. *Halab* and *Notables* also diverge in the beginning, middle, and end of their respective stories. *Halab* employed the Western-Orientalist theme of Ottoman oppression (beginning), followed by emerging national feelings and successful Arab Revolt (middle), arriving at the teleos of the story with the establishment of an authentic Arab state. In contrast, Faysal's

---

[30] Ibid., 7:605–606.
[31] Ibid., 7:606.

Arab Kingdom does not even merit a full sentence in Tabbakh's narrative. In his account, what little of the historical events of that period he does mention remains in the middle of the story, conflated with other instances of foreign occupation and humiliation: the Allied entrance into Istanbul, the treaties, and the Greek landings at Izmir. His telos, or rather Mahmud Kamil's assumed desideratum, the reestablishment of the Ottoman state in some form and the expulsion of the alien forces, was *being* written. Thus, the zenith of one narration served as the nadir of another at roughly the same time and place. The text reveals that the spirit of the Ottoman Anatolian movement had registered successfully in the Aleppine milieu. The beginnings of the movement in Anatolia, while today construed as an element of the historical genealogy of the Republic of Turkey, was, at that moment, part of Aleppo's history as well. In this light, then, the whole into which Tabbakh sought to write the city corresponded with the boundaries of the prewar Ottoman state.

Ottoman fortunes continued to decline, as did the career of Mahmud Kamil. Having resumed his post as inspector general, after the armistice he returned to Istanbul where the British Army arrested him on charges of war crimes in the postwar roundup of Young Turk politicos and officers (1919). Warned by friends of his imminent arrest, he stated with naive self-assurance, "I am not one of the men of the ministry, I did nothing that would merit culpability or retribution; I am a military man who only did his duty as was required by religion and love of country, and I am prepared if necessary to go to court and clear my name."[32] Nevertheless, the British authorities deported him with several other ranking Unionists to Malta. This low point in the life of the subject was matched only by the fate of the empire itself.

Tabbakh's description of Mahmud Kamil's imprisonment in Malta as an alleged war criminal highlights the most compelling lacuna in his account of the general's life. After the Ottomans suffered one of their greatest reversals against the Russians, the Battle of Sarıkamış, in eastern Anatolia, Mahmud Kamil took command of the Ottoman 3rd Army (10 February 1915). He had been sent as a loyal friend and ally of Young Turk junta members Talaat and Enver, in part to oversee the ethnic cleansing of eastern Anatolia's Armenians, the precipitating act in the larger Armenian Genocide. In documents that surfaced at postwar trials of the leading Unionists, a telegram signed by Mahmud Kamil was introduced as evidence of official culpability and prior planning that read in part:

---

[32] Ibid., 7:607. On the trials, see Vahakn N. Dadrian, "The Documentation of the World War I Armenian Massacres in the Proceedings of the Turkish Military Tribunal," *IJMES* 23 (1991): 549–576.

any Muslim who protects an Armenian will be hanged in front of his house which will also be burned down. If the culprit is an official he will be dismissed and court-martialed. If those who deem it worthwhile to provide protection are military officials they will be severed from the military and will be handed over to the above mentioned Court Martial to be tried before it.[33]

During the war, Mahmud Kamil had commented to a German military attaché, "After the war there will be no more Armenian Question."[34]

Several reasons exist that may explain Tabbakh's omissions on this account. First, it is most unlikely that he would have had access to secret telegrams and organizational details of Ottoman 3rd Army activities; and most of Tabbakh's information about Mahmud Kamil was given to him by his civilian family members in Aleppo, who were unlikely to cast aspersions on their illustrious relative. Likewise, while Tabbakh would have seen the deportees as they transited Aleppo, connecting them with secret command decisions in the field and the conspiracy at the capital would have been impossible with the data available to him. Second, mentioning any role he might have played in the massacres would have undermined the narrative of the biographical entry and contradicted the idealization of Mahmud Kamil; he is presented as a man beyond reproach, and any mention of these events would have given credence to accusations of war crimes and criminal culpability. Third, his role in any of these events may not have been worth mentioning. As these actions affected only Armenians, who were then perceived by some as a traitorous non-Muslim population that had sided with the empire's enemies, what Mahmud Kamil did was merely part of doing his job as defender of the Islamic community and Ottoman state. For comparison, consider how U.S. President Andrew Jackson's role in the Indian Removal Act (1830) might by rendered in a mid-nineteenth century biography written by an American nationalist.

While Mahmud Kamil was imprisoned on Malta, his colleague, Mustafa Kemal, returned to Istanbul to "organize a movement by arousing zeal and gathering around him a group of [like-minded] officers" who opposed the surrender.[35] The movement spread from the capital to the provinces: "people organized in most of the regions of Anatolia and they swore a binding oath to liberate the state and the country from the grip of the imperialists and to cleanse the body of the kingdom (*jism al-mamlaka*) of traitors and expel them to their own nations." This movement culminated in the meetings at Sivas.

---

[33] Cited in Vahakn N. Dadrian, "A Textual Analysis of the Key Indictment of the Turkish Military Tribunal Investigating the Armenian Genocide," *Journal of Political and Military Sociology* 22:1 (1994): 138.

[34] Cited in Dadrian, "The Naim-Andonian Documents," 331.

[35] *Notables*, 7:610.

Of importance in Tabbakh's explanation of the spirit of the National Pact is an absence of any *Turkish* nationalism. As explored in the previous chapter, the framers of the National Pact omitted mention of the "Turkish Nation" in the rhetoric of the declaration. Feroz Ahmad has argued that such an "omission" represented a cynical or politically motivated attempt to solidify support from "conservative" elements.[36] However, Tabbakh's use of the "body of the kingdom" suggests that, far from omitting references to the "Turkish Nation" for Machiavellian political motives, the declaration consisted of a concise statement of a consensual comprehension of the imagined Ottoman community. Or, more significantly, had the framers of the National Pact invoked references to the Turk or the Turkish nation as a sovereign political unit, it would have constituted a meaningless innovation. For Tabbakh, Turkish soldiers did attend the conference, just as Arabs rode with Faysal, yet these categories were subordinate to the more meaningful and comprehensible supraethnic identity of Muslim Ottoman. That his conflation of religion and what appeared to be the nation could strike later commentators as an inaccurate comprehension of nationalism and a marked departure from internationally sanctioned norms and standards confirms the contingent nature of those very norms and standards; that the Aleppine Mahmud Kamil had spent his adult life fighting for it remains a striking reminder of the powerful hold such imaginings—reinforced by modern bureaucratic and educational structures and Ottoman high culture—continued to have in the post-1918 world.

Meanwhile, the British authorities released Mahmud Kamil from prison on Malta. In failing health, he returned to occupied Istanbul before traveling to Germany in search of a cure.[37] Upon learning of the Greek invasion, Mahmud Kamil returned to Anatolia "against his doctors' orders," doing his duty yet again.[38] On his way to join the Anatolian forces he fell gravely ill. Kâzım Karabekir visited him in the small northern Anatolian town where he had taken refuge, and there they discussed the twenty-two-day Battle of Sakarya (August–September 1921), the turning point in the war against Greece.[39] Upon his death his relatives removed his body to the Süleymaniye Mosque in Istanbul. The symbolism of laying a man from the provinces to rest in the very heart of the imperial capital would not have been lost on Tabbakh's readers. While in retrospect an enigmatic though tragic figure, Tabbakh's Mahmud Kamil was exemplary at the time of Tabbakh's writing of the way a *modern* Muslim man of nonnotable origins could successfully navigate the rapidly changing polit-

[36] Ahmad, *Making*, 48.
[37] *Notables*, 7:613.
[38] Ibid., 7:615.
[39] Ibid., 7:616.

ical and ethical terrain of the Eastern Mediterranean. Mahmud Kamil continued to believe in the modernity of the empire and its bureaucratic and political underpinnings until his death. Conversely, in pledging allegiance to the new construct of Syria, Ibrahim Hananu had recognized the futility of any hope in the restoration of the empire, but not the implicit hierarchies and forms of distinction that the empire had buttressed. Had Mahmud Kamil lived longer he would have been faced with this Hobson's Choice, a choice in some ways akin to having to decide between serving in heaven or ruling in hell; perhaps like members of his family in the interwar period, he would have settled in Istanbul and become comfortably part of Turkey's professional and bureaucratic middle class.

THE GREAT WAR AS ETHICAL CHALLENGE: GHAZZI'S *RIVER OF GOLD*

A moment of terror gave way to wonder as a noisy flying machine appeared for the first time in Aleppo (1913). The Fokker biplane, its tail adorned with the Star and Crescent of the Ottoman Empire, flew into the city just before the sunset prayers the year before war engulfed the Sublime State. The moment's importance even showed through the normally understated prose of the Aleppine chronicler, Kamil al-Ghazzi. Under the heading of "The First Airplane in the Skies above Aleppo," he wrote,

> After circling the city for a while, two Turkish young men—skilled in the art of flying—both members of the Young Turks, Fethi and Sadik, brought their plane to rest in a field near Sabil. Government and military dignitaries, the notables of the city, and groups of regular people went out to greet them and look at [their plane]. When the plane came to rest on the ground, they let out a great cheer and applauded. Voices shouted out calling for the state's victory. The two pilots stayed for a few days and celebrations were held for them. The people bestowed great honors on them. They left Aleppo [whereupon the plane crashed near Amman] and when the people heard of this, they were sorry. The goal of sending this plane and the others which came after to this region was to announce to the Ottoman peoples that the state was concerned with advancing the art of war like any great state and to wake up its two peoples [Arabs and Turks] from their slumber and to urge them to dust themselves off and free themselves from the sloth which was upon them.[40]

---

[40] *River*, 3:535. The two pilots had intended to fly between Istanbul and Cairo, with several stops along the way. After their crash, the pilots were buried in the garden-cemetery of Saladin's mausoleum in Damascus. The projected flight, a story known by all Turkish school children, is commemorated with a memorial in the Fatih district of Istanbul. The

For the Ottoman Empire as a modernizing state, the deployment of new technologies had great symbolic importance, as evidenced by Ghazzi's understanding of the political goal of the spectacle. However, with this passage and others, especially those that presented a dispassionate catalog of the harms visited upon Aleppo in the preceding decade, the historian painted a picture of the city that asserted its membership in a broader polity, but also emphasized its special character. Ghazzi's account of Aleppo's history—completed two years after Tabbakh's volume went to press—benefited from hindsight unavailable to his colleague. By then, any hope of reestablishing the empire had been extinguished with the creation of the Republic of Turkey. The Arab Kingdom had likewise failed as an independent state, and the prospect of the return of King Faysal, at that point Britain's puppet monarch in Iraq, held little appeal. A distinct understanding of the past formed the ethical and political bases of these alternatives. As historians wrote that past, they sought to explain not only Aleppo's presence in the wider world, but also the basic logic of that wider world. In *Halab* that logic revolved around an explicitly modern ideology that vested rights and sovereignty in the nation. The editors of *Halab* had sought to persuade Aleppines that they belonged to a nation where dimensions had been formed within the nexus of language, ethnicity, and history. While Tabbakh may have recognized these dimensions, in his narrative he dismissed them and instead wrote Aleppo *back* into a stream of history that embraced a universal Islamic community in which civilization, justice, and authority derived from an authentic Ottoman past.

However, choosing either path carried certain inevitable costs, a choice made more problematic as the city fell under French control. *Halab*'s definition of Aleppo placed it in a position that made it subordinate commercially and politically to Damascus, the capital of Syria. Further, it allowed for a type of internal colonization as Arabs from other parts of the newly elaborated Arab nation had the right to exert power and authority in Aleppo. Also, the onset of a linguistic or ethnic basis for sovereignty carried with it the possibility that once-subordinate classes and groups in society—Christians, Jews, and even women—could share power. The inverse of this proposed order dominated Tabbakh's history. Cheering with unabashed exuberance the burning of Izmir, celebrating the life of Mahmud Kamil, and praising the Ottoman Anatolian resistance, Tabbakh argued for Muslim superiority in any political entity. Such a construct held great appeal to men like Ibrahim Hananu whose very *habitus* had been disrupted by the war. Conversely, it appealed little to non-Mus-

---

memorial includes a relief plaque that depicts the flight plan and shows the airplanes flying above the pyramids, representing Cairo, and the Blue Mosque, for Istanbul.

lims in Aleppo who, as a consequence of the arrival of vast numbers of Armenian refugees, now constituted more than 30 percent of the population.[41] The rejection of this basis of authority, or a fear of its radical implementation, had led many Christians and Jews to support the CUP in the prewar period. It had led even more—Armenians and Greek Catholics in particular—to voice strong support for the French Mandate.

By contrast, Ghazzi outlined in his history a modus vivendi for intercommunal, even interethnic, comity. Unlike *Halab*, in which a clearly identifiable ideology was salient and in which the act of persuasion dominated the rhetorical activity, Ghazzi's text sought to "authorize" a form of postwar social practice by employing the aesthetic of bourgeois historiography. As Hayden White argues in his discussion of Droysen's *Historik*:

> any society, in order to sustain the practices that permit it to function in the interests of its dominant groups, must devise cultural strategies to promote the identification of its subjects with the moral and legal system that "authorizes" the society's practices. Seen from this perspective, a given kind of art, literature, or historiography need not be construed as a consciously constructed instrument for convincing the members of a society of the truth of certain doctrines, for indoctrinating them into certain beliefs of an economic or political kind. On the contrary, the ideological element in art, literature, or historiography consists of the projection of the kind of subjectivity that its viewers or readers must take on in order to experience it as art, as literature, or as historiography.[42]

Ghazzi wrote a history with which his society's middle class in particular could actively identify through their own patterns of behavior. He emphasized unity between Turks and Arabs and Christians and Muslims within a hierarchical social system. He also wrote Armenians into Aleppo's present. And with a lengthy discussion of French history until the occupation of Syria, he situated Aleppo in the stream of Eurocentric history. He exhibited the same tendencies in the pivotal roles he played in the reconstitution of the Aleppo Chamber of Commerce[43] and as a founding member of the archaeological society.[44] Each formulation was calculated to reflect the inherent particularism of the city: its uniqueness and an invented tradition of tolerance and cross-sectarian cooperation.

Ghazzi had been a permanent feature of Aleppo's literary scene since the late nineteenth century. Serving on the staff of the provincial paper,

---

[41] On population figures, see Khoury, *Mandate*, 16.

[42] "Droysen, *Historik*: Historical Writing as a Bourgeois Science," in *The Content of the Form*, 86–87.

[43] *Bulletin Economique de la Chambre du Commerce d'Alep* (Aleppo: Maronite Press, 1921).

[44] See G. Rabbath's obituary for Ghazzi in the Aleppo Archeological Society's journal, *Majallat al-ʿAdiyyat al-Suriyya* 3:1–2 (January–February 1933).

Fırat, in the 1890s, he also helped to edit the province's yearbook, the *Sâlnâme*. However, along with several other officials, Ghazzi lost his position in the bureaucracy in the wake of the 1919 massacre of Armenian refugees in Aleppo. While he was not held directly responsible for the events, the authorities in Damascus had used this opportunity to remove him and other local opponents of Faysal's rule from office and replace them with Palestinians and others whom Ghazzi considered "foreigners." This left him bitter and resentful. For the first time in three decades, he was forced to leave government service, whereupon he turned to composing his magnum opus, the *River of Gold*. Published in 1926, it is a freeranging work that drew liberally on previous annals. It was also the first local Aleppine book to make reference to European primary sources, including Alexander Russell's eighteenth-century account of his decadeslong residence in the city, *The Natural History of Aleppo*.[45]

While many writers on Aleppo have used Ghazzi as a source for the history of the early modern period, he has rarely been used as a source for the history of his own time.[46] Like Tabbakh, Ghazzi's account of the rapidly changing period through which he lived is an untapped resource for understanding the *Weltanschauung* of post-Ottoman, Muslim middleclass bureaucrat-intellectuals. Likewise, while most of the sections dedicated to earlier history are a rather dry retelling of events, his discussions of events he himself witnessed are vivid, including his account of the event that transformed his life, the massacre of Armenian refugees in 1919.

In this, one of the longest and most sustained argumentative passages in his work, Ghazzi presented his readers with a formula for urban coexistence. He had developed this idea in a previous section on the 1850 outbreak of sectarian violence in Aleppo, when he wrote at length on a local tradition of tolerance and blamed the assault against the city's Christian quarter on tribal people and outsiders.[47] He even sought to exonerate his own family, noting that his father, a local cleric, had been humiliated by the perpetrators of the violence. As Masters suggests, "alGhazzi . . . used a tragic historical occurrence as an object lesson in citizenship for his contemporaries. . . . The message was . . . [G]ood Syrians do not kill their neighbors, even if they practice a different religion, and

---

[45] Alexander Russell, *The Natural History of Aleppo* (London: Robinson, 1794), 2 vols.

[46] Masters, *Origins*; Marcus, *Eve*; Sauvaget, *Alep*; and Heghnar Watenpaugh, *The Image of an Ottoman City* (Leiden: Brill, 2004).

[47] This formula is similar to that adopted by the author of the account of the 1860 massacres in Damascus and Lebanon, Mikhail Mishaqa. See his *al-Jawab ʿala iqtirah al-ahbab* [Translated as *Murder, Mayhem, Pillage and Plunder: The History of Lebanon in the 18th and 19th Centuries*], trans. W. M. Thackston, Jr. (Albany: State University of New York Press, 1988).

the rioters in 1850, having violated this, had become national pariahs."[48] For Ghazzi, narratives of civil violence would be a consummate didactic tool. His dismissal from office in 1919—and the presumption of guilt that accompanied it—redoubled his need to mount an apologia for himself and his fellow Aleppines. This process of exculpation rested on the rhetorical strategy of blaming the victim. While not unsympathetic to the Armenian refugees, Ghazzi singled out a group among them guilty of stepping beyond established rules of behavior and social practices. In his analysis of the events leading up to the massacre, Ghazzi employed a concept he labeled *husn al-mukafa'a* to define ideal social behavior. A term not easily translated, its meaning is roughly akin to equipoise, a sense of fair play, a fair exchange of favors or goods, equanimity, or social grace and signified for the author a system of well-mannered, conventional social interaction.

Under the title of "The Armenian Incident, Known by the Name, the Civil Disturbances of 28 February 1919," Ghazzi explained what happened and why in a way that would instruct readers on the way to behave in the future. It should be recalled that the massacre had likewise been used by the editors of *Halab* as a tool to distinguish Arabs from Turks and to discipline recalcitrant elements in Aleppine society. In Ghazzi's version, while "inherent" ethnic characteristics may have played a role, ultimately, those responsible for the violence were the alien Armenians who had rejected the essential principles of Aleppine social behavior.

"We cannot deny," Ghazzi began, "that among the Armenian people are men and women who are intelligent, forbearing and have *husn al-mukafa'a*," but, he rejoined, "we cannot shrink from mentioning that there are in the common people of this community a degenerate group who have descended into ignorance and have turned onto a path of vengeance." This group of "bad seeds" had emerged because "the elite of the Armenian community had lost control . . . and the troublesome faction had left its mark on the Aleppines; they have angered them and destroyed the confidence the Aleppines had in the Armenians and rage has filled them."[49] This rage was all the more bitter as the Aleppines had given refuge to the Armenians,

> the Arab community in general—and Aleppines in particular—viewed the Armenian community with an eye of compassion and mercy, and we condemn what the leaders of the Kurds did to the Armenians as an outrage, and we condemn Sultan Abdülhamid for the calamity visited on the Armenians. . . . We can not speak of a single member of the Arab community who dipped his hand

[48] Masters, "The 1850 Events in Aleppo," 10–11. Ghazzi covers the events in *River*, 3:382–388.

[49] *River*, 3:553.

in Armenian blood in these dreadful massacres and not one who failed to live up to Islamic law which guarantees to the *dhimmis* protection of their wealth, land and blood. *And perhaps if anyone in the Arab community did cooperate with the Turkish people in these massacres, then they did so because Sultan Abdülhamid had robbed them of their husn al-mukafa'a.*

He continued to catalog Aleppine generosity to Armenians who "arrived with just the shirts on their backs, . . . [T]he Arab community—and Aleppines in particular—treated them as guests and extended to them the hand of kindness . . . the opposite of what was provided to them by Cemal [which was] only sorrow and pain." Despite the *husn al-mukafa'a* that was expected from the Armenian community, they repaid Aleppo with "the exact opposite" and "incurred the rancor of the Aleppines and lit the fire of hatred."[50] Thus Aleppines, and their status as Arabs or, more important, as non-Turks and non-Kurds were innocent bystanders of the genocidal violence of the war.

Ghazzi follows this description of the ungrateful refugee community with a catalog of six specific transgressions by the Armenians. Part urban legend, part anecdote, the transgressions outline behavior deemed unacceptable by Ghazzi as a systematic departure from social grace. The "crimes" of the Armenians cross the boundaries of hospitality, commerce, and sexual and filial relations. Moreover, whereas Ghazzi makes reference to the names of people throughout his text, the Armenians—criminal or otherwise—remain anonymous and faceless. The first of these outrages occurred in Adana, then under Franco-Armenian administration. Armenian employees of the local train station beat and robbed Aleppine traders and soldiers. In a similar vein, Armenians had joined the French Army "in Lebanon and Cilicia with arrogance and impunity and had fired their rifles at some [Muslim] citizens and killed them."[51] The central crime in this last complaint was more the transgressive and threatening sight of an armed non-Muslim.

Subsequent transgressions took on a particularly Aleppine flavor. Armenians forced local merchants to accept Egyptian paper money instead of metal coinage at an inflated exchange rate, and otherwise behaved dishonestly in the marketplace. He illustrated this with a story about an Armenian who had arranged the purchase of a jerry can of butter fat. The Armenian had asked for the can to be delivered to his home where he would pay for it. The merchant agreed, sending a servant to the address

---

[50] Ibid., 3:554, emphasis mine.

[51] Ibid. In this passage, Ghazzi is making reference to the formation of the Armenian Legion. This had been given as the chief cause of the massacre by foreign observers in Aleppo at the time. PRO FO 371/4179 E 39672/2117/44. General Headquarters Egypt to War Office, 3 March 1919.

the Armenian had given him with the can. His servant delivered the can as agreed. The Armenian accepted the can and entered his house, leaving the merchant's servant outside. A long while passed and the Armenian failed to reappear. Confused, the servant knocked on the door. He subsequently learned that the house had two doors, and the Armenian who had taken the butter fat did not live there and had left by the other door. "This type of outrage was continually visited upon the Aleppine merchants . . . throughout the winter [1918–1919]. And news of these things spread amongst the Aleppines and they grew to detest the Armenians."[52]

Reason six entered the intimate spaces of the city.

> There were a large number of Armenian girls and their children living with the Aleppines. The Aleppines had given them shelter from the very first moment they took refuge in Aleppo. They had gathered them from the desert . . . and saw to their upkeep and cared for their children. Some [Muslims] took from the legally mature girls, legal wives and adopted their children.

Foreign intervention usurped this legal and accepted practice of Muslim men marrying Christian girls and widows. Ghazzi notes that upon the occupation of Aleppo by the British, the Red Cross rounded up Armenian children and women from the homes of Aleppines. "We do not rebuke the Armenian sect for wanting to return their children to their bosom, because this is what their racial traits directed them to do, yet we condemn them for the way that this prejudice aided violence and assaulted friendship."[53] As discussed in a subsequent chapter, bowing to Western pressure, Faysal had ordered Aleppo's Muslims to give up all Armenians living in their households. The "recovery" of Armenian women and children was the chief occupation of Western relief agencies in Aleppo in the immediate postwar period. In the wake of the genocide, thousands of girls, boys, and young women had been bought or incorporated into Muslim households. In Aleppo it was also thought that approximately two hundred girls had been sold into sexual slavery in the city's extensive network of brothels.[54] In "recovering" the women and children, the Armenians and the police had entered the homes of Muslims and often taken children from their adopted parents or wives from their husbands "by force." Using a technique similar to the butter-fat incident to illustrate the outrage

---

[52] Ibid., 3:555.

[53] Ibid., 3:556.

[54] PRO FO 371/3405 199352/55708/44 Sykes (Cairo) to Secretary of State (London), 2 December 1918; *Lions of Marash*, 43–48. Ghazzi's description is the only one produced by a contemporary Muslim writer on this topic. His anger seems to derive from the fact that many of the women "rescued" were wives of the men with whom they were living, and he could not understand that missionaries like Kerr saw this mixing of Armenian women with Muslim men as tantamount to miscegenation of the very worst kind.

occasioned by this behavior, Ghazzi told in vivid detail the story of an unnamed Armenian refugee woman married to a Muslim man. Eventually, the brother and the original Armenian husband of the woman, presumed dead, came to take her back. The Muslim husband refused to return her to them, "as was his right under Islamic law."[55] The police took the Muslim to jail and she, by force, to a "rescue home."[56] Locked away in a roof-top room and guarded by two nuns, the woman demanded the right to return to her Muslim husband and refused all food and drink. Meanwhile, her daughter by the Muslim husband was taken from her. In a daring escape, she leapt from her room down onto the street below and returned to her Muslim husband, who had been released. The police arrested him again and returned her to the "rescue home." Interrogated by Armenian priests, she stated that if she were not allowed to return, she would kill herself. Seeing her resolve, her Armenian husband gave up and allowed her to return. "So she returned to their house, and she has stayed with him [her Muslim husband] until today, having given him many more children."[57]

More troubling still, in addition to the Armenian children adopted by Muslims, the legitimate children of local Muslims risked "rescue" by the Red Cross. One six-year-old boy was taken from his family and, despite the testimony of the family's Muslim and Christian neighbors to the contrary, an Armenian man took him to his home. While this particular boy was eventually returned to his "true father," many others remained with Armenians. For Ghazzi this constituted interference in a Muslim's own home, own *harim*, something that was unprecedented, illegal, and a most terrible invasion of privacy. Further, he did not differentiate between "slavery" and "family," and as such seems disinclined toward some notions of emancipation and bourgeois domesticity consistent with modernity, although he remained committed to its insistence on privacy.[58]

From these antinormative insults to the nature of the Aleppine architecture of community emerges an image of correct social practices—*husn al-mukafa'a*. In its absence, the violence that erupted in 1919 was inevitable. Yet the immediate cause was one final incident of social malpractice, the stealing of a cow. Preceding the outbreak of violence by a few days, an Armenian sold a cow that did not belong to him. When the purchaser sought to resell the cow to the original owner at the Friday livestock mar-

[55] *River*, 3:557. Ghazzi's understanding of the law on this point may not have been wholly accurate.

[56] Kerr, *Lions*, 48.

[57] *River*, 3:558.

[58] Ibid. For a contrasting narrative from the perspective of some of these women and children, see Donald E. Miller and Lorna Touryan Miller, *Survivors: An Oral History of the Armenian Genocide* (Los Angeles: University of California Press, 1993), 94–136.

ket in the great plaza at the foot of the citadel, an argument broke out.
At that moment the "criminal Armenian" happened by, and they demanded of him the price of the cow. "The situation grew worse between
the two men and it attracted a crowd of thousands—Muslims, Christians,
and Jews—waiting to see what would transpire. Then the argument
changed from one of words to one of blows." This spark set off the orgy
of violence. "A crowd took up knives, steel bars and wooden bats . . .
[and] within minutes thirty Armenians lay wounded on the ground."[59]
Ghazzi is careful to note that during this *fitna* "many Muslims opened
their doors to their Armenian neighbors, sheltering them from the uprising and defending them from harm."[60] Upon the return to order, Ghazzi
asserted that the reaction of the British authorities and their Faysali allies
fell disproportionately upon the Muslim inhabitants of the city: ten notables were arrested along with the "troublemakers," many of whom were
executed or exiled to Egypt.[61] In the narrative, the people of Aleppo were
made victims twice over: first at the hands of the Armenians, and then by
the Arab government and its European supporters.

In a telling epilogue to the violence, Ghazzi described the formation of
a permanent committee of Muslim, Christian, and Jewish religious leaders. This group met shortly after the "insanity" of 28 February to "re-
affirm the love and ancient amity [*al-wala' al-qadimin*] between these
communities, to prevent a recurrence of this event which has sullied their
goodness, and to leave behind any traces of anger and rancor in their
hearts." The Muslim clerics, Jewish rabbis, and Christian priests would
gather once a week at one of their residences. "And who ever was hosting
the party would provide tea and all sorts of sweets and fresh fruits."[62]
Thus, Armenian excess and transgression, understandable Muslim reaction, and external interference had all been mitigated through the establishment of an institutionalized forum for sectarian interaction. The basis
for action by this institution itself rested upon the creation of an agreed
upon body of facts about Aleppo and Aleppines. Aleppines are tolerant;
Aleppines are honorable businessmen; Aleppines are hospitable; Aleppines possess *husn al-mukafa'a*. In sum, these virtues constitute a type of
civic technology, distinct from civil society, as a means for urban coexistence that allowed religious and ethnic difference to exist, though it did
not assert equality.

More to the point, the ideology underlying Ghazzi's *husn al-mukafa'a*
and the anti-Armenian polemic implicitly rejects notions about the indi-

---

[59] *River*, 3:558–559. Figures given by Western diplomats were higher.

[60] Ibid.

[61] Ibid., 3:561.

[62] Ibid. These meetings remained a regular occurrence in Aleppo at least through the
1930s.

vidual and the community that played a fundamental role in prevailing conceptions of middle-class modernity at the time, as evidenced in contemporary discourse. *Husn al-mukafa'a* may be fair play, but not everyone must play by the same rules; knowing one's unchanging place in the scheme of things takes priority over any kind of social mobility or societal modernization. Likewise, the story of the "bad Armenians" derives from a denial of the existence of individual rights and asserts the preeminence of communal rights. Armenians were legitimately—or at least understandably—punished communally. And likewise, the Faysali administrators, adopting the same practice, punished the whole of the Muslim community, not just those who committed the outrage. Ghazzi's vision of the future of Aleppo, while incorporating certain features of bourgeois social practice, failed to address the central middle-class dilemma of the antebellum period.[63] An ever-widening gulf continued to divide the Muslim and non-Muslim middle classes of the city. And that division appears acutely in the most personal realm. Muslim political dominance had facilitated the integration of non-Muslim refugee women and children into Muslim households. The inherently unequal position of non-Muslims in Ghazzi's Aleppo made the return of these women both illegal and immoral, while a very real demand to reclaim the community—a drive that was explained by Armenian and local Westerners as a conflict between the forces of civilization and barbarism—appeared as an equally moral *modern* imperative.

The question of "what did it mean?" or rather "what does the past mean for us now?" rested at the heart of the narrative histories that emerged in the wake of the World War I. In several venues and with various means, local intellectuals sought to answer this question. The answers themselves were not without value or power, as alternative visions of the immediate past linked Aleppo and Aleppines with the world around them in different ways. Just as *Halab's* editors chose to direct their readers down an unknown and untested nationalist path, Tabbakh had urged them to return to the sultan's fold. Ottomans like Mahmud Kamil had answered that call and rejected an ethnic definition of themselves. Bereft of either alternative, Ghazzi, sought compromise, recognizing the political super-strata of French domination by writing Aleppo politically into French history.[64] The "Incident" is followed by the final twenty pages of Ghazzi's annals, which are dedicated exclusively to French history from the time of the Celts and include a brief section on the life of Joan of Arc, in Arabic, *Jandark*, and the French Revolution. The story unfolds as though *nos*

[63] Göçek, *Rise*, 136.
[64] *River*, 3:585.

ancêtres les Gaulois had become *ajdaduna,* "our grandfathers," as well. Ultimately nostalgia, Ghazzi's history failed to take into account the social forces unleashed by the growing power of the city's non-Muslim middle class. And in Ghazzi's conservative reaction it is possible to identify streams of thought, perceptions of history, and a belief in the subordinate role of non-Muslims in Islamic society that course through recent Islamist writings.

In being modern, the middle class was able to seek in the succeeding years to use its comprehension of political organization and institutions to create alliances with the colonial powers to carve out a more substantive degree of power. Made most manifest in elections and political formations in the next two decades, this attempt again brought the middle class into conflict with the old social classes of the city. Divided and quiescent in the early 1920s, the notability would reemerge as a formidable political force in the local milieu by using many of the intellectual tools that had seemed the reserve of the middle class against it.

By 1924 Aleppo's history had also become inextricably linked to the events of the Armenian Genocide and its aftermath. Yet, while the history of the genocide is among the most controversial elements of the contemporary study of the Middle East, it has played a rather limited role in broader history writing about the region. Trapped into a sterile polemical discourse by the Turkish government's denial in the face of overwhelming evidence that the events of 1915 were a genocide, the study of the centrally organized effort to rid Anatolia of its Ottoman-Armenian citizens is burdened as well by those who see in the episodes of ethnic cleansing and campaigns of extermination evidence of inherent Muslim fanaticism or a genetic predisposition of Turks toward murder and mayhem. This last assertion, its ethnocentrism aside, is contradicted by the principled, but ultimately ineffective, stand taken by dozens of Ottoman officials like Celal and Hüseyin Kâzım, and the innumerable acts of kindness extended to refugees along the routes of deportation by townsfolk and Bedouin. That discussions of the massacres and the role of Armenians in interwar Syrian society are so prominent in much of the Arabic-language literature of the period confirms the need to integrate the genocide more thoroughly into the social and intellectual history of the Eastern Mediterranean—it is more than just a problem of Armenian history in the way the Holocaust is more than just a problem of Jewish history. Moreover, understanding the Armenian Genocide as an elemental feature of the region's encounter with modernity and not a manifestation of "age-old" sectarian and communal hatred allows its study to shed light on larger issues of citizenship, secularism, and the rule of law at a moment of revolution and world-historical change; likewise, the prominent role of educated middle-class members of a Westernizing reform movement in its implementation reveals the brutal possibilities associated with being modern.

Finally, while the *tabaqat* and *khitat* would cease to be employed in history writing in Syria, the works of Tabbakh and Ghazzi filled an emotional and intellectual need in the city's modern collective consciousness and continue to be manifestations of what Arjun Appadurai calls "imagined nostalgia."[65] Both books are still in print and can be found in the home libraries of many educated Aleppines, their longevity linked to the fact that citizens of the Gray City perceive something of themselves in the books, and keeping copies on their shelves provides a dignified sense of connection with an Aleppo that once held such promise. At the same time the Aleppines that they can see in these books are more easily recognizable than the Arabs of Orientalist-inspired fantasies or the distant Hittites, Arameans, or sundry other antique peoples.

[65] Arjun Appadurai, *Modernity at Large: Cultural Dimensions of Globalization* (Minneapolis: University of Minnesota Press, 1996), 77.

Being Modern in an Era of Colonialism

MIDDLE-CLASS MODERNITY AND THE CULTURE OF
THE FRENCH MANDATE FOR SYRIA (1925–1946)

> This traditional weakness, which is almost congenital to the
> national consciousness of underdeveloped countries, is not
> solely the result of the mutilation of the colonized people by
> the colonial regime. It is also the result of the intellectual lazi-
> ness of the national bourgeoisie, of its spiritual penury, and
> of the profoundly cosmopolitan mold that its mind is set in.
> —Frantz Fanon, *The Wretched of the Earth, 1961*

France's Mandates for Syria and Lebanon and the Britain's Mandates for
Palestine, Trans-Jordan, and Iraq were peculiar fictions created by the
League of Nations to provide diplomatic cover for the colonial ambitions
the two countries had first expressed in the Sykes-Picot Agreement of
1915. Article 22 of the League's Covenant explained the need for these
mandates:

> To those colonies and territories which as a consequence of the late war have
> ceased to be under the sovereignty of the States which formerly governed them
> and which are inhabited by peoples not yet able to stand by themselves under
> the strenuous conditions of the modern world, there should be applied the prin-
> ciple that the well-being and development of such peoples form a sacred trust
> of civilisation and that securities for the performance of this trust should be
> embodied in this *Covenant*.[1]

To bring those peoples into that "strenuous modern world," "advanced
nations who by reason of their resources, their experience or their geographical position can best undertake this responsibility" would take on
the burden of "tutelage." And while the League recognized the "existence
[of the Arab states of the Eastern Mediterranean] as independent nations," they would be "subject to the rendering of administrative advice
and assistance by a Mandatory until such time as they are able to stand

---

[1] *Covenant of the League of Nations* (Geneva: League of Nations, 1924).

alone." Ultimately, the mandate system regarded the superintending role as temporary. At the time of their establishment, however, the voluntary exit of a colonial power was unprecedented, and many considered the French and British presence open-ended, despite Wilsonian idealism to the contrary.

The British sought to rule their mandates through indirect means, while the French generally employed a more "hands-on" approach, managing elements of society with a vast network of French civil servants and a large military force of French citizens, colonial troops from Northwest Africa, Senegal, and Indochina, and the Armée du Levant—a unit cobbled together primarily from local Armenian, Alawite, and Ismaili volunteers. They also used a policy of divide and rule by creating client states where the plurality of the populations were non-Sunni Muslims, like Lebanon, or "compact minorities," including the Druzes and the Alawites, which could then be played off against Sunni Muslim majorities in the remainder of the Levant. Beyond the political expediency of divide and rule, creating Lebanon was a manifestation of France's claim to be the protector of the Eastern Mediterranean's Christians, primarily its Maronite and Greek Catholics. On administrative grounds, the state of Aleppo became for a short period a separate entity from the state of Damascus. This ministate, about the size of Kansas, was complete with its own legislature, government, and flag.

As noted in previous chapters, the French presence in the Eastern Mediterranean was initially greeted with violence in the far north of the province of Aleppo, forcing an abandonment of France's ambitions in Cilicia. Subsequently, inland Syria became a more important element of imperial policy than had been anticipated in the immediate postwar period. Employing styles of bureaucratic administration used in its other colonial possessions, France took an aggressive stance toward the reorganization of Syrian society. This contributed to the Great Syrian Revolt of 1925–1927, which would prove costly to French interests and a focus for emerging organized opposition to their rule. Beginning as a revolt against an intrusive land reform and registration program, it was led by the rural notable and Druze emir, Sultan Atrash. A guerrilla force under his command pushed the French from the Druze Mountain. Urban uprisings followed in Damascus and Homs, and while Ibrahim Hananu and others encouraged rebellion, most Aleppines demurred. The French responded to the uprising with disproportionate ferocity, shelling parts of the old city of Damascus and using airplanes to strafe civilian populations in addition to military targets. Only when reinforcements arrived from North Africa at the conclusion of the Rif War did the French regain control of the entire country. The costs of the Great Revolt in lives of French soldiers and money led France to reconsider its style of rule in Syria. One of its first acts was to draw together Aleppo and Damascus into one state. The capital would be Damascus and, consonant with a more nuanced policy, the Syrians—a designation that had gained more relevance as a result of creation of this new state and bureaucratic structures—were encouraged to contest elections and write a constitution. Though no longer an independent state, Aleppo would have a great deal of local autonomy, its own municipality, and a provincial council.

In reality, the French assistant delegate to Aleppo—an advisor in name only—ruled the city; he reported to the French high commissioner for Syria and Lebanon, located in Beirut. And while locals were often employed in various low-level capacities, French administrators filled elite technical, policing, military, cultural, and administrative positions with Europeans, creating a typical colonial "glass ceiling" that engendered a great deal of resentment from the growing ranks of middle-class Syrian engineers, educators, and bureaucrats.

Intent on regaining the kind of social and political hegemony they had enjoyed in the prerevolutionary period—the "Politics of Notables"—the old social classes of Syria's cities organized themselves into the National Bloc (1925). Joined by a cadre of middle-class intellectuals, the bloc entered into a complex political dance with the French, employing "honorable cooperation" to at times work with, and at others oppose, the French in attempts to gain independence. In the short term, they hoped to play the same intermediary role for the French that their predecessors had played for the Ottoman political elite; yet this would merely be the prologue to their formal control of the postcolonial state. "Honorable cooperation" ebbed and flowed, but, with a few exceptions, Syria remained quiet through the 1920s and 1930s. And although Syrians were given a greater political role in the running of their country with the reintroduction of elections, an assembly, a prime minister, and a president, France maintained real power through the manipulation of elections, the control of military, foreign, finance, and monetary policy, and a veto over Syrian initiatives.

The election of a left-wing government in France (1936) led to the drafting of a treaty to end the mandate on the model of the one that had ended British rule in Iraq (1932). A bloc-led general strike of that year, which was accompanied by violent street protests and the organization of fascist-type paramilitary units in the Syria's major cities, contributed to a French willingness to leave the country. The Syrian Parliament ratified the treaty that same year, but it became stalled in France as the leftist coalition came apart, and it was rejected altogether by the subsequent administration. In a cynical act calculated to garner Turkish support in the coming world war, France ceded the rich subprovince of Alexandretta, inhabited primarily by Arabs and Armenians, to Turkey (1938). As the province, and its main city Antioch were the last significant parts of Aleppo's commercial hinterland still within Syria's borders, and the town of Alexandretta the nearest deepwater seaport, their annexation by Turkey dealt a lethal blow to the city's economy. It also constituted a profound affront to emerging Syrian and Pan-Arab nationalist movements and sent another wave of refugees into Aleppo. More broadly, French economic policy and the division of the entire region into small states disrupted long-established regional trade patterns, retarded the process of industrialization that had started in the late Ottoman period, and perpetuated the underdevelopment of the Syrian financial markets and manufacturing sector; conversely, areas under cultivation expanded, especially with the introduction of irrigation networks, tractors, and mechanical harvesters in Syria's portion of Mesopotamia.

With the outbreak of World War II, Syria's limited constitution was suspended and the high commissioner ruled by decree. Briefly under Vichy control, Syria was invaded and occupied by British forces in 1941 to deny Axis landing rights. The French would seek to reestablish their preeminence in Syria after the war, though faced with British and Syrian opposition, they evacuated in 1946, but not before shelling the parliament building in Damascus, which still bears the scars—"a reminder" in the words of Philip Khoury, "of France's quarter-century of commitment to educating the people under her Mandate in the values of Western civilization and democracy."[2]

An article by Fathallah Qastun in his journal, *al-Shuʿla*, entitled "Aleppo between Terror and Hope" (1921) poignantly renders the first moments of that French presence in his city's body politic. It paints the picture of a forbearing and honorable French government acting in its and Aleppo's best interests against what Qastun viewed as a rabble of incompetent, dishonest, and uncivilized Arabs from the Hejaz. While it was possible that Qastun received a subvention from the French to author this panegyric, diplomatic accounts that revealed papers like *al-Taqaddum*, *al-Nahda*, and *al-Watan* to have received sub rosa support from the French do not list his.[3]

"When the Faysali government realized how tenuous its hold on the throne was," began Qastun, "it worked as hard as possible to turn the people against the mandatory government by using acts of terrorism, murder and aggression." And while the French under "His Excellency Henri Gouraud tried to guard the peace . . . the enmity and tyranny of the tribes increased." French ultimatums followed Faysali intitatives like

[2] Khoury, *Mandate*, 617.
[3] PRO FO 861/68 "Report on the Situation at Aleppo," 9 September 1920.

conscription and curfews. Worst yet, the Faysalis "spread lies that France and the French were the enemies of religion and civilization, but they did not deceive with their lies anyone except primitive tribesmen and naïve people."[4]

After the French announced that the day of "liberation" was near, "The Faysalis departed the Gray City to who knows where clothed in the garments of oppression." This prevented open combat, but "The Aleppines did not know this and they slept fitfully that night expecting at any moment an attack by the tribes and rabble." However, when "dawn broke on the 23rd [June 1920] voices of joy and welcome greeted the beloved French soldiers and their commander de Lamothe who spread out over Aleppo like the waves of the sea. As they entered, no blood was spilled, and they prevented a reign of terror. This established good feelings and confidence in Aleppo" toward the French. Upon occupying the city, General de Lamothe issued a proclamation, which Qastun hailed as evidence of the "magnanimity, noble compassion and high ideals for which the French are known."[5] Qastun then printed an Arabic translation of the general's words. Due to a lack of punctuation, it is hard to determine where the French officer ends and the journal editor begins.

Qastun's initial acceptance of the legitimacy of the French Mandate and the underlying language of liberation seems at odds with the self-confidence and sense of self-reliance seen in his 1910 speech to the Aleppo Mutual Aid Society. Rather, Qastun, who eagerly and confidently greeted the twentieth century by pointing with pride to the civilized modernity of the Ottoman peoples, had grown so disenchanted in the intervening years that he welcomed the French Mandate for Syria in 1920, seeing it not just as a way to end the chaos of the war years and their aftermath, but also as a logical and necessary step in the completion of the project of modernity. Qastun was representative of the portion of the middle class of Aleppo and the other cities of the region, tired of the continuing wars, lack of public security, disruptions of trade, and the seeming ineptitude of first late Ottoman and then Faysali governance, who were willing to embrace French rule.

Their decision was not a misplaced devotion to French imperialism or eagerness to collaborate for selfish or narcissistic reasons, as Frantz Fanon would argue,[6] but instead a consequence of what France meant *at that moment*. For many Aleppines the French language and sojourns in France

---

[4] Fathallah Qastun "Aleppo between Terror and Hope," *al-Shuʿla* 2:1 (August 1921): 68, 69.

[5] Ibid., 70, 71.

[6] Frantz Fanon, *The Wretched of the Earth*, Constance Farrington, trans. (New York: Grove Press, 1963), 149.

had been part of their education, and there was nothing mysterious or magical about the French; nor did they imagine simply translating facility in the French language into French citizenship. The arrival of the French, whom they had known only from a distance, presaged the resumption, perhaps even an acceleration, of the process of becoming and being modern. Moreover it held the promise of a more thorough integration into the transnational networks of trade, commerce, and thought, which played such a prominent role in the way middle-class modernity was understood and experienced. Finally, secular citizenship and the full measure of equality that had been promised but not delivered by the Revolution of 1908 was equally part of public French political discourse, and the integration of non-Muslims into the local administration, army, police forces, and government was perceived by Christians, Jews, and others as evidence of that commitment.

This is what makes Qastun's article affecting: it crystallizes the broader significance of the moment of initial colonial encounter. Dates such as 23 July 1920 in the colonial world are emblematic of perhaps not the last, but certainly among the final, instances when the colonized can believe—or have convinced themselves—that the colonizer is capable of recognizing in them equally modern people, people *just as modern* as he. Qastun's response stands in stark contrast to that of others in his class. As he welcomed the French, his former allies and acquaintances continued to fight a guerrilla war in the countryside around the city as part of a broader strategy to restore the political construct in which Qastun had lost faith. And as the realities of the colonial presence became more readily apparent, his faith in the French as agents of his modernity likewise evaporated.

The multiplicity of middle-class responses to the French occupation confirms the need to disaggregate local reactions to colonialism along communal, ethnic, and educational lines in a way that retains the ambiguity and indeterminacy within those forms of social distinction. As Rashid Khalidi has observed,

> There was a wide spectrum of modes of relating to this late form of colonialism, running from collaboration to cooperation, to accommodation, to ignoring the colonizer where possible, to noncooperation, to passive resistance, to public protest, and finally to armed resistance, with an infinite number of possible gradations between them, with individuals and groups sometimes moving back and forth along the spectrum.[7]

This section pivots on Khalidi's contention and argues that it is necessary to interrogate both middle-class forms of resistance *and* cooperation as

---

[7] Rashid Khalidi, "Concluding Remarks," in Méouchy et al., eds. *Comparative*, 703.

part of a process of theorizing colonialism and characterizing its broader historical and cultural significance.[8]

Integrating any discussion of colonial cooperation into the study of local responses to colonialism is complicated by the fact that the theme of resistance dominates historical representations of the colonial encounter among postcolonial historians. A vast theoretical and comparative literature exists to explain resistance.[9] The acts of resistance to colonialism in the Eastern Mediterranean that most rightly capture the historical imagination, such as the Palestine Revolt of the mid-1930s, are instructive examples of this phenomenon. The problem arises, however, when the historiography of these moments reifies the immediate political or ideological cause of each into a metonym for the colonial encounter in its entirety. To move beyond simple resistance narratives is to recognize the moment-to-moment, fragmentary nature of resistance; it is neither a monolithic category nor free of overt political and professional utility to both authors and their informants. And resisters and those against whom they are resisting are constantly renegotiating, re-imagining, and reconstituting their relationships. Complicating matters more, from the perspective of postcolonial textual and oral histories and memoirs written in the hegemonic discursive shadow of nationalism, it would likewise be difficult to identify with certainty most people's perceptions of European colonial domination during the periods in question.[10] Likewise, the study of the spectacular forms of elite resistance that dominate nationalist metanarratives eclipses forms of resistance in the everyday: the unglamorous—and often those acts of resistance particular to women and ethnic and religious minorities. But perhaps the most important act in understanding resistance is the acknowledgment that resistance is *exceptional*. In other words, a focus on resistance essentializes the colonized (and the colonizer) and can have a normative effect that renders the more commonplace kinds of activity, which operate outside of the structures of resistance in the least historically uninteresting or irrelevant, and in the most morally bankrupt

---

[8] This project is, in part, driven by Nicholas Thomas's contention in *Colonialism's Culture: Anthropology, Travel and Government* (Princeton: Princeton University Press, 1994) that, "If there is some disadvantage in undoing 'colonialism' as a coherent object, the compensation lies in the exclusion of a secure progressive narrative that too easily separates a colonial past and a[n allegedly] liberal present" (16–17).

[9] Rosalind O'Hanlon, "Recovering the Subject: *Subaltern Studies* and Histories of Resistance in Colonial South Asia," in Vinayak Chaturvedi, ed., *Mapping Subaltern Studies and the Postcolonial* (London: Verso, 2000), 72–115, passim.

[10] Consider Ted Swedenburg's discussion of accommodationist and collaborationist memories of the Great Revolt in Palestine (1936–1939), primarily his chapter "(Un)popular Memories: Accommodation and Collaboration," in *Memories of Revolt: The 1936–1939 Rebellion the Palestinian National Past* 2nd ed. (Lafayette: University of Arkansas Press, 2003).

or culturally inauthentic. It creates a binary construction of resistor versus colonial oppressor, which emphasizes the moral superiority of the former; likewise, this binarism can admit few categories of hybridity or layers of ambivalence. Such a structure cannot escape the same reductive Manicheanism that underlies and legitimates colonialism itself: European—Syrian, Christian—Muslim, French—Arab is reproduced in any narrative of resistance that emphasizes the dichotomy between the collaborator and the nationalist.

The historiography of French Mandate Syria often reflects this same binarism. In this historiography, the degree to which linguistic and religious minorities—most especially the middle-class components of these groups—cooperated with the colonial enterprise situates them uncomfortably in the narrative of nationalist resistance and liberation of the inter- and postwar periods. Likewise, this mode of representation creates a blind spot in our understanding of the period as it leaves large portions of the Syrian colonial population invisible to history, and where these components of society are visible, it is only in a nationalist, anticolonialist narrative's demonology.

Ironically, much of that nationalist narrative of resistance was formulated in the interwar period by middle-class, non-Sunni Muslim intellectuals. Nevertheless, the act of formulating and promoting this ideology played out against the backdrop of persisting categories of sectarian subordination and a loss of faith in the liberalism of middle-class modernity. The first chapter in this section argues that the Sunni notability of Aleppo and elsewhere in the post-Ottoman state of Syria in the course of the French Mandate (1922–1946) increasingly drew upon the literary skill, linguistic ability, communal identity, and legal training of a group of young, middle-class men—all educated in the West and conversant with the language of modern political participation—in their opposition to colonialism. The presence of these men in this opposition suggest that the old social classes had concluded that the coming of the French had authorized ways of knowing and enabled a novel political environment in which they would be at a tactical disadvantage. Yet in a fundamental turn, they hoped thereby not only to strengthen their standing vis-à-vis the colonial authorities, but also to co-opt or marginalize the very group from which these young men had been drawn.

The second chapter examines the incorporation of fascism into the broader discursive terrain of the interwar period. The introduction of fascist aesthetics, styles, and organizational techniques in the mid-1930s brings into relief the culmination of the process during the French Mandate by which urban communal and class boundaries were altered and the very nature of violence changed in the post-Ottoman Eastern Mediterranean. As portions of the middle class embraced that ideology, they rejected the liberal values upon which the modes of middle-class cohesion had been based. Critical to this chapter is the realization that not all politics, ideological debate, and class and communal interaction in the period 1925–1946 was shaped by the modalities of French colonial rule. While the French Mandate opened a space into which non-Muslims could adopt a radicalized political agenda built around fascism, the kinds of conflict that allowed that ideology to take root trace to deeper social changes within Eastern Mediterranean society.

Like others in the colonial non-West, Syrians practiced modern politics by organizing parties and incorporating into their political discourse ideologies of the Left, as well as the Right. Whereas there was no "fascist international" from which to draw on in the formation of various "shirt movements," Syria's small communist and socialist movements had strong ties to international organizations. And though often at odds with each other, becoming a fascist or communist, or for that matter a liberal nationalist, was a consummate modern act in the arena of politics. However, the leftist alternative held little appeal for the middle class at large; though, as might be expected, its intellectual vanguard had origins in the middle class or had attained middle-class status through advanced higher education abroad. This contrasts markedly with Iraq, where many prominent intellectuals, artists, and writers were members of the Iraqi Communist Party or considered themselves "independent Marxists."

Khalid Bakdash (1912–1995) was the unquestioned leader of the Syrian Communist Party, assuming leadership of it and aligning it with Stalin in the mid-1930s while still in his twenties. Of Kurdish origins, he had been expelled from law school and was initiated into the Communist Party at the age of eighteen by Haykazun Buyajyan, an Armenian refugee in Lebanon and a student of dentistry. Ordered into exile, he attended Moscow's University of the Toilers of the East and returned to Syria at the time of the 1936 general strike.[11] Though the party was small in number, its discipline, foreign support, and transnational nature helped it to realize marginal success in electoral politics in the 1940s and 1950s.

A strong leftist movement also arose among the Armenian refugee community, in particular, the Armenian Revolutionary Federation, Hay Heghapokhakan Dashnaktsutyun. More commonly, its members were known as the Dashnaks. Founded in the 1890s in Tblisi, the organization adopted a secular, socialist, and nationalist revolutionary position and even allied itself with the CUP in the opening days of the Revolution of 1908 in the Ottoman Empire. In the post–World War I period, it was the

---

[11] Batatu, *Old Social Classes*, 374; on Bakdash, see Tareq Y. Ismael and Jacqueline S. Ismael, *The Communist Movement in Syria and Lebanon* (Gainesville: University Press of Florida, 1998).

preeminent political party in the short-lived Republic of Armenia, which was absorbed into the Soviet Union and the Republic of Turkey. Bereft of a state, the Dashnaks employed cultural institutions, sports clubs, Boy and Girl Scout units, adult night school, and literacy programs to build a diasporan constituency from the refugees living in Syria, Lebanon, Palestine, and Egypt. Unlike the Syrian Communist Party, which eschewed ethnic or sectarian identification, the Dashnaks evolved into the leading representatives of the Armenian community during the mandate, often placing survival of the community above ideological consistency, negotiating with both the French and the National Bloc as the need arose.

The final chapter, which departs somewhat from the chronology of the larger work, presents a preliminary framework for understanding those kinds of negotiations and for exploring the often consciously ignored phenomenon of large-scale cooperation between local actors and the French imperial project—both before and during the French Mandate period. It seeks to move the discussion beyond the nationalist-implicated concept of the "collaborator" to a more complicated and historicized vision of this fact of colonialism. Its title flows from an implicit dimension of Qastun's 1920 essay: both he and many of his readers were members of Aleppo's large, Uniate Byzantine—Greek Catholic—community. Usually francophone and often Francophile, a significant portion of this large and prosperous community cooperated with the French imperial presence in the Levant. From the perspective of interwar Syrian nationalism, a political terrain that was dominated by the traditional Sunni oligarchies of Damascus and Aleppo, this spoke of nothing less than collaboration. It is important to point out that the act of collaboration was not unique to portions of the non-Muslim middle class; despite the animosity of the notability and its "nationalists" toward aspects of Syrian society willing to cooperate with the French, by the late 1930s that very Sunni elite had reached a modus vivendi with the French that would guarantee their power and authority and crush democratic reforms that promised a degree of empowerment for the lower and middle classes. The relationship between the French and the Greek Catholics was inflected by a style of politics I identify as the *colonial contract*. The particulars of this contract changed often, but the basic terms remained intact for most of the French Mandate: in return for the support of, or "nonopposition" to, the political, intellectual, and economic processes of imperialism, the Greek Catholic and other minority communities would receive material and discursive support for either their corporate transformation into a modern middle class or, later, the preservation of their status. Such cooperation extended as well to other religious and ethnic minorities in Aleppo, most notably the city's vast population of Armenian refugees living in and around the city as a consequence of the genocide of 1915. Ultimately, this style of colonial politics laid the groundwork for the quintessential postcolonial phenomenon of middle-class transnationality; it also was adopted and adapted by post–World War II military and authoritarian regimes as a strategy to co-opt and contain middle-class dissent.

This entire section benefits from the vast reservoir of the archives of the French Mandate stored at the Centre des Archives diplomatiques, Nantes, France, which has been completely declassified only since the late 1990s. Unlike typical diplomatic archives, the material preserved at Nantes reflect the multifaceted colonial and administrative mission of the French in Syria; and the tutelary ethos of the mandate and its style of bureaucratic organization have left a record of interaction between state and society in Syria of unprecedented detail and in an easily accessible, fully cataloged form. Among the works to take full advantage of the archive's possibilities is Elizabeth Thompson's pioneering *Colonial Citizens: Republican Rights, Paternal Privilege, and Gender in French Syria and Lebanon* (2000), which drew from this material to link paternalistic French social and educational policies with the articulation of a "colonial welfare state" that at once altered gender roles and confirmed male privilege. A rich subfield of "Mandate Studies" has since emerged, and Nadine Méouchy and Peter Sluglett's comprehensive bilingual edited volume, *The British and French Mandates in Comparative Perspectives* (2004), is only the most recent product. The concerted study of the mandates has great promise to connect the history of the Eastern Mediterranean with colonial and postcolonial studies more broadly, as long as it does not become a series of isolated explorations of the minutiae of colonial administration. The wealth of material has meant, however, that research tends to focus on the motivation, creation, and implementation of specific French policies and Syrian reactions thereto; this *problematique* itself is shaped by the manner in which information and knowledge about Syria was gathered and produced by colonial officials, recorded in triplicate, and digested in self-congratulatory and usually exaggerated reports on education, social and economic development, and other topics for the League of Nations—a requirement imposed by the League on all mandatory states. In the view of the archive, Syrians, as imperial subjects, were objects of administrative praxis and problems of policy; they were organized into categories convenient to bureaucratic knowledge and counted on the basis of their utility to the colonial state.

The following chapters reverse the view from the archive by expanding the evidentiary base and linking Syrian responses to the French Mandate to longer-term processes of social change and class formation. What follows also recognizes that the political and intellectual culture of the French Mandate contributed to new forms of middle-class politics, civil society, and conceptions of modernity.

EIGHT

Deferring to the A'yan

THE MIDDLE CLASS AND THE POLITICS OF NOTABLES

Syria belongs to us all!
—Sa'dallah al-Jabiri, 1936

From Paris in June 1928, Edmond Rabbath (1901–1991) sent to Sa'dallah al-Jabiri (1893–1947) his recently published *L'évolution politique de la Syrie sous mandat*. While the book is an early exploration of the legal underpinnings of the French Mandate, it is also the first nationalist history of Syria. Adopting a now familiar historiographical trope that the Ottoman past was a period of decadence and unjust alien rule, Rabbath organized recent episodes from the turbulent history of the Eastern Mediterranean since World War I, including Faysal's Arab Kingdom, the Syrian Arab Congress, the rebellions of Salih al-'Alawi and Ibrahim Hananu, and the Great Syrian Revolt, into a linear narrative of an unfolding modern national consciousness.[1] With a preface by a prominent figure from prewar Ottoman politics in the Levant, Shakib al-Arslan,[2] the book outlined the logic in which much of interwar Syrian opposition to French colonialism would be phrased: France must adhere to the letter and spirit of the League of Nations' Mandate and emancipate the Syrians upon their achievement of national maturity. With some reservations, Rabbath argued that this maturity had already been attained.

On the frontispiece of the copy sent to Jabiri (figure 8.1), he had added a handwritten dedication in Arabic that reads:

Ila al-mujahid al-watani
Sa'dallah bak al-Jabiri
na'ib Halab

---

[1] Edmond Rabbath, *L'évolution politique de la Syrie sous mandat* (Paris: Marcel Rivière, 1928), 19–27. See also Rifa'at Abou-al-Haj's critical reading of the uses and abuses of the Ottoman past in modern Arab historiography, in which he has shown the link between the rise of the nation-state and the vilification of the Ottoman period. "The Social Uses of the Past: Recent Arab Historiography of Ottoman Rule," *IJMES* 14 (1982): 185–201.

[2] On al-Arslan, see William L. Cleveland, *Islam against the West: Shakib Arslan and the Campaign for Islamic Nationalism* (Austin: University of Texas Press, 1985).

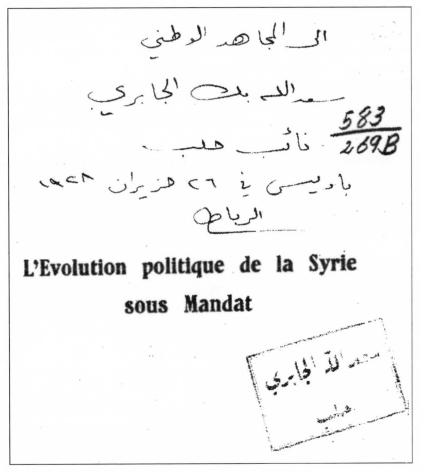

الى المجاهد الوطني

سعد الله بك الجابري

نائب حلب

باريس في ٢٦ حزيران ١٩٢٨

الرباط

L'Evolution politique de la Syrie
sous Mandat

سعد الله الجابري
حلب

FIGURE 8.1. Frontispiece of Jabiri's copy of Rabbath's *L'evolution politique de la Syrie sous mandat.*

Baris fi 26 Haziran 1928
al-Rabbat.[3]

This curious rhymed couplet encapsulates the layers of ambiguity and contradiction inherent to the complex relationship between these two men in the twenty years following the publication of Rabbath's book.

[3] Rabbath, *L'évolution*, 268–272. Translated, the inscription reads, "To the nationalist warrior / Sa'dallah bey al-Jabiri / representative from Aleppo / Paris, 26 June 1928 / [Edmond] Rabbath." The copy is housed in the National Library of Aleppo and had been presented by Jabiri's heirs upon his death in 1947.

While at once placing Jabiri, a leader of the most politically powerful family in Aleppo, in the context of a modern system of democratic representation, the Sorbonne-trained Rabbath did not address him as a fellow citizen or as an equal, but rather with the Ottoman honorific of *bey*, the meaning of which is roughly akin to "sir." More intriguing is the modification of *mujahid*—warrior—a word having religious overtones with the secular neologism *watani*—nationalist—by the Western-educated Christian lawyer, which anticipates his later efforts to appropriate powerful terms from Islamic history. Perhaps the most arresting feature of the dedication is that it is in Arabic on the frontispiece of a book written in French presumably for a French audience, connoting the fact that the fluid juxtaposition of languages, words, and meanings and an ability to self-consciously and adroitly cross linguistic and cultural boundaries would play a definitive role in the social and intellectual practice of Rabbath and other young, middle-class intellectuals in the colonial interwar period. Finally, the very association of these two individuals seems at odds with received notions about the distinct and bounded religious, social, intellectual, and educational spheres of a city where connections were often predicated by questions of class and confession and became solidified through economic cooperation, alliances by marriage, and school ties. Nevertheless, for a time the two became closely linked in the urban politics of French Mandate Aleppo.

While the relationship itself did blur many of those customary urban boundaries, it was also emblematic of the articulation of a new category of actors within the "Politics of Notables," the late Ottoman and early postwar hierarchy of power, authority, and domination. The definition of the role of these new actors—Western-educated, middle-class, liberal professionals or educators—was shaped by evolving ideas about citizenship and modern national identities, the emergence of a distinct middle stratum in the cities of Syria, and the form of elite resistance to European colonial rule. And third, notwithstanding the fact that the links between the notability and this group of lawyers, high school teachers, and college professors were based on mutual political interests, infused with a novel ideological content, and arrayed in the forms of modernity, the basic terms of the relationships were still controlled by notions of class difference and inflected with resilient conceptions of sectarian subordination. An examination of the complex connection between Sa'dallah al-Jabiri and Edmond Rabbath as it began in the late 1920s and changed through the course of mandate-era elections and political machinations brings many of these issues into relief. The vast literary output of Rabbath during the period, Jabiri's unpublished personal diary, the recently declassified reports of the French Sûreté-Générale, and other contemporary archival sources shed new light on the relationship and allow for a more meaningful understanding of the transformation and introduction of new ideas at the time—beyond the rhetoric of nationalism and League of Nations parlance—and a better comprehension of the mechanisms of social control available to the Levant's traditional ruling elite. It is also a means of illustrating how the new cultural elite of Syria that came of age in the period after World War I employed the intellectual tools of modernism in the often-subversive project of conceptualizing its relationship with France and the West at large.

Nationalist Beys and the Generation of 1900

As previously noted, historians of the early modern and modern Eastern Mediterranean tend to explain the hegemony of the local landed elite, or the *a'yan*, in terms of the "Politics of Notables."[4] While the "politics" may provide an adequate description of the calculus of power during the French Mandate for most of Syrian society, many in the emergent urban middle class of lawyers, doctors, school teachers, bureaucrats, international merchants, bankers, and their families—both its Muslim and non-Muslim wings—continued to question the claims of the customary notability to a position of hegemony in the city. Journalism, history writing, and modern forms of social and political organization had enabled this class to contest the architectures of community in the cities of the Eastern Mediterranean beginning in the period of the Revolution of 1908 and continuing with the establishment of the French Mandate for Syria and Lebanon in 1920; throughout this period, this process brought the middle class into conflict with the *a'yan*. Political parties, primarily on the Left like the Syrian Communist Party, and later the Arab Socialist Renaissance Party (al-Ba'th), in the postcolonial period would eventually become the fiercest opponents of the "Politics of Notables"; and populist land reform and wealth redistribution programs would contribute to its elimination altogether. Yet in the interwar period opposition equally found voice in the liberal political discourse emanating from institutions of middle-class civil society. Furthermore, French support and ever-increasing contacts with the West gave the middle class of the region—especially its Christian and Jewish components—even greater power in the fledgling state, adding a new dimension to the "politics" by intensifying the hostility between non-Muslims and the elite, and ultimately inflecting the conflict with sectarian overtones.

However, in the course of the 1920s and 1930s, members of the *a'yan* who had coalesced in a loose political group that called itself the National

[4] Khoury, *Syria*, 13.

Bloc turned to a cadre of young, Western-educated intellectuals in their resistance against French colonialism. Similar kinds of connections had existed in the antebellum period, the most relevant being that between the Ottoman parliamentarian Jâbirî zâde Nafiᶜ Pasha, the elder brother of Saᶜdallah al-Jabiri, and Khalil Ghanem, a Maronite deputy from Beirut and later publisher of the journals *La jeune Turquie* and *Meşveret* [Consultation], though these were far from common.[5] Yet in a fundamental turn that distinguishes this moment from comparable moments in the prewar period, the aᶜyan planned thereby not only to strengthen their standing vis-à-vis the colonial authorities, but also to marginalize politically the very group from which these young men had been drawn. Tellingly, the process by which the notables of the cities of the Levant sought to contain the political activity of the urban middle class closely parallels the methods by which the ancien régime of Europe retained so much of its authority and power despite the rapid transformation of that continent's class structure in the period before the First World War. As Arno Mayer has argued,

> Inveterate nobles firmly occupied and controlled access to the high social, cultural, and political terrain to which the bourgeoisie aspired. With characteristic flexibility and adaptability, and capitalizing on the bourgeois elements craving for social status and advancement the grand notables admitted individual postulants from business and the professions into their midst. Rather than yield institutional ground, they opted for this selective co-optation, confident of their ability to contain and defuse its attendant ideological and cultural contamination.[6]

While these young, foreign-educated intellectuals fit into the notables' broader hegemonic project in the interwar period, they were by no means the only tactic by which the notability intended to contain and control the potential threat of middle-class dissent; the ultimate failure of these young men to "deliver" the complete compliance of their class led the notables to call upon a reserve of customary urban violence to finish the task of ensuring middle-class quiescence.

This is not to cast Edmond Rabbath as a passive actor in this relationship, drawn into it *solely* on the basis of ambition or the cultural and religious prestige of the notability. Rather, beginning in the late 1920s— as evidenced by both his writings and his political activism—and along with other young men in Aleppo and elsewhere in the Levant, who had been born within a few years of the turn of the century and come of age after the war, he asserted the modernity of an Arab Syria and sought

---

[5] See Kayal, *Arabs and Young Turks*, 26–27, 40–44.

[6] Arno J. Mayer, *The Persistence of the Old Regime: Europe to the Great War* (New York: Pantheon Books, 1981), 81.

nothing less than to bring it into alignment with what he saw as the political foundations of bourgeois democratic Western Europe. Among those with whom this new vision for Syria resonated were Rabbath's fellow middle-class Aleppines, Na'im al-Antaki[7] and Nazim al-Qudsi.[8] Each had been born at the turn of the century and had attained an advanced Western education in law or the social sciences; in the course of the interwar period, each became closely associated with the National Bloc and its notable leadership, and in the case of the latter two, ministers in the post-independence period.

Based in two worlds, men like Rabbath were mediating figures capable of comprehending both the basic terms of the "Politics of Notables" and the organizing principles and modes of political activity of middle-class civil society; likewise, they could serve as interlocutors in the kinds of discussions and negotiations that typified the style of interwar elite colonial resistance in Syria. Critically, they contributed to the transformation of Ottoman-era customary authority into a recognizably modern vernacular of power through a redefinition or modification of the concept of "natural leadership." Rabbath went even further and was among the first to elaborate the idea that a positivist view of a religion, in this case Islam, could be welded with a modern national identity, the Arab, and then serve

[7] Na'im al-Antaki, a Greek Catholic, was born in 1903 in Aleppo. After graduating from the local Jesuit school he attended the American University in Beirut. Subsequently, he studied literature and law at the Sorbonne. He returned to Aleppo and became a practicing attorney in 1928—the same year he joined the National Bloc—and was elected to the syndicate of lawyers. In 1936 the bloc engineered his election as president of the syndicate. He accompanied the bloc delegation to Paris that same year. In Aleppo he was most often associated with Ibrahim Hananu. During World War II he settled in Damascus where he was elected deputy from that city (1942–1944). While in parliament he served as the finance minister, and after the war he was part of the Syrian delegation to the San Francisco Conference, which led to the founding of the United Nations. In 1948 he was Syrian President Hashim al-Atasi's representative to the United Nations on the Palestine conflict. Khoury, *Mandate*, 421; *Man Huwa fi Suriyya* [Who's Who Syria] (Dimasq: Hashimi ikhwan, 1951), 73–74.

[8] Nazim al-Qudsi, a Sunni Muslim, was born in 1906 in Aleppo. After attending the local imperial high school, he attended the American University of Beirut. Upon completing postgraduate work in the faculty of law at the Syrian National University in Damascus, he joined the Aleppo syndicate of lawyers. He pursued further studies at the University of Geneva, earning a doctorate in international law (1929). Elected twice to the Syrian Parliament as a member of the National Bloc, he served during the war years as Syria's chargé d'affaires in Washington, D.C. Elected several times in the 1940s, he was both Syria's foreign minister and briefly prime minister in 1950 and again in 1960–1963. Members of the Qudsi family were *ashraf*, peripheral members of the Aleppine notability and woven into the bureaucracy of the prewar Ottoman provincial administration and secret police. In many ways, Nazim, considered the most radical of the bloc's young lawyers, represented a transitional type between the more traditional Istanbul-educated and younger Western-educated members of his family. Khoury, *Mandate*, 422; *Man Huwa*, 602–603.

as a legitimate basis for rule.[9] In this he prefigured other Christian or non-Sunni Muslim Arab nationalist intellectuals of the interwar and postwar period who sought to secularize and historicize Islam as a definitive cultural practice of the Arabs. Among these were Michel ʿAflaq,[10] Constantine Zurayk,[11] and Zaki al-Arsuzi.[12] Ironically, in the case of the founders of the Baʿth—ʿAflaq and al-Arsuzi—this connection of Islam to the conception of a broader Arab nation would serve as a basis for their dissent from the elite and often parochial nationalism of the old notables.

Understanding the terms of the relationship between the Sunni Muslim bloc notable Jabiri and the Greek Catholic Rabbath helps to fill a lacuna in the theory of the "Politics of Notables" for the late Ottoman and interwar period and complicates our understanding of the changing historical experience of the middle-class secular intellectual in the post-Ottoman Eastern Mediterranean.[13] Unlike Qastun, Ghazzi, or Tabbakh, Rabbath was part of the first generation to be educated after the shift of the region's educational and cultural métropole from Istanbul to multiple ones in the Arab Middle East, Western Europe, and North America; at the same time, he was among the first to confront the reality that the practice of the "intellectual's craft" itself had become transformed by a Western colonial presence. Like others in his generation, for Rabbath the critical ambivalence of this colonial encounter consisted of a simultaneous belief in the

---

[9] See Hourani, *Arabic Thought*: Rabbath's work "is an attempt to define the nature and limits of the Arab nation. 'There is no Syrian nation, there is an Arab nation,' he proclaims and defines the Arab nation in terms of several different factors: blood and origin . . . for the Arab nation, even outside the peninsula, has been formed by successive waves of immigration; language, the 'national factor *par excellence*'; and religion. His view of the political function of religion is that of the positivists: it plays a considerable part in the initial formation of nations, and religious solidarity is a forerunner of national solidarity, which prepares the way for political association and draws men together against a foreign invader. The religion which has played this role in Arab history is undoubtedly Islam, 'une religion d'essence nationale,' and the Islamic community was an embryonic Arab community" (310).

[10] Michel ʿAflaq, a Greek Orthodox Christian born in Damascus (1910), attended the Sorbonne in the 1930s. In a speech delivered at the Syrian National University in 1943 entitled "In Remembrance of the Arab Prophet," he argued, "To the Arabs, the Islamic movement embodied in the life of [Muhammad] is not merely a historical occurrence . . . rather, it is at the very depths . . . and bound fiercely into the life of the Arab"; further, he concluded that "Islam has renewed Arabism and completed it." Mishil ʿAflaq, *Fi sabil al-baʿth* [For the Cause of the Baʿth], 8th ed. (Beirut: Dar al-taliʿa lil-tibaʿa wa al-nashr, 1972; orig. pub. 1959), 127–138. See also Hourani, *Arabic Thought*, 357; Hanna Batatu, *Old Social Classes*, 727–737.

[11] For Constantine Zurayk, an Orthodox Christian born in Damascus in 1909, see Hourani, *Arabic Thought*, 309–311.

[12] On Zaki al-Arsuzi, an Alawite born in Lattakia in 1901 and educated in philosophy at the Sorbonne in the 1920s, see Batatu, *Old Social Classes*, 722–724; also my, "'Creating Phantoms.'"

[13] Khoury, "The Urban Notables Paradigm Revisited," 226.

vitality and modernity of the emancipatory, republican, and universalist impulses of the French "civilizing mission" and the historical necessity of opposition to French imperialism.[14]

Edmond Rabbath had begun to carve out a role for himself in the intellectual life of Aleppo as a young man. Born at the turn of the century to a middle-class merchant-ecclesiastical family, at the age of twenty-six he and fellow young intellectual, Sami al-Kayyali—a relative of the bloc notable ʿAbd al-Rahman al-Kayyali—founded the journal *al-Hadith* [The Modern].[15] Aleppo's version of *Esquire*, it was one of the most stable magazines in Syria, continuing with few breaks through the 1950s. Founded to "do battle with ignorance and backwardness," it enjoyed a wide readership among the educated middle class of young men and women in Aleppo.[16] In addition to publishing short stories and think pieces, it covered the Cairene literary scene and evidenced a fascination with Republican Turkey and Kemalism. While regularly publishing photographs and engravings of scantily clad young Western women on its final pages, it championed Arab women's rights and franchise and featured articles about men's and women's European fashion and proper bourgeois manners. Editions published in the first year contained several sections, including "al-nisa'iyyat" (Women's Issues), "al-adab" (Literature), and "al-ʿulum wa al-funun" (Arts and Sciences). The focus on manners, fashion, and "women's issues" functioned for the authors and readers of the journal as simulacra of modernity, archaizing customary behavior and thereby marking their ideas and practice as modern.

Rabbath brought this process into the political realm in another of these sections, "al-ijtimaʿiyyat," (Sociology). One of his earliest articles, "The Decline of Democracy," revealed his commitment to modernist conceptions of patriotism, civic participation, and authority. Ostensibly, the article was a discussion of constitutional monarchy and the universal franchise, though at its core it presented a definition of democracy and an identification of the historical role played by the middle class in both its formulation and implementation. "Democracy," he argued, "is the order which seeks its power from the community at large (*al-umma al-saha*) expressed through universal franchise (*al-iqtiraʿ al-ʿamm*) in its multiple forms, and it is distinguished from other forms of rule in the real equality

---

[14] For a contrasting sense of the dualism of the colonial encounter in Africa, see Alice Conklin, *A Mission to Civilize: The Republican Idea of Empire in France and West Africa 1895–1930* (Stanford: Stanford University Press, 1997).

[15] Suhayl al-Malathi, *al-Tibaʿa wa al-sahafa fi Halab* [Printing and Journalism in Aleppo] (Damascus: Dar yʿaribu, 1996), 304. Sami al-Kayyali (1898–1972) served as director of the Dar al-Kutub at the time of the donation of Saʿdallah al-Jabiri's library and represented Syria for a time in the late 1960s at UNESCO.

[16] Ibid., 307.

of individual rights and responsibilities, and [people] are judged in it in a way which is not diminished or abrogated by an unrestricted general will (*al-idara al-'amma*)." "The democracy of the nineteenth century had" consequently "sprung forth from the efforts of the middle class—the class of the age (*al-tabaqa min al-zaman*). . . . It is the class made up of those who were industrious and built their wealth on trade and invented the tools of modern life." According to Rabbath, this class first articulated democracy in Holland and England, later in the early 1800s in France, and by the second half of the nineteenth century in Germany. Central to each case was a middle-class effort to "monopolize capital and gain political power." Rabbath warned that various political strategies could subvert the middle classes' hold on power. The most threatening, the "teutonic form," appeared in Prussia where it became impossible to "distinguish between nationalism and conservatism, between absolutist power and political action, and between king and religion . . . ultimately," he concluded, "this led to the outbreak of the world war."[17] The significance of this early article lies in the fact that it is a manifesto of sorts for the Syrian middle class, who had grown wealthy and had begun to regard themselves as a class similar to, if not indistinct from, their European bourgeois cognate. It also linked the project of modernity with both democratic participation and bourgeois conceptions of the citizen. Rabbath's linking of modernity with middle-class political dominance seems at odds with his later support of the reactionary tendencies of the aristocratic notability embodied in the continued hegemony of Jabiri.

Rabbath left the journal in late 1927 to defend his thesis in law at the Sorbonne. The thesis, published as *L'évolution*, was reviewed in the pages of *al-Hadith* the following year. Sami al-Kayyali dedicated the July 1928 edition to Rabbath, and under the young lawyer's photograph, he described him as "among the most intelligent of our cultured young men. He is a shining example in these trying times of exceptional intelligence and manners. We wish for him a successful future in the service of his nation and in his intellectual pursuits." The review was no less adulatory: "His book . . . has produced an outcry in French and Syrian political circles. It is important in this period of awakening to imbue our enlightened youth with an understanding of Europeans. . . . He paints a true picture of Syria, which to many Europeans . . . still resembles the land of Waq-Waq."[18] Kayyali continued his review with an outline of Rabbath's future work including an Arabic translation of *L évolution*, the compilation of a volume of documents about Syria, and a French translation of

---

[17] Idmun al-Rabbat (Edmond Rabbath), "The Decline of Democracy" 100–101, 104.

[18] Sami al-Kayyali, introductory dedication, *al-Hadith* 7 (June 1928). "Waq-waq" is used to mean an unknown and fantastical land.

important Arabic literature, "in order to inform the French . . . about the treasures of Arabic."[19]

As a consequence of his literary output, Rabbath had been befriended by Sa'dallah al-Jabiri by 1927 or 1928. Jabiri, though only a decade older than Rabbath, was born at a time when Aleppine notables, who had grown wealthy in the nineteenth century on tax farming, land rents, and agriculture, still sent their sons to be educated as Ottomans in order to serve the expanding imperial bureaucracy and their families' interests therein.[20] Jabiri's father Jâbirî zâde 'Abd al-Qadir served briefly as the mufti of Aleppo (1879–1880) and divided the remainder of his time between his activities as a *muhaddith* and a gentleman farmer. One of 'Abd al-Qadir's elder sons, the aforementioned Nafi', served in the first and second Ottoman Parliaments, and his brothers Ihsan, Fakhr, and Sa'dallah each obtained an imperial education. Sa'dallah was one of the first graduates of the local Ottoman secondary school, the Thanawiyyat al-Ma'mun, and shortly before the First World War he began to study law at the Mekteb-i Hukuk-u Şhahane in Istanbul. During the war, but before he completed his studies, Sa'dallah left school and joined the Ottoman Army as a *küçük zâbit* (noncommissioned officer). Serving with the commissary corps in Erzerum, he probably fought in the disastrous campaign against the Russians of the winter of 1915. He left the army upon demobilization in 1918, returned to Aleppo, and served in the Syrian Congress of 1919. His elder brother, Ihsan, was one of Sharif Husayn's chamberlains while the Hashemites resided in Istanbul and briefly served as mayor of Aleppo during the Arab Kingdom. With the French occupation of Syria the brothers fled, Sa'dallah to Cairo. He later returned to Aleppo to ensure the family's leading role in any political structure taking shape in what was to become Syria. Consequently, he numbered among the founding members of the National Bloc.[21]

The Arabic-language daily journal Jabiri kept for the pivotal year 1929, a previously untapped archival source (and the only year available), reveals him to be a middle-aged bachelor uncomfortable with the public role that had fallen to him in the absence of his brother Ihsan, who had been tried and sentenced to death in absentia in 1920 and could not return to Syria.[22] He was continually concerned about a lack of cash,[23] and plagued by various family difficulties such as the public insinuation of the

[19] Ibid., 499. None of these projects ever materialized.

[20] Khoury, *Urban Notables*, 1–52.

[21] On the origins of the National Bloc, see 'Abd al-Rahman al-Kayyali, *al-Marahil fi al-intidab al-faransi wa fi nidalina al-watani* [The Stages of the French Mandate and Our National Struggle] (Aleppo: Dad, 1958), 1:64–71.

[22] MWT-Qkh Folder 95: "Private Papers of Sa'dallah al-Jabiri," entry for 8 June 1929.

[23] Ibid., entry for 4 March 1929.

homosexuality of one of his nephews.[24] Perhaps the most arresting feature of his diary is his acute consciousness of sectarian and class differences in the city and his complex and often contradictory feelings about this phenomenon. At once obsessed and repelled by the sexual allure of un-veiled Jewish and Christian women, he expressed jealousy of the apparent ease with which middle-class non-Muslim men and women mixed in pub-lic. For example, he noted wistfully in his entry for 12 May 1929, "There was a soirée [at the Aleppo Club] and Christian men came with their women and I flirted with some of them with my eyes. Especially pleasant were the Jewish girls who were eyeing me and I was looking at them, but I could not go over to them because [where they were sitting] is not avail-able to me as a single man."[25] "On more than one occasion he expressed the conviction that Christians hated him and his class.[26] In this context of perceived Christian animus, he singled out three young Christian middle-class men for their "lack of bigotry": Michel Elian, Na'im al-Antaki, and Edmond Rabbath.[27] Over the course of 1929, he and Rabbath met several times a week at the Aleppo Club, the institution that was the focus of the city's middle-class social interaction, or at Ibrahim Hananu's home, which served as a makeshift bloc headquarters, and discussed culture and politics. On at least one occasion Jabiri went to the cinema, another locus of modern middle-class activity, with Rabbath, Antaki, and Antaki's un-named female companion.[28] From Jabiri's entries, it is clear that Rabbath played a large role in his public social and intellectual life, with Jabiri at one point concluding that his friendship with the young lawyer had changed him.[29] However, in the period covered by the diary, Jabiri never visited Rabbath at the latter's home; nor was Rabbath ever invited to Jabiri's house, facts that show the very real limits to their "friendship."

[24] Ibid. entry for 13 January 1929: In this entry, Jabiri complained about fellow notable 'Abd al-Rahman al-Kayyali, who had been spreading homophobic rumors in Aleppo about one of Ihsan al-Jabiri's sons. Like other families, the Hananus in particular, the Jabiris were cash-poor and land-rich. As if to confirm this problem, the Syrian archives also contain Sa'dallah's unpaid—and very large—bar-bills from a hotel in Bludan in the late 1940s, sug-gesting that money problems continued to plague him throughout his career.

[25] Ibid., entry for 12 May 1929. Jabiri was apparently sitting in the area of the Aleppo Club reserved for single men. Men accompanied by female family members or girlfriends could sit in the mixed-sex area. This practice of segregating males unaccompanied by women in public places was prevalent in the 1930s, as it is today. Possibly it was more difficult for Jabiri to come to the club accompanied by female members of his family because of the practice of seclusion imposed on Muslims of the highest social status.

[26] Ibid., entry for 31 March 1929 in which he recounts the courtesy visits he made on the occasion of Easter to several ecclesiastical leaders.

[27] Ibid., entry for 2 Februrary 1929. Elian would later serve as a commander of Aleppo's National Guard; see following chapter.

[28] Ibid., entry for 15 May 1929. While the name of the movie is not mentioned, he re-called its "beauty in portraying the injustice of the oppression of the people."

[29] Ibid., entry for 24 June 1929.

Clearly, many of the same spatial-communal obstacles of the prewar period had persisted well into the 1930s.

Their acquaintance took on a fundamentally different character when
Jabiri introduced Rabbath to national politics at a secret meeting attended
by the two other leading notables of the National Bloc in Aleppo, 'Abd
al-Rahman al-Kayyali and Ibrahim Hananu. This meeting, which took
place sometime in January 1931, confirmed the opposition of the Aleppine wing of the bloc to the mandate.[30] It must have been an inspiring
moment for Rabbath. He was a generation younger than most of the men
in the room; he was the only non-Muslim, and the only one with a French
education; and he differed from the other participants in terms of class,
clan, and upbringing. That he was there as an equal is unlikely, although
he may have considered himself as such. Most likely, Jabiri had brought
him to the meeting to reinforce his position with the other notables
through the introduction of an impeccably modern protégé. Rabbath represented no "constituency" other than himself; he was not part of the vast
urban and rural networks of patrons and clients that the others in the
room controlled; he could not use their customary means of mobilization.
Rather, Rabbath's usefulness lay in his potential to intervene skillfully and
persuasively in the constituent elements of the city's public sphere. In a
very real sense, the notables were absent from this place of critical-rational discourse by virtue of their training and cultural prerogatives and
collectively did not have the kinds of talents or social credentials of someone like the young lawyer. For Rabbath, being so close to power, so close
to a group of men who presented a credible opposition to the hated mandate, may have eased his egalitarian conscience and allowed him to consider delaying his devotion to the ideals of democracy and representation
expressed in his previous literary output; it revealed as well, perhaps, the
greatest weakness of the middle class: the ease with which members of
an ancien régime could exploit the bourgeois anxiety of individuals like
Rabbath for their own ends.

Alternatively, by recruiting Rabbath, Jabiri could have been signaling
his support for Rabbath's ideas about nationalism and the future of Syria.
Central to these, as explicated in his various writings, is a belief in the
unity of Syria, though ironically within French Orientalist–defined geographical and cultural boundaries. Upon the occupation of the region,
French policymakers had separated the area into states that roughly corresponded with the old systems of *sancaks* and *vilayets* of the Ottoman
period, and Rabbath agitated for their unification.[31] Rabbath's Syria, conversely, was united and part of an imagined Arab community with bound-

[30] PRO FO 371/15364 E1187/656/89 Monck-Mason (Aleppo) to Secretary of State for
Foreign Affairs, 4 February 1931.

[31] Edmond Rabbath, *Les états-unis de Syrie!* (Aleppo: Maronite Press, 1925).

aries defined and reinforced by language, race, and Islam and Eastern
Christianity; his nationalism, when viewed in the context of the period,
was not particularly radical and reflected both his French education and
his concerns as a member of a religious minority.[32]

While Philip Khoury has suggested that Jabiri had been an advocate of
"Arab nationalism before the First World War while still in his teens"
and was a member of the Arab nationalist secret society, al-Fatat, this
was probably not the case.[33] Certainly, however, of the leading notables
of Aleppo, he was the first to embrace a nationalist ideology. His association with Rabbath could be construed as proof of this, although such a
claim merits close examination. The evidence equally proves that Jabiri,
through his teens and young adulthood, saw himself as a member of an
urban, urbane, aristocratic class that reinforced its local authority
through links with Istanbul and metropolitan Ottoman society. He probably saw himself as an Ottoman while a student in the capital and in the
army. Neither Ihsan nor Sa'dallah participated in early Arab nationalist
activities such as the First Arab Congress in Paris (1912), to which several
Aleppines sent telegrams of support.[34] The Jabiri family's subsequent participation in the Syrian Congress of 1919 need not signal anything more
than its resolve to participate in any and all structures of power forming
in interwar Syria. Specifically, it is unproductive to confuse the clans's
pro-Faysal stance with an ideological commitment to Arabism. While
there is evidence of a tactical alliance, there is no evidence of an ideological engagement, and these two ought not to be conflated.

However, Jabiri's journal entries do indicate that by the late 1920s he
had been exposed to the idea of a Pan-Arab nation. This was due largely
to Rabbath's influence, as can be seen in a diary entry that recounts a
lengthy discussion of the subject with Rabbath over coffee after the two
men attended a play in French that Jabiri had been unable to follow due
to his limited capacity in that language.[35] That his Arabism acquired a
level of sophistication and a grounding in Western nationalist theory at
the same time he and Rabbath had grown closer is more than a coincidence, although it would be difficult to prove a direct causal link; never-

---

[32] Rabbath later developed a theory of a "true France," in a construction similar to
"true civilization," which was dedicated to liberal principles and would eventually find
itself again and aid the Arabs in their national awakening. The imperialistic form of the
French Mandate, he would argue, was only temporary and derived from the French experience with North Africans, a people Rabbath considered inferior to Syrians. Hourani,
Arabic Thought, 311.

[33] Khoury, *Mandate*, 126.

[34] See Muhammad Kamil al-Khatib, ed., *al-Mu'tamar al-'arabi al-awwal* [The First Arab
Congress] (Cairo: Ministry of Culture, 1913; reprint Damascus, 1996), 166–167.

[35] MWT-QK 95, "Private Papers of Sa'dallah al-Jabiri," entry for 18 June 1929.

theless, the coincidence confirms the value to the notability of the knowledge possessed by someone like Rabbath as the former began to recognize
the broad utility of nationalism as a tool for popular mobilization and
rhetorical engagement with the French. A further clue to the scope of his
nationalist consciousness is seen in his dismay that one of Nafi'Pasha's
sons, Cevdet, who resided in Istanbul and visited Aleppo in the spring
of 1929, wore a brimmed hat rather than a fez and had taken Turkish
citizenship. The passage does not reveal whether his concern was that
Cevdet had turned his back on his family or his presumed "nation."[36]
There is no evidence, however, that this incipient nationalism translated
fully into the liberal ideology espoused by Rabbath. In addition to his
clear notion of being distinct from most members of non-Muslim Arab
groups, as outlined above, his diary reveals an unmistakable aristocratic
bent: the "common people" are described as contemptible and labeled
the "rabble" (al-ra'a'), and he often complained of the amount needed to
manipulate them through the use of cash subsidies.[37]

A critical reading of Jabiri's relationship with Rabbath rests on an understanding of the transformation of the logic of power that had begun
in the later part of the nineteenth century but had accelerated in the 1920s
and 1930s. The bases of Jabiri's power and influence in Aleppine society
were custom and precedent supported by the religious order and the family's connection with the Ottoman state and its ruling class. The family's
leadership in the fields of administration and religion is evidenced by the
various salaried positions it held and the appointments it received from
the central state. And members of the family owned vast tracts of land.[38]
Customary reasoning held that the family ought to have power because
it had "always" had power through its control of resources, access to the
Ottoman elite, religious authority, and wealth. Taken as a whole, these
categories form the constituent elements of this class's "natural leadership." It was with this authority, through complex networks of clientage,
that the family maintained its power and dominance. For those within
the boundaries of these notable networks, however, Rabbath's discussion
of national sovereignty and his refutation of French claims that Syrians
were legally a "minor" people would have seemed so much logorrhea or
simply irrelevant. Their support for Jabiri was based on a much older
ideology—incoherent in the idiom of modernity—and one that was not
predicated upon the logic and rhetoric that were Maître Rabbath's stock-
in-trade. Thus, Jabiri did not need Rabbath's services to control or influ-

[36] Ibid., entry for 14 April 1929.
[37] Ibid., entry for 12 January 1929.
[38] Muhammad As'ad Pasha Jabiri alone possessed more than 17 square kilometers in the
area of Jabal al-Ghazalat at the time of the Revolution of 1908. Tabbakh, Notables, 7:582.

ence this part of Aleppine society. Rather, as noted above, Jabiri needed Rabbath to reach novel parts of the Syrian polity and beyond. This included not just the French and the broader international community in the form of the League of Nations, but also the city's large Christian community and the powerful Muslim and Christian commercial middle class and educated young men and women in the liberal professions who peopled the Aleppine public sphere. Rabbath's origin in a well-established Greek Catholic family, education, and linguistic abilities gave him access to these constituent elements of the city's political and social landscape. Most especially, he held the credentials of a transnational *modern*.

The relative success of his early writings recommended his services to Jabiri in the first of these requirements, reaching the French. The mandate system cloaked European colonialism with a naive Wilsonian idealism, thereby infusing the discourse of imperialism with questions about rights and responsibilities, freedoms and national self-determination. To Jabiri, Rabbath's books and articles indicated his ability to understand these concepts and perhaps eventually to turn the legal tables on the French authorities. Within the penumbra of the theory of mandate, the "natives" could appeal to the League of Nations for assistance. The experience of colonized peoples from Senegal to Indochina also showed that to have any chance of relevance within the Palace of Nations in Geneva, one had to speak the same language of modernism that the imperial powers spoke.

This language had been gaining currency in Aleppo as well. Those who could speak it were the readers of *al-Hadith* and *L'evolution politique de la Syrie sous mandat*, the graduates of the Western missionary schools and those recently returned from the Sorbonne or other French institutions of higher learning. The education they had received had taught them that the appeals to tradition at the core of notable power were archaic and hollow, and instead, political authority must proceed from a rational basis and should be open to their participation. As explored in earlier chapters, this jaundiced view of notable authority had been a hallmark of middle-class political activity in the revolutionary period. Thus, ironically or willfully, Jabiri co-opted (or recruited) the young man in Aleppine society most capable of criticizing him. For precisely this reason, Rabbath's task was not simple, as Jabiri's claim to power was based on aristocratic precedent and theocratic privilege. Such a warrant had to be recast in the language of public opinion and of Ottoman-cum-Syrian noblesse oblige. The electoral politics of the late Ottoman and Mandate period, especially elections that guaranteed a large representation for Christians, had intensified the need to legitimize the notables in this manner. Vis-à-vis the city's Christians, a group whose stock had risen with the French occupation, Rabbath's role proved equally complex. Rabbath had to persuade them that they, as Syrian citizens, had a stake in the type of government proposed by the National Bloc. He also constituted a personal example that the bloc had some commitment to a secular state that would guarantee that gains in personal status made by Christians under the French would not erode and there would not be a return to what Rabbath himself had labeled in *L'évolution*, a state "for and by the Muslims."[39]

The ideologically flexible and pragmatic response of Jabiri acting on his family's and class's behalf was not uncommon; like others of their class in Syria and elsewhere, they were more interested in co-opting such movements and "covering their bets." Simply put, in the early years of the mandate, the process of maintaining, or in this case, recovering, hegemony required the notables to use an ideology—liberal nationalism—that taken to its logical extent would erode the very bases of their hegemony. The nature of these bases, as Geoff Eley has observed, taking his cue from Antonio Gramsci, are "always open to modification, and under specific circumstances may be more radically transformed or even . . . break down altogether,"[40] suggesting that the elite component of the "Politics of Notables" could turn to new ideologies and recruit and employ talent from outside its customary pool of resources, even if the acceptance of such ideologies and the use of such talents could ultimately undermine its very existence. This telling note of irony does not call into question whether the notables actually understood the ideology articulated by intellectuals like Rabbath, but rather should lead to doubt as to the depth of their commitment to it. That they understood it as a threat to their hegemony is likely; they felt confident that matters would never be allowed to mature beyond a certain point and that they could control the social forces unleashed.

NOTABLE DEMOCRATS AND MIDDLE-CLASS RESISTANCE IN THE ELECTORAL POLITICS OF THE 1930s

The full contours of the contradictory and ultimately unstable relationship between Jabiri and Rabbath became visible during the most important political events of the early 1930s: the constituent assembly elections of December 1931 and January 1932, the delegation to France of 1936, and the elections that took place that same year. Similarly, a clearer

[39] Rabbath, *L'evolution*, 15.

[40] Eley, "Nations," 324. See also, Khoury: "The point is that the nationalist elite was aware of nationalist feelings and constructs different from their own. When they were not able to ignore them or reinterpret them, they tried to co-opt them. The process of doing so tells us something about the nationalist elite, about ideological hegemony, and about available alternatives." "The Paradoxical in Arab Nationalism: Inter-war Syria Reconsidered," in James Jankowski and Israel Gershoni, *Rethinking*, 275.

picture of the way the middle class sought to contest the city's architectures of community emerged in this period, as did the full extent of the discursive environment in which Rabbath's services were needed.

The form of Syrian elections during most of the mandate, which were modeled on the old Ottoman system of tiered representation, contributed in no small way to the shape of that discursive environment. Such a system was calculated both to help maintain the status quo and facilitate official manipulation. In principle, the system worked as follows: all adult males voluntarily registered by neighborhood. The *mukhtar* or "head man" of the quarter certified this list, after checking it for duplication and the registration of the dead or ineligible. The mukhtar then passed the list on to the central authorities, who authorized the vote. The voting took place at public places around the city, mosques, schools, churches, synagogues, and cafés.[41] Individuals voted for electors of the second degree rather than any specific party although, like a caucus-style vote, the secondary electors were generally identified with a certain faction or individual. These electors then met and chose from among themselves the final delegates (table 8.1). They were allowed to cast as many votes as there were seats in the district. Corruption of the process could occur at any step—most easily at the level of registration.

Mandate-era elections resembled pre-1908 Ottoman elections in an additional way: confessional representation was guaranteed. In other words, on the basis of preliminary calculation, and regardless of the eventual vote totals, religious communities were awarded representatives. The electors of the second degree in 1932 filled six seats assigned to "Muslims" (conceived as a monolithic group), two "Armenian Orthodox," one "Armenian Catholic," one "Greek Catholic," and one "Syrian Catholic." In subsequent elections a seat would be reserved for "Aleppo's minorities," that is Jews, Chaldeans, and Greek and Syrian Orthodox. For example, Rabbath ran as a "Greek Catholic" and lost in that category to Latif al-Ghanima by a margin of 174 to 293 in the secondary elections.[42] The authorities juggled such allotments throughout the mandate period.

Direct vote rigging was unnecessary to gain an outcome favorable to those who were least antagonistic to the mandate; rather, French efforts indicate that they had identified, supported, and protected a cross-confessional constituency within Aleppine society—Muslim, Christian, and Jewish—unwilling to support the notables of the bloc. Indeed, the group of Christians identified as "moderate candidates" by the French were, for

---

[41] CADN-MAE Fonds Beyrouth, Cabinet Politique 399, Assistant Delegate (Aleppo) to High Commissioner (Beirut), no. 61/13, 9 January 1932. For an earlier discussion of the Aleppine electoral politics at this time, see Sluglett, "Urban Dissidence in Mandatory Syria," 301–316.

[42] CADN-MAE Fonds Beyrouth, Cabinet Politique 399, High Commissioner (Damascus) to Minister of Foreign Affairs, no. 87, 29 January 1932.

TABLE 8.1.
Table of Electors of the First Degree in Aleppo, 1932

Sunni		
Shiite		
Druze		
Alawite		
Yezidi		
[Total Muslim]	27,471	(55%)
Jewish	1,759	
Armenian Catholic	3,029	
Armenian Orthodox	9,104	
Greek Catholic	2,426	
Greek Orthodox	560	
Syrian Catholic	1,171	
Syrian Orthodox	1,379	
Maronite	625	
Chaldean	351	
Latin	502	
Protestant	1,202	
[Total non-Muslim]	22,378	(45%)
Total	49,849	

While the French noted different Muslim sects in the census data, they did differentiate among these groups in the final count.
Source: CADN-MAE Fonds Beyrouth, Cabinet Politique 399, Assistant Delegate (Aleppo) to High Commissioner (Beirut), no. 61/13, 9 January 1932.

the most part, similar to the secondary electors themselves in terms of class and the economic role they played in the city.[43] Among these were Salim Janbart, the sixty-year-old president of the Chamber of Commerce, and Henri Hindiyya, a local businessman in one of the more successful international trading-houses of Aleppo, Frères Hindié.[44] Of the Muslims elected, however, each was a notable who had collaborated with the French or historically had been involved with a conservative Ottoman resistance in the immediate postwar period.[45]

---

[43] Ibid., Assistant Delegate (Aleppo) to High Commissioner (Beirut), no. 61/13, 9 January 1932.

[44] PRO FO 371/23280 E5572/1291/89, "Records of Leading Personalities in Syria and the Lebanon," 9 August 1939, 10–11.

[45] PRO FO 371/7847 E 8200/274/89, Morgan (Aleppo) to Secretary of State for Foreign Affairs, 26 July 1922.

On the eve of the 1931–1932 elections, it became clear that the bloc could not repeat its victory of 1928.[46] The primary cause for their anxiety was a list of candidates headed by Subhi bey Barakat and calling itself the Liberal Constitutionalists who enjoyed French support. The Liberal Constitutionalists embraced the nonnationalist notables of the city, especially the Mudarris family, and advocated greater autonomy for the province of Aleppo. This policy had a broad appeal to the merchant community as manifested by the defection of the majority of the bloc's non-Muslim supporters. For example, the aforementioned Greek Catholic merchant Latif al-Ghanima, who had run with the bloc list in 1928, left it for this new grouping. Aware of the strength of the Liberal Constitutionalists and of an emboldened middle-class electorate, the bloc sensed that their chances of electoral success were slim.[47]

"The extremists [the term employed by the French to denote those who did not cooperate] did all they could to gain control of the ballot boxes, upon failing this they attempted a boycott," reads the terse Sûreté Générale report of the first day's balloting sent to the Aleppo assistant delegate.[48] Rabbath was one of the few bloc partisans to agitate actively for

[46] Drawing primarily on electoral networks established in the late Ottoman period, the bloc's notables had been elected in 1928 without much opposition. See CADN-MAE Fonds Beyrouth Cabinet Politique 398, "Elections 1928," 10 April 1928.

[47] The nationalist notables of Aleppo had tried to organize boycotts in the elections of 1923 and 1926. In 1923 turnout in the first degree was estimated at 40 percent despite the boycott. The election of 1926 saw the most successful of these boycotts, with turnout reduced to around 23 percent of the total, though this reduction can also be attributed to wide-scale Christian fears of violence and retaliation. The elections of 1928 also saw widespread attempts at intimidation, and again Christians stayed away from the polls, thereby assuring a near-sweep by the bloc. CADN-MAE Fonds Beyrouth Cabinet Politique 396, "Summary of the Elections to the Representative Councils of the States of Syria, October 1923"; PRO FO 371/11515 E641/146/89 Hough (Aleppo) to Chamberlain, 15 January 1926; CADN-MAE Fonds Beyrouth Cabinet Politique 398, "Political Situation in Aleppo" Collet (Damascus) to High Commissioner, 21 March 1928; CADN-MAE Fonds Beyrouth Cabinet Politique 398, "1928 Elections" Protche (Aleppo) to Chief, Sûreté Générale, 27 April 1926. In his report, Protche discusses the intimidation of two Christian electors of the second degree by operatives of Hananu. Hananu, with the assistance of Na'im al-Anflaki, asked for the release of the alleged perpetrators; Khoury, *Mandate*, 335. Armenian refugees who had recently been given the right to vote by Ponsot were also singled out for attack by the nationalists. Stephen H. Longrigg, *Syria and Lebanon under French Mandate* (Oxford: Oxford University Press, 1958), 181; PRO FO 371/13074 E 5338/141/8 Monck-Mason (Aleppo) to Lord Cushendon, 30 October 1928. Monck-Mason enclosed a copy of an anonymous pamphlet that proclaimed in part, "Not satisfied with these acts of oppression, they have recently introduced unto our land 100,000 Armenian refugees, of whom many have been raised to high rank. . . . All our commerce and finance have gone to these usurpers." CADN-MAE Fonds Beyrouth Cabinet Politique 399, Chief, Sûreté Générale (Aleppo) to Assistant Delegate (Aleppo), no. 110/S.G., 9 January 1932. The Sûreté's informants were aware of the decision to organize a boycott on 16 December 1931.

[48] CADN-MAE Fonds Beyrouth Cabinet Politique 399, Chief, Sûreté Générale (Aleppo) to Assistant Delegate (Aleppo), no. 5.368/S.G., 21 December 1931.

the boycott on the day of the election, but even his efforts appeared desperate and no doubt reinforced the impression among the city's middle
class that the bloc had begun to represent a threat to urban peace. According to the report filed that day by Mahmud Khulussi 'Isa, vice president of the electoral commission of al-Dudu, an extramural, mostly Muslim lower-class neighborhood to the east of the old city,

> At 4:00 p.m. Edmond Rabbath came in a private automobile to the voting bu-
> reau of Doudou [the café of Mahmud Misri at Bariyat al-Maslakh] and [ex-
> claimed]: "Long live the Boycott. . . . Let us grab the box, and break it so no
> one can be elected.". . . The inhabitants responded with calm telling him that
> its not up to him to intervene in this election. . . . Edmond did not pay attention
> to these words. . . . Thus according to the law I arrested him.[49]

Rabbath confirmed the basic outline of this event during an oral history
interview in 1975.[50] More important, this moment of drive-by politicking
highlights the conclusion that Rabbath personally lacked the kinds of
skills, charisma, or authority needed to successfully mobilize the inhabitants of the less middle-class districts of the city.

Despite the call to boycott, 40 percent of the electorate voted. More
telling, however, was the fact that the three modern suburban middle-class
neighborhoods, 'Aziziyya, Hamidiyya, and Sulaymaniyya, had voted at
a rate averaging over 50 percent, representing the highest per capita
voting in the city.[51] While these results may not have been representative
of Aleppo as a whole, they could be interpreted as reflecting the middle
class's distrust of the notables who opposed the mandate. This distrust
seemed even more justifiable the next day. To punish the middle class of
the city, young toughs in the employ of the bloc forced shopkeepers to
close their establishments. By 22 December 1932 all shops had been
closed out of fear of retaliation, looting, and mayhem.[52] And for the first
time, middle-class candidates began to receive death threats. Latif al-Ghanima and Henri Hindiyya were sent letters, signed in blood for added
effect, that read, "If you do not quit now you will die along with your
family." To confuse matters even more, Henri Hindiyya's opponent and
a bloc candidate in the Armenian Catholic category, Fathallah Assiyun,
also received a similar note, believed to have been from the same source.[53]

---

[49] Ibid., Mahmoud Khouloussi Issa (Aleppo) to President of the Electoral Commission
(Aleppo).

[50] Khoury, *Mandate*, 372. Khoury cites his conversation with Rabbath (Beirut, 21 August
1975): "Rabbath, a Christian, remembers inciting many Muslims to break electoral boxes."

[51] CADN-MAE Fonds Beyrouth, Cabinet Politique 399, Assistant Delegate (Aleppo) to
High Commissioner (Beirut), no. 61/13, 9 January 1932.

[52] Ibid., Chief, Sûreté Générale (Aleppo) to Assistant Delegate (Aleppo), no. 110/S.G., 9
January 1932.

[53] Ibid., Sûreté Générale (Aleppo), no. 189, 24 December 1931.

That all of these candidates were also Christians reinforces the conclusion that sectarianism had infused the conflict as well. Despite such threats, a demonstration in the courtyard of the Thanawiyyat al-Ma'mun led by Hananu's son, and a deputation to the Aleppo Deputy Delegate Lavastre by the female members of the families of bloc notables Kayyali, Jabiri, and Hananu, the secondary elections took place without incident.[54]

Having lost the election, the bloc contended that it had been stolen. Its position found voice in *La question syrienne: Les élections d'Alep*.[55] Written as a complaint to the League of Nations in Hananu's name, the pamphlet may have actually been penned by Rabbath or Antaki, both of whom figure prominently in the tract and who had better French language skills. It contains an extraordinary catalog of alleged French offenses, including interference in the both the first and second rounds of voting and their brutal treatment of local nationalists. It also names collaborators and pro-French journals and newspapers. The document abounds with references to the League's legal requirements and how the French were acting in contravention of these, a feature that could indicate the authorship of the lawyers Rabbath and Antaki. By placing the complaints within the legal framework of the League's rules and regulations, the author(s) were hoping to translate their demands into a forum beyond their immediate interaction with the local French authorities. Thus, in an exquisite act of subversion, the *évolué* author of the work used a French vocabulary of nationalism and the legalistic grammar of the mandate against the occupier.

The pamphlet's author(s) also sought to reinvent the notables simultaneously for audiences both outside and inside Aleppine society. A principal example of this is seen in the labeling of the notables who contested the elections (Hananu, Jamal Ibrahim-Basha, ʿAbd al-Rahman al-Kayyali, and Fakhr and Saʿdallah al-Jabiri) as "patriotic candidates."[56] For those within the customary sphere of political activity, such a designation was superfluous to the way they already saw themselves in relation to the *aʿyan*. However, the designation had meaning for some other audience or multiple audiences; quite simply, it is a term that only has meaning in a modern discursive environment.

The elections of 1931–1932 also proved the Aleppine bloc's organizational weakness in the Christian community. Rabbath himself reflected upon this problem in his unpublished manuscript, *Courte histoire du*

[54] Ibid., Chief, Sûreté Générale (Aleppo) to Assistant Delegate (Aleppo), no. 110/S.G., 9 January 1932.

[55] Ibrahim Hanano [Ibrahim Hananu], *La question syrienne: Les élections d'Alep* (Toulouse: Societé Meridional d'Impression, 1932).

[56] Ibid., 20.

mandat en Syrie et au Liban. In his recollections of the period, he came to the conclusion that the French had persuaded his coreligionists that they were involved in a sectarian conflict of "cross versus crescent" rather than resistance to colonialism. And were they to support the bloc they risked immersion in a "sea of Islam."[57] A recurring complaint in the bloc's statement addressed to the League of Nations voiced a similar concern, primarily that the French Mandate authority had conspired to manipulate the vote through appeals to sectarian fears. "They [the French and their collaborators] repeated over and over again as they [the secondary electors] went to vote that the success of the patriots would mean the massacre of the Christians, the expulsion of the Armenians and the conspiracy with the Turks for their [the Turk's] return to Syria."[58] While the tone of the author of the pamphlet implies that such fears were baseless, the growing frequency of violent incidents in the city and the general low regard in which those Armenians who had fled to Aleppo as refugees were held contributed to a climate of fear in which such agitation found resonance. The bloc's failure could also be explained by its "rather complacent attitude toward the Christian vote, which it all but ignored."[59]

For Rabbath, a French colonial policy that emphasized communalism and the protection of minorities had implications broader than electoral politics. In his estimation, such a policy undermined the long-term goal of creating a national(ist) identity for Syria. Rather than protecting minorities like himself, such a policy condemned Syria to continue as a *régime de cloisons étanches*, a system of watertight compartments of religious communities in which the state was officially Muslim and in which Muslims and non-Muslims alike lived within their own bounded religio-legal fictions rather than in the same state as its citizens. He had first explored this idea in *L'évolution*, writing, "The absolute liberty of conscience is incompatible with the existence of a state religion." Likewise, "freedom of conscience . . . can not find its total application under the Syrian communitarian régime. [Such] freedom is indirectly reduced to the liberty of believing in an official religion and precludes either adhesion to an unofficial faith or the freeing of oneself from any confessional group."[60] This statement carried with it profound implications; had Syrian legal structures been altered in a way to remedy such an obvious barrier to freedom of conscience—a process of laicization—conceivably, the *religious* basis of notable authority would crumble, leaving the other bases upon which their power rested increasingly unstable. The temporal power of Christian

---

[57] Cited in Khoury, *Mandate*, 362.

[58] Hanano, *La question syrienne*, 15.

[59] Khoury, *Syria*, 372.

[60] Rabbath, *L'evolution*, 19, 101, 202.

ecclesiastical leaders would likewise vanish, as much of their authority arose from their ability to dominate their flocks as supreme arbiters of issues of family law or laws of personal status. Establishing society on the basis of secular citizenship could assure equality more readily than the status quo and no doubt appealed to those in the middle class like Rabbath. Conversely, it could have had little appeal to someone like Jabiri, whose "natural leadership" derived in general from the institutional domination of society by Sunni Muslims and was legitimized by his clan's claim to descent from the family of the Prophet Muhammad.

Similarly, what Rabbath considered a colonialist-inspired division of society made improbable the formation of a Syrian national identity: "Does this mean," he asked,

> there do not exist collective sentiments other than those which follow from this very regime [communalism]? Such a conclusion would singularly support the thesis of those who declared that there does not exist in Syria anything but confessions which act in the place of national sentiment and fatherland and that the Syrians are still far from conceiving and realizing the national sovereignty and liberty to which their leaders lay claim.[61]

Election results broadly reflecting an unwillingness of much of the Aleppine middle class, especially its Christian wing, to support the notables of the National Bloc and their nationalism reinforced such a conclusion. Creating nationalist sentiment, a key moment in the claiming of modernity, was therefore blocked by the perpetuation of confessional division by the French imperialists and those whom Rabbath would label collaborators. He had come to believe that the French had vested in the local Christian population a false consciousness of the centrality and essential nature of sectarianism in Syria. In reaction, his writings reveal that he had imagined by the mid-1920s a type of Syrian citizenship that was at variance with both colonial policy and the dominant conception of Ottoman-style institutionalized Muslim dominance of the state.[62] Such a secular interpretation of citizenship was an expression of both his middle-class origins and his intellectual training. However, in Rabbath's estimation, the Sunni notables who opposed the French represented the best means to the ends of the formation of a national identity in Syria; hence, association, with the elite bloc represented a short-term concession on his part in order to serve a more important long-term goal.

[61] Ibid., 20.

[62] Unlike many of his co-religionists, Rabbath, had renounced his own right to hold a foreign passport—in his case Greek—in favor of sole Syrian nationality sometime in the 1920s; until today, Aleppine Christians often hold dual (or multiple) nationality as a type of "insurance policy." PRO FO 371/23280 E5572/1291/89 "Records of Leading Personalities in Syria and the Lebanon," 9 August 1939, 16.

A new opening for both Jabiri and Rabbath seemed possible after the bloc's well-enforced General Strike of 1936. In response to the strike, the left-wing French government of Léon Blum invited the bloc and others to Paris to renegotiate the terms of the mandate in anticipation of granting Syrian independence. The Aleppines in the ranks of the National Bloc delegation included Sa'dallah al-Jabiri, the banker Edmond Homsy, Syrian Communist Party leader Khalid Bakdash, and the delegation's secretaries, Na'im al-Antaki and Rabbath.[63] Following the seemingly successful negotiation of the treaty, the delegation returned to Syria and prepared to conduct an election that they hoped would solidify their gains. In the days before the race, the National Bloc opened a new newspaper in Aleppo, *al-Nazir* [The Herald]. This paper, which began publishing in November 1936, is the primary textual evidence of the ongoing efforts to transform Jabiri and other notables into something even more than "patriotic candidates." Hananu's death in 1935 had paved the way for Jabiri to assume control of the Aleppine wing of the bloc. Glossing over the fact that Jabiri had always had a poor relationship with Hananu, the editorial staff of *al-Nazir* immediately heralded Jabiri as his legitimate successor. Banner headlines labeled "The *za'im* Sa'dallah Jabiri, the *khalifa* of Hananu."[64] The process of transforming an Ottoman notable into a modern nationalist leader was under way—though it used two of the oldest words in the Arabic-Islamic lexicon of power to do so.

Other efforts to legitimate the notables in modern terms understandable in the new discursive environment included a series of speaking engagements in two institutions at the very heart of middle-class Aleppo. On 20 October 1936 the professional syndicates of the city organized a tea in Jabiri's honor at the Aleppo Club. Approximately 800 people attended, including all the nationalist leaders, the president of the Chamber of Commerce, Salim Janbart, as well as journalists, lawyers, doctors, and bureaucrats. During the ceremony, speakers—including Rabbath's co-editor at *al-Hadith*, Sami al-Kayyali—eulogized Sa'dallah al-Jabiri. Finally taking the stage at the end of the ornate hall, he began his speech by asserting the bloc's commitment to an egalitarian Syrian citizenship: "there does not exist among us the great and the small. We are all equal and there is no difference between us especially between those who work for the Syrian cause."[65] After the tea, he traversed the two blocks between the Aleppo Club and the Cercle de la jeunesse Catholique. There he gave another speech to an audience that included the bloc leadership, Rabbath

[63] Khoury, *Syria*, 464–468.

[64] *al-Nazir* (Aleppo), 15 November 1936.

[65] CADN-MAE Fonds Beyrouth Cabinet Politique 400 Sûreté Générale (Aleppo), no. 3999, 21 October 1936.

among them, the local bishops and archbishops, leaders of the various Christian quarters, and the young men and women who made up the membership of the consummate Francophile bourgeois club itself. Echoing his earlier address, Jabiri declared, among other things:

> we concluded the Franco-Syrian Treaty in which the rights of Christians are safeguarded. . . . We know very well that you are better educated than we are, we do not ignore that. . . . Religion is God's and the fatherland is to all. I do not want anyone to say that this person is Christian and that one is Muslim. We are all Arabs and Syria belongs to us all. Fanaticism must disappear to save this country and to give it the prosperity it used to have.[66]

He then translated his text into Turkish for the Armenians in the room, showing that the very linguistic basis of the Arab Syrian nation he had just described was itself precarious.

With these speeches and the meetings, the first to take place in the officially apolitical clubs, Jabiri hoped to demonstrate the extent to which the public ideology of the bloc reflected a liberal-nationalist orientation, as well as the bloc's realization of its need to "reach out" to the urban middle class, to whom they assured that power would be shared. However, the internal contradictions of the speeches, which call to mind the persistence of forms of inequality and distinction found in Rabbath's inscription eight years earlier, confirm that this sharing would take place within the framework of continued notable domination. While there may be "no difference between" the classes and religious communities, the audience may well have been left wondering if "Syria belongs to us all," why did people like Jabiri have a right to more of that all?

An effort to reconcile such contradictions—the persistence of class and sectarian distinction alongside the assertion of the irrelevance of such differences—had motivated Rabbath to write a series of newspaper articles on the subject in the spring of 1936. These articles were an attempt to "spin" bloc pronouncements like Jabiri's speeches into a more coherent policy on Syrian minorities. Appearing in the "Tribune Libre" section of the Lebanese French-language journal Le Jour,[67] the series both outlined the bloc's public interpretation of the French policy toward minorities and employed an Orientalist argument that true Islam, and a state dominated by Muslims, would tolerate Christians who would prosper as long

---

[66] Ibid., Sûreté Générale (Aleppo), no. 3998, 23 October 1936. It is interesting to note the resurrection of the Arab Kingdom era slogan "religion is to God, the fatherland is to all." For a discussion of the origins of this slogan, see Gelvin, *Divided*, 181–186.

[67] The author of *La question syrienne* accuses various papers, among them Aleppo's *al-Taqaddum* and Beirut's *L' Orient*, of taking subsidies from the French authorities; see CADN-MAE Fonds Beyrouth Cabinet Politique 445.

as they willingly cooperated with it.[68] Writing in French and using almost exclusively French Orientalist and legal sources, Rabbath inflected his argument in a way that pandered to the cultural snobbery of the Levant's Francophone Christian middle class. For many, French was approaching a near-native tongue, defining those who spoke it as members of a separate community within a non-French milieu. It did not define them as French per se but presented them with an identity in antagonism with the identity of Arab or Syrian advocated by Rabbath. His central aim in the articles was to leave the Christian middle class in no doubt that a nationalist government would—while protecting their rights as fellow citizens—deny to them access to this alternative identity; this identity, he sought to show, had no basis in the historical past, nor would it have any meaning in the politics of the postcolonial future.

Entitled "Les Minorités," the articles ran from 6 March through 10 March 1936. Rabbath began the first installment, subtitled "Muslim Tolerance," arguing that the Christians of the Levant had always viewed the Arab Muslim conquerors as just rulers: "We can honestly say that . . . [French] prejudice against majoritarian Islam is profoundly unjust."[69] Things only began to fall apart, the history lesson continued, upon the accession to the throne of the Abbasid Caliph al-Mutawakkil (847–861) when "a phenomenon similar to Hitlerian [*sic*] anti-Semitism arose" and "persecution became more generalized because Islam was no longer well understood by its adherents." Moving swiftly from the medieval to the modern period, Rabbath assigned blame for the sundry massacres of Christians by Muslims in the midnineteenth century on outsiders, that is non-Arabs. The son of the Albanian Mehmet Ali, Ibrahim Pasha, the Janissaries, and rapacious and corrupt "Turkish" governors all come under indictment: "In 1860 what has been called massacres were merely . . . revolts of a popular and agrarian nature which pitted feudal lords against exasperated serfs and which were encouraged, as if for fun, by the Turkish pashas."[70] Nevertheless, the late Ottoman reforms, presaged by "the habit of the Great Powers to insert themselves in the relationships of the Ottoman Empire with its non-Muslim subjects," assisted the cause of the Christians in the empire. "They [the Christians and Jews] tri-

---

[68] Rabbath's Orientalist sources include L Bréhier, *L'eglise et l'orient au moyen-age: Les Croisades* (Paris, 1921); Henri Lammens, *La Syrie: précis historique* (Paris, 1913); and Antoine Rabbath-Tournebize, *Documents inédits pour pour servir à l'histoire du christianisme en Orient* (Paris: A. Picard et Fils, 1905).

[69] *Le Jour* (Beirut), 6 March 1936. Rabbath's initial paragraph was a refutation of Édouard Daladier's widely quoted statement to the French Chamber on 30 March 1929: "why . . . must we maintain troops in Syria? . . . [B]ecause the day when you recall these forces you will risk seeing these different races attacking each other as it has happened very regularly in their history."

[70] Ibid., 7 March 1936.

umphed in commerce and banking, their privileged domain," he wrote of
the period after 1878—adopting the dominant historiographical prejudices about the position of Christians and Jews in Ottoman society. "In
the great cities they lived in the best quarters and in the most beautiful
buildings. . . . Many Christians became ministers, senators, magistrates
and members of official bodies. They exerted a definite political influence,
their patriarchs were treated as the equals of viziers." In the waning days
of the empire, "Rights, conscription, taxes were equally imposed on all."
Similarly, Cemal Pasha executed both Christian and Muslim "nationalists" in 1915; "The gibbet was set up for everyone, without distinction of
religion." The Great War, concluded Rabbath, ushered in an era of the
"conflict of races and that of religions seemed a thing of the past." As
Syria was a "racially homogeneous" state under King Faysal, the question
of minorities was not an issue, "the Damascus cabinet [included] four
Christians out of eight ministers." And "Public spirit was steering itself
towards Arabism and unity." This final thought is an explicit criticism of
the French presence, which he saw as both a disruption in the natural
evolution of an Arab Syria, but also a return to the period in which outsiders employed sectarianism to deter the modernization of his nation. Paraphrasing a passage from Ernest Renan's 1882 Sorbonne lecture "Qu'est-
ce qu'une nation?" "[F]orgetfulness . . . the essence of a nation is that all
the individuals have many things in common and thus they have forgotten
many things," Rabbath argued that a kind of conscious amnesia and an
enlightened censorship would be the final act which would return Syria
to the correct historical trajectory.[71] This necessary "forgetfulness" segued
into the final article, "The 'protection' of minorities," and Rabbath's chill-
ing warning to his fellow Christian minorities of Syria. Following a complex and pedantic argument about the role of the League of Nations in
protecting minorities, Rabbath shifted into the first person and addressed
his co-religionists directly: "The future is not in Europe . . . but in Islam
in which we are immersed." A Bible verse ends the series: "[the Old Testament prophet] Jeremiah's words remain meaningful 'But seek the welfare
of the city where I have sent you into exile, and pray to the Lord on its
behalf, for in its welfare you will find your welfare.' "[72]

In this sweeping history, Rabbath bound the Orientalist trope of an
essential Islamic community to the nationalist construct of a timeless Arab
race, thereby making a striking historicist argument. Further developed
in his last overtly political text, *Unité syrienne et devenir arabe*, a gloss
of this argument unfolds as follows: Arab history is a history of intersectarian comity where the responsibility for provoking sectarianism

[71] Ibid., 8 March 1936.
[72] Ibid., 10 March 1936. Jeremiah 29:7 "Recherchez le bien de la ville où je vous ai menés
en captivité, et priez l'Éternel en sa faveur, parce que votre bonheur dépend du sien."

rested on non-Arabs.[73] Since Islam by definition is a tolerant religion, if there were no outside interference then Arabs would live in harmony together. Christians had nothing to fear because historical strife has its origins in the lands beyond the Arab-Islamic world. Regardless, the violence of the past, and the trepidation of survivors of the massacres, should be forgotten because that forgetting is the basis of the nation, a nation within which one's condition as a minority would have no standing; rather, the law would protect the legitimate rights of all. Minorities would not be allowed any special status and would have no appeal to an outside power because they would not need such protection. Nevertheless, with the implications of the Prophet Jeremiah's words in mind, Syrian minorities—like the Hebrews during the Babylonian captivity—would remain in a subordinate condition as not quite Syrians, still exiles in their own land. In return for the support of the minorities and their middle class, the bloc then would also protect their access to the public sphere. Consequently, key components of a public sphere—free association, speech, and religion—were enshrined in their statements and promises to the French dating from this period. It is unlikely that the bloc would have made such promises in the absence of the growing power of the Syrian middle class, especially its Christian wing, whose fears Rabbath had sought to assuage in these articles.

MIDDLE-CLASS QUIESCENCE AND A RETREAT FROM THE PUBLIC SPHERE

Despite the promises and public devotion to these ideals, the events of the 1936 election showed that Rabbath's arguments found little resonance in his own community and that ultimately, in lieu of persuasion, the bloc would take recourse to much less subtle means. That the bloc abandoned such ideals may have caused Rabbath's eventual disenchantment with its leadership and led to his distancing himself from Jabiri. In the end, his system of belief was based on the rule of law and the logos of modernity; he was ill prepared for the grim realities of the late 1930s' Syrian urban politics.[74]

Having arrogated most municipal authority to itself following the return of the delegation to Syria, the bloc ran the city of Aleppo from its titular headquarters, the House of Hananu. From this vantage point, it sought to assure itself an electoral victory by any means necessary. Such a victory would mean the reassertion of notable hegemony in Aleppine

---

[73] Edmond Rabbath, *Unité syrienne et devenir arabe* (Paris: Marcel Rivière, 1937).

[74] PRO FO 371/23280 E5572/1291/89, "Records of Leading Personalities in Syria and the Lebanon," 9 August 1939, 16. Even British diplomatic observers noticed his growing "moderation" in this period.

society through the complete dominance of government structures by the families that constituted the bloc leadership. Just as in the previous elections, the battle to control the ballot box began by deciding who was allowed to vote. The French had successfully encouraged a high voter turnout for what they called "moderate candidates" in the 1932 election in part through the control of the lists. From 1928 until 1936 the bloc leadership had complained about the overrepresentation of Christians on the rolls.[75] As if to correct this historical overrepresentation, the bloc had the names of Christian electors reduced from 22,000 to 12,000, with Armenians representing about three-quarters of the entire amount, simply by destroying the records of certain neighborhoods.[76] This reduction was possible because all lists had first to go through the bloc headquarters before being presented to the government.[77]

The alteration of such lists was by no means limited to the middle-class parts of the city. By the end of November, mukhtars of the poorer quarters of Kallasa, Mashariqa, Jallum, and Bab al-Nayrab, who had connections with notable families outside of the bloc's orbit, complained that the bloc had no right to erase some names and replace them with others without their consultation, and they threatened to boycott or run an alternative list.[78] Such calls for boycott were echoed in complaints made in the Christian and Armenian neighborhoods about the candidates who had been imposed on them by the bloc. Perhaps the most unpopular candidate was Edmond Rabbath himself. The bloc had selected him to represent "Aleppo's minorities," that is Jews, Maronites, Syrian Orthodox, Latins, and Protestants.[79] Despite the public outcry, the bloc refused to alter its list. A low turnout was predicted, and all involved recognized the inevitability of the bloc's victory.

Ultimately, this victory was not assured by the persuasive nature of the new dimensions of the bloc's political discourse. Rather, the French had ceded enough ground to the notables, who used the opportunity to create

---

[75] CADN-MAE Fonds Beyrouth Cabinet Politique 398 Reseignements, 29 March 1928. During this election ʿAbd al-Rahman al-Kayyali and Ibrahim Hananu had complained to the interior minister that the superior number of seats accorded to minorities created an "unfavorable impression in the Muslim milieu of Aleppo."

[76] CADN-MAE Fonds Beyrouth Cabinet Politique 400 Sûreté Générale (Aleppo), no. 4022, 22 October 1936.

[77] Ibid., no. 4343, 9 October 1936. Disturbed by this occurrence, Arman Mazlumyan, the owner of the Baron Hotel, approached the mayor (24 October 1936), complaining that the lists could not reflect the true number of Armenians living in the refugee camps turned suburban neighborhoods of Midan and Dawudiyya. Inscription was then renewed, and the number of Armenians on the rolls expanded to 11,000. CADN-MAE Fonds Beyrouth Cabinet Politique 400 Sûreté Générale (Aleppo), no. 3739, 9 October 1936.

[78] Ibid., no. 4448, 16 November 1936; no. 4684, 30 November 1936; and no. 4445, 16 November 1936.

[79] Ibid., no. 4448, 16 November 1936.

social formations to reduce or even eliminate the range of activity of the Aleppine middle class. The primary feature of this was the *al-haris al-watani*, the National Guard, the subject of the following chapter. Following the lead of several European countries, the bloc in Aleppo outfitted, trained, drilled, and marched through the city a group of young men and boys. By mid-1936 the group, an analog of the Damascene *al-qumsan al-hadidiyya*, the Steel Shirts, had become a familiar and daunting presence in the streets of Aleppo through their weekly exercise schedule. The most violent Guard contingent was led by Jabiri's traditional lieutenant, 'Abd al-Rahman "'Abduh" Misri. 'Abduh Misri seems to have been the foil of Edmond Rabbath. He was Muslim, a member of the underclass, from a much different part of the city, and had under his command young men capable of violence; he seemed immune from any retribution, and far from representing a new actor in the "Politics of Notables," he served the Jabiri family as its enforcer, its *qabaday*. Indeed, as the bloc gained power, and the notables came to thoroughly dominate Aleppo, the fading of Rabbath and the evolution of a neighborhood tough like 'Abduh Misri into a political activist, as explored in the following chapter, is evidence of shifting terms of where and when being modern was relevant in the period.

Taken as a whole, the bloc's actions presented the average middle-class Aleppine with little room to maneuver, as many aspects of what had been the public sphere now fell under the direct control of the bloc. In the first round of voting on 18 November, less than 60 percent of eligible Muslims, not more than 20 percent of Christians, and 10 percent of Armenians voted, proving that an antibloc counterboycott had taken place.[80] The bloc itself had not anticipated such recalcitrance on the part of the electorate. Such totals, far less than any previous election, confirmed, among other things, that Rabbath had failed to do his job. Nevertheless, the young lawyer was included in the electoral list as it appeared in *al-Nazir*.

The list ran:

Sa'dallah al-Jabiri
'Abd al-Rahman al-Kayyali
'Abd al-Qadir al-Sarmini
Hasan Fu'ad Ibrahim-Basha
Nazim al-Qudsi
Rushdi Kikhiya
Edmond Rabbath
Edmond Homsy
Fathallah Asiyyun
Bidrus Millatbashiyan
Hrant Sulahiyan

[80] Ibid., no. 4493, 19 November 1936.

A note beneath the list made more ominous by the underlying threat of urban violence read, "o honored secondary electors, this list of the National Bloc is given to you, and remember it as you give your voice [cast your vote] . . . and may God and the nation bless you."[81] The order of the list was not a random choice, however, and reinforces the notion that the egalitarian rhetoric of the bloc's political discourse cloaked a more illiberal reality: it made visible a hierarchy that any Aleppine reading the paper would understand—the first six candidates are Muslim, and each was a prototypical member of the aʿyan, the possible exception being al-Qudsi, who had older notable relatives; the next three, including Rabbath, are from the city's established Christian middle class; and the last two names on the list are Armenians—albeit middle class—who had arrived in Aleppo as refugees following the First World War.

Nevertheless, the entire list won, and the National Bloc went into government. Such a success would seem to have vindicated the bloc's claims of fraud at the time of the 1932 election. Certainly the "people" had chosen the bloc to represent them. However, the bloc's success more accurately reflected its ability to minimize the voting power of those Aleppines unwilling to support it. Further debilitating to the middle class was a shift during the post-1936 period in French colonial discourse away from an emphasis on republican values toward a program of pragmatic cooperation with the notability.[82] Thus having lost the backing of the French imperial administration as a check to unencumbered notable hegemony, ideas of rights, citizenship, even of nation tended to fade in importance.

In their drive to marginalize and/or co-opt elements of society that threatened the persistence of their hegemony, the Syrian notability sought subordinates who could intervene in the middle-class public sphere taking shape in the urban centers of Syria. Inflected both by League of Nations' demands on the Mandate state and by a decades-long process during which this middle class had contested the civil society, this space had grown to incorporate often dissonant discussions about rights, legitimacy, and nationalism. Likewise, the manner in which the notables sought to interface with the new discursive elements of the architectures of interwar community is a valuable line of inquiry, not only because it can reveal the vertical links between classes and sects, but because it also highlights the fluidity of hegemonic processes subsumed under the rubric

---

[81] *al-Nazir* (Aleppo), 29 November 1936.

[82] "After World War I, these same values weakened as the Third Republic attempted to come to terms with the losses and traumas of the war and the growth of nationalist protest throughout the empire. Colonial discourse echoed this shift: established republican verities now surfaced in a more attenuated from." Conklin, *Mission*, 24.

سعدالله الجابري
Saadallah Djâbry

واني من قوم كأن نفوسهم   بها انف ان تسكن اللحم والعظما

FIGURE 8.2. Political caricature of Jabiri from 'Abd al-Latif al-Dashwali's *Miraya*.

of the "Politics of Notables." In addition, it shows how new ideas like nation and altered conceptions of history were used by the political elite of Syria and elsewhere in the post-Ottoman Eastern Mediterranean to control aspects of their societies heretofore novel and beyond the immediacy of their experience.

Ultimately Edmond Rabbath was something more than a Syrian mimic-man in Homi Bhabha's sense of the term;[83] his ambivalence toward the colonial state *and* the bases of notable power points to a double act of subversion. His commitment to a positivist and progressivist program of middle-class modernity was inconsistent not only with French colonialism but ultimately with notable hegemony. Still he understood the value of a strategic, though presumably temporary, alliance with the notables; that he had something to offer Jabiri also reflects the changing function of the intellectual in the interwar Eastern Mediterranean. The establishment of a French colonial presence in Syria had empowered men like Rabbath who could translate, formulate, or adapt modern conceptions of the nation and citizen into that moment's epistemic lingua franca.

The Aleppine political cartoonist ʿAbd al-Latif al-Dashwali drew a particularly satirical rendering of Jabiri for his 1947 collection of caricatures, *Miraya* [Mirrors] (fig. 8.2). The slender notable is portrayed wearing a tuxedo, head held high, with a question mark forming his ear. The couplet beneath reads, in a rough translation: "I am from a people whose souls turn up their noses / at living in flesh and bones."[84] Perhaps to contemporary middle-class critics like Dashwali (an engineer in his day job), Jabiri's populist pose in the late 1930s and his status as a patriotic candidate in the elections thereafter seemed improbable. His premature death in 1947, however, a few months after stepping down from the post of prime minister assured his status in the pantheon of Syrian nationalists. His friend and patron gone, and generally disillusioned with postindependence Syria, Rabbath spent the rest of his years in Beirut, becoming Lebanon's premier constitutional scholar. On the eve of the 1975 Lebanese civil war he completed the hauntingly prescient *La formation historique du Liban politique et constitutionne*,[85] and finished his career with the multivolume *Les Chrétiens dans l'Islam des premiers temps*.[86] He never returned to live in Aleppo.

[83] Bhabha, *Location*, 85–92.

[84] ʿAbd al-Latif al-Dashwali, *Maraya* [Mirrors] (Damascus, 1947), 65.

[85] Edmond Rabbath, *La formation historique du Liban politique et constitutionnel: Essai de synthèse* (Beyrouth: Publications de l'Université Libanaise, 1973).

[86] Edmond Rabbath, vol. 1, *L'Orient chrétien à la veille de l'Islam* (1980); vol. 2, *Mahomet, Prophète arabe et fondateur d'état* (1981); and the two-part vol. 3, *La Conquête arabe sous les quarte premiers califes* (Beyrouth: Publications de l'Université Libanaise, 1985).

NINE

Middle-Class Fascism and the Transformation of Civil Violence

STEEL SHIRTS, WHITE BADGES, AND THE LAST *QABADAY*

> "We made the Christians eat it."
> —Abu Yasin, recalling the street fighting of 1936

In the late morning of 12 October 1936, two uniformed paramilitary groups, the White Badge and the Steel Shirts, clashed in Aleppo's open-air Sunday market. Fighting spilled over into the blind alleys and narrow streets of the old city as fists gave way to brickbats, pavement stones, knives, and a few firearms. By the late afternoon, when the French colonial police force restored order, Artin ʿUbaji, Jurji Ilyas Mura, and Muhammad Bashir Zayn lay dead; two more participants would die of their wounds the following day: Danyil Sarkis Santurliyan and Kasbar Manukhiyan. This sanguinary outburst marked the most significant moment of Aleppine-on-Aleppine violence since the 1919 massacre of Armenian refugees. On its surface, this civil disorder could be seen as a variation on a theme familiar to the streets of many European, African, and South and Central American cities in the 1930s. Instead of the White Badge in their starched white shirts, blue neckerchiefs, and berets, or the Steel Shirts with their battleship gray tunics and plus-fours, it could have been *fasci* Black Shirts and anarchists attacking one another in Parma, Iron Guards in Bucharest, Orange Shirts in Johannesburg, Brown Shirts in Munich, *Falangistes* marching in Madrid, Integralists in São Paulo, or *chemises vertes* of France's long hot summers of 1936 and 1937. This worldwide diffusion of fascist idealism, aesthetics, and forms of organization is a recognized phenomenon;[1] and in many of the post-Ottoman states of the

---

[1] For the purposes of this chapter, I have employed a typological definition, useful in distinguishing generic fascism from racial National Socialism. In this definition, fascism embraces a positive evaluation of the use of violence and war, tends to be antiliberal, anticommunist, and anticonservative. Yet its most important marker is its technique and style of organization. It attempts to mass mobilize and militarize human interaction; it stresses the holding of well-orchestrated mass meetings impregnated with the movement's semiotics, which in turn seek to create a mystical and emotional reaction; it celebrates youth over all else; masculinity and male-domination are key, as is charismatic and authoritarian leader-

Eastern Mediterranean, fascist organizations formed accordingly, most notably the "Green Shirts" of the Egyptian Ahmad Husayn and the Brazilian-Lebanese Antun Saʿada's Syrian People's Party.[2]

Yet unlike these more obviously fascist groups, the formation of the Steel Shirts and the White Badge in Aleppo, while representing a successful interpolation of the language of fascist paramilitary organization, carried with it little engagement with the rather amorphous ideological dimensions of fascism. Rather, the limited incorporation of fascist forms in the mid-1930s brings into relief the changing nature of the communal and class aspects of violence in the cities of the post-Ottoman Eastern Mediterranean. The specific impulse to use these forms grew from the desire of a traditional elite masquerading as nationalists to contain forces and groups increasingly outside of the locus of its control; while simultaneously, the plastic nature of such forms provided an emergent middle-class minority with the means to demarcate the terms of its identity, gain momentarily a measure of power within the urban milieu, and dissent from dominant forms of Arabism and Syrian citizenship.

Understanding the role of these movements in Aleppo during this period is a way to characterize more broadly the Levant's encounter with what Philipe Burrin has called "the magnetic field of fascism."[3] At the core of the experience with fascism's magnetism in the era of colonialism is a striking disenchantment with liberalism and middle-class modernity, seeing the former as impotent and fragile and the latter as frail and inauthentic, and the acute awareness of the usefulness of fascist aesthetics, cultural politics, and styles of organization for the purposes of nationalist, anticolonial mass mobilization and social control.

More significantly, the fascist interlude points to a critical moment of urban dissonance in the city's architectures of community. Those who saw themselves as modern, the elite, and middle-class elements of these movements—nationalist or otherwise—drew legitimacy from mimicking European, primarily German and Italian, models, as closely as possible—

ship. See Stanley G. Payne, *A History of Fascism, 1914–1945* (Madison: University of Wisconsin Press, 1995), 14–18.

[2] James P. Jankowski, *Egypt's Young Rebels : "Young Egypt," 1933–1952* (Stanford: Hoover Institution Press, 1975), and Husayn's version of *Mein Kampf, Imani* [My Faith] (Cairo, 1936). For a compelling account of Antun Saʿada's life and influence, see Christoph Schumann, *Radikalnationalismus in Syrien und Libanon; Politische Sozialisation und Elitenbildung, 1930–1958* (Hamburg: Deutsches Orient Institut, 2001), and his "The Generation of Broad Expectations: Nationalism, Education and Autobiography in Syria and Lebanon, 1930–58," *Die Welt des Islam* 41:2 (2001).

[3] Philippe Burrin, "La France dans le champ magnétique des fascismes," *Le Débat* 32 (November 1984): 52–72.

and thereby indicating that being fascist had become for some evidence of being modern. At the same time, by locating these groups within colonial resistance to or collaboration with the French presence, this chapter can eschew what Robert Paxton labels the "'bestiary' approach" to the comparative study of fascism.[4] Often what fascism meant for these groups was in conflict with the terms of participation with nonelite city people. And as these people were integrated into the fascist movements, much to the dismay of their elite animators, they sought to authenticate their own participation by using religious symbols and signs and customary patterns of organization vested with meaning in the context of their own class and communal boundaries. The idiom of nonelite participation was not essentially *traditional*, however; it did clash with a middle-class sense of the centrality of secularism and an identifiable national identity to the public modern self.

The defining moment of the last years of that French presence in Syria was the General Strike of January and February 1936. Similar to the Cairo riots a year earlier, and the first stirrings of the Great Revolt in Palestine some months later, the extreme level of violence that accompanied the strike in the major cities of Syria, and the involvement of people who generally did not participate in street fighting, primarily secondary and university students, distinguished the strike from previous instances of urban discord. The General Strike, unlike the more regionalized and limited uprising in 1925, provides evidence that a "Syrian" national community had begun to make sense and had become more of a tangible reality for segments of the populations of Damascus, Aleppo, Homs, and Hama. As these demonstrations grew in their ferocity, especially in Damascus over the course of February, it became apparent that the notables who directed the National Bloc were unable to control the social forces unleashed. Instead, student leaders associated with the newly formed League of National Action and the traditional quarter toughs, the *qabadayat*, dominated the streets.[5] By the time the bloc's notables had acquired some measure of control of the strike, they had already begun behind-the-scenes meetings with the French colonial authorities. Upon the announcement that the delegation of notables and others, including Edmond Rabbath and Khalid Bakdash, would travel to France to negotiate a treaty to end the mandate, the forty-three-day strike concluded. While the bloc's de-

---

[4] Robert O. Paxton, "The Five Stages of Fascism," *The Journal of Modern History* 70:1 (March 1998): 10.

[5] On the General Strike, especially how the notables of the National Bloc in Damascus were caught unawares by the extreme nature of the demonstrations and rioting, see Khoury, *Mandate*, 457–481 passim. "The National Bloc was not in charge of the situation in Damascus. Rather, student leaders mostly from the League of National Action, *qabadayat* in the quarters were at the forefront of political agitation (458).

mands fell short of those of the more fervent demonstrators, the level of group solidarity, the ability of a modern ideology to motivate young men and boys, and the responsiveness of the Quai d'Orsay to this form of popular political action comprised a series of lessons not lost on the constituent elements of an emerging Syrian society.

Within days of the strike's conclusion, in an apparent effort to capture some of the energy of the strikers, the Damascus leaders of the National Bloc formed an organization known as the Steel Shirts (in Arabic, *al-qumsan al-hadidiyya*). Underwritten by Fakhri al-Barudi and led by a young nationalist firebrand, Munir al-Ajlani, the group adopted the basic uniform of European fascist groups.[6] The records of the Steel Shirts housed in the Syrian National Archives depict a highly organized and hierarchical movement, complete with a borrowed language of symbols and signs; they also recount mass meetings where leaders sought to create the emotional feel of similar events in Italy or Germany.[7] While the Steel Shirts became an increasingly prominent feature of public ceremonies in the Syrian capital, they never succeeded in capturing the imagination or support of the city's youth. Rather, scout organizations, as discussed in the subsequent chapter, and the youth wing of the League tended attracted many more adherents from young intellectuals, university and secondary students, and the children of the middle class. Furthermore, in Damascus, the bloc leadership did not use the Steel Shirts to organize young men from subaltern groups, that is, uneducated working men or unemployed city dwellers. This "classism" is often singled out as a reason for the relative failure of the Steel Shirts.[8]

Old Notables—New Clothes: Violence and the Containment of Middle-Class Dissent

If the elitist overtones of the Steel Shirt movement in Damascus contributed to the bloc's inability to successfully engage the potential of youth

---

[6] Khoury argues that the magazine *al-Musawwar* was fundamental to disseminating images of European youth groups in the Middle East. Certainly, as Khoury also points out, the elite of the bloc need look no farther than Cairo, where the Wafd—a political movement upon which the bloc often modeled itself—had organized its own paramilitary group. Students returning from Europe were an additional vector for this information. On the uniforms and salutes of the various paramilitary groups of the period, see M. Lecerf et al., "Transformation en orient, sous l'influence de l'occident, du costume et des modes: Insignes et saluts," in R. Montagne, ed., *Entretiens sur l'évolution des pays de civilisation arabe* (Paris: Imprimerie Alençonnaise, 1938), 80–104.

[7] MWT-QKh, "National Guard."

[8] Khoury, *Syria*, 470–472.

violence, it did not prevent the movement's spread to the other major cities of Syria: Homs, Hama, and Aleppo. However, the Aleppine version of the Steel Shirts, the National Guard (*al-haris al-watani*), differed somewhat. The more cosmopolitan nature of Aleppine society, its complex non-Muslim middle class and the presence of a large population of refugees, contributed to this difference. The local response to the General Strike confirmed that these variables challenged the Aleppine Sunni notables' drive to employ a nationalist agenda to regain local hegemony; the unwillingness of many non-Muslim members of the business community to participate in the strike was foremost among these challenges. Put simply, their unwillingness to cooperate threatened the bloc's strategy in Aleppo, of attempting to make the city unmanageable except by them.

When local merchants resisted the call to strike, the bloc organized neighborhood toughs and secondary school boys into *squadristi*, to borrow a term from Italian fascism, to shut the doors of recalcitrant shopkeepers.[9] The Steel Shirts were an outgrowth and an institutionalization of those young men. More than just a means of enforcing future strikes, they ultimately constituted an effort to confront public political activity and restrain the freedom of action of the local bureaucratic, commercial, and primarily non-Muslim middle class, the only significant part of Aleppine society challenging the notables of the National Bloc. The use of the Guard for this purpose constitutes a heretofore unrecognized dimension of Steel Shirt activity in Syria. While the Steel Shirts had been organized in Damascus "in the face of new challenges from radicals and, in particular the League of National Action"; enforcing political orthodoxy on the middle class was the Guard's main mission in Aleppo.[10] It was called upon to coerce and compel cooperation from Syrians more willing to cooperate with the French, and, more important, those elements of Aleppine society who felt threatened by the potential establishment of a Sunni-dominated polity—be it Arab nationalist or otherwise. It also served as a way to shape and control ideological consciousness in parts of the city usually marginal to such discussions.

To affect this multidimensional mission, the Steel Shirts of the National Guard imposed themselves on the streets of Aleppo through noisy marches and, most notably, mass rallies of young men in uniform. The first of these rallies—known locally as a *hafla*—took place in the Qarlik quarter's sheep market in early April 1936. Some 600 young men attended, 500 from various quarters and 100 students from the local schools, including the state high school, the Thanawiyyat al-Ma'mun,

---

[9] PRO FO 371/200065 E702/195/89, Parr (Aleppo) to Eden, 29 January, 1936.
[10] Khoury, *Syria*, 472.

Mission Laïque Française, and the applied arts school. Under the command of six ex-Ottoman officers, *anciens combattants* on the losing side in World War I, the young men drilled for two and half hours. Accounts of the period portray these first gatherings as rather disorganized, and bemused onlookers would gather at the assembly site.[11]

As the spring progressed, however, the mass meetings grew more sophisticated, and by mid-1936 the group had become a familiar and daunting presence in the streets of the city.[12] Meeting on Fridays after noon prayers in the Qadi ʿAskar neighborhood, the rallies successfully re-created the choreographic precision dictated by generic forms of fascism in Europe. Most were like that of June 26, in which over 1,000 young men gathered, about half in uniform. For several hours, they marched, sang nationalist anthems, chanted slogans, and practiced their salutes. Around 5:00 p.m. a car brought members of the central committee. The ranks saluted them fascist-style for several minutes; then, headed by a drum and bugle corps, they marched through the various neighborhoods of Aleppo.

The *hafla*s and marches spoke to both participants and observers in unprecedented ways. While Aleppo constituted a municipality from an administrative standpoint, quarter identification and other more limited and circumscribed understandings of the city still dominated the consciousness of most people. By drawing men and boys from various neighborhoods and classes, the organization replicated other technological innovations, most notably, street-cars and automobiles, that were breaking down boundaries of time and space between disparate parts of the city. The implicit meaning of the marches—and indeed the identity of those who marched—marked the formation of a new conceptual understanding of the city. As the Steel Shirts coursed through the streets of Aleppo, they stitched it together as a political unit in their own imaginations and in that of their observers. The organized cacophony, the uniforms, the precision and the kinetic energy of the vigorous young men made corporeal a new vision of Aleppo. In this manner, the notables who controlled the Shirts asserted that their authority permeated the city in its entirety.

To keep control of the organization, the executive body of the Guard, which included members of Aleppo's elite Sunni families—Rushdi Kikhiya, Ahmad Munir Wafa'i, and Jamil Ibrahim-Basha—as well as a charismatic cleric/educator and future Syrian Prime Minister Maʿruf Dawalibi and Naʿim Qudsi, a lawyer in the National Bloc's leadership, regularized the membership and structure of the units. More important, following a central tenet of fascist tactics, they worked to militarize the hierarchical

---

[11] CADN-MAE Fonds Beyrouth Cabinet Politique 400 Sûreté Générale (Aleppo), no. 3468, 28 April 1936.

[12] Ibid.

relations between the young participants and the notables directing the National Bloc by explicitly tying the Guard to the bloc. Placing the young men under a central, anonymous authority within the framework of a paramilitary organization blurred the lines of older quarter-based relationships between patrons and clients, though in many cases this meant a mere retooling of those relationships. More significantly, in the case of Muslim middle-class students and university graduates, it acted to bind them back into the "Politics of Notables," a structure from which, as shown in the previous chapter, they and their class had been growing increasingly distant in the post-Tanzimat period.

The executive levied a fee of one franc per month on the members of the guard, payable at the weekly exercise, and divided the troops into three divisions: a motorcycle brigade, a "scout" group for boys under eighteen, and an "infantry." In a more significant development, and in a radical departure from the totalizing and leveling impulses of European fascism, they further divided the group into two wings along lines of class and education: first, educated boys and men, primarily high school students or those recently graduated, middle-class *moderns* as it were, and second, the subaltern classes, designated as the illiterate in the mandate archives, who could more accurately be called the "unlettered." Different uniforms distinguished the educated from the others. The uniform for the *effendiya* resembled that worn by the Steel Shirts in Damascus, a steel-gray tunic with matching pants, shirt, and hat. From among this wing, an "honor guard" was later founded who would wear the *faysaliyya* hat, a modified pith-helmet made popular by King Faysal, which had become associated with Arabism, and plus-fours, known in the French secret police reports as "pantalons golfe."[13] Led by German-educated engineer and nephew of Hasan Fu'ad Ibrahim-Basha, Rashid Rustum, the honor guard was made up of young men from the "best families."[14] This division of the young men reflects a tension in nationalist imaginings in Syria and other Middle Eastern countries that was equally present in the relationship between Jabiri and Rabbath. Namely, while the nation may belong to all, paraphrasing a common trope in Syrian nationalist rhetoric, kinship would ultimately determine who had the right to more of that all.

The uniform of the subaltern "unlettered" also represented a significant departure from the dominant fascist "shirt" motif. These guardsmen wore garments unrecognizable in the idiom of modern or Western uniforms: rather, they tapped into a local sartorial lexicon of power. Instead of the gray outfit, they wore a red 'abaya—a traditional three-quarter-

[13] Ibid.
[14] CADN-MAE Fonds Beyrouth Cabinet Politique 400 Sûreté Générale (Aleppo), no. 2126, 30 November 1936.

FIGURE 9.1. Steel Shirt honor guard welcoming returning delegates, Aleppo, 1936. On the far left is Jabiri, preceding Hananu.

length wool coat—black sharwals—baggy trousers with tapered lower legs—sleeves embroidered with gold piping, and a black felt skull-cap with a white scarf coiled around it. Clearly, the outfit reproduced on a massive scale the ceremonial garb of quarter toughs, the *qabadayat*.[15] This second group, known as the *firqat Hananu*, in honor of Ibrahim Hananu, was not required to wear their uniforms at the weekly Friday exercises, while the middle-class young men were to wear at least their gray shirts.

To assuage merchants' concerns about roving bands of young men in uniform, the Guard were to wear their uniforms only during officially sanctioned activities and not in public establishments. This last decision may have seemed an empty promise as one of the group's sanctioned activities was collecting "donations" from members of the merchant community and "guarding" their stores in times of discord. The potential for violence of disciplined paramilitary uniformed young men, the mass meetings and marches, and the Guards' ubiquitous presence left little ideological room between collaboration and complete obedience to the bloc line. French unwillingness to suppress the marches or the Guard likewise proved persuasive.

[15] Ibid., no. 3468, 28 April 1936. Also oral history interview with "Abu Yasin" ('Abd al-'Aziz 'Ik), Aleppo, 12 June 1999, conducted in Arabic by author. Abu Yasin of Asile was member of the Hananu Brigade and remembers the uniform.

Chief among those employed by the bloc for the purposes of more forceful persuasion was the shadowy figure ʿAbd al-Rahman "ʿAbdu Misri," whose family had long been associated with the leading clan of the National Bloc in Aleppo, the Jabiris.[16] ʿAbdu Misri, like his father before him, was the *qabaday*—in the Aleppine patois, *ʿagid*—of the neighborhood of al-Qasila south of the citadel.[17] In the summer of 1936, ʿAbdu Misri organized the young men of al-Qasila into a Guard unit. Faced with some initial resistance from the elitist animators of the group in the city, he traveled to Damascus to demand the right to organize his boys. This act alone signals how far ʿAbdu Misri had transcended the "traditional" bounds of the *qabaday*: availing himself of advanced technologies, he was aware of how he could use modern political and bureaucratic forms taking shape in the national capital to his advantage. The Guards' integration of the subaltern young men into the organization was a testament to ʿAbdu Misri's success. This incident may also reflect an intranotable struggle between the Jabiris and the Kayyalis. Dr. ʿAbd al-Rahman al-Kayyali was one of the more active supporters of the Guard and could have used them in a struggle for control of the Aleppine bloc. Fearing this, Saʿdallah Jabiri may have encouraged ʿAbdu Misri in some fashion to create a counterweight to the Guard that would remain under his control. The continuing relationship of the ʿagid and Jabiri after the collapse of the Guard proves that relationships other than those manifest in the terms of the modernist paramilitary organization of the Steel Shirts bound the two.

As noted above, upon the conclusion of the General Strike, *qabadayat* like ʿAbdu Misri were not integrated in the Damascene Steel Shirts. The exception to this in Aleppo suggests that (1) greater popular resistance to the bloc's efforts necessitated a more thorough apparatus of power to enforce bloc hegemony, and (2) the *qabadayat* of Aleppo, far from being restrained by "tradition," were active agents in expanding their connection to power, willing to recast ceremonial authority in modern modes, and conscious of how they could maintain their positions of leadership by integrating themselves into the bloc's networks. In other words, as the *zuʿama* of Syria became the patriotic nationalist leaders of the National Bloc, the *qabadayat* could likewise become political activists. None of these alterations required an adoption of the nationalism of the bloc's intellectuals. Indeed, a simple quid pro quo can account for

---

[16] ʿAbdu Misri is referred to in the French diplomatic archives as the family's *homme à tout faire*. CADN-MAE Fonds Beyrouth Cabinet Politique 400, Assistant Delegate Aleppo to High Commissioner Beirut, 13 June 1938.

[17] Oral history interview with Mahmud al-Misri (son of ʿAbdu Misri), Aleppo, 12 June 1999, conducted in Arabic by author.

the *qabaday*'s realignment with the nationalists in the framework of the Steel Shirts. Upon the successful assertion of bloc hegemony, the *qabadayat* assumed that they would receive a freer hand in the quarters they controlled, as well as an expansion of their areas of control—their turf—into places heretofore off limits like the Christian extramural neighborhoods and the newly established refugee camps. Likewise, the use of a *qabaday* in a position of citywide leadership illustrates the fact that not only could the bloc use fascist paramilitary forms to channel the energy of the children of the middle class, they could also integrate them into a structure in which they would be able to make use of the "skills" of the more traditional exponents of urban violence.

The *qabaday*, a term of Turkish origin, has a colorful and complex history in the cities of the Levant.[18] In spite of the self-consciously anachronistic, honor-bound presentations of self, many of them were ruthlessly effective at assessing the shifting bases of power in urban society and altering their behavior accordingly. Generally despised by small-scale merchants and the educated middle class due to their running of protection rackets, arms smuggling, and drug trafficking, the *qabadayat* were nevertheless a fundamental element of the connection between the Sunni notability and the mass of urban society.[19] Having arrived in the city at the time of the Egyptian occupation (hence his patronymic), ʿAbdu Misri's father had established himself in al-Qasila by gradually strong-arming the control of a caravansary complex, now known as Khan ʿAbdu Misri. Today, his son portrays him as a counselor to Saʿdallah al-Jabiri, who would come to him for advice in time of need; likewise, he bristles at hearing his father labeled a mere *qabaday*, instead of the more exalted *zaʿim*.[20] At the time of the General Strike he had just been released from prison after serving a two-year term for the illegal possession of a firearm.[21] His "turf" included the commercially significant eastern entrance of Aleppo's massive covered bazaar, which he successfully closed during

---

[18] Ira Lapidus, *Muslim Cities in the Later Middle Ages* (Cambridge: Harvard University Press, 1967), 163–165 and 170–177; also Ahmad Hilmi al-ʿAllaf, *Dimashq fi matlaʿ al-qarn al-ʿashrin*, [Damascus at the Turn of the Twentieth Century] (Damascus: Ministry of Culture Publications, 1976), 244.

[19] For a discussion of the role of the *qabaday* in Damascene interwar politics, see Khoury, *Syria*: "One figure in the quarter who could give the nationalist leader a decisive edge in the competition for clientele was the local gang leader, the *qabaday*" (302). See also Michael Johnson's discussion of the evolution of the *qabadayat* in Beirut until the mid-1970s, "Political Bosses and Their Gangs, " in Ernest Gellner and John Waterbury, eds., *Patrons and Clients in Mediterranean Societies* (Duckworth: London, 1977), 207–224.

[20] Oral History interview with Mahmud al-Misri, Aleppo, 12 June 1999, conducted in Arabic by author.

[21] CADN-MAE Fonds Beyrouth Cabinet Politique 400 Sûreté Générale (Aleppo), no. 2421, 8 July 1936.

the strike. At the same time, he is credited for having organized the purchase and distribution of foodstuffs "out of his own pocket" for those affected by the strike, though the amount of cash needed to accomplish this suggests that he was being funded by sources higher on the ladder of patrons and clients.[22]

While the Guard's patrons sought to portray the movement as modern, nonsectarian, inclusive, and unified, the presence of 'Abdu Misri and others like him called such an image into question for many. 'Abdu Misri and his men often broke ranks and disobeyed orders from the leadership of the Steel Shirts.[23] Significantly, when he first convened his young men as a Guard unit, he had them place on their shirts the star and crescent of the old Ottoman Empire embroidered in beige silk. As nonsectarianism was at the core of the public ideology of the National Bloc, this clearly sectarian symbol was met with a quick reaction. Steel Shirt leaders demanded that it be removed. Insulted, 'Abdu Misri refused. Thereupon a heated discussion took place, in the course of which 'Abdu Misri declared to bloc notable Dr. Hasan Fu'ad Ibrahim-Basha, "If you are an extremist [or perhaps nationalist], I am the god of extremists and I am a more influential leader than you are."[24] Already fearful and resentful of what was interpreted in some circles as the abandonment of the non-Muslim communities of Syria in the text of the draft treaty, the members of Aleppo's Christian community would have regarded the use of the star and crescent as having a great deal of significance and interpreted it in the worst possible light. 'Abdu Misri's reaction confirms that Ottoman-Islamic symbols remained meaningful for many Muslims in Aleppo despite nationalist efforts toward secularization, and that these symbols also operated in a universe of meaning where Muslim political dominance still persisted. While 'Abdu Misri may have overstated his importance, he certainly was closer to "the people" than a medical doctor educated at the American University in Beirut and could influence men like himself not unwilling to employ violence.

Aleppo's non-Muslims received further proof of a sectarian dimension of the Steel Shirts in statements emanating from the pulpit of one of the

[22] Oral History interview with Mahmud al-Misri, Aleppo, 12 June 1999, conducted in Arabic by author.

[23] CADN-MAE Fonds Beyrouth Cabinet Politique 492 Sûreté Générale (Aleppo), no. 3350, 17 September 1936. Upon word of the bloc delegation's signing of a draft treaty with France, a great ceremony of welcome was planned for the delegates upon their return. It was also decided that the Guard would feature as the centerpiece of a great triumphal procession throughout the city. Apparently concerned about the marching skills of the young men, the leaders of the Guard ordered members to assemble every night to practice marching.

[24] CADN-MAE Fonds Beyrouth Cabinet Politique 492 Sûreté Générale (Aleppo), no. 2421, 8 July 1936.

original organizers of the Guard in Aleppo, Dawalibi. In the spring of 1936 he publicly advocated the boycott not just of Zionist settlers' products but also of the cloth manufactured by native Christian and Jewish weaving establishments. More significantly, he called for the use of the Steel Shirts to enforce the boycott. While the record of this *khutba* message appeared in an editorial condemning it, it nevertheless typified the ambiguous discourse of National Bloc rhetoric.[25] The fact that many Aleppine Christians could have learned of Dawlibi's pronouncements from the pages of a newspaper also shows the means by which modern media allowed information often produced to be consumed within specific communal boundaries to cross those very boundaries.

Despite the obvious sectarian overtones of elements of the bloc's paramilitary units, many non-Muslim young men were attracted by the modern, fascist style of the Steel Shirts. On 6 September 1936, thirty Christian young men accompanied by two local doctors, Riyad Makhmalji and Camille 'Aris, joined the guard,[26] and a few days later, twenty Armenians did likewise, led by Ardashes Bughikiyan, the Ottoman-era newspaper editor who had connections with Ibrahim Hananu. After taking the usual oath—though presumably not on the Qur'an—they were fitted out for their uniforms.[27] The return of the delegates from France provided another moment of intersectarian comity in which any tensions for the present seemed subsumed beneath a wave of happiness at the prospect of a French withdrawal. In celebration of the draft treaty, a grand youth assembly took place on the grounds of the city's state high school in the extramural neighborhood of Jamiliyya. Members of the National Guard in their Steel Shirts met in formation alongside Muslim, Armenian, Jewish, and Catholic Boy Scouts. Once in formation, the ranks, estimated at 1,650, marched through modern Aleppo, skirting the old city. The gathering of these groups reflected the nationalists' efforts to lay the fears of the city's middle class to rest; it also allowed groups heretofore resistant to National Bloc hegemony to express solidarity and good will toward the notables, the apparent winners of the negotiations with the French and presumably the future rulers of Syria. The subaltern elements of the Guard, the 'Abdu Misri's Hananu Brigades, were not present. In the end, even this moment of communal harmony was disturbed by the fact that the boys of the Catholic Scouts de France movement marched to the strains of "La Marseillaise."[28]

[25] *al-Jihad* (Aleppo), 13 May 1936.
[26] CADN-MAE Fonds Beyrouth Cabinet Politique 492 Sûreté Générale (Aleppo), no. 3294, 11 September 1936.
[27] Ibid., no. 3417, 21 September 1936.
[28] Ibid., no. 2421, 8 July 1936.

CATHOLIC FASCISTS AND MIDDLE-CLASS FEAR: THE WHITE BADGE

One group officially barred from the celebration was the Party of the Order of the White Badge.[29] In the course of 1936 perhaps a hundred young Christians joined the Steel Shirts of Aleppo; however, by far the vast majority of non-Muslim youth—educated or otherwise—who participated in any form of paramilitary organization did so as members of the White Badge (in French, *l'Insigne Blanc*; in Arabic, *al-Shara al-Bayda'*. Formed in reaction to the National Guard, the White Badge attracted a larger membership than its rival.[30] Founded by a former colonial police officer, Greek Catholic and *ancien combattant* of the winning side of the Great War 'Abbud Qumbaz,[31] the group drew its membership from all of Aleppo's Christian sects and would number at one point 3,500.

The rapid growth of the movement at the time of the Paris negotiations reveals the heightened tension that some in Aleppo felt in the face of the looming treaty with France; or, as French intelligence concluded in the fall of 1936, "the Christians [of Aleppo] believe that they have been abandoned by France following the conclusion of the treaty and they have grouped en masse around this idea [the White Badge]. The clergy, the wealthy merchants and the influential Christians in general have aided and encouraged this novel formation."[32] At its most basic, then, the formation of the White Badge signaled a perceived need to create a way for Christians to participate in urban violence in an act of "self-defense" in anticipation of France's departure. Moreover, in the minds of those organizing the group, it served as a means to limit the Sunni elite's domination of Aleppo's Christian middle class. In this sense, the formation of the White Badge was a physical manifestation of elements of a middle-class Aleppine Catholic identity that had developed over the previous decades. This identity layered Catholicism and francophilia, and it mobilized archeology and history to define an Aleppine particularism in which non-

[29] CADN-MAE Fonds Beyrouth Cabinet Politique 392 Sûreté Générale (Aleppo), no. 3287, 14 September 1936. Denied a place in the parade, they mounted a countermarch in 'Aziziyya.

[30] Ibid., no. 2359, 15 July 1936.

[31] Oral History interview with Firyal Qumbaz (daughter of 'Abbud Qumbaz), Aleppo, 9 June 1999, interview conducted by author in Arabic and French. Ms. Qumbaz provided a copy of her father's lengthy police service personnel file that details his various awards and commendations. Qumbaz had emigrated to America around 1908. His business failed and he left New York to return to Aleppo via France. He arrived in Marseilles in late 1914 and was interned as an enemy national—he was still an Ottoman subject. Seizing the opportunity to join the French regular army, he was given French citizenship.

[32] CADN-MAE Fonds Beyrouth Cabinet Politique 492 Sûreté Générale (Aleppo), "Notes: Insigne Blanc," 17 October 1936, 4.

Muslims played a central role. Far more than a rejection of bloc political initiatives, the organization of the White Badge acted as a metonym for this identity by asserting the community's "subnational" sovereignty and its right thereby to authorize its members to use violence. It figured as a part of the process by which some Christians sought detachment from the "Syrian nation" as imagined by the bloc and its intellectuals like Edmond Rabbath, which the marches of its Steel Shirts expressed. This detachment is inconceivable without the culture of the French mandate, itself, and the reciprocity inherent to in the colonial *civilizing mission*, a central feature of which was the tendency of colonial officials to encourage and support separatist impulses in compradorial formations within minority groups.

Fully conversant with this culture, ʿAbbud Qumbaz, identifying himself as "le président du parti de l'Insigne Blanc" and as "Médaillé Militaire, Ancien Combattant," wrote a solicitous letter to the assistant delegate for the province of Aleppo, the chief local French functionary, which sought to align France's expressed support for Aleppo's Christians with the White Badge.[33] The White Badge was a "parti politique Syrien Chrétien"; it would "safe guard the interests of Christians without distinction of rite," protect their "political and cultural rights by collaboration with the French government in all areas which concern communal and economic affairs," and prepare for the coming parliamentary elections by combating the influence of the "extremists" on the youth of Aleppo.[34]

Qumbaz claimed that the Badge already included some 345 active dues-paying members, of whom 165 formed the actual paramilitary guard. Drawn from the "classes ouvrière et moyenne," and provisionally divided into six squads, they met each morning on the plaza at the northern end of Tilal street in their official uniform of white pants, shirts, shoes, and socks, topped off by a sky-blue scarf and a beret. In a parallel to the use of sectarian symbols by ʿAbdu Misri's men, the White Badge affixed a cross to their right breast pocket.[35] They marched in formation up and down the streets of the Christian districts of Saliba and ʿAziziyya, often with a drum core. From among the rank-and-file, they had formed bicycle, motorcycle, and automobile squads, and a soccer team. New members, whose numbers, according Qumbaz, increased daily, swore an oath of allegiance and were "prepared to sacrifice body and soul for the cause of the party."[36]

---

[33] Qumbaz had been awarded this medal as a consequence of being wounded at the Battle of the Marne. He was also a member of the Légion d'honneur. Oral history interview with Firyal Qumbaz, Aleppo, 9 June 1999, conducted by author in Arabic and French. In the course of the interview, I was shown the certificates and the medals.

[34] Ibid., Combaz (Qumbaz) to Assistant Delegate (in Sûreté Générale file), 22 July 1936.

[35] Oral History interview with Firyal Qumbaz, Aleppo, 9 June 1999, conducted by author in Arabic and French.

[36] Combaz to Assistant Delegate (in Sûreté Générale file) dated 22 July 1936.

In spite of these advances, Qumbaz explained that the group was under threat from the nationalists, who "were attacking it with great energy and by all means imaginable." Newspaper articles, even some authored by "chrétiens esclaves du 'Bloc Nationaliste,' " "slandered" the Badge. Threats of physical violence accompanied the press campaign. Thus, concluded Qumbaz in his letter to the assistant delegate, he requested a disbursement from a "secret fund" to support the White Badge.[37] While no evidence exists to suggest that the High Commission dispersed monies from this secret fund (if indeed such a fund existed), the mere fact that the organization was allowed to continue to recruit members, wear uniforms, drill, and march—all of which was in contravention to rules regulating clubs and social organizations—conveys the sense that the French colonial authorities tacitly tolerated the movement, just as they tolerated the Steel Shirts.

Regardless of its rather tenuous connection with the colonial authorities, the White Badge manifested unambiguous links with the local Catholic community, often holding ceremonies on Sunday mornings in the large plaza, Sahat Farhat, that abuts the three major uniate churches of the city: Maronite, Armenian Catholic, and Greek Catholic. For example, on Sunday, 23 August 1936, ʿAbbud Qumbaz attended mass at the Greek Catholic Church in his White Badge uniform. As he entered and left the sanctuary, twenty young men, also in uniform, raised their arms in the fascist salute and cried "vive ʿAbbud Qumbaz!" Ancillary to this local expression of *Führerprinzip*, two White Badges stood at the entrances of the Maronite and Greek Catholic churches to collect donations.[38] More significantly, the Badge garnered support from the various uniate bishops of the city and Mgr. Habib Naʿsani, the Syrian Catholic bishop, had even spoken in favor of the unit from the pulpit. As the summer progressed, even non-Catholic Christians began to join the movement, especially disaffected Armenians and Assyrians.[39]

Throughout June and July 1936, the White Badge continued its marches on the streets of Aleppo, although only in the Christian neighborhoods and refugee camps. Forming behind a stark white flag, in white shirts with blue neckerchiefs, the group sought to convey a sense of security and separate-

[37] Ibid.

[38] CADN-MAE Fonds Beyrouth Cabinet Politique 392 Sûreté Générale (Aleppo), no. 3042, 27 August 1936.

[39] Ibid. Very early in the formation of the White Badge, socialist and leftist organizations within the Armenian community had warned their young men not to join the group. This is especially the case for the Armenian Revolutionary Federation, the Dashnaks, who had reached an informal arrangement with the bloc, and the small, Armenian-dominated Syrian Communist Party. Both groups tended to be more politically sophisticated than the dominant political formations in Syria and were tied into a worldwide socialist, antifascist, anticlerical discourse.

ness to the city's Christians. Unlike the vision of Aleppo conveyed in the Steel Shirt marches, the Badge's efforts made visible a much smaller, distinct community and demarcated a separate sphere within the larger whole. A remarkable testament to the resilience of communal boundaries even in the modern period is the fact that the Steel Shirts and White Badges never clashed in Aleppo's own "long hot summer."

This changed in September when the executive of the Badge sent a delegation led by two middle-class intellectuals, Homère Hakim and Yurji Hallaq (later editor of *Majallat al-Dad*), to the Jazira to recruit members from the local Assyrian and Armenian refugee communities. This move was part of a broader plan to create a quasi-independent non-Muslim/non-Arab state in upper Mesopotamia for which Aleppo would serve as capital.[40] In a letter to the assistant delegate (6 October 1936), Hallaq reported that they had been set upon by a large mob of Steel Shirts and nationalist supporters while making a stopover in Dayr al-Zawr. Beaten by batons and fists, the twenty-five members of the Badge retreated to the headquarters of the secret police. In the course of the mêlée the Steel Shirts seized a folder containing the photographs of 500 new members that the delegation had recruited in Hasaka and Qamishli. Several letters implicating the uniate bishops of the Jazira in supporting the group were also taken. Only with the intervention of the local gendarmerie could the men escape and return to Aleppo.[41] In what must have been seen as the ultimate act of abandonment, the French colonial authorities did not react to the attack on the White Badge. Fearing that the lack of response would signal to the nationalists that their Steel Shirts could act with impunity against

---

[40] Generally ignored by the nationalists in Damascus, upper Mesopotamia, the Syrian Jazira, was an ethnically heterogeneous region, culturally and economically linked to Anatolia, Mosul, and Aleppo. In the late 1930s a small but vigorous separatist movement emerged in the area centered on the mixed Armenian-Kurdish town of Qamishli. With some support from French Mandate officials, the movement actively lobbied for autonomy under direct French rule and separation from Syria on the grounds that the majority of the inhabitants were not Arabs. Gaining force in the period after the Paris negotiations, the notable nationalists saw the movement as a profound threat to their eventual rule. Beyond the implications for Syrian sovereignty, the region was agriculturally rich, and while this was less important at that moment, it turned out to be home to Syria's small oil reserves. The nationalists supported a local Arab Shammar tribal leader, Daham al-Hadi, with small arms and money; in turn, his allied Kurdish tribes sacked and burned the Assyrian town of Amuda (1937). The French responded with an airborne assault on a nearby Kurdish village. By 1939 the Jazira enjoyed a special administrative régime that awarded it a great deal of autonomy. This special status was reversed by the postcolonial government of Syria. See Khoury, *Mandate*, 525–534; L. Dillemann, "Les Français en Haute-Djezireh—Une réussite ignorée en marge de l'échec syrien, " CHEAM 50538 (n.d.); and Christian Velud's masterful, *Une expérience d'administration régionale en Syrie durant le mandat français: conquête, colonisation et mise en valeur de la Gasirah 1920–1936* (Thèse en doctorat, Lyon II, 1991).

[41] Hallak (Hallaq) to Assistant Delegate (in Sûreté Générale file), dated 6 October 1936.

them throughout Syria, the White Badge took a provocative step that they hoped would force the hand of the French. A turf battle remembered in Aleppo as the Sunday Market incident ensued the following week.

THE SUNDAY MARKET INCIDENT

What set off the Sunday Market conflagration of 12 October 1936 is unclear. In the days following, however, the Aleppine press put forward several explanations for what had happened. A theme running through many of the accounts suggested that the White Badge had acted in league with mandate functionaries, most notably a police commander named Moretti. In these versions, as they appeared in *al-Jihad* [Struggle] and *al-Shabab* [Youth], colonial officials had created the White Badge to foment a revolt in the French colonies that would lead to the overthrow of the French socialist government of Léon Blum. As proof the papers pointed out that the White Badge began the incident while the French military garrison of Aleppo was in the field, and weapons of government issue were found on the wounded.[42] While many colonial officials may have sympathized with the antisocialist party of the Croix de Feu in France, French intelligence reports dismissed these versions and concluded that the White Badge had provoked the Steel Shirts.[43]

The White Badge and their supporters argued that they merely had been trying to protect an Armenian merchant under assault by some Steel Shirts. Elsewhere, in the recollection of ʿAbbud Qumbaz's daughter Firyal Qumbaz, the White Badge had stopped a young Muslim woman from being assaulted by a mob of Muslim men—an account that casts the White Badge in a nonsectarian, chivalrous pose.[44] An investigation by French Prosecutor General Bocquet determined that the White Badge's effort to extort a *taxe d'étalage* (or in American slang, "protection money") from the Muslim merchants of the Sunday Market had precipitated the outbreak of violence. The White Badge certainly understood that any effort to expand their territory into this predominately Muslim domain would be considered a broach of intersectarian protocol. It was Muslim turf and only people like ʿAbdu Misri had the "right" to extort unofficial taxes from the merchants. Regardless of the actual facts of the case, the mere appearance of members of the White Badge—that is, Chris-

---

[42] *al-Jihad* (Aleppo), 13 October 1936; *al-Shabab* (Aleppo), 13 October 1936.

[43] CADN-MAE Fonds Beyrouth Cabinet Politique 492 Assistant Delegate (Aleppo) to High Commissioner (Beruit), no. 3370 (October 1936).

[44] Oral history interview with Firyal Qumbaz, Aleppo, 9 June 1999, interview conducted by author in Arabic and French.

tians in paramilitary uniforms—in the public Muslim spaces of Aleppo had a transgressive and provocative feel. They had stepped beyond the bounds of tolerable public activity and, as far as many were concerned, the reaction of the nationalists, Steel Shirts, and *qabadayat* was appropriate, even moderate.

Upon hearing of the White Badge's shakedown efforts, ʿAbd al-Rahman al-Kayyali dispatched several patrols of Steel Shirts. As mentioned above, by the end of the day five had been killed and the number of wounded reached into the hundreds. In a reaction the White Badge had hoped to avoid, local diplomats credited the Steel Shirts with restoring order and preventing a large-scale massacre.[45] Groups of Steel Shirts patrolled the marketplace, allowing most business to resume Monday, though over the next few days isolated and sporadic attacks on Christian merchants and family members of White Badges took place.[46] In a final and humiliating act, the bloc ordered its Steel Shirts to "arrest" members of the White Badge wearing their uniforms in public.[47] More devastating to the White Badge, however, was the French reaction. At the time of the disturbance the colonial authorities arrested twenty members of the group, many of whom languished in prison for several months.[48] Following Bocquet's report, the police raided the headquarters of the movement and arrested three members of the executive, including ʿAbbud Qumbaz, despite the fact that he had resigned some weeks before the Sunday Market incident.[49]

The apparent lack of support for the White Badge from the French also prompted leading ecclesiastics and members of the city's merchant middle class to disavow it. The most abrupt denunciation occurred following Saʿdallah Jabiri's address to a meeting of the Cercle de la jeunesse catholique. The bishop of the Syrian Catholic community, Mgr. Naʿsani, who a mere three months earlier had encouraged the young men of his flock to join the White Badge, responded by agreeing with the notable: "Christians and Muslims have lived together for centuries and will continue to live in this way. The deplorable events that took place in the Sunday Market were caused by troublemakers and agitators."[50] The Armenian Ortho-

---

[45] PRO FO 371/20066 E 6610/195/89 Parr (Aleppo) to Eden, 20 October 1936. "Dr. Khayali [*sic*], the leader of the Nationalist party in Aleppo, dispatched his 'Steel Shirts' to restore and maintain order, and it seems likely that his prompt intervention averted what might have been a serious massacre. He acted with decision and effectiveness."

[46] CADN-MAE Fonds Beyrouth Cabinet Politique 392 Sûreté Générale (Aleppo), no. 3939, 21 October 1936.

[47] Ibid., no. 3941, 21 October 1936.

[48] Ibid., no. 3370, October 1936.

[49] Ibid., no. 4544/36, 31 October 1936; no. 3848, 15 October, 1936.

[50] Ibid., no. 3848, 15 October, 1936.

dox Bishop Ardavazd Surmeyan sounded a note reminiscent of Ghazzi's notion of *husn al-mukafa'a* in his address to an assembly in the Armenian refugee camp north of the city:

> I came here with the nationalist leaders in order to invite you all to be calm and to return to your work. We have every interest in having cordial relations with the Muslims. The incident of last Sunday Market had their origin in the "White Shirts"[*sic*] . . . who are bought and paid for by certain traitors; they create trouble to spread discord between the elements of the country in order to obtain their goal. I ask therefore all Armenians to have no relations with the "White Badge" and to prevent even that these people circulate around [the tent-city].[51]

Members of the business community responded likewise. A telegram addressed to the high commissioner in Beirut from Aleppo's leading Christian businessmen labeled the Sunday Market incident "nothing more than a plot by some malcontents opposed to the accord and the alliance realized between France and the Syrian people." They condemned the Badge and echoed the nationalist rhetoric of Jabiri: "We proclaim [our] solidarity with all of the populations of the beloved fatherland and [our] approval of the Franco-Syrian treaty."[52] Nevertheless, one can imagine that had the French response to the White Badge's efforts been different, the community would not have turned its back on it so forcefully and quickly. Quite simply, for the Christian middle class of Aleppo, tacit support of the Badge had, in the fall of 1936 seemed at least superfluous and at most dangerously provocative. On the surface, the bloc, using an explicitly liberal nationalist rhetoric, had successfully reconciled various communities to their vision of "Syria"; more important, the violent potential of the Steel Shirts—realized in the course of the rumble—denied to them the validity or even viability of alternatives.

This rapprochement was short-lived. Bereft of opponents in Aleppo, the bloc could and did act with greater impunity. Steel Shirts or "red 'abayas" were employed to protect bloc interests and, if necessary, terrorize voters into compliance during the lead-up to the December 1936 parliamentary elections.[53] In the most egregious case, the bloc decided to replace the universally respected scion of the Aleppine business community,

---

[51] CADN-MAE Fonds Beyrouth Cabinet Politique 392 Sûreté Générale (Aleppo), no. 3829, 16 October 1936.

[52] CADN-MAE Fonds Beyrouth Cabinet Politique 392 Sûreté Générale (Aleppo), copy of telegram to high commissioner in Beirut enclosed, 13 October 1936. Signatories include Raphael Hindiyya, Vincent Balit, Salim Janbart, Louis Ziyada, Butrus Millatbashiyan, Antoine 'Aris, César Khayyat, Georges Antaki, Albert Homsy, Georges Salim, and Yusuf Aswad.

[53] CADN-MAE Fonds Beyrouth Cabinet Politique 400 Sûreté Générale (Aleppo), no. 4448, 16 November 1936.

Salim Janbart, as the candidate of the Greek Catholic community with Edmond Homsy, whose probloc credentials were more established. During the meeting of the electors of the second degree who were to choose between the two, members of the Hananu Brigade led by ʿAbdu Misri, bats at the ready, stood at the back of the room as a formidable reminder of the fate that would await those who opposed the wishes of the bloc.[54] Citywide, in the election the bloc assigned to each of the polling stations a contingent of "national guardsmen . . . [to] watch the voting."[55]

Owing to the bloc's seeming retreat from the promise of open political participation and the outbreak of communal violence in Beirut in late 1936, some of those who had abandoned the White Badge reconsidered their position and the organization enjoyed a brief revival in the winter of 1936–1937. Released from prison, the executive of the group held new elections that returned Homère Hakim and Subhi Zahlana to office. Several leading Christian Aleppine merchants and liberal professionals—including lawyers Georges Sabbagh and Henri Saqqal and banker Razzuq Hindi—openly expressed the desire that the White Badge be reformed in the style of the Lebanese phalange and serve as the Christian community's militia.[56] However, bloc power at that moment was too great.[57] Without active support from the churches, and with a lack of sanction from the French and a growing sense of resignation in the Christian communities of northern Syria, the White Badge faded. In place of an active attempt to oppose the nationalist agenda, large groups of Christians allied themselves to it or made a quiescent retreat from politics altogether. Local observers marked an increase in emigration from the city to Lebanon, where French policies provided incentives for Christian resettlement, or to the West, primarily Central and South America, as immigration controls instituted as a reaction to the Great Depression closed the doors to the United States. Though emigration had ebbed and flowed since the previous century, the rate at which Aleppo's Christian middle class sought to leave at this moment signaled the real beginning of their permanent absence from the city's architectures of community.

The Steel Shirts' moment of greatest accomplishment was the beginning of its decline as well. With the notable-nationalists' victory at the polls,

---

[54] Ibid., "Elections 1936," Sûreté Générale (Aleppo), no. 4411, 12 November 1936.

[55] Ibid., no. 3738, 9 October 1936.

[56] CADN-MAE Fonds Beyrouth Cabinet Politique 492 Sûreté Générale (Aleppo), no. 492, 11 December 1936.

[57] An aspect of this was bloc control of most press outlets. Fearing retribution from Steel Shirts, papers once sympathetic to the movement refused to publish its new manifesto. Indeed, when the editor of *al-Taqaddum* gave Dr. Kayyali a copy of the Order's statement, the bloc notable declared, "As soon as we take power, all these factious groups will be dissolved and muzzled." Ibid.

the leadership of the Steel Shirts sought to transform their movement into a postcolonial civil guard. Steel Shirts bosses approached Saʿdallah Jabiri, the newly appointed minister of the interior in the National Bloc's government, demanding training in the use of firearms, jobs in the public sector, and the appointment of a Syrian as director of the secret police rather than a colonial official. The delegation received a cool reception from the minister, creating a great deal of anxiety among the group's leadership.[58] Returning to Aleppo, some members of the Steel Shirt executive, especially Hasan Fu'ad Ibrahim-Basha, sought permission to organize all the youth of Aleppo into the National Guard via the school system, though this proposal too was met with little bloc support.[59]

An editorial in the nationalist mouthpiece *al-Nazir* gives some hint as to the reasons why the bloc had begun this policy of distancing itself from the National Guard. Written by the newspaper's editor, Ahmad Qanbar, the piece praised the work of the Steel Shirts while it laid the groundwork for their eventual demobilization. For Qanbar, the Steel Shirts were "among the most brilliant works which have been created in the city, the formation and triumph [of the movement] in the sister cities of Syria, and the way it gathered the youth of the nation under the banner of the National Guard are all efforts in which Aleppo the Gray has a right take pride." He then identified and dismissed various accusations leveled against the Steel Shirts—which may, nonetheless, have been an accurate statement of popular perceptions of the paramilitary units—namely, that the youth of the Guard had "acquired a taste for order without imposing it on themselves and . . . it infused their hearts with a love of discipline and order with the provision that neither applies to them." Nevertheless, the "*haflat* may have grown out of hand [and thus] . . . it is clear that the circumstances do not support the continuation of these assemblies in this manner."[60] In other words, the Steel Shirts were no longer needed. The bloc matched its local undermining of the Steel Shirts with an explicitly antifascist press campaign throughout the winter of 1936–1937. Several articles in *al-Nazir* belittled fascist leaders Adolf Hitler and Benito Mussolini and cataloged the excesses of Franco in Spain.[61]

With the political marginalization of the Aleppine middle class and the suppression of alternative opposition to their rule, the leadership of the bloc in Aleppo had a great deal to fear from the potential power of a fascist-type organization. It should be recalled that the notables compris-

[58] CADN-MAE Fonds Beyrouth Cabinet Politique 492 Sûreté Générale (Aleppo), no. 5230, 29 December 1936.
[59] Ibid., no. 317, 21 January 1937.
[60] *al-Nazir* (Aleppo), 10 December 1936.
[61] *al-Nazir* (Aleppo), 13 December 1936.

FIGURE 9.2. Editorial cartoon, "Hitler and Mussolini Roast the World," *al-Nazir*, Aleppo, 13 December 1936. The caption beneath reads: "Caricature representing the current world situation, in which Hitler is seen standing on a cannon and Mussolini on a box of shells. The two are turning the Earth on a spit under which the flames of fascism are roasting it."

ing the National Bloc still largely maintained themselves around a reactionary illiberal gerontocratic view of society, so that for a patrician ruling elite, a radicalizing, youth-oriented movement that could generate cults of personality around figures outside of the old social classes occasioned great concern. Furthermore, the bourgeois sensibilities that motivated the bloc's intellectuals, Na'im Antaki and Edmond Rabbath in particular, led them to create a public ideological program for the notables that was essentially liberal nationalist and antagonistic to fascism.

Troubled intellectually and ideologically by fascism, and threatened functionally by the ideology's ability to achieve a measure of mass mobilization, the bloc allowed the National Guard to wither. As 1937 approached, the number of young men attending Guard rallies dropped precipitously. Only 200 attended the meeting of 24 April 1937,[62] and a year later the total had dwindled to a handful. A police report from July 1938 noted that a mere 28 Steel Shirts attended the commemoration of the Battle of Maysalun. In June 1938 the bloc canceled any further meetings of the Guard.[63] By the end of that year, all that was left of the Aleppo Steel Shirts was the soccer team that played against the Armenian sports club HoMenEtMen and the Sporting Union of the Catholic Circle.

Despite their inglorious endings, the Steel Shirts and the White Badge did hold sway on the streets of Aleppo for a few tremulous months in 1936. A persistent feature of the National Guard was the continuing utility of men like ʿAbdu Misri. The ʿagid was a reminder of the ability of the notables to deliver brute force when necessary. In 1938 the bloc again employed the "muscle" of ʿAbdu Misri to assure the election of its candidate to replace the Armenian delegate Millatbashiyan, who had died with two years of his term remaining. Reconvening the secondary electors from the 1936 election to select a successor, the bloc had ʿAbdu Misri stand at the doorway of the meeting hall with a bat-wielding "goon squad." In the words of a frustrated French bureaucrat, he was "inviting, with an insistence to which it is not usual to resist, the electors to vote for" the bloc-sanctioned candidate, the elderly Ardashes Bughikiyan, instead of the more popular Hirash Babaziyan.[64] That Bughikiyan was to "represent" the Apostolic (Orthodox) Armenian community of Aleppo seems incommensurate with such a prominent role reserved for the Muslim ʿAbdu Misri in the facilitation of his election. The mechanism of representation, flawed in favor of communal reservation in the first instance, had been rendered a sham by the interference of the bloc, and the action that typified middle-class participation in civil society itself had been successfully circumscribed. The reappearance of the former avant garde journalist of the revolutionary period as a representative of the conservative establishment is a striking reminder of the concessions and compromises required of ethnic minorities in the charged sectarian environment of the mandate and later.

The continued use of men like ʿAbdu Misri in Aleppo is likewise out of phase with the growing distancing of structures of power from the *qabadayat* in other parts of Syria.[65] Nevertheless, the ability of ʿAbdu Misri to

---

[62] CADN-MAE Fonds Beyrouth Cabinet Politique 492 Sûreté Générale (Aleppo), no. 2164, 26 April 1937.

[63] Ibid., no. 265, 14 May 1938.

[64] CADN-MAE Fonds Beyrouth Cabinet Politique 400 Assistant Delegate (Aleppo) to High Commissioner (Beirut), 13 June 1938. The archives and local accounts shed no light on this peculiar popular volte face concerning Bughikian. Perhaps hoping to tap into his general popularity in the Armenian community, the bloc nominated him, an act that subsequently tainted him.

[65] See Khoury, "Abu Ali: A Damascus *Qabaday*" in Gellner and Waterbury, *Patrons.*

integrate himself into the emerging modernist style of political and bureau-cratic organization may be the exception that tests the rule. More signifi-cantly, the Aleppine experience with the Steel Shirts is further proof of reluctance on the part of the Sunni-Muslim notability of Aleppo to partici-pate in modern social formations or middle-class structures of civil society. While employing modern forms—fascism, democratic participation, public opinion—as the need arose, the notables of the National Bloc generally resisted any action that would permit the underlying modernity of each to become a permanent feature of society. They also exhibited a more general resistance to sharing power, and as such their behavior continued to create resentment among the city's middle class and a young, educated, and in-creasingly fervent Arab nationalist cadre. The failure of the notability to embrace these new forms of organization and channel the violent potential of paramilitary groups drove many of these young men into the arms of the League of National Action and subsequently to Ba'thism.

By arming itself, the White Badge dissented from the bloc's hegemony and articulated patterns of identification antithetical to emerging forms of Arabism and resulting definitions of Syrian citizenship. More signifi-cantly, the language of European fascist militancy authorized and legiti-mized their access to violence in defense of this dissent. Their militancy was, nonetheless, illegitimate in the customary theory of Islamic political dominance in which Muslims had a monopoly on urban violence. Or, as one of 'Abdu Misri's men, Abu Yasin, recalled—defining this theory in the most basic of terms—the street fighting of 1936 was a time when "we made the Christians eat it."[66]

The Sunday Market incident was a moment in which two groups driven by a modernist ideology clashed, but it also had the hallmarks of inter-communal strife and was part of a continuing and radical transformation of the structures of urban violence dating from the "Events" of 1850. These changes allowed objectively modern forms of violence to develop alongside more customary forms, though they changed inexorably the rules of who could be violent, or who had the social sanction to be violent. However, where fascism, and its antagonism toward liberalism, had its greatest impact would be on young men in their twenties and thirties, attracted by the power and sense of dignity membership in these move-ments gave them, who would translate their disenchantment and anger into support for the brutish régimes of the postcolonial period and the modernity of authoritarianism.

---

[66] Oral history interview with 'Abd al-'Aziz 'Ik ("Abu Yasin"), Aleppo, 12 June 1999, conducted in Arabic by author.

TEN

Not Quite Syrians

ALEPPO'S COMMUNITIES OF COLLABORATION

> Est-ce parce que mon père en parlait sans cesse? Tout ce qui
> concerne le Mandat me fait regretter d'être née un peu trop
> tard. . . . Le Mandat raconté par mon père m'évoquait le
> monde fascinant de Casablanca, où Ingrid Bergman et
> Humphrey Bogart jouent leur éternelle scène d'amour sous
> le ventilateurs.[1]
> —Marie Seurat née Ma'marbashi, "Mandat, mon
> beau Mandat"

The French colonial strategy for ruling the cities of the Eastern Mediterranean under their mandate was a part-purposeful, part-accidental intensification of preexisting categories of religious and ethnic difference.[2] However, less well understood is how that strategy intersected with questions of class or even the manner in which the colonizers' comprehension of— or indeed anxiety about—their own modernity shaped the local experience of these phenomena. An example of this intersection is the recognition that being modern and middle class contributed to the political discourse and ideological terms upon which Edmond Rabbath based his opposition to French rule (but not "French civilization") and by which ʿAbbud Qumbaz sought accommodation with it. The inherent ambivalence of Rabbath toward the French and French culture, language, and political theory, in particular, reinforce Homi Bhabha's contention that

> Resistance [to colonialism] is not necessarily an oppositional act of political
> intention, nor is it the simple negation or exclusion of the "content" of another
> culture, as a difference once perceived. It is the effect of an ambivalence pro
> duced within the rules or recognition of dominating discourse as they articulate

---

[1] "Is this because my father spoke about it unceasingly? All that relates to the Mandate makes me regret having been born a little too late. . . . The Mandate, as told by my father, evoked for me the fascinating world of 'Casablanca,' where Ingrid Bergman and Humphrey Bogart play their eternal love scene under the ceiling fans."

[2] Khoury, *Mandate*, 1–94 passim.

the signs of cultural difference and reimplicate them within the deferential rela-tions of colonial power.[3]

Moreover, it is easy to imagine how collaboration could be conceptualized along the same lines: it too is not simply a matter of affirming or accepting the culture of the colonizer but carries with it a complex and multilayered engagement with power and cultural difference; it too is not only a mi-metic process or the reversal of resistance.

By focusing on a series of discrete moments in the seemingly collabora-tionist response of two minority communities in Aleppo, the Byzantine-rite Greek Catholics and the Armenians, this chapter moves issues of class and modernity outside the political narrative of the interwar period and into the spheres of domesticity, education, and communal identity. And while I have sought in previous chapters to integrate the history of Arme-nians and Arabic-speaking Christians and Jews into the larger history of the Eastern Mediterranean, the encapsulated nature of these communi-ties, especially their middle class, a condition that had grown in intensity by the late 1930s, and the intimacy of their relationship with the French and other foreign communities mark the unique importance of their en-counter with the cultural and ideological dimensions of colonialism. As previously noted, each case highlights the formation in the story of the middle class of a body of complex social, political, and economic ex-changes that constitute a phenomenon I call the "colonial contract." In this context, the contract constituted an exchange of the active or passive support for colonialism by members of these communities for a series of distinct social and communal privileges. For the Armenians, the terms of this exchange included French protection of the community as a distinct ethnicity and transformation from abject poverty into an urban proto-middle class; for the Greek Catholics, the exchange guaranteed the com-pletion of the process of "nearing the summit of civilization," outlined by Fathallah Qastun in 1910. For that community, cooperation with the French and participation in the civilizing mission allowed the community to draw closer and even seek to close completely the "distance" between it and its metropolitan exemplar; likewise, it secured their position in a separate sphere within the city's colonial architecture of community. Ultimately, as the contours of this contract become visible, so does the realization that the neither the Greek Catholics nor the Armenians of Aleppo were passive recipients of French paternalism. Rather they were active agents in the negotiation and reformulation of their role in the colonial encounter.

---

[3] Bhabha, "Signs Taken for Wonders: Questions of Ambivalence and Authority under a Tree Outside Delhi, May 1817," in *Location*, 110.

THE ARMENIANS: FROM REFUGEES INTO AN URBAN MIDDLE CLASS

The complex relationships between the French colonial authorities in Syria and the Armenian refugee community constitutes a vital field within which to begin the interrogation of colonial cooperation. By 1922, as a consequence of a genocidal program undertaken by the Ottoman authorities that exterminated a vast portion of the Armenian population of the empire, a stateless, non-Muslim, non-Arabic-speaking, primarily rural, and disproportionately female group of survivors had been violently uprooted and forced to flee Anatolia and were living on the margins of Syria's major cities.[4] The vast bulk of these displaced individuals—more than 50,000—found refuge in and around Aleppo, altering it forever.[5] The emergent community that took shape was caught in a political and social no-man's-land: on one side was the memory of the killing fields of Anatolia and the newly formed ultranationalist Republic of Turkey that barred a return to their homeland, and on the other side was an often hostile Syrian population that generally viewed these refugees as ethnic, linguistic, and religious outsiders. The ambiguous and vulnerable status of the Armenians in Syria forced community representatives and leaders to mobilize political and cultural resources and to accept governmental and nongovernmental, paternal, albeit often-altruistic aid to survive. That strategy for survival took the form of a complex arrangement, which transcended mere collaboration. This relationship first took shape in the immediate context of the humanitarian and tutelary aspects of the mandate between the refugee communities and the French authorities, and in a second and broader way, between the Armenians and the West writ large. Ellen Lust-Okar has argued that the connection between the French and Armenian refugees was initially predicated upon a French plan to use the latter as "compradorial agents of rule"—primarily as a colonial armed force or gendarmerie—in the Levant and that this plan failed as a consequence of the cost to both parties in maintaining it. By explaining the link between the two in such a way, she calls into question the stability and static nature of the comprador in the interwar Eastern Mediterranean.[6]

---

[4] See Siwrmeian, *Patmut'iwn Halepi Hayots.*

[5] The mandate authorities estimated that by 1923 approximately 200,000 Armenians had passed through Aleppo. Over 75,000 had resettled in the post-Ottoman province of Aleppo, with 50,000 of these in the city. The remainder settled in camps near Damascus and Beirut; large portions of this population subsequently emigrated to North and South America. CADN-MAE Fonds Beyrouth Cabinet Politique 575, "Installation de réfugiés arméniens à Alep," Assistant Delegate, Aleppo to Puaux, High Commissioner, Beirut, no. 3754, 8 July 1940. On the Armenian Genocide, see Dadrian, *Armenian Genocide*; Richard G. Hovannisian, *The Armenian Genocide in Perspective.*

[6] Ellen Marie Lust-Okar, "Failure of Collaboration: Armenian refugees in Syria," *Middle Eastern Studies* 32:1 (1996): 53.

However, questions about motivation and intent—beyond the basic needs of colonial administration—remain unresolved in such an analysis. For example, did the Armenians ever imagine themselves as a compradors, beholden as it were to the French? Was the political status of Armenians in Syria mediated solely by the French, or were other actors involved? In what ways did it matter that this population was neither Muslim nor Arabic-speaking? Similarly, how did the changing relationship between the two groups of actors contribute to French conceptions of their own *civilizing mission* at home and abroad, as well as to the evolving concept of international humanitarianism? How did the Ottoman Armenians, a community with a history of complex objective institutions, including religious hierarchies, political formations of both the Right and Left, middle-class social and philanthropic organizations, and youth movements like the Boy and Girl Scouts, re-create these institutions in a transnational diaspora and colonial context? Moreover, does a parallel exist between the way the Armenian community of Syria sought to build a relationship with the French and the modes of communal cooperation between Armenians and the prewar Ottoman state?[7]

As the Armenian community created and structured relationships with power within the framework of the mandate system, it both redefined its members' political and class status and transformed their corporate identity. In so doing they created a space for cooperation with what Elizabeth Thompson labels "paternal" colonial authority, thereby preserving the community itself in the wake of a brutal attempt to destroy it by the Ottoman authorities and in the face of a host population that viewed their presence, for the most part, as a sectarian, political, and economic threat.[8] This translated distinctly into the movement to "rescue" Armenian orphans and girls from Muslim households and then to integrate them into urban society that had so offended Kamil al-Ghazzi, and the massive building projects that replaced the refugee camps with paved streets and proper middle-class homes. Underlying these moments—and complicating the terms of the contract—was an international humanitarian effort of pro-Armenian groups and the League of Nation's Nansen International Office for Refugees that sought to preserve the Armenian community by developing it in partial isolation from the remainder of an emerging Syrian national community.[9]

---

[7] On pre-Genocide relations between Armenians and the Ottoman state in Syria, see Avedis Krikor Sanjian, *The Armenian Communities in Syria under Ottoman Dominion* (Cambridge: Harvard University Press, 1965).

[8] Thompson, *Colonial*, 67.

[9] On the Nansen Office, see *Convention Relating to the Status of Refugees* (Paris, Nansen Office for Refugees, 1938); Fridtjof Nansen, "Armenian Refugees," League of Nations C:237 (1924).

An arresting portrayal of the Armenian experience in Syria—the missionary-inspired effort to find and retrieve Armenian women, girls, and boys from Muslim households in rural and urban areas—is a filmed reenactment of the "rescue" of a pair of young Armenian women from the tent of a Bedouin chieftain made for fund raising by a Danish missionary in the late 1930s.[10] The film opens with the Armenian driver of a Ford Model T owned by a relief agency drawing water for his overheated radiator from a pond somewhere in the Syrian Jazira. A woman dressed in Bedouin clothes filling water skins beside him informs him that she is Armenian and named Lucia and wants to escape. They agree to meet at that spot later. The scene shifts to a Bedouin's tent, where another Armenian woman, Astrid, is forced to perform menial labor and is even beaten. Lucia invites Astrid to leave with her and, after much hesitation, she agrees. Returning to the pond at the appointed date, the two find the driver and effect a daring escape. A chase ensues, but the Bedouins on horseback are no match for the Armenian in his technologically superior Model T. Upon reaching Aleppo, the film focuses on Astrid, who is brought into a building identified as a rescue house while still in Bedouin garb. A few moments later, she reemerges wearing a dropped-waist calico dress, toped off with a stylish bobbed haircut. The use of the clothes as simulacra of modernity is obvious and functions in way similar to the deployment of examples of technology.

Meanwhile, Astrid is shown around the rescue home where young women are being taught to read Armenian, to clean and to cook, and to crochet lace. They are taught modern housekeeping skills, as well as a craft in anticipation of entering the workforce or, as was often the case, traveling to the West as mail-order brides for immigrant American-Armenian men. In a fundamental moment, Astrid tells her life story to a clerk who writes it down, and thereby she acquires a written past. A tearful reunion ends the film as an old woman recognizes Astrid as her own long lost granddaughter on the basis of a birthmark. Astrid is thus reunited with the remnants of her biological family and, more important, with modern urban society; to do this she has had to abandon/escape her adopted family in the desert, coded by the filmmakers as antimodern, brutal, and barbaric.

Mark Sykes had estimated in 1918 that between 4,000 and 5,000 children of both sexes had been sold along the route of the death caravans to Bedouin, *fellahin*, and townspeople. In addition to this number, he be-

[10] The film has no visible copyright or bibliographic information. It is no doubt similar to the now-lost docudrama, "Ravished Armenia" (Selig, 1919) directed by Oscar Apfel. See Anthony Slide, *Ravished Armenia and the Story of Aurora Mardiganian* (London: Scarecrow Press, 1997).

lieved that some 200 girls had been purchased as de facto slaves for Aleppo's extensive network of brothels.[11] By 1927, as the period of rescue drew to a close, Karen Jeppe, a Danish missionary and the director in Aleppo of the Commission for the Protection of Women and Children in the Near East, estimated that her agency had participated in the rescue of over 1,600 people.[12]

Central to the process of rescue were the several rescue homes in the city, similar to the one run by the Near East Relief described by Kerr:

> On reaching Aleppo the children were given a warm welcome by members of the NER [Near East Relief] reception staff. . . . At this center the children were checked by NER medical personnel, with special attention to contagious diseases and intestinal parasites, and were then grouped according to sex and age and prepared for transport to orphanages in the districts where they had been born. Girls who had been violated (some, indeed, were pregnant) were placed in "rescue homes" which had the facilities for infant care.[13]

These homes were places wherein, according to Jeppe, the rescued would be "restored . . . to a normal life in their *own* world."[14] The missionaries would define the boundaries of this world in ethnographic, if not racist, terms. Again Jeppe, noting that many of the rescued Armenian boys who had been between the ages of 6 and 12 in 1915 escaped the rescue home to return to the Bedouin, observed:

> An interesting feature is that many of them, after a short stay with us, returned to the Arabs. It seemed too difficult for them to adapt themselves to Armenian life, which means learning and thinking and in general a good deal of toil, as all civilized life does. The vast steppes and the aimless nomadic life with the cattle lured them back. In the beginning this filled us with despair; but we soon learned that they would be sure to return to us again. After all, they could not forget their people and their faith and the spiritual atmosphere that was their birthright. Sometimes they would stay away a year or two, but finally they came home, this time to settle down among their own people.[15]

---

[11] PRO FO 371/3405, 199352/55708/44 Sykes (Cairo) to Secretary of State (London), 2 December 1918. Stanley Kerr had been sent to Aleppo on behalf of Near East Relief. Before arriving in Marash he participated in the rescue of young women from a Bedouin encampment and narrates the rescue of some fifty children from another tribal chief in his *Lions*, 43–48.

[12] League of Nations A.29.1927.IV Social, Karen Jeppe, "Report of the Commission for the Protection of Women and Children in the Near East: Aleppo, 1 July 1926–30 June 1927," 2.

[13] Kerr, *Lions*, 48

[14] Jeppe, "Report," 2, emphasis mine.

[15] Ibid., 4.

Contemporary conceptions of the inherent moral and racial superiority of the Christian Armenians, whose "national purity" should not be sullied by intercourse with, in Jeppe's words, the Bedouin "cattle," obviously shaped this missionary worldview. Also, an underlying paternalistic assumption of the missionary effort was that they knew the "real" wishes of the "rescuees" even if they did not know them themselves. Thus, for racially inflected humanitarian reasons, the Armenians deserved intervention for the restoration of their community. Crucially, it could be argued that this notion of rescuing the community was unprecedented in the Armenian community and only existed as a peculiar feature of missionary paternalism. As might be expected, most nonmissionary rescue efforts were conducted by immediate family members, acting not as representatives of a community, but rather as individuals seeking to locate their surviving relatives. Further, while the large number of potential "rescuees" and the sheer scale of the horror of the genocide with its mass deportations and policy of systematic rape was unparalleled, the abduction and enslavement of girls and young women from settlements by rural nomads was less so. The attempt to rehabilitate women who had been raped or who had entered into common-law relationships or legal marriages with non-Armenian men and had had children with them proved problematic. In these cases, the missionaries, with the backing of first the Faysali and later the French authorities, broke apart families in the name of community, racial purity, and Christianity. Nevertheless, the rescue movement both reflected and reinforced an international sanction for the idea of distinct and relatively superior—in racial and religious terms— ethnic Armenian community. In the writings of Jeppe and others, this community had attained, or could attain, a national character and possessed a level of civilization not necessarily shared by the broader Muslim society, by definition, and deserved protection from that majority.

The rescue movement was a popular cause in the West. In fiscal year 1926 alone, tens of thousands of pounds from various organizations were sent to the rescue commission in Aleppo. Among these organizations were the (London) Lord Mayor's Fund, the Armenian Ladies Guild, the Friends of Armenia, and the Bible Lands Society. The remaining cost of the enterprise was provided not by the Syrian state, but rather by the League of Nations.[16] Consequently, the rescue movement became an unprecedented international cause that far transcended its local context.[17]

[16] Ibid., 1.

[17] For a popular account of the American efforts on behalf of the Armenian communities of Anatolia, see Peter Balakian, *Burning the Tigris: The Armenian Genocide and America's Response* (New York: Harper Collins, 2003); also, Joseph L. Grabell, *Protestant Diplomacy and the Near East: Missionary Influence on American Policy, 1920–1927* (Minneapolis:

Rarely were French officials directly involved in the process, though they often lent gendarmes to rescue efforts. The conclusion of Jeppe's 1927 report to the League of Nations provides a hint to the utility of French support for the rescue movement and the alignment with the missionaries:

> And now nothing remains but to thank . . . the Mandatory Power for Syria for their enduring sympathy and most valuable aid in the work that has lasted so many years. . . . It has been a light in the darkness and a source of happiness to many people who have suffered terribly from those evils which it is the special aim of the League of Nations to root out or at least to mitigate.[18]

The fiction of the mandate system imposed humanitarian responsibilities on colonial authorities. In this vein, supporting the rescue movement aided French efforts to define and defend their presence in the Levant on a broader international stage. This almost gestural place of the Armenians in the matrix of colonial legitimization was relatively new, although Great Power politics of the nineteenth-century "Armenian Question" often justified increased involvement in Ottoman affairs on the basis of the protection of Christian minorities. In the late 1920s—especially after the criticism leveled against the French in the wake of the Great Syria Revolt—the French pointed to their support for the refugees as evidence of both a civilizing and humanitarian dimension to their rule.[19]

The rescue movement also dovetailed neatly into the preexisting conceptions of an Armenian national community as articulated by the various Western phil-Armenian groups and Armenian exilic political parties of the time.[20] However, rarely could they marshal the resources of organizations like Near East Relief. Indeed, several of these groups voiced concern that the success of the missionaries undermined the authority of the Armenian organizations in Aleppo. An early example of such a conflict is seen in the outrage evidenced when American missionaries translated the Bible into Turkish—the spoken language of vast numbers of the refugees—written in the Armenian script and even began to publish a newspaper, *Maranata*, using the same format. Conversely, the Armenian organizations asserted that the refugees should be taught modern literary Western

---

University of Minnesota Press, 1971); and Frank Ross, C. Luther Fry, and Elbridge Sibley, *The Near East and American Philanthropy: A Survey Conducted under the Guidance of the General Committee of the Near East Survey* (New York: Columbia Press, 1929).

[18] Jeppe, "Report," 4.

[19] CADN-MAE Fonds Beyrouth Cabinet Politique 573 "Note au sujet des Arméniens," 26 October 1929, 2.

[20] See, for example, CADN-MAE Fonds Beyrouth Cabinet Politque 577 Enclosure: "Note de l'Union Générale Arménienne de Bienfaisance à son Excellence Monsieur de Martel, Haut Commissaire en Syrie & au Liban," 12 October 1934.

Armenian. Regardless, the rescue movement was both a product of and contributing factor to the drawing of a boundary around the Armenian community in Aleppo, demarcating it culturally and politically, and assuring its alignment with both European civilization and modernity.

The rescue movement, beyond aligning the community with the West, equally contributed to a cementing of the distance between Aleppo's Armenians and the Arab Muslim community of the city.[21] As noted in the historian Ghazzi's discussion of this period—the only contemporary Muslim account of the movement—the return of these women to their prewar families was unwarranted and un-Islamic. Finally, despite the intervention of the missionaries, an intervention that was supported by Armenian political and cultural organizations in Syria and elsewhere, a tradition of gratitude toward the Bedouins for saving orphans from death along the banks of the Euphrates permeates the modern historical consciousness of Armenians of Aleppo.

The placing of the Armenian community more squarely into the discursive framework of French colonialism occurred in 1928 when High Commissioner Henri Ponsot affirmed that the Armenian refugees residing in Syria had the right to vote in the constituent assembly elections that year. Armenians in Syria had been granted Syrian citizenship in the wake of the Treaty of Lausanne, although their integration into Syrian political structures remained in doubt in the period prior to those elections. This change, which significantly altered the sectarian demographics of the Syrian electorate, provoked a great deal of local outrage and points to the changing nature of citizenship in the post-Ottoman states of the Eastern Mediterranean.[22] The Armenians, like the Syrians had possessed Ottoman citizenship in the period before the war. Indeed many of the Armenians in the city of Aleppo were originally from the province of Aleppo, albeit from the portion that had become part of the Republic of Turkey, primarily Marʿash, Urfa, and ʿAyntab. Nevertheless, with the drawing of the new boundaries they became stateless and their status an issue of both local and international politics. Inasmuch as the granting of citizenship to the Armenians was couched in humanitarian terms, the techniques of the French intervention in the shadow public sphere of the Syrian electoral process points to another motive. The French had concluded that increased levels of Christian political participation were fundamental to their attempts to suppress the political power of the National Bloc. As

[21] Ghazzi, *River*, 3:553.

[22] Longrigg, *Syria*, 181; PRO FO 371/13074 E 5338/141/8 Monck-Mason (Aleppo) to Lord Cushendon, 30 October 1928; CADN-MAE Fonds Beyrouth Cabinet Politique 399, Chief, Sûreté Générale (Aleppo) to Assistant Delegate (Aleppo), no. 110/S.G., 9 January 1932.

noted previously, French political activism in Syria found and promoted a cross-confessional constituency within urban society—Muslim, Christian, and Jewish—to oppose the National Bloc, which at the same time did not resist the tutelary fiction of the mandate. Conversely, the National Bloc often excluded this part of the electorate from participation with a combination of boycotts and terror campaigns against potential voters.[23] Indeed, an anonymous pamphlet appeared in the city at the time of the elections that read: "Not satisfied with these acts of oppression, they [the French] have recently introduced unto our land 100,000 Armenian refugees, of whom many have been raised to a high rank. . . . All our commerce and finance have gone to these usurpers";[24] and a later Damascus newspaper headline read: "The Zionists are better than the Armenians."[25]

The effort to align the Armenian refugee population with the French Mandate authorities was based on integrating the refugees into modern urban society as members of what French policymakers identified as the respectable lower middle class. This process was explained by Ponsot during a meeting of the Central Committee for Refugee Aid in Beirut, 24 June 1931:

> One must lend support to the real distress which this situation [refugee-hood] creates. This is what has been done in Syria and Lebanon. This [situation] has been brought under control in material terms through loans of money, and in moral terms, by a humane welcome which has allowed them to acquire the national status [i.e., citizenship] of the country which has opened its doors to them. It is necessary to help the refugees primarily to establish them permanently. This is what the goal is. With the Armenians, what one fears is that as soon as they have a little savings, they will wish to go elsewhere. This must be avoided, and to avoid it, we must make of them small-property owners, of a house, of a land or of a field. This task is underway: what has been done in the Levant toward this goal does honor to the League of Nations.[26]

---

[23] CADN-MAE Fonds Beyrouth Cabinet Politique 396, "Summary of the Elections to the Representative Councils of the States of Syria, October 1923"; PRO FO 371/11515 E641/146/89 Hough (Aleppo) to Chamberlain, 15 January 1926; CADN-MAE Fonds Beyrouth Cabinet Politique 398, "Political Situation in Aleppo" Collet (Damascus) to High Commissioner, 21 March 1928; CADN-MAE Fonds Beyrouth Cabinet Politique 398 "1928 Elections" Protche (Aleppo) to Chief, Sûreté Générale, 27 April 1926.

[24] PRO FO 371/13074 E 5338/141/8 Monck-Mason (Aleppo) to Lord Cushendon, 30 October 1928.

[25] al-Qabas (Damascus), 16 March 1931. The article made a connection between Zionist claims to the creation of a state in Palestine and Armenian, Kurdish, and Cherkess desires to found similar national homes in Syria. It warned that Syria risked transformation into a "Tower of Babel."

[26] CADN-MAE Fonds Beyrouth Cabinet Politique 575, "Comité de secours aux refugiés arméniens, Procès-verbal," 24 June 1931.

More concretely, early 1930s' French refugee policy was devised on a four-point plan: (1) The purchase of urban land and the construction of homes and then the transfer of these homes and land to the refugees for sale or rent; (2) the placement of refugees in public and private enterprises; (3) professional apprenticeships; and (4) the organization of a "credit agricole et la petite industrie" to aid the refugees[27] In total, these measures were intended to integrate the Armenians by providing them with property, a trade, or a profession in a way that intensified their linkage with the French state, the local economy, and agriculture.

The most visible manifestation of this process was the transformation of the refugee camps to the north of Aleppo into urban neighborhoods. The building of these new neighborhoods in the city accompanied similar projects in Beirut and Damascus, as well as agricultural installations, primarily along the Turkish border and in the province of Alexandretta.[28] Indeed, in the self-congratulatory view of the author of the 1936 Nansen Office *Report* to the League of Nations, the building of these new neighborhoods had transformed "Aleppo and Beyrouth from Oriental into modern cities."[29]

It was estimated that at the beginning of the process of the *installation définitive*, some 4,000 shanties existed in Aleppo housing approximately 20,000 people. By 1936, 2,061 new residential structures had been built, housing some 3,121 families or 15,644 people. In that same year, 356 houses were under construction, leaving only 583 shanties standing and occupied by 2,995 people.[30] The architecture of the homes themselves— multistoried with separate sleeping rooms for different family members— imposed a middle-class lifestyle and notions of privacy. The semidetached or detached structures often had indoor plumbing, had running water, and were on Aleppo's electrical grid. In addition to the homes, part of the development of the neighborhoods included the establishment of public/ civic institutions, primarily intended to ease the transition to urban life. In addition new churches for Orthodox, Catholic, and Protestant congregations were built, and private organizations started schools, a maternity hospital, a clinic, and a community center for adult orphans.[31] Addition-

---

[27] CADN-MAE Fonds Unions Internationales 2ème versement no. 1902, "Rapport de M.B. Nicolsky sur l'oeuvre d'établissement de réfugiés arméniens en Syrie," 30 June 1936.

[28] Ibid.

[29] Ibid. On the linkage between urban forms and French Colonial modernity, see Gwendolyn Wright, "Tradition in the Service of Modernity: Architecture and Urbanism in French Colonial Policy, 1900–1930," in Cooper and Stoler, *Colonial Cultures*, 322–345.

[30] CADN-MAE Fonds Unions Internationales 2ème versement no. 1902, "Rapport de M. B. Nicolsky sur l'oeuvre d'établissement de réfugiés Arméniens en Syrie," 30 June 1936.

[31] Andranik Zaroukian's *Mankut'iwn ch'unets'ogh mardik* [Men without Childhood] trans. Elise Bayizian and Marzbed Margossian (New York: Ashod Press, 1985), provides a touching first-hand account of orphanage life in Aleppo during the interwar period.

ally, the Nansen Office opened settlement/welfare offices in the camps, and the mandate authorities built a municipal police station. By 1930 upwards of 1,000 workshops had opened for carpet weaving or embroidery, the chief means of support of the female survivors of the Genocide.[32] These were planned communities, the very forms of which reflected the intention of their planners to formulate modern, efficient social spaces that would assure the class ascendance of their inhabitants.

In addition, the relative success of the building projects aided the formulation in French bureaucratic culture of an edifice of stereotypical ideas about Armenian industriousness, work ethic, and compliance that accompanied a uniform belief that as a whole the community "always looked to France to help it in its struggle against problems."[33] Or as Charles Godard, municipal counselor of urban affairs of Aleppo in the late 1930s, explained in his description of the new neighborhoods, "the history of the development of these quarters speaks to the qualities of the Armenian people, who, beneath the protection of the Syrian and French flags have recovered a nation. The 'bidons à pétrole' and the shanties of wood and paper have been replaced by houses of fired brick."[34] A visitor to contemporary Aleppo is still struck by the form of suburban Armenian neighborhoods like Midan, known to its inhabitants as Nor Giwgh, the New Town. The district's wide thoroughfares, its rectilinear street plan, the preponderance of signage in the Armenian script, the use of Armenian and Turkish speech, and the relative lack of Muslim religious establishments all mark it as a space different from the rest of the city as well as evidence of the persistence of the distinct nature of the Armenian community in Syria.

Ultimately, the complex relationship between the French and Armenians in the postwar period shows the difficulty in generalizing the position of non-Muslim minorities during the Mandate period. The French secured their position vis à vis the League of Nations with their support of the rescue movement as it couched the occupation of the country within an emerging discourse of humanitarianism. Likewise, it phrased the French Mandate—perhaps for French domestic consumption—in the nationalist-inflected conception of France as the "protector" of the Christians of the Orient. It played into ideas about race and hierarchies of racial distinction, a conception of particular concern to American missionaries like E. Stanley Kerr, who conceived the rescue of young Armenian women

---

[32] CADN-MAE Fonds Beyrouth Dossiers Isolés no. 2387, "Installation des refugiés Arméniens 1930."

[33] CADN-MAE Fonds Beyrouth Cabinet Politique 575 "Arméniens d'Alep." ca.1924, 3.

[34] Godard, *Alep*, 20.

in ways that recalled the genre of nineteenth-century American Indian captivity narratives.

In sum, the realization in the late 1920s and early 1930s that the Armenians were not going to "go home," a profound and deeply troubling moment for the refugees, was seized by the mandate authorities as a way of reinvigorating the colonial contract. The French, drawing upon the support of international organizations, settled the refugees in separate, distinct communities. The settlement of the refugees in such a way reinforced both the notion of the uniqueness of the Armenians in Syria and a commitment to exchange support for French interests for a commitment to the establishment of this community as both modern and middle class. It also contributed to French efforts to alter the demographics of Syria and Lebanon in a way that aided their political efforts and hindered the possible formation of unified opposition to their rule. When only viewed in this manner, the Armenians emerge as vulgar tools of French policy, placing parochial community self-interest before national exigency. However, when this discursive strategy is pushed aside, a much more textured account emerges that also contributes to broader understanding of issues that continue to haunt other refugee and displaced populations in the Middle East and elsewhere.

When viewed from outside a resistance narrative structure, however, the terms of the colonial contract, the rescue movement, and the creation of these neighborhoods were emblematic of a formation of separate space for Armenians within the political culture of interwar Syria. This was something more than ghetto politics or colonial strategies; the formation of this new physical and social space for the refugee community bound the Armenians to an idealized middle-class modernity and made a complete break with Ottoman-era structures of political subordination, as well as the broader Sunni Muslim Arabic-speaking majority. Had the community been allowed a "natural" process of integration and assimilation, the profile of the Armenian community in the increasingly violent urban politics of Syria would have been significantly reduced. Instead, by navigating the fluid uncertainties of French colonial domination, and later those of the equally perilous independent postwar regimes, the Armenian community *survived*—perhaps the ultimate act of resistance.

THE SCOUTS ET GUIDES DE FRANCE OF ALEPPO

Among Maggie Homsy's most prized possessions is a photograph of her at the age of fifteen as a patrol leader in a flag ceremony at the yearly mass

FIGURE 10.1. Maggie Homsy (center) during a 1946 joint Scout and Guide de France celebration in Aleppo.

meeting of her Scout group the Scouts et Guides de France ca. 1946.[35] In the image, the symbols and signs on the uniforms and flags differed little from other Scouting movements of the interwar period: fleurs-de-lys, shorts, and campaign hats for boys, and culottes and berets for girls. This remarkable consistency and the fact that thousands of middle-class teenaged Arabs had been part of a French Catholic youth movement is not just a consummate moment of hybridity in the relationship between colonialism and the colonized, but also evokes the "cultural cringe" that often accompanies moments of seeming undiluted mimicry of the cultural forms of the colonial powers.

The movement was poorly received at the time outside Christian circles and was eventually banned altogether by the independent Syrian state (ca. 1950). For Arab nationalists and many in the Sunni elite, it provided evidence of both Christian complicity with the foreign occupiers and a self-conscious distancing of the Christian community, primarily Uniate Catholics from Syrian society. That conclusion was made more acute by the fact that the Scouts de France of Aleppo vehemently rejected any association with the growing and equally middle-class Arab Scout movement in the Levant. The young people in the movement, however, often remember their years as Scouts or Guides as among the happiest in their lives, and moreover as proof of their clear attainment of middle-class status and

---

[35] This section is derived from an essay-in-progress about the role of Scouting movements in the Eastern Mediterranean in the formation of a transnational middle class.

modernity. For them, their parents, and community leaders, it was not an abnegation of their status as Syrians or for that matter Arabs, but rather a natural sign of their membership in a transnational middle class. Nevertheless, the Scouts de France movement, especially as it manifested itself in Aleppo in the 1930s and early 1940s, is a testament to the how thoroughly the Greek Catholic middle class of the city relied on the idiom of French cultural practice to assert their modernity. And it also shows how the act of attaining undisputed middle-class status had become contingent on being *seamlessly* European. And while this form of practice—which extended to the realms of education, given names, and fashion—eased this wing of the middle class's entrance into globalized networks of emigration and commerce, it rendered members of this class increasingly irrelevant in the immediate architectures of urban and national community; the price of membership in the transnational middle class—the terms of the colonial contract—would be the ultimate, though gradual, effacement of this community from the city, especially as the French Mandate itself was drawn to a close.

Aleppo's Uniate Christian middle class was far from the only group in the Ottoman and post-Ottoman Eastern Mediterranean to have adopted and adapted Scouting. Indeed within a decade of its organization in Britain in 1908, ostensibly with the goal of preserving the British Empire,[36] the movement had spread to Istanbul and other Ottoman cities.[37] The movement's seemingly universal appeal as both an educational device and a tool for making citizens in the successor states of Syria, Turkey, Leba-

[36] See Michael Rosenthal, *The Character Factory: Baden-Powell and the Origins of the Boy Scout Movement* (New York: Pantheon Books, 1986). Rosenthal argues that though Baden-Powell, the "Hero of Mafeking," had founded the movement to instill a sense of patriotism and paramilitary preparation among Britain's lower and working classes, the solid middle class embraced and grew to dominate the movement in a way that was surprising even to its founder. Further, he contends that Scouting's success and its rapid spread throughout bourgeois Western Europe and North America was a consequence of the way it eased middle-class anxieties about masculinity in the face of urbanization and passive office-work (2–14 passim).

[37] Images of British Boy Scouts appeared in the Istanbul press in 1908–1909. The first Ottoman Scout group was founded by the curiously named Ahmet Robinson, an Anglo-Ottoman teacher at the Imperial Galatasaray High School in Istanbul. Robinson coined the Turkish word for Boy Scout, *Izci* (Scouting being *Izcilik*). The first Ottoman translation of Baden-Powell's *Scouting for Boys* appeared shortly thereafter: *Izci Ocağnin Iç Nizamnamesi* [Scouting Hearth's Internal Organization] (Istanbul: Matbaa-i hayriye ve Sirketsi, 1330); Gökhan Uzgören, *Izcilik Tarihi* [The History of Scouting] (Istanbul: Istanbul Lisesi Sakarya Izciligi Kitapları, 1984), 59. After the war, Scouting was integrated fully into the Kemalist project—see Mustafa Resmi's introduction to his 1925 translation of *Scouting for Boys*, *Izcilik* (Istanbul: Matbaa-i Amiri, 1342). Resmi makes an explicit link between the reform of Turkish society and the kinds of reforms envisioned by the Baden-Powell in Britain.

non, Egypt, Jordan, Palestine, and Israel and the manifestation of Jewish, Armenian, Orthodox, Catholic, and Muslim groups suggests a viable common denominator with which to understand the way non-Western middle classes sought to be modern.[38] Moreover, the lack of modifications in the adaptation to the basic structure of Scouting and its attendant symbols, signs, and shibboleths complicates our understanding of the emergence of a transnational middle class in the cities of the Eastern Mediterranean, as it unravels the complex knot of anxieties about class status and gender roles, as well as notions of history and progress that played such a fundamental role in the experience of members of that stratum. It may seem difficult to take seriously a youth movement like Scouting. The kind of distaste that such movements elicit, with their seeming lack of authenticity and active cooperation with the colonial enterprise, has likewise led many to look past Scouting and other youth groups to focus exclusively on more violent paramilitary and nationalist organizations that drew far fewer adherents, as seen in the previous chapter. Ultimately this neglect is inconsistent with the value modern middle-class society places upon the need to create and control institutions intended to train, discipline, and socialize its boys and girls, and to use such institutions as performative sites in which to be modern.

Scouting was not a simple case of slavish derivation or unreflective collaboration. Diverse middle classes not just in the interwar Middle East but throughout the world self-consciously and actively employed the movement to assert their position in an emerging modern urban order and claim for themselves the kind of distinction and class identity that membership in these organizations signaled in the métropole. And just as middle-class modernity reformulated definitive feminine and masculine identities, it has also constructed the identity of youth; the sine qua non of being modern and middle class was and is that one's children, to paraphrase Hobsbawm, have childhoods, or rather that one's children should be teenagers before becoming adults—a luxury not shared by the vast majority of people in the colonial and postcolonial non-West where young people entered the workforce or agriculture at an early age. Scouting played a part in that construction of youth.

---

[38] On the origins of Arab Scouting, al-Kashafa, Scout being Kashaf, which began at the American University in Beirut in the prewar period, see Shafiq Naqash and ʿAli Khalifa, Al-Haraka al-Kashfiyya fi al-iqtar al-ʿarabiyya [The Scouting Movement in the Arab regions] (Beirut: Matbʿat al-kashaf Bayrut, 1936), and Anonymous, "Note sur le Scoutisme musulman en Syrie et au Liban," CHEAM 684, Beirut, 4 April 1944. The earliest Arabic translation of Scouting for Boys is probably that of the Aleppine high school teacher Mamduh Haqqi, al-Kashafa [Scouting] (Damascus, 1929). See Syrian Director General of Public Instruction's 1940 report "Note sur le scoutisme musulman dans le Mohafazat d'Alep" in CADN-MAE Fonds Beyrouth 2ème verserment Instruction Publique no. 189. Alongside Arab Scouting, which tended to be dominated by Muslims, Jewish groups associated with

In the Scout de France movement all the colonial concerns about language, sect, community preservation, and distinction coalesced.[39] Founded by French officers in Aleppo, it grew in the course of the 1920s and 1930s under local leadership until it encompassed twelve boy groups and three girl groups made up almost exclusively of Uniate Catholic children and adolescents by the time the postcolonial Syrian state forcibly disbanded the movement in 1948. Moreover, the memory of the movement has been successfully obliterated from the official history of Syria, and any historical documentation about it is in the hands of former members or in brief notices in the French Mandate archives.[40]

Meeting twice a week, on Sundays and Thursdays, the boys and girls gathered to speak French, work on badges and skills, play games, and read books. Among the books mentioned in oral history interviews are French translations of Kipling's *Kim* and stories about Mowgli from *The Jungle Book*, as well as Cooper's *Last of the Mohicans*. Books in Arabic about Scouting were of little interest as, in the words of one respondent, "they reflected a completely different mentality."[41] Members of the units came exclusively from the city's professional and commercial middle class. Attempts to form organizations among poorer Christians, primarily Syrian Orthodox, failed because the boys were expected to earn a living and could not spare the time to participate in group activities—they did not have childhoods.[42] The units sought to create and reinforce patterns of association, promoting the horizontal linkages so fundamental to Aleppo's middle-class society. In the words of one oral history, "Scouting gave us the ability to succeed in society; honest, strong, don't be afraid to be yourself. We were from middle-class families. . . . In politics no one became important; all of us became doctors, pharmacists, engineers, businessmen and bankers."[43]

Alliance Israélite also formed; Armenian Scouting was linked to organizations like the HoMenEtMen or the more middle-class Armenian General Benevolent Union.

[39] On the history of the Scout de France movement, see Philippe Laneyrie, *Les Scouts de France: L'évolution du mouvement des origines aux années quatre-vingt* (Paris: Les éditions du cerf, 1985). Unlike Scouting in the Anglo Saxon world, where unique national Scouting movements emerged, in France and other European countries, Scouting tended to follow religious divisions. Hence the Catholic Scout de France were founded in 1919 by Père Sevin in opposition to the secular Les Éclaireuses et Éclaireurs de France, the Jewish Les Éclaireuses et Éclaireurs Israélites de France, and most recently, Scouts Musulmans de France. Unlike the other Scout movements in France, the Scout de France integrated bellicose Catholic imagery into their repertoire of symbols, including Crusaders.

[40] CADN-MAE Fonds Beyrouth 2ème versement Instruction Publique no. 189.

[41] Oral History interview with Henri Ayyub, 12 December 1995, conducted by author in Arabic and French. Henri Ayyub was a senior youth leader of a Scout de France Group associated with Aleppo's Marist Brothers high school.

[42] Oral history interview with Elie and Lora Hindie, 7 December 1995, conducted by author in Arabic, English, and French.

[43] Oral history interview with Pierre Khoury, 10 December 1995, conducted by author in English.

Public marches were a central feature of Scout de France activity, and it was through these marches and parades that they inscribed themselves on Aleppo's urban fabric. By the late 1930s these marches, like those of the White Badge, had grown to form a central ritual of the city's Christian community, allowing it to have a public persona in the Christian neighborhoods of the city. Like the case of the White Badge, such a presence, nevertheless, constituted a transgressive act in a place and time where organized public activity by members of religious minorities had been historically circumscribed and certainly contributed to the sectarian tension underlying its relationship with the Muslim majority.

Marching in Aleppo was not reserved only to Scout de France. The funeral of Saʿdallah Jabiri, who had died in 1947, occasioned a massive parade. Pierre Khoury, a Cub Scout at the time of the funeral, recalled: "All the Boy Scouts of Aleppo marched, even the Jews, Armenians, and Christians. There were Muslim Boy Scouts, their shorts covered their knees just because of a religious prohibition . . . we saw them so few times."[44] The young adult leader, Henri Ayyub remembers it differently: despite not being invited by the national authorities, "we imposed ourselves, or else they would have said 'the Christian Scouts do not love their country.' "[45]

It is understandable that the Scouts de France were viewed as outsiders or even traitors in Syria. The use of French and the centrality of Catholicism clearly identified them with the imperial power that had occupied the region. The Scout de France's symbols—symbols that identified them with, among other things, the Frankish crusaders of the Middle Ages, were antagonistic—if not inflammatory.[46] Yet, for the Scouts de France in Aleppo, the use of this language of symbols connected the Scouts in France with the boys and girls in Syria. Hence, the boundaries of the community made legible in the movement indicate that the conception of an Arab Syria had little relevance for the Christian middle class of Aleppo. Rather, they took the idea of a mimicked bourgeoisie to its logical conclusion. Seeking to create a community on the basis of their conception of their reified European cognate, they moved to the next step, obliterating the barriers and distance between themselves and the ideal. Thus, the Scouts de France did not create Frenchmen, but rather young men and women who believed themselves to be modern, albeit modern à la Française. In such a construct

---

[44] Ibid.

[45] Oral history interview with Henri Ayyub, 12 December 1995, conducted by author in Arabic and French.

[46] See, for example, the premier issue of the organization's journal, *Le Scout de France* 1:1 (15 January 1923). The cover shows a Crusader, most likely the French king Saint Louis, standing behind a Scout dressed in campaign hat, shorts, and neckerchief. The knight's crown and the boy's hat share the elaborate Jerusalem Cross.

FIGURE 10.2. Henri Ayyub (second row left) and his Scout de France patrol, ca. 1936, Aleppo.

lies the brilliance—or insidious nature—of the culture of the mandate and the entire edifice of the civilizing mission. While presenting itself as the best of all possible worlds and as an absolute set of values and definitions, this world and these values—when scrutinized more closely—reappear diffracted through a manifestly French imperial lens.

Still, attributing the force of the movement merely to French imperial machinations would deny the agency of the middle class shown by the persistence of the movement in postcolonial Syria. Upon independence the Scouts de France in Aleppo recreated themselves as the Catholic Syrian Scouts and gave themselves an Arabic name and emblem. That same year, the leader of the Arab Scouting movement in Damascus moved to bring all the Scout movements under his direct control. The Armenian Scout movements compromised with the authorities in Damascus, agreeing to use Arabic in public, though in private they continued to use Armenian. The former Scouts de France in Aleppo were unwilling to make such a deal. Leaders of the movement in the city who continued to press their case were arrested.[47] To those of the movement still alive in Syria, this event remains a fresh and painful memory.

---

[47] Appealing to a provision in the postcolonial Syrian constitution that guaranteed freedom of association, Henri Ayyub filed a formal written complaint against the Ministry of Education in 1952.

In contrast to the fond associations of Maggie Homsy with her photo-graph, while looking at this image of his Scouts de France troop, Henri Ayyub passed his finger across it, mournfully noting as he reached each head who had emigrated and to where. Few of the former Scouts re-mained in Syria, and most had left for North America, primarily Quebec or metropolitan France. The same holds for the Franco-Aleppine author and memoirist Marie Seurat, whose ambivalent and romantic vision of interwar Aleppo, as seen through the eyes of her father, also portrays a late-1930s' and early 1940s' lifestyle where Francophone cultural practice assured cultural mobility and the secure possession of middle-class status that ultimately made ephemeral continued association with Aleppo and permanent the relationship with the métropole.[48] For many in the middle class, the true cost of being modern was alienation and exile from the Gray City.

[48] In addition to *Salons*, see also her *Les Corbeaux d'Alep* (Paris: Gallimard-lieu Com-mun, 1988).

ELEVEN

Coda: The Incomplete Project of Middle-Class Modernity and the Paradox of Metropolitan Desire

The French evacuation from Syria (1946) set the stage for the complete political ascendance of the a'yan of the National Bloc. Shukri al-Quwwatli, a Damascene notable, served as Syria's first postindependent, president, and Aleppo's Sa'dallah al-Jabiri, its prime minister. The notability, while possessed of substantial political acumen, had very little direct experience with governing—French policies had assured that. Consequently, their coalition fractured almost immediately along a Damascus-Aleppo axis. These divisions in the notability created an opportunity for Aleppo's middle and entrepreneurial class to form Hizb al-Sha'b, the People's Party, which contested elections in the late 1940s. Centered on opposition to Quwwatli's pro-large-landowner policies and in support of the reestablishment of late Ottoman-era networks of trade, primarily with Iraq, the formation of the People's Party provides a momentary glimpse of the potential of the commercial and bureaucratic middle class, when allied with petty industrialists, to exert its will on the postcolonial political scene.

The 1948 war between the fledgling state of Israel and the neighboring Arab countries spelled the undoing of the Quwwatli government. Syria's military blamed the failures on the civilian leadership and Husni Za'im, an officer of Kurdish origins led the first of many coups that extinguished civilian parliamentary rule in Syria and ended the dominant role for the notability in the country's politics, though it continued to play a part until 1963. Likewise, the domination of Syrian political life by the military forestalled indefinitely a middle-class role, especially as the majority of Syria's indigenous officer corps was drawn from the rural peasantry or refugees and had few historical or familial connections with that class. While during brief moments of parliamentary rule in 1950s several of the important middle-class intellectuals of the interwar period, contemporaries of Edmond Rabbath, emerged as political leaders, the inherent instability of Syrian politics rendered their cumulative role insufficient to secure a permanent place for their class in the exercise of power.

Early in the postwar period the Arab Socialists Renaissance Party, al-Ba'th, was first formulated by a trio of Western-educated high school philosophy teachers of middle-class origin, Michel 'Aflaq, Zaki al-Arsuzi, and Salah al-Din Bitar. Drawing on an eclectic mixture of interwar fascism and socialism, the ideology had great appeal to younger, disaffected, and modernizing students, intellectuals, military men, and bureaucrats, especially as it articulated a notion of Arab political and economic unity as a tool to return the Arabs to the path of modernization and development that they had been forced to leave by the colonial occupations of the interwar era, as well as by what the Baʿthists and others saw as an act of neocolonialism in the form of the state of Israel. Members of al-Baʿth took control of Syria through electoral means (1963), but as a consequence of Syria's defeat in the 1967 war with Israel, the civilian leadership was deposed in favor of the military dictatorship of Hafiz al-Assad (1968). The populist impulses of these régimes expanded the opportunities for larger and larger portions of Syrian society to move into the middle class during the 1960s, primarily through mass compulsory schooling and the establishment and expansion of regional public universities and the immense growth of the public sector and white-collar office jobs.

Despite the ideology of rebirth associated with al-Baʿth, Syria has been ruled for four decades as an old-fashioned police state, which suppresses dissent and opposition and routinely denies basic human rights to its citizens. And while often victims of the state's oppressive policies, especially of its clumsily programs of central economic planning, the middle class continues to be a growing cultural and social presence in Syria. A peculiar modus vivendi has emerged between it and the ruling elite, elements of which can be traced to the interwar period and earlier: in exchange for political quietism and the surrender of anything resembling civil society and political freedoms, the middle class is guaranteed many of the *material* elements of middle-class modernity and thereby can maintain the intra- and interclass forms of distinction crucial to the "hierarchy of exclusiveness." The Syrian middle class can send its children to state universities for free; it can maintain a middle-class lifestyle through subsidies of basic commodities like rice, milk, and oil; white-collar government jobs, though low paying, are plentiful; and local industry and the retail sector are protected from competition and the disruptive vagaries of globalization. Brand-name or knock-off consumer goods are available; rents are controlled; and conspicuous consumption is frowned upon but practiced. Albeit increasingly difficult, it is at once possible to live in a middle-class way in Syria, even to aspire to middle-class status from the lower classes, and still have no political rights whatsoever. And Syria's large Christian population, though declining as a consequence of patterns of emigration established in the late Ottoman period, is protected and allowed to create institutions of civil society—as long as those institutions serve only the members of its own community. This protection binds the Christians to the minority Alawite-controlled state, perpetuating aspects of the *colonial contract* of the interwar period. In the wake of the founding of Israel and the rise of vitriolic state anti-Zionism that often crosses into a vulgar and populist anti-Semitism, the Jewish community has abandoned Syria, leaving Aleppo altogether for opportunities in the West, primarily New York City, though a small community remains in Damascus.

For the most part, the status quo in Syria simply produces a vacuous middle-class ennui that is replicated throughout the Middle East and resonates in other parts of the postcolonial non-West. However, it possesses an explosive underside, whose full measure is only now beginning to be understood. As Sami Zubaida has observed of one of the key byproducts of these postcolonial authoritarian régimes' concessions to middle-class modernity: "Mass higher education produces a proletarianized, poorly educated intelligentsia, poor and resentful, directing its 're-sentiment' against the Westernized elites, seen as the agents of cultural invasion. These are the main cadres of nationalist and religious xenophobia, currently so powerful in the region."[1] As a consequence, radicalized contemporary Islamist movements have appealed to members of the middle class in unanticipated ways; the raw material of violent movements that have emanated from the region in the last two decades are not the poor, but are rather those who, by virtue of education, wealth, or profession, are the middle class. Coming to terms with the reality of a modern middle-class Islamism, its antipathy toward the West, and the possibility of middle-class Islamist revolutions in the major states of the region are perhaps the greatest intellectual challenges facing students of the contemporary Middle East and moreover mark a fundamental turn in middle-class history writ-large. Less a problem of "What Went Wrong?" as Bernard Lewis asks, these issues unfold against questions about the power of persisting forms of colonial subordination, unequal access to natural resources, capital, and economic opportunity, Western support for régimes that oppress their own citizens or occupy the lands of others with unremitting brutality, and the arrogant exercise of military might on people whose belief in their ability to change their and their children's world for the better, to live and to prosper, has virtually disappeared. A primary feature of middle-class modernity has been a steadfast faith in an individual, familial, and societal "plot line" of progress, and hope mixed with personal, professional, and social ambition; loss of that hope as a tangible reality—and not Islam—is among the motives compelling middle-class college students to strap dynamite to their waists, explode themselves, and kill those around them on public buses or crash jet airplanes into buildings. Not so

[1] Sami Zubaida, "Cosmopolitans, Nationalists, and Fundamentalists in the Modern Middle East" Inaugural Lecture, Birkbeck College, 5 May 2004.

ironically, their understanding of the institutional forms of civil society, history, access to technology, primarily computers and the Internet, knowledge of mass media, the power of spectacle, and the role of public opinion, and fluency in Western languages—cumulatively evidence of being modern—enhances their ability to act with such reckless disregard for human life.

Toward a Theory of the Middle Class

Issues of resiliency and continuity in the history of the middle class in the period 1908–1946 can serve as a basis for a series conceptual axioms I offer here as a starting point for the future comparative study of the history of the middle class as a social and cultural phenomenon of the West *and* non-West:

1. Middle-class identity was formulated in dialog with an idealized metropolitan middle-class practice. Particular elements of that middle-class identity were contingent and not fixed and rather changed in accordance with shifts in dominant high-cultural forms, tastes, fashions and ideologies at work or practiced in a variety of *métropoles*. However the framework for being middle class—middle-class praxis—remained static and centered on advanced education, transgenerational class reproduction, patterns of consumption, kinds of professions, and a general commitment to being modern.

2. The middle class was expert in forming institutions of civil society, bringing to these institutional forms shared expectations of participation, equality, and accountability. While a template for larger participation in society, the bonds the middle class created in the universe of voluntary association were weak. Other bonds of religion, ethnicity, and family were stronger, so that the bonds its members made in civil society, likewise, were too enfeebled to challenge the state or withstand hostile interference by it and rarely translated directly into political ascendance. This weakness made the individual members of the middle class vulnerable to forms of cultural and economic cooptation by colonialist, conservative, and authoritarian elites.

3. The middle class was fascinated with history. This fascination was not just a response to a need to establish a genealogy of their own and society's modernity by identifying an unmodern past, but also a function of their propensity to "think with history." Middle-class historicism has been a key feature in the successful formation of imagined national communities, confirming the pivotal role of the formation of the middle class and the way its members thought to the broader imposition/adoption of nationalism.

4. The middle class maintained a pragmatic relationship to power, while its members resorted to idealism to oppose it or support it. Issues of citizenship, liberalism, secularism, and egalitarianism were fundamental to middle-class expectations from state and society; however, each of these concepts was negotiable. Where the middle class put a premium on all of them, it would not necessarily insist on their universal or complete implementation were it to have meant a concomitant loss of security or the undermining of their relative economic status.

5. Middle-class modernity as a form of cultural practice eased the transnational movement of members of the middle class, from the colonial periphery to the *métropole* with which they most identified. While the motives for making this transition vary, it was often a result of a generalized deracination of ethnic and religious minorities from the majority society. This disconnection can have violent origins or result from persistent forms of social discrimination and insurmountable economic barriers. The fluidity of this process and its recurrence over the last century has a deleterious effect on the vitality of the societies "left behind" and has altered indelibly metropolitan societies as well.

As I observed at the start of this book, the middle class as a historical problem has been ignored; the vital nature of its role in the past and clear presence in the future demands greater attention.

The Incomplete Project of Middle-Class Modernity

Though its path is littered with broken promises and false starts, the emergence of an urban middle class in the Eastern Mediterranean was neither a simple function of the introduction of new technologies or economic categories nor an unchallenged shift in the dynamics of urban society, but rather it constituted the species of change at the heart of the historical experience of modernity in the world beyond the West. In claiming modernity, the members of the middle class established themselves as a novel and permanent feature of the region's architecture of community. And by *being modern*, new types and proportionally larger numbers of people began *to speak*—in the sense of both public opinion and self-representation; *to remember*—that is, explaining the present through an historicist comprehension of the past; and *to produce culture*—primarily secular, religiously unsanctioned high culture.

By being modern, the middle class brought to urban society expectations of openness and rationality that at once undermined customary politics and produced civil society. Ultimately, the inability of the middle class to maintain a dominant role in civil society led to its debasement in the hands of a traditional Sunni oligarchy and elimination altogether by the

postcolonial military regimes, using a combination of internal secret policing and the threat of extreme violence. Likewise, while meaningful and
relevant to the thousands of men, women, and children associated with
institutions like the Aleppo Mutual Aid Society, the Scouts de France, the
Alliance Israélite, the Chamber of Commerce, even the League of National Action, throughout the late Ottoman and interwar Eastern Mediterranean, these central elements of middle-class civic and cultural life
could not, by their very nature, resonate with the vast remainder of the
region's population. Their participation in these middle-class elements of
civil society betokened ascendancy into the "hierarchy of exclusiveness."
This is especially the case in the forms of middle-class education. On a
very basic level, such a luxury was unavailable to most Syrians, whose
children did not have childhoods. Ultimately, this highlights what is unfinished about the project of modernity in the non-West, and the way it
has unraveled in the West. As Habermas contends, the obvious patholo-
gies of modernity are not necessarily preordained. Modernity's incompleteness is a consequence of the failure to check the excesses of societal
modernization with a parallel dedication to cultural modernization.[2]

Modernity, which articulates a universal discourse of rationality, emancipation, progress, and liberalism, tends to exclude those who are illiterate
in its idiom. The means by which modernity spread in Eastern Mediterranean society did not always lead to the creation of secular, democratic,
and rational institutions, rather its local variations cemented distance,
alienation, and cultural impoverishment. This central irony has not gone
unnoticed by critics like Göçek: "the Enlightenment ideas inherent [to]
Western education led Ottoman officials to develop ties with one another
at the expense of the sultan."[3] These ideas and a mastery of modern ways
of knowing allowed these men to consolidate social forms of organization
that the patriarchal sultan could no longer control. Once created, however, these social forms were used to facilitate the destruction of the Ottoman minority commercial middle class immediately before and after the
creation of the Republic of Turkey. Justified in part by an understanding
of modern forms of ethnic and cultural distinction, the state that emerged
based itself on modernity, secularism, and nationalism, but, nevertheless,
"excluded cosmopolitan non-Muslim Ottoman minorities from the national bourgeoisie."[4]

A continuing failure to incorporate the middle-class segments of these
groups into a pluralistic order threatens, in Göçek's words, to doom "Tur-

---

[2] Jürgen Habermas, "Modernity: An Unfinished Project," in Maurizio Passerin d'Entrèves and Seyla Benhabib, eds., *Habermas and the Unfinished Project of Modernity: Critical Essays on the Philosophical Discourse of Modernity* (Cambridge: MIT Press, 1997); see
also Maurizio Passerin d'Entrèves' "Introduction," 3.

[3] Göçek, "Rise of Bourgeoisie," 138.

[4] Ibid., 141.

key to the periphery once again."[5] Ranajit Guha identifies a variation on this theme in the experience of the postcolonial Indian middle class. He attacks the class not just for its propensity to accommodate the colonial presence but also for "its failure to measure up to the heroism of the European bourgeoisie in its period of ascendancy" and confront the local semifeudal order at the same time.

> The liberalism they professed was never strong enough to exceed the limitations of the half-hearted initiatives for reform which issued from the colonial administration. This mediocre liberalism, a caricature of the vigorous democratic culture of the rise of the bourgeoisie in the West, operated throughout the colonial period in a symbiotic relationship with the still active and vigorous forces of the semi-feudal cultures of India.[6]

The middle-class experience of the Eastern Mediterranean shares tendencies with both conclusions and cannot escape similar criticism. While, in what became Turkey, the marginalization, deportation, and extermination of local Christians and the subsequent religious homogenization of Anatolia and Thrace reduced a potential variable in the construction of a national middle class, in Aleppo, religious difference continued to interfere with attempts to create intraclass solidarity. The apparent ease with which the non-Muslim middle class of Aleppo transcended national boundaries contributed to the improbability of cooperation. That in every upper-middle and most middle-class non-Muslim family at least one person possesses a foreign passport, and that the Armenian community, while integrating Syrian society economically and politically, vigorously and successfully withstood linguistic and cultural assimilation into an Arab Syria, are both manifestations of this phenomenon. As in the case of Turkey, it is possible to show a gradual merging of the upper segments of the Muslim middle-class with the local notability. Far from reducing the role of Islam in defining the parameters of legitimacy, it enhanced it, adding to the mix a middle-class insistence on the text-based and monistic Sunni Islam of Islamic modernism. This further marginalized extra textual Islam, Sufi brotherhoods in particular, and more importantly Syria's heterogeneous Muslim sects, the Ismailis, Druze, and the group dominant in Syria at the time of writing, the Alawites.

The erasure of the boundary between the Muslim upper middle class and the notability—a process of mutual co-optation—meant as well, accommodation with the illiberal dimensions of the politics of notables. Eliminated in the Republic of Turkey, except in parts of Turkish Kurdistan, the Anatolian variation of the politics of notables disappeared as a viable technique to comprehend center/periphery relations by the mid-

---

[5] Ibid.
[6] Guha, *Dominance*, 5.

FIGURE 11.1. Advertisements from *Aleppo and Its Environs*.

1920s. Its perpetuation in Syria into the post–World War II era by the postcolonial elite in cooperation with the urban middle class, and indeed its postmodern manifestation in Lebanon, bears a striking resemblance to Guha's "mediocre bourgeois liberalism."

THE PARADOX OF METROPOLITAN DESIRE

During the Second World War, as Aleppo enjoyed a brief economic upswing as a consequence of wartime restrictions of international trade, the Aleppo Chamber of Commerce produced a pocket-sized pamphlet entitled *Aleppo and Its Environs*, destined for the British troops who were occupying the city.[7] Edited by two local Anglo-Irish Jesuits, its eighty pages were intended to introduce Aleppo to the soldiers with sections on the city's history, places of interest, food, flowers, and local customs. A striking feature of the pamphlet is the advertisement section, which enfolds the text. The Roxy and Rex Cinemas promise "ALWAYS THE BEST

[7] J. Brindley Kingdon S.J. and Christopher Devlin S.J., eds, *Aleppo and Its Environs*, 2nd ed. (Aleppo: Maronite Press, 1944).

AND LATEST ENGLISH AND AMERICAN FILMS"; George Notarkis, "Bakers and Grocers—caterers for fêtes" could provide "First class pastries and cakes, sweets, ices, biscuits, hams, sausages and preserved meat, wines, liqueurs, whisky, champagne—all first quality." Watches were to be repaired at Toros'; the Librarie du Nord and Pelican Book shop carried current English and American magazines. Western consumer goods were to be had at Orosdi Back's department store; Persian carpets, camel hair fabric, and silk brocade woven on jacquard looms were sold at Marco Polo's. The Hotel Baron pledged "All modern comforts / Bar and Restaurant." Despite—or more accurately in spite of—the visibly modern middle-class taste and consumerism manifest in the advertisements, the last five sections continue the natural historical format of the preceding chapters in an "attempt to explain some of the customs and traditions, racial and religious, both Muslim and Christian, which unless they are explained often act as a barrier to true understanding between East and West" and in so doing cast doubt on the degree to which the inhabitants of the Eastern Mediterranean were modern in the eyes of the resident Westerners, their most immediate metropolitan exemplars.[8] Alford Carleton, the principal of the local American Protestant high school, Aleppo College, wrote in an article suitably entitled "East and West: Their Modes and Manners,"

> All types are to be found in the East, as in the West, and the western-educated, Paris-dressed, English-speaking young Arab is miles away from his staid turban-wearing grandfather. There is still enough basic difference between East and West, however, that the new comer to the Orient will do well to study men's minds and manners patiently and long before venturing a familiar relationship with anyone in the East.[9]

While he distinguishes between traditional and modern "Orientals," Carleton's piece still exemplifies a phenomenon that I call the *paradox of metropolitan desire*. In many ways this paradox defines the relationship between modernity and the moderns of the non-West: the West's impulse to assert the universality of modernity exists simultaneously with the denial that the non-Westerner—no matter how successfully he or she incorporated into their lives the constituent elements of being modern—could ever be *really* modern. In this case, the multilingual and sartorially correct "young Arab" is condemned, in perpetuity, to a hyphenated existence somewhere between a "real" modernity and its exquisite shadow in the East. The paradox itself hinges on a belief in a congenital inadequacy: in

[8] Ibid., preface.
[9] Ibid., 76.

the American principal's phlegmatic appraisal, "The cardinal virtue of the Orient is 'graciousness' or 'courtesy' rather than moral courage as in the West."[10] A more likely origin of the paradox is the fear that were the non-Westerner allowed to be modern, it would eliminate the distance necessary for continued European hegemony—a miscegenation of modernity. If allowed to stand, the overt mixing or admission of the non-Westerner to the ranks of the elect would deny the historical specificity of Europe (or North America) as the permanent home of what is modern and Occidentals as the "high priests" of modernity.

From within the terms of that very paradox and intrinsic to this book has been an exploration of the possibilities of a radical critique of the question of modernity through the prism of the non-West—a necessary first step toward what Dipesh Chakrabarty calls "the provincializing of Europe."[11] In this critique of modernity, what is conveyed and received as universal and complete in the metropolitan and the colonial visions of what it means to be modern reemerges as contingent, limited, and particular. Out of the critique as well, I have sought to retrieve the ornate chaos of human difference.

[10] Ibid.

[11] Dipesh Chakrabarty, *Provincializing Europe: Postcolonial Thought and Historical Difference* (Princeton: Princeton University Press, 2000).

Select Bibliography

ARCHIVES

France

Centre des archives diplomatiques. Nantes Ministère des affairs etrangères. (CADN-MAE)

DIPLOMATIC RECORDS
Consulat Alep Série "A."—1914 (Correspondences from the French Consulate in Aleppo to the French Embassy in Constantinople)

ARCHIVES OF THE FRENCH MANDATE
Fonds Beyrouth. Cabinet Politique
Fonds Beyrouth. Cilicie 1919–1921
Fonds Beyrouth. Petit Fonds Political et Adminstratif
Fonds Unions Internationales 2ème versement
Fonds Beyrouth 2ème versement Instruction Publique

Centre de Hautes Études Administratives sur l'Afrique et l'Asie Modernes. Paris. (CHEAM)

Ministère de la Défense: Service historique de l'armée de terre. Vincennes. (MD-SHAT)
Series 4 H
Series 6 N

Syrian Arab Republic

Markaz al-watha'iq al-tarikhiyya. Al-Qism al-khass. Damascus. (MWT-QKh)
Hananu's Revolt
Private Papers of Saʿdallah al-Jabiri
National Guard

Republic of Turkey

Başbakanlık Arşivi. Osmanl Dairesi. Istanbul. (BBA)
Dahilye Nezareti (Interior Ministry) (DH-)
Muhâberât-ı Umûmiye Idaresi (MUI)
Mütenevvî (MTV)

United Kingdom

Public Record Office. Foreign Office. Kew. (PRO FO)

DIPLOMATIC RECORDS
FO 195. Embassy and Consular Archives, Turkey: Correspondences
FO 371. General Correspondences Aleppo Consulate

FO 372. Embassy and Consular Archives. Turkey; Aleppo
FO 608. Papers Relating to the Paris Peace Conference
FO 684. France-Damascus, Embassy and Consular Archives
FO 861. Embassy and Consular Archives. Turkey; Aleppo, General Correspondences (Outgoing and Incoming)

United States of America

United States National Archives. Department of State. College Park, Maryland. (USNA II)

DIPLOMATIC RECORDS

Records of the Department of State Relating to the Internal Affairs of Asia: Record Group 59 Syria (Microform) 860.d 00/01 . . .
Record Group 84 Aleppo Consulate 10044/01 . . .

League of Nations

League of Nations A.29.1927.IV Social

Other Archives or Private Collections

Archives of the Cercle de la jeunesse Catholique, Aleppo, Syria.
Archives of the Violette Jebebjian Library, Aleppo, Syria.
Private Papers of Henri Ayyub, Aleppo, Syria.
Private Papers of Firyal Qumbaz, Aleppo, Syria.

NEWSPAPERS AND MAGAZINES

al-ʿAsima (Damascus)
al-Furat / Ghadîr-i Fırat (Aleppo)
al-Hadith (Aleppo)
Halab (Aleppo)
Le Jour (Beirut)
Lisân-ı Ahâlî / Lisan al-Ahali (Aleppo)
al-Nahda (Aleppo)
al-Nazir (Aleppo)
al-Shudhur (Aleppo)
al-Shuʿla (Aleppo)
Sedâ-yı Şehbâ / Sadaʾ al-Shahbaʾ (Aleppo)
Şefak (Aleppo)
al-Taqaddum (Aleppo)
Times (New York)
al-Jihad (Aleppo)
al-Shaʿb (Aleppo)
al-Shabab (Aleppo)

BOOKS, ARTICLES, AND ORAL HISTORY INTERVIEWS

ʿAflaq, Mishil. *Fi sabil al-baʿth* [For the cause of the Baʿth] 8th edition. Beirut: Dar al-taliʿa lil-tibaʿa wa al-nashr, 1972. Originally published in 1959.

al-Asadi, Khayr al-Din. *Masuʿat Halab* [Encyclopedia of Aleppo]. Aleppo: Aleppo University Press, 1992.

al-ʿAyntabi, Fuʿad and Najwa ʿUthman. *Halab fi miʾt ʿam* [One Hundred Years of Aleppo]. 3 vols. Aleppo: University of Aleppo Press, 1993.

Bakhash, Naum. *Yawmiyyat Halab* [Aleppo Diary]. Aleppo: Maronite Press, 1990.

Bell, Getrude. *The Desert and the Sown*. London: Heinemann, 1907.

Berkes, Niyazi. *The Development of Secularism in Turkey*. Montréal: McGill University Press, 1961.

Biru, Tawfiq. *Al-ʿarab wa al-turk fi al-ahd al-dust, ri al-ʿuthmani* [The Arabs and Turks in the Era of the Ottoman Constitution]. Cairo, 1960.

Bodman, Herbert. *Political Factions in Aleppo, 1760–1826*. Chapel Hill: University of North Carolina Press, 1963.

Brémond, Édouard. *La Cilicie en 1919–1920*. Paris: Imprimerie nationale, 1921.

Brummett, Palmira Johnson. *Image and Imperialism in the Ottoman Revolutionary Press, 1908–1911*. Albany: State University of New York, 2001.

Bulletin Economique de la Chambre du Commerce d'Alep. Aleppo: Maronite Press, 1921.

Charle, Christophe. *Naissance des intellectuels, 1880–1900*. Paris: Editions de minuit, 1990.

Charles-Roux, François. *Les Échelles de Syrie et de Palestine au XVIIIe siècle*. Paris: Librarie Orientaliste Paul Geuthner, 1928.

Chatterjee, Partha. *Nationalist Thought and the Colonial World: A Derivative Discourse*. London: Zed Books, 1986.

———. *The Nation and Its Fragments: Colonial and Postcolonial Histories*. Princeton: Princeton University Press, 1993.

Chaturvedi, Vinayak, ed. *Mapping Subaltern Studies and the Postcolonial*. London: Verso, 2000.

Conklin, Alice. *A Mission to Civilize: The Republican Idea of Empire in France and West Africa 1895–1930*. Stanford: Stanford University Press, 1997.

Cioeta, Donald J. "Ottoman Censorship in Lebanon and Syria, 1876–1908," *International Journal of Middle East Studies* 10:2 (May 1979): 167–186.

Clayer, Nathalie, Alexandre Popovic and Thierry Zarcone, eds. *Presse Turque et Presse de Turquie*. Istanbul: Isis Press, 1992.

Committee for the Commemorative Volume. *Al-Dhikra al-miʾawi al-Maʾmun* [Centennial Memorial: al-Maʾmun]. Aleppo: Arab Pen Publishing House, 1994.

Copeaux, Étienne. *Espaces et temps de la nation turque: analyse d'une historiographie nationaliste, 1931–1993*. Paris: CNRS Editions, 1997.

al-Dabbagh, ʿAʾisha. *al-Haraka al-fikriyya fi Halab* [The Intellectual Movement in Aleppo]. Beirut, 1972.

Dashwali, ʿAbd al-Latif. *Maraya* [Mirrors]. Damascus, 1947.

David, Jean-Claude. "Alep, dégradation et tentative actuelle de réadaptation des structures urbaines traditionelles," *BEO* 28 (1975): 19–56.

David, Jean-Claude, and Dominique Hubert. "Maisons et immeubles du début du XXe siècle à Alep." *Les cahiers de la recherche architecturale* 10/11 (April 1982): 94–101.

Davis, Ralph. *Aleppo in Devonshire Square*. London: Macmillan, 1967.

Duman, Hasan. *Osmanl Y ll klar (Salnameler ve Nevsaller)* (Ottoman Year-Books). Istanbul: Renkler, 1982.

———, ed. *Istanbul Kütüphaneleri Arap Harfl Süreli Yay nlar Toplu Katalogu 1828–1928* [Union Catalog of the Periodicals in the Arabic Script in the Libraries of Istanbul]. Istanbul: Islâm Tarih, Sanat, ve Kültür Arastirma Merkezi, 1986.

Dwek, Jacob Saul. *Derekh Emuna*. Aleppo, 1913/14.

Eldem, Edhem, Daniel Goffman, and Bruce Masters. *The Ottoman City between East and West: Aleppo, Izmir and Istanbul*. London: Cambridge University Press, 1999.

Eley, Geoff. "Nations, Publics and Political Cultures: Placing Habermas in the Nineteenth Century." In *Habermas and the Public Sphere*. Edited by Craig Calhoun, 289–339. Cambridge: M.I.T. Press, 1994.

Eley, Geoff, and Ronald Grigor Suny. "Introduction." In *Becoming National: A Reader*. Edited by Geoff Eley and Ronald Grigor Suny. Oxford: Oxford University Press, 1996.

d'Entrèves, Maurizio Passerin, and Seyla Benhabib, ed. *Habermas and the Unfinished Project of Modernity: Critical Essays on the Philosophical Discourse of Modernity*. Cambridge: MIT Press, 1997.

Fani, Seyh Muhsin (Hüseyin Kâzim Kadri). *Istikbale Dogru* [Straight Toward the Future]. Istanbul, 1915.

Faris, Jurj, ed. *Man huwa fi Suriyya* [Who's Who in Syria]. Damascus, 1951.

Fawaz, Leila Tarazi. and C. A. Bayly. *Modernity and Culture from the Mediterranean to the Indian Ocean, 1890–1920*. New York: Columbia University Press, 2001.

Findley, Carter. *Ottoman Civil Officialdom: A Social History*. Princeton: Princeton University Press, 1989.

Frisby, David. *Fragments of Modernity: Theories of Modernity in the Work of Simmel, Kracauer, and Benjamin*. Cambridge: Polity, 1985.

Gautherot, Gustave. *La France en Syrie et en Cilicie*. Courbevoie: Librairie indépendante, 1920.

Gay, Peter. *The Bourgeois Experience: Victoria to Freud*. Vol. 3, *The Cultivation of Hatred*. New York: W. W. Norton, 1993.

———. *The Bourgeois Experience: Victoria to Freud*. Vol. 5, *Pleasure Wars*. New York: W. W. Norton, 1998.

Gelvin. James. *Divided Loyalties: Nationalism and Mass Politics in Syria at the Close of Empire*. Berkeley: University of California Press, 1998.

al-Ghazzi, Kamil. *Kitab Nahr al-Dhahab fi Tarikh Halab* [The River of Gold in the History of Aleppo] 2nd ed. Edited by Shawqi Sha'th and Mahmud Fakhuri. 3 vols. Aleppo: Arab Pen Press, 1991–1993.

Göçek, Fatma Müge. *Rise of the Bourgeoisie, Demise of Empire: Ottoman Westernization and Social Change*. Oxford: Oxford University Press, 1996.

Godard, Charles. *Alep: Essai de géographie urbaine et d'économie politique et sociale*. Aleppo: Aleppo Municipality, 1938.

Goffman, Daniel. *Izmir and the Leventine World, 1550–1650*. Seattle: University of Washington Press, 1990.

Göle, Nilufer. *The Forbidden Modern: Civilization and Veiling.* Ann Arbor: University of Michigan Press, 1996.

Guha, Ranajit. *Dominance without Hegemony: History and Power in Colonial India.* Cambridge: Harvard University Press, 1997.

———. *History at the Limit of World History.* New York: Columbia University Press, 2002.

Habermas, Jürgen. *The Structural Transformation of the Public Sphere: An Inquiry into a Category of Bourgeois Society.* Translated by Thomas Burger with Fredrick Lawrence. Cambridge: MIT Press, 1994.

———. "Modernity: an Unfinished Project." *Habermas and the Unfinished Project of Modernity: Critical Essays on the Philosophical Discourse of Modernity.* Edited by Maurizio Passerin d'Entrèves and Seyla Benhabib. Cambridge: MIT Press, 1997.

———. "Modernity's Consciousness of Time and Its Need for Self-Reassurance." In *The Philosophical Discourse of Modernity: Twelve Lectures.* Translated by Frredrick Lawrence. Cambridge: MIT Press, 2000.

Hallaq, ʿAbdallah Yurki. *Al-thawrat al-suriyya al-kubra fi rubʿ qarn 1918–1945* [The Great Syrian Revolts in the Quarter Century 1918–1945]. Aleppo: Dad, 1990.

Hamidé, Abdul-Rahman. *La région d'Alep: Etude de géographie urbaine.* Paris: n.p., 1959.

Hanano, Ibrahim. *La question syrienne: Les élections d'Alep.* Toulouse: Societé Meridional d'Impression, 1932.

Harootunian, Harry. *Overcome by Modernity: History, Culture, and Community in Interwar Japan.* Princeton: Princeton University Press, 2000.

Harrison, Carol. *The Bourgeois Citizen in the 19th Century: Gender, Sociability, and the Uses of Emulation.* London: Oxford University Press, 1999.

Himsi, Qustaki. *Udabaʾ Halab dhu al-athar fi al-qarn al-tasiʿ ʿashar* [Aleppo's Men of Letters in the Nineteenth Century]. Aleppo: Maronite Press, 1925.

Hobsbawn, Eric. *The Age of Empire: 1875–1914.* New York: Vintage Books, 1989.

———. *Nations and Nationalism since 1780: Programme, Myth, Reality.* Cambridge: Canto, 1990.

Hobsbawn, Eric, and Terence Ranger, eds. *The Invention of Tradition.* Cambridge: Cambridge University Press, 1983.

Hodgson, Marshall G. S. *The Venture of Islam: Conscience and History in a World Civilization.* Vol. 2: *The Expansion of Islam in the Middle Period.* Chicago: University of Chicago Press, 1974.

———. *Rethinking World History: Essays on Europe, Islam, and World History.* Edited, with an introduction and conclusion, by Edmund Burke, III. Cambridge: Cambridge University Press, 1993.

Hourani, Albert. *Arabic Thought in the Liberal Age 1798–1939.* Cambridge: Cambridge University Press, 1983. Originally published by Oxford University Press in 1962.

———. "Ottoman Reform and the Politics of Notables." In *Beginnings of Modernization in the Middle East.* Edited by William R. Polk and Richard L. Chambers, 41–68. Chicago: University of Chicago Press, 1968.

Ibrahim-Basha, Jamil. *Nidal al-ahrar fi sabil al-istiqlal* [Struggle of the Freeborn on the Path of Independence]. Aleppo: Dad Publishing, 1959.

Jebedjian, Robert. "Armenian Syrian Deputies." *Geghard 5* (1996).

Joshi, Sanjay. *Fractured Modernity: Making of a Middle Class in Colonial North India*. New Delhi: Oxford University Press, 2001.

Judge, Joan. "Public Opinion in the New Politics of Contestation in the Late Qing, 1904–1911." *Modern China* 20:1 (1994).

Jundi, Adham. *Tarikh al-thawrat al-suriyya fi ʿahd al-intidab al-faransi* [The History of the Syrian Revolts in the Era of the French Mandate]. Damascus, 1960.

Kansu, Aykut. *The Revolution of 1908 in Turkey*. Leiden: Brill, 1997.

Kayalı, Hasan. "Elections and the Electoral Process in the Ottoman Empire, 1876–1919." *International Journal of Middle East Studies* 27 (1995): 265–286.

———. *Arabs and Young Turks: Ottomanism, Arabism and Islamism in the Ottoman Empire*. Los Angeles: University of California Press, 1997.

Kayyali, ʿAbd al-Rahman. *al-Marahil fi al-intidab al-faransi wa fi nidalina al-watani* [The Stages of the French Mandate and Our National Struggle]. 4 vols. Aleppo: Dad Publishing House, 1958–1962.

Kerr, E. Stanely. *The Lions of Marash*. Albany: Syracuse University Press, 1973.

Khairallah, K. T. *La Syrie: territoire, origines ethnique et politiques*. Paris, 1912.

Khalidi, Rashid. *Palestinian Identity*. New York: Columbia University Press, 1997.

Khater, Akram Fouad. *Inventing Home; Emigration, Gender, and the Middle Class in Lebanon, 1870–1920*. Berkeley: University of California Press, 2001.

Khoury, Philip. *Urban Notables and Arab Nationalism: The Politics of Damascus*. Cambridge: Cambridge University Press, 1983.

———. *Syria and the French Mandate: The Politics of Arab Nationalism 1920–1945*. Princeton: Princeton University Press, 1987.

———. "The Urban Notables Paradigm Revisited." *Revue du Monde Musulman et de la Méditerranée* (January and February 1990).

———. "Continuity and Change in Syrian Political Life: The Nineteenth and Twentieth Centuries," *The American Historical Review* 96:5 (December 1991): 1374–1395.

———. "The Paradoxical in Arab Nationalism: Inter-war Syria Reconsidered." In *Rethinking Nationalism in the Arab Middle East*. Edited by Israel Gershoni and James Jankowski. New York: Columbia University Press, 1997.

Kingdon, J. Brindley, and Christopher Devlin, ed. *Aleppo and Its Environs*. 2nd ed. Aleppo: Maronite Press, 1944.

Kocka, Jürgen. *Industrial Culture and Bourgeois Society: Business, Labor, and Bureaucracy in Modern Germany*. New York: Berghan Books, 1999.

Kologlu, Orhan. "La formation des intellectuels à la culture journalistique dans l'Empire ottoman et l'influence de la presse étrangère." In *Presse Turque et Presse de Turquie*. Edited by Nathalie Clayer, Alexandre Popovic and Thierry Zarcone, 123–142. Istanbul: Isis, 1992.

Lammens, Henri. *La Syrie: précis historique*. Paris, 1913.

Lecerf, M., et al.. "Transformation en orient, sous l'influence de l'occident, du costume et des modes: Insignes et saluts." *Entretiens sur l'évolution des pays de civilisation arabe*. Edited by R. Montagne, 80–104. Paris: Imprimerie Alençonnaise, 1938.

Lewis, Bernard. *The Emergence of Modern Turkey*. Oxford: Oxford University Press, 1968.

———. *The Muslim Discovery of Europe*. New York: W. W. Norton, 1982.

Longrigg, Stephen H. *Syria and Lebanon under French Mandate*. Oxford: Oxford University Press, 1958.

Lyotard, Jean-Francois. *The Postmodern Condition: A Report on Knowledge*. Translated by Geoff Bennington and Brian Massumi. Minneapolis: University of Minnesota Press, 1984.

Malathi, Suhayl. *al-Tibaʿa wa al-sihafa fi Halab* [Printing and Journalism in Aleppo]. Damascus, 1996.

Mayer, Arno. "The Lower Middle Class as Historical Problem," *The Journal of Modern History* 47:3 (September 1975).

———. *The Persistence of the Old Regime: Europe to the Great War*. New York: Pantheon Books, 1981.

———. *The Furies: Violence and Terror in the French and Russian Revolutions*. Princeton: Princeton University Press, 2002.

Méouchy, Nadine. "Les mobilisations urbaines et rurales à l'époque mandataire." *France, Syrie et Liban 1918–1946: les ambiguïtés et les dynamiques de la relation mandataire*. Edited by Nadine Méouchy. Damascus: Institute Français d'Études Arabes de Damas Press, 2002.

——— ed. *France, Syrie et Liban 1918–1946: les ambiguïties et les dynmaiques de la relation mandataire*. Damascus: Institute Français d'Études Arabes de Damas Press, 2002.

Méouchy, Nadine and Peter Sluglett, eds. *The British and French Mandates in Comparative Perspective / Les mandats français et anglais dans une perspective comparative*. Brill: Leiden, 2004.

Meriwether, Margaret Lee. *The Kin Who Count: Family and Society in Ottoman Aleppo, 1770–1840*. Austin: University of Texas Press, 1999.

Miller, Donald E., and Lorna Touryan Miller. *Survivors: An Oral History of the Armenian Genocide*. Los Angeles: University of California Press, 1993.

Mishaqa, Mikhail. al-*Jawab ʿala iqtirah al-ahbab* [Translated as *Murder, Mayhem, Pillage and Plunder: The History of Lebanon in the 18th and 19th Centuries*]. Translated by W. M. Thackston, Jr. Albany: State University of New York Press, 1988.

Mitchell, Timothy. *Colonising Egypt*. Los Angeles: University of California Press, 1991.

———. "The Stage of Modernity," in *Questions of Modernity*. Edited by Timothy Mitchell. Minneapolis: University of Minnesota Press, 2000.

———, ed. *Questions of Modernity*. Minneapolis: University of Minnesota Press, 2000.

———, *Rule of Experts: Egypt, Techno-Politics, Modernity*. Berkeley: University of California Press, 2002.

Muʿallim, Walid. *Suriyya: al-tariq ila al-huriyya (1916–1946)* [Syria on the Road to Freedom.] Damascus, 1988.

Owensby, Brian P. *Intimate Ironies: Modernity and the Making of Middle-Class Lives in Brazil*. Stanford: Stanford University Press, 1999.

Paxton, Robert O. "The Five Stages of Fascism," *The Journal of Modern History* 70:1 (March 1998).

Rabbath, Edmond. *Les états-unis de Syrie!* Aleppo: Maronite Press, 1925.

Rabbath, Gabriel. "Obituary Notice for Kamil al-Ghazzi." *Majallat al-ʿAdiyyat al-Suriyya* 3:1–2 (January–February 1933).

Saqqal, Antuan. *Min Dhikrayati fi al-muhama fi Misr wa Suriyya* [My Memoirs of the Legal Profession in Egypt and Syria]. Aleppo: Maronite Press, 1963.

Schorske, Carl E. *Thinking with History: Explorations in the Passage to Modernism*. Princeton: Princeton University Press, 1998.

Shit, Ihsan. "Madaris al-fatra al-ʿuthmaniyya fi Halab" [Schools of the Ottoman Period in Aleppo]. In *al-Dhikra al-miʾawi al-Maʾmun* [Centennial Memorial: al-Maʾmun]. Edited by Committee for Commemorative Volume, 53–59. Aleppo: Arab Pen Publishing House, 1994.

Sluglett, Peter. "Urban Dissidence in Mandatory Syria: Aleppo 1918–1936." In *Etat, ville et mouvements sociaux au Maghreb et au Moyen Orient* Urban Crises and Social Movements in the Middle East. Edited by Kenneth Brown et al., 301–316. Paris: L'Harmattan: 1986.

———. "Aspects of Economy and Society in the Syrian Provinces: Aleppo in Transition, 1880–1925." In *Modernity and Culture from the Mediterranean to the Indian Ocean, 1890–1920*. Edited by Leila Fawaz and C. A. Bayly, 144–157. New York: Columbia University Press, 2001.

———. "Will the Real Nationalists Stand Up? The Political Activities of the Notables of Aleppo. 1918–1946." In *France, Syrie et Liban 1918–1946: les ambiguïties et les dynmaiques de la relation mandataire*. Edited by Nadine Méochy, 273–290. Damascus: Institute Français d'Études Arabes de Damas Press, 2002.

al-Sultan, ʿAli. *Tarikh Suriyya 1908–1918* [History of Syria: 1908–1918]. Damascus: 1987.

al-Tabbakh, Raghib. *Iʿlam al-nubalaʾ bi-tarikh Halab al-shahbaʾ* [Information of the Notables in the History of Aleppo the Gray]. 2nd ed. Edited by Muhammad Kamal. 7 vols. Aleppo: Arab Pen Press 1988–1992. [Orig. ed. Aleppo: Maronite Press, 1923–1926.]

di Tarazi, Filib (Philippe de Tarazi). *Tarikh al-sahafa al-ʿarabiyya* [History of Arabic Journalism]. 4 vols. Beirut: al-ʿAdabiyya Press, 1933.

Thompson, Elizabeth. *Colonial Citizens: Republican Rights and Paternal Privilege in French Syria and Lebanon*. New York: Columbia University Press, 2001.

Valter, Stéphane. *La construction nationale syrienne: Légitimation de la nature communautaire du ouvoir par le discours historique*. Paris: CNRS Editions, 2002.

Index

'Abduh, Muhammad, 101
Abdülhamid II, 2, 50, 54, 55, 58, 70, 96, 122, 185, 190, 191, 202, 203
adab, 23, 229
Adana, 4, 33, 35, 125, 171, 176, 203
Adoian, Vosdanik (Arshile Gorky), 118
'Aflaq, Michel 51, 228, 228n10, 300
'agid, 263, 277
Ahmad, Feroz, 27n52, 99n10, 101, 197
airplanes, 86, 198, 198n40, 212, 301
al-Alabawi, 'Isa, 84–85
Alawites, 36, 177, 212, 228, 239, 300, 305
Alawite Mountains, 177
alcohol: consumption of, 52, 230n24, 307; and sociability, 60
Aleppo: architecture of 31; demography of, 36, 239; economy of, 32, 33, 34, 36; ethnic diversity of, 9, 31, 36, 115, 139, 152, 281; histories of, 127n6, 138, 148, 148n34, 185–186, 198–207, 208; urban geography of, 33, 46–49, 260, 266
Aleppo Club, 49, 50, 232, 245; as successor to the Aleppo Mutual Aid society, 93
Aleppo College, 307
Aleppo, Ottoman Province of, 4, 35, 48, 99, 125, 143, 154, 157, 171, 173, 180, 210, 240, 268, 287
Alexandretta, 76, 173n33, 213, 214, 289
Alexandria, 25, 27, 27n55, 32, 33
al-'Ali, Salih, 178–180, 222
American University in Beirut, 51, 227n7, 227n8, 265, 294.
America, America, 118
America, North, 51, 65, 87, 88, 89, 155, 226, 291, 307, 308; emigration to, 9, 117, 118, 265n31, 279n5, 296, 298; scouting in, 291n36.
America, Latin, 9. *See also* Mexico
America, South: immigration to, 272n5, 279. *See also* Brazil
Amin, Qasim, 91
ancien régime, 21,169, 226; Ottoman, 5, 58; Syrian, 233. *See also* a'yan, notables
Anderson, Benedict, 137n12, 145, 183
Ankara Accord (1921), 173n31, 180

Antioch, 35, 96, 107, 172, 177, 178, 214
anti-Semitism, 169, 247, 301
Antonius, George, 59n5, 134,
al-Antaki, 'Abd al-Masih, 44–47
al-Antaki, Na'im, 227, 227n7, 232, 242, 245, 276
Antaki family, 107
Appadurai, Arjun, 209
Arabic, 2, 3, 6, 8, 9, 20, 44, 51, 56, 57, 59, 76, 99, 111, 112, 114, 115, 116, 117, 123, 126, 127, 129, 135, 138, 143–145, 147, 148, 158, 186, 187, 190, 207, 215, 231, 245, 280, 282, 291, 295, 297
Arabic Thought in the Liberal Age (Hourani), 6–7
"The Arab," 117, 135, 140, 143, 144, 147, 227
Arab Kingdom, 10, 60, 128, 138, 162, 163, 164, 165, 174, 176, 184, 187, 195, 199, 222, 231
Arab Revolt, 122, 134, 135, 136, 138, 141, 146, 147, 158, 188, 194, 194
Arabs, 6, 34, 88, 115, 122, 127, 134, 135,139, 141–149, 162, 179, 194, 197, 198, 199, 200, 202, 203, 209, 213, 214, 228, 246, 249, 284, 74, 293, 300
archaeology, 138
"architectures of community," 29, 63, 70, 80, 109, 130, 159, 163, 174, 225, 238, 256, 274
archives: Ottoman, 66, 76, 77; of the French Mandate, 221, 261; of the Syrian state, 180, 258
Armée du Levant, 212
Armenia, Republic of, 160, 166, 167
Armenian language, 2, 8, 20, 42, 51, 76, 281, 288, 297
Armenians, 4, 26, 32, 34, 36, 51, 55, 57, 60, 82, 104, 112, 113, 118, 144, 153, 154, 166, 172, 176, 180, 196, 220, 238, 241, 269, 271, 277, 282; nationalism of, 59; as refugees, 124, 125, 126, 168, 200, 201–206, 207, 208, 212, 219, 220, 255, 270, 281–291, 305; neighborhoods of, 49, 250, 275; political organization of